Created and Directed by Hans Höfer

INSIGHT
GUIDES

NORWAY

Edited by Doreen Taylor-Wilkie
Editorial Director: Brian Bell

APA PUBLICATIONS

NORWAY

First Edition (2nd Reprint)
© **1992 APA PUBLICATIONS (HK) LTD**
All Rights Reserved
Printed in Singapore by Höfer Press Pte. Ltd

ABOUT THIS BOOK

Somebody once described Norway as "like Scotland, only more so," and this was something that struck project editor **Doreen Taylor-Wilkie** when she first visited Norway in the late 1970s. Taylor-Wilkie should know: as a Scottish journalist, broadcaster and travel writer, it was easy for her to feel a kinship between Norway and her own home country "even if the fjords were deeper and the mountains higher."

Even the languages had strong similarities, a relic perhaps from the early presence of the Vikings and the continuing influence from Norway, which ruled the northern islands of Orkney and Shetland until the 15th century. But more than anything else, Taylor-Wilkie leapt at the chance to edit *Insight Guide: Norway* because it was the country that had first fired her imagination to write about travel. In addition to acting as project editor, Taylor-Wilkie wrote the chapters on the fjord country from Stavanger and Rogaland in the south, through the world-famous Sogn, Nord and Geirangerfjords, to Trondheim – only a quarter of the way up the long, serrated edge of Norway's west coast but the gateway to the north.

The writing team

The Vikings, and Snorri Sturlusson – the Icelander who chronicled their great deeds – became a compulsive preoccupation for **Rowlinson Carter,** who wrote the history chapters of the book. Carter is a journalist with his roots in philosophy and history and with strong Norwegian connections. Over the weeks of writing, he vanished frequently into the London Library and emerged with ever-growing armfuls of ancient books that accompanied him around London.

But though the fjords, the midnight sun, and the Vikings are the aspects people most identified with Norway, Taylor-Wilkie and her team of specialist writers knew the country held a great deal more. Norway is both one of the world's oldest countries and one of the youngest European states, emerging only in 1905 from 400 years of Danish rule followed by nearly a century sharing a Swedish monarch.

This makes the Norwegians ever ready to wave their national flags and sing their songs, and gives them a fierce pride in everything Norwegian, as **Michael Brady** is well qualified to describe. Brady arrived in 1958 from the United States, with skis, hiking books and a Fulbright Fellowship. As an active outdoor man, specialising in books and articles on skiing and fitness, Brady loves the open air life that Norwegians favour. He describes his adopted countryfolk as "privileged to live where they do and knowing it, but afflicted sometimes with an inferiority complex." His knowledge and experience fits him to write with authority and enthusiasm about national customs and traditions, sport and the outdoor life.

The environment and conservation are the main preoccupations of **Inga Wallerius**, one of Sweden's most eminent journalists. She studied social anthropology, human ecology and control of the environment at the University of Gothenburg, and has a deep interest in ethnic cultures. She writes perceptively about the Sami people of Northern Norway, who acknowledge no national boundaries and move between Sweden and Finland, and even as far as Russia.

Taylor-Wilkie

Carter

Brady

Wallerius

Bobby Tulloch, who comes from those same Shetland Islands that the Norwegians held, was a natural for the chapter on Spitsbergen (or Svalbard, to use its correct Norwegian title). He is one of Scotland's best known ornithologists, and writes extensively about birds, animals such as otters, and Shetland. He is also deeply interested in the strong links with Norway that hold firm in his islands. Tulloch has led birdwatching expeditions as far south as the Falkland Islands and as far north as the Arctic, but his favourite area is Norway's northern coasts, and especially Spitsbergen. The chapter is a result of his most recent expedition there.

After nearly two decades in Scandinavia, **Jim Hardy** made a lengthy visit to his native New England a year ago and discovered that he was more Scandinavian than American. Years in neighbouring Sweden had subtly changed his views ("moved me slightly left of centre as far as social welfare and nationalised medicine goes") and his family were shocked that he no longer subscribed to the "pull yourself up by the bootstraps" policy. Safely back in Stockholm, where he writes about garden design and architecture as well as the Scandinavian arts, he provided the book's arts chapter.

Karen Fossli, who wrote about the oil industry, film, and Norway's neighbours, is also American and is the Oslo correspondent for London's *Financial Times*.

The fourth American, **Anita Peltonen**, who provided the chapters on Oslo and its surrounding countryside, jokes that she keeps moving up in the world – at least in terms of latitude. Born in New York City, she ascended to Montreal, then London and is now roving in Scandinavia, based in Finland. Visiting Olso for her research and trying out the vibrant new artistic life and nightspots that open and close and re-open, Peltonen marvelled at the swiftness of the change from a very "provincial" capital to the glass and painted steel of a modern cosmopolitan city.

Fascinating trek

Important though the capital and the fjord country are, Norway is much more and called for the rare writer who knew Norway's great distances well. **Robert Spark** was an ideal choice, a man whose interest was first awakened by a visit to Narvik 30 years ago and who has since driven all over Norway for his own motoring guides to Scandinavia. For *Insight Guide: Norway*, he undertook the fascinating trek north from Lake Mjøsa, less than 100 miles from Oslo, through the centre of Norway and the great massifs of the Hardangervidda and Jotunheimen and, from Trondheim, ever north to Kirkenes on the Soviet border.

Despite these wanderings on roads both major and so minor they were little more than a track, Spark comments: "Some recent developments have made it easier for the visitor to get around the less accessible regions, but it is to be hoped that this trend will not be taken too far. On the other hand it is a pity that many visitors cling to one or two more popular areas when there is so much more to see." This ambivalent view, he believes, is one shared by many Norwegians.

In London, the editorial centre for this book, **Jill Anderson** marshalled the text through a variety of Macintosh computers and **Christopher Catling** handled proofreading and indexing. In Scotland, **Kirsti Dinnis** was the Norwegian reader.

Hardy   *Peltonen*   *Spark*

CONTENTS

TRAVEL TIPS

"I'm Norwegian," proclaims one of the characters in a Hans Christian Andersen story, "and when I say I'm Norwegian, I think I've said enough. I'm as firm in my foundations as the ancient mountains of old Norway... It thrills me to the marrow to think what I am, and let my thoughts ring out in words of granite."

Andersen was, of course, a Dane, and he was teasing the Norwegians, as their Scandinavian neighbours are apt to do. In much the same way as Italians are satirically reduced to being tearful opera and ice cream fiends, and Frenchmen become obtuse philosophers in onion necklaces, so the typical Norwegian is portrayed as a simple, stubborn peasant who from time to time needs a comforting pat on the head.

Naturally enough, Norwegians see themselves rather differently. A Gallup poll once asked 200 people from each of 12 countries to rank themselves in terms of culture, food, living standards, natural beauty, female beauty, joie de vivre, and national pride. The Norwegian contingent gave themselves top marks in virtually every category. While few dispassionate observers would wish to quibble with the natural and female beauty assessment, it is more difficult to envisage Norway racing ahead in the culinary stakes. Various preparation of herring are undeniably tasty, but the colours would also be carried by exceedingly dark horses like fiske pudding, a substance which uninitiated palates might well be unable to distinguish from polystyrene foam. This sweeping victory for the home side was surpassed only by the conceit of the American entry.

Generous hospitality: The Norwegian character is of course far more complex than Andersen would allow or Gallup could measure. It is sometimes said that Norwegians are xenophobic. While this may be an exaggeration, it is certainly the case that they do not accept outside criticism. Yet the hospitality

shown towards foreign visitors far exceeds the demands of mere good manners. An English visitor was whisked off spontaneously to a wedding party in Oslo. As the only foreigner among 200 guests, he was disarmed when the bride's father, advised of his surprise presence, gave away his daughter in English. Although the younger Norwegian guests were, as usual, fluent in English, some older ones were left in the dark, but they thoroughly approved of the gesture.

The same English visitor, immobilised by

skis around his neck after capsizing on a narrow cross-country ski trail, brought down a party of local skiers who descended on his predicament too fast and too late to stop. The victims of the concertina pile-up were disgruntled until they made sense of his choked apologies, in English of course, at which point they tried to make him feel that, in the circumstances, the violent introduction was an unexpected pleasure, not to say privilege.

Other signs of welcome are given without thinking. A visitor in the house is the signal for lighting candles, probably a throwback to the days when, compounded by the long hours of winter darkness, houses shuttered against the cold were gloomy. Until quite recently, most of Norway's population of little more than four million was scattered across a vast landscape in a patchwork of tiny communities, so visitors invariably arrived after a long and exhausting journey, sometimes on skis. The assumption was that they arrived hungry, and restorative food and drink still appear as if by magic. A planned meal for guests requires elaborate place-settings showing off the finest silver, glassware and candlesticks in the house.

Visitors will not be allowed to leave without a look at the family photograph album plus a tour of the house. This demands close attention to detail and appreciative com-

is the double-edged nature of life in such a community: mutual support in adversity weighed against a suffocating lack of privacy at other times.

The lesser-known Aksel Sandemose wrote Ten Commandments for village life, the essence being humility bordering on self-abasement. A sample: "You must not think that you are worth anything; you must not think that you are better than anyone else; you must not think yourself capable of anything worthwhile, and you must not think that you are in any way exceptional."

Jingoistic chest-pounding of the sort noted by Hans Christian Andersen is derived to some extent from Norway's peculiar posi-

ments about any object which is obviously new. Norway's vaunted standard of living is a relatively recent phenomenon, and many people are still on the rebound from pre-war shortages and poverty. This may explain the otherwise inordinate desire to acquire the latest model of anything and everything.

Critical eye: The more enigmatic aspects of the Norwegian psyche—including the Nordic gloom which descends after a drink too many—have been famously scrutinised by a native, Henrik Ibsen. He was brought up in small communities and, during a long exile, turned his critical eye on the experience. One of the themes running through Ibsen's work

tion as both one of the oldest, if not the oldest, nation in Europe and at the same time one of the youngest. It is oldest in the sense that the Norwegians can trace an unbroken line of descent from people who inhabited their territory in prehistoric times, a homogeneity whose origins antedate the beginnings of Western civilisation in the Aegean.

Yet the present state of Norway was reconstituted only in 1905, which makes it younger than many of the junior members in the United Nations, themselves pasted together by the imperial powers in the 19th century. Having been relegated to a back seat in Scandinavian affairs for hundreds of years, these distant descendants of the illustrious Vikings need to pinch themselves—or blow a trumpet—as if they nervously expect to wake up and discover that their independence was a cruel dream.

Norwegians enjoy amazing longevity. They manage to look remarkably healthy all their lives, and the octagenarian grandma whizzing by on skis is not a myth. In any case, there are Norwegians alive who can remember, or have had drummed into them, the euphoria of liberation from their domineering Scandinavian partners. Practically every house has a private flag pole, and the flag is run up on the slightest pretext, if only to indicate that the owner is in residence.

thought of their revered flag being desecrated as a pair of underpants or on shopping bags. Their dignity as a sovereign state is not to be trivialised. The Swedish king who reluctantly oversaw Norway's independence predicted that bureaucratic incompetence would soon have Norwegians begging to be returned to the fold. The response, even now, is a reluctance to admit (to outsiders) that they are capable of making a mistake, as if to do so would vindicate the Swedish king's forebodings.

As long as authority was vested in foreigners, Norwegians did not regard it too highly. On assuming it themselves, however, authority was allowed to assume the aura of

Frenetic flag-waving could be construed as a rude gesture to the Swedes who, under the union, decided when, where and how the Norwegian colours were to be shown in foreign waters, relegating it to no more than a patch on a much larger Swedish flag. The flag flown on Norwegian shipping was, like separate consular representation and the establishment of a national bank, a perennial bone of contention before independence.

Norwegians would be distressed at the

Far left, at 89, Tormod Finner still cuts grass the traditional way. **Left**, great-grandmother with grandchild number 19. **Above**, September sun.

divine right, before which loyal citizens should willingly prostrate themselves. Norwegian history is full of swings from one extreme to another. Pagans who held out against Christianity until a surprisingly late date became—and in some cases remain—dogged fundamentalists after seeing the light. A nation which was once thought to be in danger of drinking itself to death has by no means buried the bottle, but drinking is now treated as a vice and for the sake of appearances most people go along with austere state measures to inhibit it.

Visitors sampling the state television service might wonder, too, at the litany of self-congratulation in almost daily items about the excellence of the health and welfare services. Programmes about children—for example, choirs singing carols at Christmas—are bound to include an unrealistic proportion of Third World immigrants. The way the camera seeks out and locks on to black, brown or yellow faces—possibly in difficulty with unfamiliar tunes and words—seems a rather contrived message to the effect that Norway can show the world a thing or two about charitable, liberal decency. This is a role which many are pleased to play; appeals by international agencies, when famine or disaster strikes, are always met with astonishing generosity, and the

most sensitive. There is no alarm about the predatory impact of, say, satellite television on a language which hardly exists outside Norway. Far from resenting visitors who presume to address them in a foreign language, Norwegians positively relish the challenge, and usually very fluently.

Confidence in the hardiness of their language is curiously at odds with the historical background. Language was a burning issue in Norwegian politics until the 1950s, having forced a prime minister to resign in 1912. The long-running controversy started as a form of agitation against Danish rule, throughout which Danish was the language of the civil service, schools and the church.

country spends more per capita on foreign aid than any other in the west.

Such open-handedness has inevitably attracted abuse, and questions are increasingly asked about the real credentials of political "refugees" who flock in for their share of the largesse on offer. If proved, the evidence would be difficult to swallow, as it was when statistics revealed that suicides had overtaken the number of traffic deaths in a certain period. Was that not, an apologist ventured, excellent proof of road safety standards?

In contrast with these examples of mild paranoia, Norwegians can be remarkably robust where they might be expected to be

For a long time after the Reformation the revised Bible was available only in Danish, as were all the new hymns. Denmark got its first printing press in 1480 but Norway had to wait until 1643. Until then books were imported and in Danish.

When reading aloud, Norwegians modified standard Danish through the use of their own pronunciation and intonation. This mixture eventually produced a hybrid known as *bokmål* (book language). The 19th-century nationalists still saw it as fundamentally Danish, however, and wanted a national language which was authentically Norwegian. Unfortunately, there was no single Norwegian substitute, because the language had developed many dialects. Rather than choose one dialect at the expense of the others, the language reformers concentrated on developing a composite.

The early language reformers included Ivar Aasen and Knut Knudsen, the latter a schoolmaster driven by his pupils' frustration in trying to work out Danish spelling. They worked on what became known as a *landsmål* or *nynorsk*, but their efforts were not unreservedly welcomed. Danish was the language of society and the theatre, and if Norwegian had to be spoken, a Danicised pronunciation was fashionable. These tendencies eroded as intellectuals like Ibsen lent

Progress towards *samnorsk* was given a nudge in the 1950s with a proposal to have school textbooks converted into it. There was such an outcry, however, that the government backed down. Subsequent policy has been to treat the two languages evenhandedly, still with the hope that they will one day converge. In spite of attempts to shore up *nynorsk* through radio and television, it looks as if it is losing ground.

Individualistic tongue: Educated speech is distinctly that of the southeast, although that does not prevent country dwellers on a visit to the capital, say, from laying on their regional accents thick for effect. The Bergensere—people from Bergen—at the heart

respectability to the campaign for the revivification of a purely Norwegian language.

In 1929 *bokmål* and *nynorsk* were recognised as dual official languages, the hope being that they would drift towards a blend which would be known as *samnorsk*. The names of cities and towns lost their Danish connotations. Christiania, for example, reverted to a good old Norwegian name, Oslo. The reformers also tackled the habit of referring to the number 25 as "five-and-twenty". It became "twenty-five".

Left, winter in the Nordmarka. **Above**, the summer goal is the beach.

of the *nynorsk* area, are certainly proud of their individualistic tongue.

The regional fragmentation at the heart of the language debate extends to most facets of cultural and economic life. While Norway has since Viking times been pointedly a single nation—an identity unshaken by ostensible absorption into Denmark and Sweden—it has been a confederation of many parts. Norway can be divided north-south, east-west or a dozen different ways. Like the Renaissance, the Industrial Revolution hardly intruded, so there was not the rapid urbanisation which occurred elsewhere. Trondheim, Bergen and Oslo were towns rather than cities. A later creation like Stavanger owed its existence to the arrival of vast shoals of herring, which were the basis of jobs, trade and other pre-requisities of a cash economy. Most of Norway remained rooted in subsistence agriculture.

Rural families tended to be isolated and self-sufficient. Their lives depended on agriculture, and the land was not good enough to support more than a family or two in a single valley. Separated from their neighbours by mountains which were ironically easier to cross in winter (on skis) than in summer, they effectively lived in worlds apart. There were hardly any villages where tradesmen could be found and paid in cash. The versatile

family managed on its own, a resourcefulness which still runs in the blood. It is not unknown for young couples living in Oslo today to solicit the help of friends to build their first home with their own hands.

The need to spread the population thin is a recurring imperative in Norwegian history. The Viking expeditions were to a large extent inspired by the pangs of land starvation. The modern Norwegian makes a virtue out of what used to be necessity. The ideal *hytte*, as a country cottage is known, is isolated. It will probably have electricity, but running water may be considered effete. Visitors who decide, sensibly, to rent a *hytte* will

almost certainly come round to the view that water drawn from a stream is not merely an exercise in rural nostalgia but also doubly delicious. In winter there is the added joy of first having to drill a hole through the ice to reach it.

The old necessities carry over to the passion for owning a boat. On gentle summer evenings, Oslo fjord is alive with private boats, a pattern repeated everywhere. Although Norwegians are said to grow up on skis, messing about in boats is equally ingrained. Both used to represent basic transport in a land where road and rail construction is prohibitively expensive because of the mountainous terrain and fjords which penetrate deep inland.

Although the country is now well served in both departments and, of course, by air links, the boat once represented (on inland lakes, as well as along the coast) a tool of daily life as well as a source of recreation. Far easier to cross a fjord by boat than walk around it, which was the only alternative. Norwegian skill and daring at sea, which began in the 8th century when the Vikings designed ships capable of crossing the open seas to Britain, mainland Europe and, eventually, to America, was on tap during World War II when Norwegian guerrillas applied their small boats to an ancient route and nonchalantly called it the "Shetland bus".

Modern Norway has the reputation of being an enlightened, progressive state on the Scandinavian model, but it does Norwegians no disservice to recognise the old Viking strains that lurk below. A man found sitting in a hole on the snowbound Oslo golf course said with a twinkle that his ancestors had devised a system of digging holes which, taking into account the direction of the wind and other factors, provided an emergency—and actually quite comfortable—refuge in the event of snowstorms. He felt he was doing his bit, preserving some of his heritage for posterity. He put his palms to his temples and waggled his outstretched fingers.

That the Vikings wore horns is doubtful, if not an outright fallacy, but only the most churlish observer would wish to deny someone who saw sport in sitting in a hole in the snow a certain degree of historical licence.

Left, close of a day out. Right, Norwegian *bunad*s (national costume) worn for church.

Life in Norway has been influenced to an extraordinary degree by the terrain and the weather. The original inhabitants hugged the coastal areas which, warmed by the Gulf Stream, made life more bearable. With the gradual recession of the last Ice Age about 12,000 years ago, the hunters and fishers inched northwards—but again only along the coast because the interior remained frigidly inhospitable.

The thaw was followed by mild weather, unknown before or since. Around 500 BC, however, just as iron was beginning to replace bronze and the Athenians were getting ready to build the Parthenon, it inexplicably deteriorated. The impact of suddenly colder, wetter weather was not unlike the predictions of what would happen now in the event of a "nuclear winter".

During the preceding Bronze Age considerable progress had been made in weapons, ornaments and utensils made out of metal imported from Britain and Continental Europe. Contemporary drawings chiselled into rock and burial slabs show boats capable of carrying 30 men (although not yet with sails), warriors on horseback and either two or four-wheeled carts drawn by horses or oxen. Progress was thrown into reverse by the climatic change and a large part of the population perished.

Survival in the new Ice Age demanded cultural adjustments. Men, who until then had usually worn a kind of belted cloak, pulled on underwear and trousers. Instead of the semi-nomadic existence which many preferred to lead, all had to settle on farms in order to secure winter fodder and shelter for livestock which had previously grazed outside all year round. People and animals occupied either end of the same house, an unhygienic but necessary form of early central heating.

In common with most of Europe, Norway was again struck by the weather in the 14th century. The economic decline then was exacerbated terribly by the Black Death. Apart from the general consequences, the

Preceding pages: Viking gold. **Left**, Odin, king of the Norse Gods.

acute shortage of labour led to the collapse of the aristocratic estates, demoting the owners to peasantry. The number of knights in Norway dropped from 270 to 60.

History starts late: Who were these people? The recorded history of Norway begins remarkably late, only in about AD 800, and the archaeological pointers towards specific events in earlier times are comparatively scanty. The ancient world had curious opinions about the ancient northerners: one, advanced by Pomponius Mela (AD 43), was that, living on birds' eggs, the people had hooved feet and ears so large that they covered their bodies, thereby dispensing with the need for clothing.

Another, Greek in origin, had the territory populated by Hyperboreans, a jolly race who lived in forests and sang and danced their way to incredible longevity. When eventually tired of life, they feasted, bedecked themselves with flowers—and threw themselves off cliffs. Norwegians continue to live longer than practically anyone else. Furthermore, they remain energetic to the end. It is one thing for a foreigner struggling on skis to be overtaken by a blasé six-year-old, quite another if the speed demon turns out to be a venerable grandmother.

Lieutenant W.H. Breton, a 19th-century tourist, was amazed by reports of a man who married at 113 and lasted until he was 146. Another early visitor commented on four peasants who were the principal dancers at an entertainment laid on for King Christian VI. All of them were well over 100. One Derwent Conway, in about 1820, asked a fit 74-year-old in Telemark for the secret of his robust health. Pouring himself a fifth glass of home-made corn brandy, he replied that it was due to "this excellent drink".

New blood: That the original inhabitants of Norway received infusions of new blood, probably from the east, is indicated by artefacts which have given their name to their respective cultures: Funnel-Beaker, Battle-Axe and Boat-Axe peoples. Changing burial practices are another reliable sign of influential immigration.

It was once thought, although the theory is now discredited, that the Sami (Lapps of

Finnmark) were the original inhabitants. Being Mongoloid and short of stature, they are very different from the familiar Scandinavian stereotype. It seems theirs was a relatively recent migration from Siberia, long after European types had moved in. The great majority of Norwegians are undoubtedly in a direct descent from the people who were occupying their territory long before 3000 BC, the date customarily taken as the beginning of Western civilisation.

Like a Nordic Rip van Winkle, Norway slept through the millennium in which Greece and then Rome flourished, although the runic alphabet did appear around the 3rd century AD. It was Latin in origin but dis-

pensed with the curved Latin letters because, perhaps, straight lines were easier to cut into wood, stone and metal, as runic inscriptions invariably were.

Norway was ignored by the civilised world until the late 8th century, by which time the Muslim tide had been turned back and Charlemagne was building his empire. Nowhere in Pliny the Elder, Tacitus, Ptolemy or any of the celebrated descriptions of the then known world are the Norwegian people mentioned by name. Even the term "Scandinavia" is a misreading of a manuscript by Pliny, who referred to the unknown land beyond Jutland as "Scatinavia".

Foreign ignorance, however, did not mean that nothing was happening locally. The evolution of ship design was the most potent of these hidden developments. The Phoenicians had undertaken stupendous voyages very much earlier, but they routinely stayed within sight of land.

The Norwegians were working on vessels capable of crossing oceans. The Gokstad ship, found in a burial mound near Sandefjord in 1880, was a masterpiece. Made out of oak planks, it was 80 ft long and 16 ft wide (25 metres by 5 metres). It had a mast and 16 pairs of oars. The crew handled one oar each which left enough room for an equal number of marines. The rudder, hung on the starboard side, could be raised for fast beaching. A modern replica crossed the Atlantic in just four weeks and attained a maximum speed of 12 knots. These ships represented a menacing mobility, and once the Norwegians had cause to take their unsuspecting neighbours to the south by surprise, they were able to do so with stunning efficiency.

Vikings appear: The Norwegians introduced themselves to the rest of the world with deceptive tranquillity. *The Anglo-Saxon Chronicle* for the year 787 contains the laconic entry: "In this year King Breohtric married King Offa's daughter Eadburge. And in his days came the first three ships of the Northmen from Hereoalande" (i.e. Hordaland, on the west coast of Norway).

In 793 the Vikings opened their account in earnest by plundering the monastery of Lindisfarne, one of the great sanctuaries of the Western Christian church. The next year they attacked the monastery of Jarrow in Northumbria, and the year after that they arrived in South Wales in a fleet of more than 100 ships. They were driven off by King Maredudd and that, together with the resistance they had encountered in England, persuaded them, for a period of 40 years, to turn their attention to softer targets in Ireland.

Various opinions prevail about the origin of the name "Viking", but there was no doubt among their victims in the 9th and 10th centuries that it meant "pirate" or "sea-robber". The terminology is further confused by the tendency in English chronicles to call all Vikings "Danes", while many of them were actually "Northmen", "Norsemen" or, in present terminology, Norwegians.

In Continental records, Norwegians take

all the credit (or blame) for what was usually the work of Danes. Swedish Vikings were busy too, but they tended to direct their attentions overland via Russia.

Proper outside investigation into the geography and demography of Norway began with Alfred the Great of England, who had every reason to wonder about people who had become painful tormentors. He was enlightened by Ottar, a rich Norwegian from Hålogaland. He told the king that Norway was a very long and narrow country, full of rocks and mountains.

The only places which could be pastured or ploughed were those close to the sea; the inhabitants kept sheep and swine and bred

The monastic chroniclers at the receiving end of their devotion registered complete helplessness. The only explanation they could think of was that they were feeling the Wrath of God for some unexplained sin. They prayed for "deliverance from the fury of the Northmen" and, specifically, their indiscriminate throat-cutting.

Truculent population: While Christians put their faith in the sign of the Cross, the Vikings trusted the hammer of Thor the Thunderer, defender of heaven against giants, men against monsters, and themselves from "the followers of the White Cross", as they called Christians. Small Viking raiding parties faced with a large and truculent popula-

tame deer, which they called reindeer. In the Arthurian romances of medieval England, the Norwegians were adamantly "wild and savage and had not in them the love of God nor of their neighbours."

In reality, the Vikings were land-hungry adventurers for whom rich and undefended coastal abbeys were irresistible business opportunities. They had no scruples about violating their supposed sacrosanctity; on the contrary, they saw Christianity as a heretical threat to their heathen beliefs.

<u>Left</u>, early sailing equipment. <u>Above</u>, Viking ship in Oslo's Viking Museum.

tion found that a reputation for uncompromising destruction and cruelty served their purposes well, encouraging the enemy to flee rather than put up a fight. Viking victory celebrations—"wild outbursts of triumphant rejoicing"—included the proven intimidatory techniques of transfixing captured children with spears and drinking out of the skulls of fallen enemies.

The Vikings also have apologists who prefer to concentrate on their apparent managerial talents in occupied territory and an artistic streak manifested in the finely-worked ornaments recovered from excavated ships. Montesquieu praised them as an army of free men in an age when armies were usually press-ganged.

The historian Snorre Sturluson is disarmingly indifferent to matters which others might consider to be grave flaws in their heroes. The royal pretender Harald Gille is summarised as "friendly, jovial, playful, unassuming, generous, accommodating and easily led," which glosses over the fact, which Snorre himself recounts with relish, that he blinded and castrated a rival, hanged a bishop and died drunk in the arms of his mistress with his wife standing by. After cataloguing this list of crimes, Snorre gaily refers to him on the next page as a saint!

The reason sometimes given for the sud-

den explosion of controversial Viking activity abroad is that it was the result of another explosion, that of population because of uniform polygamy. Over-population was certainly the case in western Norway where agricultural land was so scarce, but the problem was less acute elsewhere.

Nevertheless, all sons, legitimate and otherwise, were entitled to equal shares of an inheritance, and as political power and social standing were invested in property, the aristocracy especially were reluctant to carve land up into smaller and smaller parcels. The surfeit of sons was thus encouraged to seek a fortune abroad.

Annihilating the natives: Women and children often accompanied the men but they were usually parked in fortified camps while the men "harried". Occasionally they did join in and one of them, an amazon who rose to command her own army in Ireland, was acclaimed as the fearsome "Red Maiden".

When the Vikings came across unoccupied land or, as in the Orkneys, rendered it so by annihilating the natives, they were keen to settle it. If that proved to be impractical, a raid might at least produce some slaves who could either be sold or, increasingly, put to good use at home. When piracy could not be made to pay, however, the Vikings were willing to engage in conventional trade.

Profits from piracy and trade generated in Norway the nucleus of a merchant class which complemented the traditional structure of aristocratic earls, free men and thralls (i.e. slaves). The pecking order was reflected in Western Norway by *wergild*, a system which stipulated the compensation due in the event of murder. A slave was worth half the value of an ordinary peasant and a quarter of that of a land-owner, who in turn was worth only a quarter of a chieftain and one-eighth of a king.

Slaves must have been worked hard because there was a provision in law which absolved owners of guilt if a slave died through exhaustion or ill-treatment. Owners were permitted, when slaves died, to throw their children into an open grave to die from exposure. They were obliged, however, to step in and rescue the last one left alive. Some slaves were captured craftsmen who turned out valuable goods for local consumption and export. They were prized, as were young women with whom masters could replenish or increase the labour pool. Unlike the custom in Sweden, the child of a Norwegian master and slave woman remained a slave.

Viking women made an impression abroad in a way which hints at the "liberated" attitudes ascribed to them in the 20th century, albeit a reputation bestowed less frequently on Norwegian women than on the other Scandinavians. In 844 a Norwegian king ruling in Dublin exchanged envoys with Emir Abderrhaman II, the Moorish leader in Spain.

Alghazal, a poet, was appointed to the court of the "King of the Pagans" and became enchanted by the queen. While keen to further their acquaintance, he was alarmed at the prospect of the king finding out. The queen reassured him that "it is not customary with us to be jealous. Our women stay with their husbands only as long as they please, and leave them whenever they choose." She seems not to have added that Viking husbands reciprocated in kind. Men traded wives, or gave them away to friends if they bored or displeased them.

Daughter's dowry: The renewed Viking campaigns were launched from the west coast of Norway, from strongholds on the Scottish islands or from the Norwegian kingdom in Ireland, centred on a castle built in

The Viking raids into Europe were conducted like annual summer holidays, and year after year the fleets grew larger. An alarmed Charlemagne threw up military posts along his northern borders to guard against them. The defence of Paris against the Vikings was led by another King Charles who, perhaps to distinguish him from "the Great", was known as Charles the Bald.

The city was attacked in 857 and sacked in 861. Charles offered one lot of Vikings 3,000 lb (1,360 kg) of silver to go and fight some of their compatriots instead of him. In 885, however, both were back and it cost a further 700 lb (318 kg) of silver to get rid of them. To sweeten the deal, they were given permis-

Dublin in 841 by Torgisl. The Vikings were overlords rather than settlers in Ireland, although some intermarried—with sometimes explosive results.

Norway might still have overseas territories today if a Danish king, as we shall see, had not mortgaged the Orkney and Shetland Isles to raise money for his daughter's dowry. The Viking kingdom in the Isle of Man lasted until 1405, when the island submitted to Henry IV of England.

Left, a bloody confrontation from the Frithiof Saga by E. Tégnér, illustration Knut Ekwall. **Above**, Runic inscription on a Viking monument.

sion to plunder Burgundy on their way home. The most enduring Viking presence in France was in Normandy which, of course, was named after them. It began with Rolf the Ganger, a Viking who claimed descent from Harald Hårfagre, and was so corpulent that no horse could carry him. He was forced to pursue his considerable travel on foot. These Viking armies on the continent, of which Rolf's was only one, grew to massive proportions and were not driven off until 891, by the German emperor Arnulf.

Although the Vikings were active wherever the pickings looked promising (at one point they laid siege to Lisbon), geographical proximity recommended the British Isles. They attacked them in earnest from 834. Their most spectacular effort was in 851 when they took 350 ships up the Thames, stopping off to capture Canterbury before storming London. Wessex in the southwest was then the dominant kingdom in England, and it was from there that Ethelwulf and his son Ethelbald advanced to defeat the invaders at the battle of Aclea.

Winter campaign: The Vikings were back three years later and every summer thereafter, and in 866 a strong force put most of England under Viking control. What's more, they gave every indication of wanting to stay. Independent Wessex, which had

decisive battle with Harold of England near Hastings, Harald Hådråde had already tried to accomplish the same feat but had been stopped and killed at the battle of Stamford Bridge in Lincolnshire.

Viking territorial ambitions were not limited to Britain and Continental Europe. They sailed east to Iceland, Greenland and eventually to the American continent. As many as 20,000 Norwegians emigrated to Iceland; by the latter half of the 10th century there were no fewer than 39 petty kingdoms established there. They penetrated the Mediterranean as far as Constantinople.

This surging mixture of colonialism, plunder, trade and adventurism lasted for two

passed on to Alfred the Great, remained the greatest obstacle.

In 878 the Vikings took the unprecedented step of launching a winter campaign, setting off a panic which forced Alfred into hiding on an island in the Perrot River in Somerset. This is the historical context of the fanciful tale about his burning the cakes. In his subsequent victory, the defeated Viking leaders had to submit to Christian baptism, but the treaty acknowledged their right to rule a large swathe of England and to maintain a Northumbrian kingdom based in York.

In 1066, the same year in which William the Conqueror crossed from France for his

centuries between the fall of the western Roman Empire and the First Crusade, and it nearly brought about the overthrow of Christianity in Europe (as the Moslems had been close to doing earlier). The benefits to those left at home were considerable. The period produced unprecedented wealth and provided the cultural impulse which welded unruly petty kingdoms and chieftainships into what was recognisably the country which Norway is today.

Above, from Snorri Sturlusson's *Norse Kings*. Drawing by Halvfdan Egedins. **Right**, romantic view of a Viking (1828).

A VIKING BURIAL

In the year AD 921, a peripatetic Arab named Ahmad bin Fudlan came across Vikings who had settled on the banks of the Volga river. They were trading with Constantinople: furs and slaves for gold and silver ornaments, silks and other luxuries. A chieftain died while he was with them, and his account of the funeral is an antidote to some of the over-romantic nonsense that has been written about the Vikings.

When the chieftain died, Ahmad reported, his maidservants were asked: "Who will die with him?" The first to volunteer was immediately put under guard in case she changed her mind, not that she gave any indication of wishing to do so. To Ahmad's amazement, she "spent every day drinking and singing, happy and cheerful."

The elaborate formalities began with the division of the chieftain's estate into three equal parts. One went to his family, the second to cover the cost of the funeral, and the last on drink. "They are much addicted to wine," Ahmad observed, "which they drink night and day, and often one of them dies with a cup in his hand".

The boat in which the chieftain was to be despatched was drawn out of the water and decorated with quilts and cushions. Ahmad then met "the angel of death";

he described her as "dusky, hale, strongly built and austere." Austere she might well have been, for it was her function eventually to kill the carousing maidservant.

The chieftain's body was removed from the temporary grave where it had lain for 10 days. Ahmad had a good look at it. "I saw that he had gone black, because of the cold climate of the country," he said; but otherwise "the corpse had in no way altered." The body was dressed in finery and propped up on cushions in a tent erected on the boat.

"They now brought liquor, fruit, and herbs and put them by him, then they brought bread, meat, and onions, and threw them down in front of him. They brought a dog, cut it in half, and threw it into the boat, then brought all his weapons, and put them by his side. After that they took two beasts of burden, drove them along until they sweated, then cut them up with swords and threw their flesh into the boat. Then they brought two cows, cut them up also, and threw them into the boat. The girl who was to be killed, meanwhile, was going up and down, entering one tent after another, and one man after another had intercourse with her. Each one said to her, 'Tell your master that I only do this for love of him'."

The girl was later taken to the boat, where she handed over her bracelets and anklets to the "angel of death" and the two girls who had been guarding her. They were joined by men carrying shields and pieces of wood. Farewell drinks and songs followed until, Ahmad wrote, "I saw that she had become bewildered and wished to enter the tent."

The old woman followed her into the tent, whereupon "the men began beating the shields with the pieces of wood so that the sound of her screams should not be heard, and the other girls be afraid and not wish to die with their masters. Six men then entered the tent, and all of them had intercourse with her. They then made her lie down by the side of her dead master, and took hold of her hands and two her feet. The old woman called the 'angel of death' put a rope done into a noose round her neck, and gave it to two men to pull. She came forward with a large, broad-bladed knife and began thrusting it in and out between the girl's ribs in place after place, while the two men strangled her until she died."

Walking backwards, the next of kin then went naked to the boat and lit kindling which had been placed beneath it. The rest of the men followed suit. "At this moment, an awe-inspiring gale got up, so that the flames of the fire grew stronger and its blaze fiercer. One of the Vikings chose to compare the funeral arrangements with what he had heard about Islamic rites. 'You Arabs are stupid,' he remarked to Ahmad, 'because you take your dearest and most honourable men and cast them into the dust, so that creeping things and worms eat them. We burn them with fire in a twinkling and they enter Paradise the very same hour'." Then, according to Ahmad bin Fudlan, "he laughed heartily".

BORGUND CHURCH.

With Snorre Sturluson, Norwegian history begins to speak for itself instead of relying on outsiders who observed or passed on fantastic tales about the land and its people. Snorre's epic *Heimskringla*, the Sagas of the Norse Kings, is a work of genius.

He visited Norway only twice, but working on his remote saga island in Iceland he compiled an almost inconceivable mass of information which begins with the mythology of prehistoric times and continues until 1177 (two years before he was born), by which time the Vikings had been tamed, Christianity had taken hold in Norway and the country had been forced to endure a century of civil war.

Amusing tale: Although Snorre was himself a foreigner, he drew on the oral history of the scalds at the courts of the Norwegian kings. He was obviously a discriminating historian although, like Herodotus, never one to exclude an amusing tale because he did not believe it either: "It is the way of scalds, of course, to give most praise to him for whom they composed, but no one would dare tell the king himself such deeds of his as all listeners and the king himself knew to be lies and loose talk; that would be mockery, but not praise."

There are no fewer than 2,000 names of persons and places in his saga and he gives his readers a vivid sense of what was happening, as it were, at home. But Snorre's unlucky recompense was to be put to death by the King of Norway's men in 1241.

Snorre introduces the Norwegian royal line in the person of Halvdan the Black, a king troubled by his inability to dream. He consulted Torleiv the Wise, who said he had suffered from the same complaint and had cured it by sleeping in a pig sty. The king followed his example "and then it always happened that he dreamed".

More prosaically, Halvdan was descended from the Swedish Ynglinger family who ruled in Uppsala. His branch had moved to Norway about a century before the Viking period, when the concept of Norway as an entity existed only in the term "Norovegr", or North Way, the coastal stretch from Vestfold to Hålogaland.

A king dreaming in a pigsty might seem to belong to mythology rather than history, but he was real enough. The Oseberg ship unearthed in Vestfold in 1904 proved to be that in which his mother, a Danish princess, was actually buried. When Halvdan died, his body was chopped up so that the pieces could be more widely distributed to bring good luck to the recipients.

Female demands: Halvdan's son, known as Harald Hårfagre (Fair Hair), became the first ruler of a united Norway. It was said of this subsequent unification that he was put up to it by a woman whom he wished to take to bed. Her reply to his proposition, conveyed by messengers, was that she could not possibly "waste her maidenhood" on a man who ruled over a kingdom which compared so unfavourably in size with those in Denmark and Sweden.

His messengers nervously reported her comment but were relieved by the philosophical manner in which he took it. "She has reminded me of those things," he said,

Left, one of the oldest stave churches, Borgund. **Right**, Harald Hårfagre (*circa* 1200).

"which it now seems strange I have not thought of before."

Harald advanced north from Vestfold to improve his conjugal prospects. He made contact with the powerful Earl Håkon, whose interests extended south from Trøndelag, the region surrounding what was eventually to become Trondheim. The cold facts, never as much fun as Snorre, are that Harald and Håkon saw the mutual benefits of trade but first had to suppress unruly Viking bands along the coast who would have disrupted it.

Harald needed assistance and set the precedent for long intercourse between the Norwegian and English thrones by turning to

Athelstan, King of England. As a pledge of friendship, accompanied by some mutual chicanery, he initiated what was to become another quite common practice: he sent his infant son Håkon to be fostered at Athelstan's court.

Harald's campaigns sent many of his dispossessed opponents looking for alternative accommodation in Iceland, Shetland, the Orkney Islands and the Hebrides. The decisive battle was at Hafrsfjord, near present-day Stavanger, in southwestern Norway about AD 900. The victory made him, Snorre says, the first king of the Norwegians, and also won him the postponed hand of the

"large-minded maid", who proceeded to bear him five children. As a love story, however, the conclusion is not completely satisfactory. "King Harald had many wives and many children," Snorre says. "They say that when he took Ragnhild the Mighty (daughter of King Erik of Jutland), he had divorced himself from nine other women.

Too many children: The awesome number of royal progeny was to prove a constant source of havoc in the matter of choosing a successor. The English chronicler Roger of Hoveden wrote: "it is the custom of the kingdom of Norway… that everyone who is recognised to be the son of any King of Norway, even though he be a bastard and born of a serving wench, can claim for himself as great a right to the kingdom of Norway as the son of a wedded king and one born of a free woman. And so fighting goes on incessantly between them, till one of them is vanquished and slain."

Harald Hårfagre's umpteenth son, but the only one by the final, mighty Ragnhild, was the wretched Erik Bloodaxe, who advanced his succession by murdering all but one of his legitimate half-brothers. The exception was Håkon, the boy who had been fostered by King Athelstan in England.

Erik had none of his father's authority and the united kingdom quickly degenerated into squabbling petty kingdoms ruled by various of Harald's bastard sons. On Håkon's return from England, Erik was forced to flee in the opposite direction. In what the English may well have regarded as a thoroughly inequitable exchange, Erik ended up as King of Northumberland.

First Christian: Håkon den Gode (the Good) was more successful than Erik at holding hostile factions together and before he died was acknowledged as king over the whole coastal area from Oslo to Hålogaland. He was a notable reformer of law and defence; he was also the first Norwegian Christian king, having been baptised while in England. He imported an English bishop and missionaries with a view to converting his countrymen, but that did not prove to be easy.

Nowhere was resistance to Christianity more forcibly expressed than in Trondheim, which was then notably against any form of imposed authority whether by Håkon or, as they had just convincingly demonstrated, by the rival King Øystein of Opplandene. Øystein, to some "the Mighty" and to others "the Evil", had offered them as king a choice between one of his thralls, known as Tore the Hairy, or his dog, Saur.

They chose the dog. "Then they bewitched the dog with the wit of three men"—sufficient to enable the hound to communicate through a mixture of barking and speech: one word, apparently, for every two barks. The king lived in a palatial kennel and was carried around "when it was muddy" on the shoulders of its subjects.

It was into this unorthodox regal set-up that Håkon tried to introduce Christianity. He urged people to "believe in one God, Christ, the son of Mary, and give up all blood

from toasting their gods morning, noon and night. They were concerned, too, that their potential parishioners would drink themselves into extinction and, by instructing them in the cultivation of fruit and vegetables, hoped to persuade them to consume at least some solids. In fact, the seemingly unquenchable thirst was probably attributable to what they did eat, which was bountifully salted to preserve it.

In the end the missionaries realised that pious sobriety was unattainable. The best they could hope for was to have the toasting converted to Christian saints rather than pagan gods. They provided a long list of saints' names and it seems that some of their

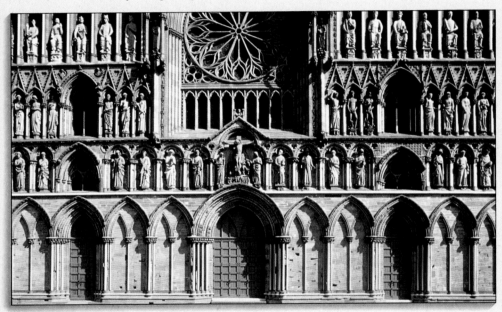

offerings and heathen gods, keep holy the seventh day and not work, and fast every seventh day." From the typical audience "there was straightaway a mighty uproar", followed by devious ploys to trick Håkon into eating a morsel of horse flesh on a day when he was self-righteously fasting or to make him participate in a toast to one or other of their beloved pagan gods.

Håkon's imported missionaries despaired. Their targets would not deviate

Left, the monument at Hafrsfjord, where Harald Hårfagre first united Norway. **Above**, the main door and rose window at Nidaros Cathedral.

parishioners were content to drink to them with undiminished frequency and pleasure.

Missionaries' fate: The missionaries had less luck in suppressing traditions like blood sacrifices (usually animals but occasionally humans), polygamy, feuds, the exposure of unwanted infants and some of the excesses associated with slavery. In Trondheim the obdurate response to the message they preached was to send out four ships looking for tiresome missionaries: they "slew three priests and burned three churches; they then went home".

Even when Christianity was finally adopted in Norway, much of the old religion lingered until the Reformation and beyond. The early Christian clergy, for instance, ignored papal injunctions about celibacy. The medieval stave churches are another case in point. Their intricate construction resembles nothing if not the keel of a Viking ship, and they are festooned with dragon heads and scenes from heathen mythology. Many of these churches were pulled down in a torrent of 19th-century Pietism, a kind of Christian fundamentalism which still holds sway in many rural areas and is responsible for a total ban on alcohol in some (usually rural) communities.

On the military front, Håkon in the 10th century was under constant threat from Erik Bloodaxe's avenging sons coming over from Northumberland. In defeat they had turned to their uncle, the Danish King, Harald Bluetooth, who wanted to reassert himself over old Danish territories at the mouth of Oslo fjord. At a decisive battle in 960 Håkon was defeated and killed. With him, for the time being, went Christianity's immediate prospects in Norway.

Christianity had to wait for its next champion until Olav Tryggvason, later King Olav I and a monument in Norwegian history. Snorre says he was a great sportsman who could walk on the oars along the outside of a ship, "smote equally well with both hands" and could hurl two spears at a time. He was "the gladdest of all men and very playful, blithe and forgiving, very heated in all things, generous and prominent amongst his fellows, bold before all in battle…"

By the age of 12 he was a full-blooded Viking, cruising the Baltic in command of five longships and later moving west to terrorise the English coast. His personality changed through a chance meeting in the Scilly Isles, where he was resting after some strenuous atrocities. A wise old man took him aside and explained the True Path. Transformed overnight, Olav returned to England "and now went about peacefully, for England was a Christian country and he was also a Christian".

Militant conversions: He was not so peaceful when he got round to converting his compatriots at home. Those who opposed him "he dealt with hard; some he slew, some he maimed and some he drove away from the land". He advertised his determination to propagate the faith by carting about the sev-ered heads of those who disagreed. In the circumstances, it is understandable that a man who was elected to argue theological niceties with the king stood up only to develop "such a cough and choking in the chest that he could not bring forth one word and he sat himself down."

Olav Tryggvason was unlucky in love. In proposing marriage to the wealthy Queen Sigrid of Sweden, he insisted she would first have to be baptised. She demurred. "King Olav was very wroth and answered hastily, 'Why should I wed thee, thou heathen bitch?'" reinforcing his point with a smack in the face. "That may well be thy death", she observed – with truth, as it proved.

She was a crafty enemy. Her wealth attracted a procession of proposals from minor kings, which she found irksome. King Swein Forkbeard of Denmark, son of Harald Bluetooth, was the type she preferred, and as soon as they were married she began to mention a small matter which she wished to settle with Olav. She talked Swein Forkbeard into an alliance with the Swedish King Olav the Tax Gatherer to achieve the desired result. A great sea battle ensued, at the climax of which Olav, who was being assisted by King Boleslav of Poland, was forced to jump overboard. He was never seen again and the victors, including the gratified queen, divided Norway among themselves.

First saint: The man who would soon restore Norway's integrity had, like Olav Tryggvason, embarked on a naval career at 12. Olav Haraldson, later St Olav, was in England when the same Swein Forkbeard landed his forces and was responsible for the then King of England, Ethelred, being castigated ever more as "the Unready".

Olav allied himself with Ethelred in an anti-Danish war which came to a head at London Bridge across the Thames. The Danish forces looked, and probably felt, impregnable in the fortifications which they occupied on the bridge, but they reckoned without Olav's well-built Vikings. Having fastened ropes to the piles under the bridge, they heaved at the oars and brought the whole thing down. (Several churches in England, which still exist, were dedicated to St Olav for this remarkable feat.)

Olav managed to lay the foundations of the Church, even in petulant Trøndelag, but in so doing antagonised many potential rivals. He faced a greater threat from abroad in the person of the expansionist King Canute of Denmark who, with the clear intention of annexing Norway, invaded in 1028 with overwhelming forces.

Olav fled to Kiev until he learned that the earl whom Canute had appointed to govern Norway was dead. He returned to regain his kingdom but miscalculated his level of support in Trøndelag. He was killed. Canute sent his son with his English concubine mother to run the country.

Olav was elevated to sainthood and his body placed in the church of St Clement in Trondheim (later to be moved). In spite of his insensitive missionary zeal, the memory of

abroad to enrich themselves. He signed up as a Varangian mercenary for the Byzantine emperor in Constantinople and saw service in Syria, Armenia, Palestine, Sicily and Africa. He was an enterprising warrior. During one siege he faked his own funeral and, emulating the Trojan Horse, his men persuaded the townspeople to open the gates to admit his coffin which, they promised, would work powerful magic to their benefit.

All of this was immensely profitable because the mercenaries were entitled to keep as much treasure from captured palaces as they could grab with both hands. An oblique memorial to Norwegians like Harald who served with the Varangians exists on the

Olav kept alive the notion of a united and independent kingdom of Norway through the troubled centuries ahead.

King Canute's kingdom fell apart after his death, the Scandinavian component reforming into three distinct and generally hostile kingdoms. Norway was ruled first by Magnus I and then by Harald Hådråda, whom we have met before as the man who failed to do what William the Conqueror achieved in the very same year, 1066.

Noble mercenary: Harald was typical of the young nobles who were forced to look

Runic script at Skjeberg, south of Oslo.

great Pireaus marble lion which the Venetians carried away after their conquest of Athens in 1687 and which stands now at the entrance to the Arsenal in Venice. Very faded but still visible is an example of Varangian graffiti: a runic inscription etched into its flanks.

Harald consolidated the kingdom of Norway. Troubled as Norwegian kings invariably were by the people of Trøndelag and its capital, Trondheim, he founded Oslo in 1048 as a counterbalance. He provided the town with a patron saint, Hallvard, whose main claim to sainthood seems to have been the refusal of his body to sink after being thrown into a fjord with a stone around the neck.

Defeat in England: As King Canute's sovereignty over England was still within living memory, it was possibly inevitable that a confident Harald would develop similar ambitions. In any case, there had been so much to-ing and fro-ing between the west coast of Norway and Britain that the affinities between them were as close, or closer, than those between settlements scattered over the vastness of Norway. Harald therefore probably felt he was exercising a natural right in his invasion of England.

His approach was from the north and he was stopped at Stamford Bridge, in Lincolnshire. (It should not be confused—a com-

Magnus's death produced the familiar pattern of multiple heirs, in this case three simultaneously acclaimed kings who were all minors. One died young, Sigurd went off to the Holy Land to earn his title, "the Crusader", and Øystein mixed Viking raids with improvements to fisheries, harbours and roads and the establishment of monasteries. Sigurd had the throne to himself after Øystein's death, though he continued to be confronted by the complicated rules of succession throughout his reign.

Battles for the throne: These battles to occupy the Norwegian throne went on and on. There were brilliant interludes under a king like Sverre, but more often than not the suc-

mon failing in lesser guidebooks—with its namesake in London, the home of the Chelsea soccer club.) Some historians argue that the English army's need to rush north to meet Harald weakened its ability to resist William when he materialised in the south.

After Harald's death in this abortive conquest of England, he was succeeded by his sons Magnus and Olav the Peaceful, the latter founding the towns of Bergen and Stavanger before being succeeded by his son, yet another Magnus but in this instance unforgettably "the Bareleg" because, after visiting Scotland (which he dearly wanted to annex), he took to wearing a kilt.

cession was a squabble between the powers behind official contestants who might be children not yet six years old. With the stability of Håkon IV's 46-year reign and that of his son, Magnus the Lawmender, however, Norway achieved its 13th-century "Period of Greatness".

Money was spent on cathedrals and churches, the arts flourished and Norwegians assiduously studied and followed European fashions. This cultural awakening was to some extent through the creation of a wealthy upper class and the consolidation of state and Church. It was not so beneficial for the peasants; riches were not evenly spread, and the number of independent farmers dropped significantly as they defaulted on mortgages, leaving the Church and big land-owners free to step in and take over the land.

Norway's overseas empire contributed to a sense of greatness. Jämtland in Sweden was a Norwegian possession, as were the Orkney and Shetland Islands. In 1262 Iceland accepted Norwegian sovereignty, as did Greenland. It was the period, too, which saw the growth of towns like Bergen with a rich trade in dried fish from the north. Foreign trade, to begin with, was mainly with Britain but it then tilted towards the Baltic coast, especially Lübeck. The Germans had plenty of corn but a shortage of fish; a perfect trade balance with Norway.

The Lübeck merchants grew ever more powerful because of Norway's almost total reliance on them. They were allowed to buy property in Bergen and settle there. If their demands were not met, they simply threatened to cut off corn supplies. Reliance on imported food was effectively costing the country a degree of independence, an unsettling vulnerability which persists in the current national obsession about subsidising agriculture wherever it is remotely possible.

Black Death: The whole of Europe had to tighten belts in the 14th century. Icelandic chronicles, which kept track of the weather, recorded volcanic eruptions, earthquakes, abnormally heavy winter snowfalls and consequently spring floods. To compound the misery, a galley arriving in Sicily from the Far East in October 1347 brought the Black Death. Within a couple of years, a third of the European population was dead.

The plague was carried to Bergen in 1349 in the hold of an English ship. The effect on isolated Norwegian farming communities, especially, was catastrophic: farms which had been painfully created in conditions difficult at the best of times were reduced to waste, in some cases to this day.

The estates generating the wealth which was the necessary platform for general economic development could not be maintained while labourers dropped dead. The nobles who survived were reduced to scratching a

Left, the Ring of Brogar, Viking remains in Orkney, Scotland. **Right**, Akershus Fortress, scene of the treacherous murder of the Norwegian patriot Knut Alvsson.

living out of the land like everyone else. The effect of *force majeure* acting as a social leveller assumed a pattern in Norwegian history which cannot be discounted in explaining the easy-going classlessness which pertains today.

The decimation of the nobility removed the impetus behind the normally turbulent activity around the Norwegian throne. Unchallenged, two successive kings sat out long reigns, a foretaste of the comparative stability about to the foisted on all Scandinavia in the late 14th century through the cunning manipulation of Margareta, widow of King Håkon.

A Danish princess, she was married to him

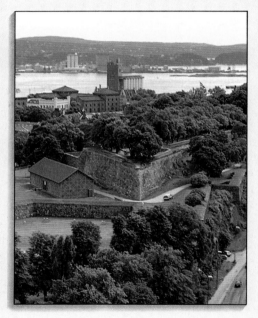

at the age of 10 and was thus steeped in the machinery of monarchy. She has been credited with "the greatest personal position ever achieved in Scandinavia" and was sometimes addressed as "Lady King". She first persuaded the Danes to accept as king her son Olav, then aged five.

With mother active behind the scenes, Olav also took over the crown of Norway at 10, and not long afterwards inherited the claim of the dispossessed Folkung dynasty in Sweden. He died suddenly at 17 and Margareta found a suitable substitute to don the united crowns in Erik of Pomerania, her five-year-old nephew.

The union of the three crowns was formalised at a coronation in the Swedish town of Kalmar, close to the then border with Denmark. The date, appropriately, was Trinity Sunday, 1397. The coronation was performed by the Danish and Swedish archbishops; Norway was represented by the Bishop of Orkney, by chance an Englishman.

Although there may have been an attempt to draft a constitution which would have united the three realms forever under a single king, the rules of succession adopted left a

cially fellow Pomeranians. He also tried to squeeze the Hanseatic merchants for money. Their response included an attack on Copenhagen, where they were seen off by 200 examples of a new invention, the cannon. He was less successful when the merchants retaliated with a blockade. The worst sufferers were the nobility and wealthy merchants who, holding Erik responsible for their misfortune, conspired to dethrone him.

Erik retreated to the island of Gotland in the hope that they would change their minds

gaping loophole. Erik was given full rights to dispose of the crown as he saw fit, a recipe for reversion to the old royal uncertainties after his death.

In the event, the union collapsed in his lifetime. His greatest difficulty was paying for the court and centralised administration in Copenhagen. The united crown had no significant estates of its own; the nobility did and was comparatively well off, but it was not inclined to surrender its wealth. Erik tried to circumvent the authority of the nobility by giving the position of castellan or bailiff—local military commander—to persons of lower rank or even foreigners, espe-

and invite him back. Norway would have done so, but the Danish nobles wanted to make a fresh start. The invitation went to Christian of Oldenburg, who thereupon rose from the title of count in an obscure part of Germany to found a dynasty which was to last for more than four centuries. Sweden resisted the choice, but Norway went along with it.

Christian I was almost as short of money as Erik had been. His attempts to make up shortfalls were notoriously at the expense of Norway, the weaker partner. Expected to hand over 60,000 guilders as a dowry for his daughter Margaret's marriage to the heir to the Scottish throne, he mortgaged the Orkney Islands to Scotland for 50,000.

When the time came for the wedding, he was still 8,000 guilders short—and mortgaged Shetland to make up the difference. To put 8,000 guilders into perspective, he spent three times that sum on a trip to Rome a few years later (which he had to borrow from the Hanseatics). The Scots gloated over the transaction; not merely the trifling price but that Margaret "deemed it a greater thing to be queen in Scotland than daughter of a king who wears three crowns".

Treacherous murder: Norway's resentment at such exploitation eventually boiled over. On the turn of the 16th century, Knut Alvsson, a Swedish-Norwegian nobleman, led an uprising which created a potentially independent state stretching from Oslo to Bergen. Danish troops were sent to put a stop to it. The outcome, however, was thoroughly dishonourable. Alvsson had established himself in Akershus Castle in Oslo. He was invited to negotiate under a flag of truce and promptly murdered. In the poem *At Akershus*, Ibsen called his death a blow to Norway's heart.

Norwegian resentment at the treatment meted out to Alvsson was exacerbated by punitive taxes to pay for Christian II of Denmark's wars with the restless Swedes. Norwegians were not altogether sorry to see him toppled and bundled off into exile, but they were not ready to extend a welcome to his successor, Frederik I.

Norway was nominally Roman Catholic and there was not much spontaneous interest in the forces of the Reformation which lay beneath the tussle for the Danish throne. The country did not have the urban bourgeoisie who elsewhere were the first to adopt Lutheranism. Norway's peasant culture was deeply conservative, not to say backward, so much so that many scholars classify Norway as "medieval" until the early 16th century.

It could be said that the Reformation, when it reached Norway, was the first of the

great European cultural swathes that had any meaningful impact on the country. Feudalism passed it by (never a Norwegian knight in armour rescuing damsels in distress) as did the Renaissance. Most of rural Norway remained doggedly in its past, Christianity providing only a light sprinkling on what were fundamentally old heathen ways. Peasants were still scratching their heads over Christianity as they knew it when elsewhere in Europe the enthusiasm was for a radically different version, which Norwegians were

for the most part in no hurry to contemplate.

New leader: It was at this point that a new Norwegian leader emerged. He was Olav Engelbrektsson, the Archbishop of Trondheim (or Nidaros, as it was then known). Olav raised an army with a view to getting Christian II back. The exiled king was able to muster a fleet with Dutch help and in 1531 set sail for Oslo. A storm scattered the fleet so that only a small part of it went into action against Akershus Castle. The attack was futile. Christian was captured and imprisoned, and the Norwegians were forced to acclaim Frederik I as their king.

Christian II was still in prison when

Frederik died and was replaced by Christian III, a Protestant. He rounded up the Danish bishops and then ordered the Archbishopric of Trondheim to be abolished, if necessary by force. Olav thought of resisting but, having weighed up the likely repercussions, fled to the Netherlands.

Any further hope of Norwegian independence was firmly squashed by Christian III's 1536 edict demoting the country to the status of an ordinary Danish province—"and it shall henceforth neither be nor be called a kingdom in itself". The humbled status was intended to last in perpetuity; in the event, it lasted for a little less than 300 years, culminating not in independence but in an 1814

takeover by Sweden after Norway had become a coveted prize bobbing between its more powerful neighbours.

The loss of political sovereignty under Denmark could not obliterate Norway's separate identity at once. People went on speaking the same language as before and local administration retained many traditional features, but the creeping effects of the Reformation, and Christian III's determination to Danicise Norway, could not forever be postponed.

The Danish influence: Most of the new Protestant clergy were Danes. The revised version of the Bible was in Danish and so were the hymns. Official jobs were invariably given to Danes, who conducted them in the Danish language and reported back to the administration in Copenhagen.

With the spread of schooling and therefore literacy in books imported from Denmark (the first printing press was late in arriving in Norway), the anomaly arose of people speaking one language among themselves but reading—albeit with characteristic Norwegian pronunciation—and writing in another. The result was a hybrid Dano-Norwegian and the genesis of a language dispute which has not been settled to this day.

Norway won a measure of Danish respect in the latter's frequent wars with Sweden, in which the Norwegian contingents invariably acquitted themselves well. Denmark began to realise that Norway could only be governed in its own way. Sweden was forever peering enviously over Denmark's shoulder at Norway. Too much antagonism could result in Norway accepting a more attractive offer of union with Sweden.

The Norwegian economy began to recover from its long decline, partly as the result of vast shoals of herring which materialised off the Norwegian coast and partly because of the invention of the water-driven saw, which made exploitation of the timber forests lucrative. Christian IV was far more positive about Norway than his predecessors. He visited the country at least 30 times, making a special trip on learning of the discovery of silver at what is now Kongsberg. He supervised the founding of the town, hence the name, which translates as "King's Mountain". He founded and attached his name to Kristiansand, as he did "Christiania" to the new city built on the site where the former Oslo burned down in 1624.

Nevertheless, Christian ran the country as if it were a private company. He cracked down on the Hanseatic traders, making them take out Norwegian citizenship, if they had not already done so of their own accord, or leave. Foreigners from other parts were encouraged to bring to Norway their skills, enterprise and, best of all, their money. Under his encouragement, former trading posts became towns in places like Drammen, Moss, Larvik, Mandal and Arendal.

The Norwegians did not always receive these foreigners with uncritical joy. In 1700, for example, a simple fight between two men in Arendal escalated into a splendid brawl which pitched all 900 resident foreigners against everyone else. It lasted a week. Nevertheless, a population which had been reduced by the Black Death to something like 180,000 picked up under Christian's energetic policies, reaching 440,000 in 1665 and nearly 900,000 by 1801.

Not all of Christian IV's successors shared his delicate touch with regard to Norwegian sensibilities. There were periods when the Danish crown was autocratically absolute, and respite depended on having an independently-minded Stattholder, the crown agent with responsibility for Norway.

Ulrik Frederik Gyldenløve, the illegiti-

edly shed the mantle of medievalism and got to grips with Protestantism, it adopted the faith as zealously as it had once defended paganism. The rural areas, especially, embraced Pietism, real hellfire-and-brimstone stuff which persuaded peasants that their austere existence was actually abominably frivolous. Gripped by a kind of manic fundamentalism, they despised their folk culture and—particularly in the 19th century, when Pietism was still going strong—were encouraged to tear down the ornate stave churches. Confirmation and church attendance on Sunday were made compulsory.

Looking around them, the Pietists were appalled by the realisation that in their midst,

mate son of Frederik III, conscientiously protected his Norwegian charges. He intervened to save peasants from the more rapacious taxes sought by Copenhagen, and he built up the Norwegian armed forces so that at Kvistrum in 1677 they were able to humiliate a far larger force of Swedes. Peter Wessel Tordenskiold became a great naval hero for many daring feats, the best of which was sailing a small squadron up a fjord (Dynekilen) and destroying a Swedish fleet.

Hellfire and brimstone: As Norway belat-

Left, an old rose-painted *stuene* (living room). **Above**, a traditional Norwegian Sunday.

or anyway within the national boundaries, there were still heathens. Thomas von Weston, a superb linguist, took it on himself to remedy the situation among the Lapps of Finnmark. Hans Egede went further afield to save souls in Greenland and, although he worked tirelessly, it took him eight years to win his first Innuit convert.

The legacy of Pietism is to be found not so much in the numerically small but fanatical sects still beating the drum for prohibition but (in so far as the result is likely to affect visitors) in the state's feeble acquiescence to such pressure.

On the other hand, when a liberal wind

blew in Copenhagen, it was also felt in Norway. For example, Christian VII's going mad put the affairs of state into the hands of his physician, a German named Johann Friedrich Struensee. He believed in unrestricted trade, freedom of the press and so on.

Norway was gratified to see the abolition of a system which put a fixed and artificially low value on Norwegian iron imported into Denmark, whereas Danish corn exports to Norway were sold at whatever the market would bear. Correcting the imbalance helped, but prospects of additional economic reforms ended abruptly when it was discovered that Struensee had been having an affair with Caroline Mathilde, the wife of his de-

leaving at the age of 21, and it is a pithy comment on the difficulty of drawing a line between specifically Norwegian and Danish history during the four centuries when the countries were so closely tied that both countries now claim him as their own.

Nelson attacks: Co-existence between Denmark and Norway was traumatised from the unlikely quarter of Napoleon Bonaparte. Britain had fallen out with Denmark (and hence Norway) over the Danish alliance with Prussia and Russia. A total of 149 Danish and Norwegian vessels were seized in British ports; in response, a Danish force marched into Hamburg and appropriated British property worth £15 million.

ranged patient. Strunsee was executed.

Against a backdrop of Pietism and the death penalty for sexual irregularity, one of the first chinks of the Enlightenment shone through in the person of Ludvig Holberg. He was born in Bergen but later became a resident of Copenhagen, a playwright, historian and satirist (in Latin) who, according to the distinguished historian T.K. Derry, "in his own generation had no obvious superior in range of intellect except Voltaire". Holberg's impressive output included 26 plays for the newly founded Copenhagen theatre between 1722 and 1727.

Holberg never returned to Bergen after

Nelson moved on Copenhagen with a powerful fleet. Danish and Norwegian crews manning a line of blockships put up a spirited defence, and after a six-hour battle Nelson urged the Danish Crown Prince Regent to capitulate, failing which he would have to destroy the blockships "without having the power to save the brave Danes who have defended them". The Prince agreed.

A few years later Napoleon insisted that Denmark-Norway join his continental system and close their ports to British ships. A large British fleet demanded the handing-over of the Danish navy, which Napoleon sorely needed after losing his at Trafalgar, and when this met with refusal, Copenhagen was bombarded with at least 14,000 rounds over three days.

British troops occupied the capital for six weeks, after which the expedition went home with the Danish fleet and vast quantities of naval stores. The enormity of such an attack on what was a neutral country put Denmark and Norway firmly into Napoleon's camp, a position which required them to join him in attacking Sweden.

The division thus rendered between Sweden and Denmark was bound to have serious consequences. The impotent "pig in the middle" was Norway. The inevitable was set rolling in 1810 when Sweden's King Karl

The Danish Crown Prince Christian Frederik tried to rally Norwegian loyalty, *inter alia* by agreeing to let Norway have the national bank it had long craved. In the end, though, the decision did not rest in either Norwegian or Danish hands. Union between Sweden and Norway was imposed by the Peace of Kiel (following Napoleon's defeat at Leipzig) in 1814.

Battle for throne: Christian Frederik was not going to surrender Norway without a struggle. He entertained the idea of getting himself popularly acclaimed as king (he thought his chances best in Trondheim) but the general feeling among the population at large was that the Danish line had renounced

XIII appointed as his heir (of all people, considering the events which had just passed) Jean-Baptiste Bernadotte, one of Napoleon's marshals. Bernadotte assumed slightly more plausible Swedish credentials by changing his name to Karl Johan and succeeded to the throne in 1818.

Karl Johan conceived a plan whereby Russia and Britain would support Swedish claims on Norway. They agreed, with the result that Norwegian ports were blockaded to secure a "voluntary" union with Sweden.

Left, the old mining town of Røros. **Above**, a northern graveyard in Andøy, Vesterålen.

its sovereignty and the Norwegians were now entitled to choose their own king.

In April 1814, an assembly of 37 farmers, 16 businessmen, and 59 bureaucrats met in Eidsvoll to decide what that future should be. The constitution they prepared was signed on 17 May, still the biggest day of the year in Norway. On the same day a new king was elected; to his immense satisfaction, it was the tenacious Christian Frederik. Sweden would have none of it. The Norwegians fought well in a one-sided contest but Christian Frederik soon had to sue for peace. Karl Johan, *née* Bernadotte, stepped forward to occupy his double throne.

Divorce from Denmark was followed by a quarrel over the division of joint assets and liabilities. The assets were Iceland, Greenland and the Faroes which, Norway claimed, were Norwegian colonies long before marriage with Denmark. The liabilities were the Danish-Norwegian national debt.

Who owed what? The Norwegian position was not only that Denmark alone should shoulder the burden but that compensation was due to Norway for centuries of exploitation. Assuming powers granted under the Treaty of Kiel which had brought about the new union, Karl Johan declared that Norway would pay off some of the debt. The matter of the colonies was not finally resolved until 1931, when the International Court at The Hague found in favour of Denmark.

Two kingdoms: Friction between Karl Johan and the Norwegian half of his kingdom was present right from the start because they were pulling in opposite directions: Karl Johan envisaged a gradual merging of the two kingdoms, while Norway was determined to consolidate the independence ratified by the 1814 Constitution.

A constitutional battle took place over a bill to abolish all noble titles and privileges. Again and again the Storting (Norway's parliament) presented the bill—and the king refused to sanction it. The constitution said he could refuse a bill only twice; the third time it automatically become law. Karl Johan objected strongly to what was clearly a limitation on his authority which did not exist in Sweden.

A fundamental principle was at stake and the dispute was not to be resolved easily. Indeed, it remained the biggest bone of contention for the life of the union and, as much as anything else, was the author of its eventual dissolution. Norwegian pride was prickly. Merchant ships could fly the Norwegian flag close to home but not in waters notoriously under the sway of North African pirates. Sweden had bought off the pirates but the immunity extended only to the Swedish flag; if Norwegian ships wanted to take advantage of it, they had to switch flags.

Sweden's dogged refusal to allow Norway its own diplomatic and consular representation abroad was not only an insult but a practical handicap because the Norwegian merchant fleet was well on its way to becoming, by 1880, the third largest in the world. Its far-flung crews wanted and needed a purely Norwegian diplomatic service.

Oslo once again: Karl Johan was adept at making a concession here and there to court

popularity, and the welcome he received on visiting Christiania in 1838 was probably sincere, as was the manifestation of grief when he died six years later. Although changing Christiania's name back to Oslo obliterated a Danish memory, the capital was, and is, content to leave its main street named after Karl Johan.

His successor, Oskar I, immediately tried to placate Norway through gestures such as his title which, locally, became King of Norway and Sweden, rather than the other way round. He also agreed to a new union flag which gave equal prominence to the Swedish and Norwegian colours.

Left, Eidsvoll, where the Norwegian Constitution was agreed in 1814. Right, King Karl XIV Johan of Norway and Sweden.

Norwegian politics in the 19th century were dominated at first by the Venstre party which carried the banner of separatism and rallied against the royal veto. Its leader, Johan Sverdrup, was a lawyer who worked at creating an alliance between urban radicals and wealthy farmers. Their interests were too divergent, however, and the party split, leaving room for the strong labour movement which has characterised most of the present century.

It dawned on poorer farmers and peasants who had previously let the land-owning and merchant classes get on with government, that their special interests, especially a reduction in taxes, could be advanced only if

being too poor in the lean times to pay the fare. In 1882 a record 29,000 Norwegians left, and by 1910 there were more than 400,000 people of Norwegian birth in the United States, their numbers growing right the way through to World War I.

The arts flourish: The rise of nationalism throughout Europe produced in Norway an unprecedented, and subsequently unequalled, flowering of the arts. Ibsen and Kielland, giants among an extraordinarily talented assortment of writers (not forgetting composers like Grieg and the artist Munch) came along just in time to present the world with a clearer insight into Norway than was available from best-selling romantic writers

they became involved in the process. They were assisted by a mood of national romanticism, a Nordic adaptation of the French philosopher Rousseau's belief in the nobility of savages. The Norwegian peasant farmer was portrayed as the salt of the earth. The farmers' grip on the national heart-strings—and purse—has never been relinquished.

Putting peasants on a pedestal, however, did not ameliorate the hard facts of life. Emigration to the United States began in 1825, although statistics reveal the irony that emigration was highest when the economic conditions at home were good, and lowest when they were bad. Perhaps it was a case of

who began to churn out the most extraordinary rubbish about the country.

It may be worth summarising, for strong stomachs, the plot of one such work, *Thelma: A Norwegian Princess*, by Miss Marie Corelli, which ran to no fewer than 47 editions. Sir Philip Bruce-Errington encounters in Altenfjord, in the northernmost part of Norway, a crazy dwarf who lives in a cavern illuminated by antique Etruscan lamps. Sir Philip and the dwarf converse comfortably

Above, emigrants leave Stavanger for the New World. **Right**, this boy, aged 8, crossed the Atlantic alone in 1907 after his mother died.

THE GREAT EXODUS

One thousand years after the first Norwegian Vikings turned their longships towards the west, pushing out as far as North America, a second wave of Norwegians began to cast their eyes in the same direction.

The motives of these new emigrants were similar—lack of opportunity and poverty—but they had none of the warlike excitement of the earlier exodus. These new "Vikings" sought a place where they could work and prosper rather than exploration and conquest.

Yet the first small emigrant boat, the 54-ft (16-metre) sloop *Restauration*, must have been scarcely more sea-worthy than the superbly built longships. With 52 crew and passengers crammed into its hold, even degrees of comfort could only have been comparative and the sufferings of the pregnant woman who gave birth to a daughter on board are better left unimagined.

But these early "sloopers", who set sail from Stavanger in July 1825, were idealistic and highly motivated. The leader, Lars Larsen Geilane, was a Quaker and there were members of the religious Haugeans sect among these pioneers. Their intention to found a classless society where they could follow their own religion had been further encouraged when the previous year another Norwegian pioneer, Cleng Peerson, returned with reports of the promised land.

The *Restauration* reached New York in October of the same year and these farming people, mostly from Rogaland *fylke*, the county around Stavanger, lost no time in settling on land bought for them by Cleng Peerson at Kendall on the shores of Lake Ontario. This settlement became a staging post on the road to Illinois, where many Norwegian emigrants made their homes.

When the *Restauration* left in 1825, Norway's population was only one million, yet the next three generations sent 750,000 Norwegians to North America, reflecting a population increase at home rather than an emptying of the Norwegian countryside, though early industrialists began to campaign against such a dribbling away of potential labour.

The early "sloopers" had more in common with the Pilgrim Fathers who left Plymouth in the *Mayflower* two centuries earlier than with the Norwegian emigrants who came after them. The main motive among the second and later waves of country people was good land and good farming prospects rather than religious or political repression. To be an *odelsbonde*, who owned his own land, was to be a free man and the goal of every Norwegian peasant.

Many who had worked for wages or at sea in Norway were able to own their farms in the new country. The American merchant fleets were also eager to make use of the superior skills of the Norwegian seamen, bred from generations who had lived off the sea. The newcomers prospered and regular letters home, reports, and Norwegian visitors from the New World increased the fever. The letters were printed in newspapers all over the country and one or two mid-Western American states began to use agents to encourage emigration.

By the middle of the 1830s new emigrants and some of the original "sloopers" had moved on to Illinois where the hardy Norwegians were bred to endure the freezing temperatures of a mid-Western winter. By the middle of the 19th century, Illinois had 2,500 Norwegians among its 80,000 population. Twenty years later, they numbered more than 12,500. The 1862 Homestead Law, which granted land to immigrants, turned the early trickle into a steady flow, and Cleg Peerson founded Norwegian settlements in Iowa.

For many patriotic Norwegians it became *de rigueur* to help the expansion. The great violinist, Ole Bull, who had travelled the world, had a well-intentioned but crashing failure with a planned settlement, "Oleana", in Pennsylvania. He was too far from his Norwegian farming roots. The soil was ungrateful, communications impossible, and Bull lost more than $40,000.

Later, Norwegians also settled in Canada; but by the 1930s emigration had dwindled to a trickle. Yet the Norwegian influence was strong in the places where they settled; many communities taught the Norwegian tongue in their schools for generations, the distinctive Lutheran tradition continued —and they brought their skis and skiing skills. Today, the overt "Norwegian-ness" may have disappeared, but anyone who doubts it still exists need only read Garrison Keillor's winsome tales of life around Lake Wobegon.

in English but that does not prevent Sir Philip from being amazed by the dwarf's intellect, when he correctly guesses his nationality.

Sir Philip then makes the acquaintance of old Olaf Guldmar, Princess Thelma's father. He is a wretched peasant farmer who, like the mad dwarf, is fluent in English which he even uses to address his servant. Sir Philip is understandably full of admiration and respect when he discovers Olaf's library. It contains, for example, the works of Shakespeare, Scott, Byron, Keats, Gibbon, Plutarch and Chapman's translation of Homer. It turns out that he is an accomplished Latin scholar, although in religious belief still a devout pagan, "by Valhalla!"

being his favourite oath.

Not a moment too soon, Olaf feels death coming on and, following custom, is carried aboard his vessel which is set on fire and pushed out to sea. "He raised his arms as though in ecstasy: 'Glory! – joy! – victory!' And, like a noble tree struck down by lightning, he fell—dead."

That the reality of Norway might be different from the picture conveyed above was first mooted, at least in England, by a short article which appeared in the *Spectator* magazine in 1872 about a previously unheard of Norwegian poet named Ibsen who had written "short songs of irregular meas-

ure after the manner of Heine". The poet wrote a note of thanks to the writer, Edmund Gosse, adding "I shall consider myself most fortunate if you decide to translate one or more of my books," a modest hint that he may have written more than poems.

Poet and playwright: At home Ibsen and others like Bjørnstjerne Bjørnson were leading lights in agitation against Danish domination in the arts. The campaign included, for example, that Danish actors should no longer be employed on the Norwegian stage.

Henrik Johan Ibsen was born in the small town of Skien in Telemark in 1828. His father's financial indiscretions plunged the family into poverty, and Ibsen was apprenticed at an early age to a chemist in the even smaller town of Grimstad. His first poems, with titles like *Resignation*, *Doubt* and *The Corpse's Ball*, give a clue to the majestic gloom—punctuated, nevertheless by delicious wit—of his later work.

After working in the theatre in Bergen, he joined the Christiania (Oslo) Norske Theater, which had been founded to promote specifically Norwegian theatre. He fared miserably with one failure after another, poor health and no money. In the depths of depression he began to question the deplorable position of the creative artist in society and that, ironically, put him on the road to better things. *The Pretenders*, first performed in 1864, was a great success and helped him to a travelling scholarship. He went abroad, first to Italy, and did not live in Norway again until 27 years later.

The plays for which he is best remembered were produced from about 1877 onwards. The first of these, *Pillars of Society*, broke new ground in dealing with the untruth and humbug of a small provincial town. In creating any number of great female roles, Ibsen touched on subjects that theatre audiences and critics were not ready for.

If his work was controversial at home, it was considered outrageous when eventually it travelled abroad. The *Daily Telegraph* in London seems not to have enjoyed the first overseas production of *Ghosts*: "positively abominable... this disgusting presentation... a dirty act done publicly, a (lavatory) with all its doors and windows open... gross, almost putrid indecorum... literary carrion... crapulous stuff." Another critic went even further: "Lugubrious diagnosis of sordid impropriety... maunderings of nook-shotten Norwegians."

There were other points of view, however, like that of Havelock Ellis and, when the dust had settled, in George Bernard Shaw's appraisal of Ibsen's work: "The influence which Ibsen has had in England is almost equal to the influence which three revolutions, six crusades, a couple of foreign invasions, and an earthquake would produce. The Norman conquest was a mere nothing compared with the Norwegian Conquest."

While the Norwegian element in the work of the great Holberg in the previous century could hardly be told apart from the Danish, there was no ambiguity about Ibsen. As a

over Norway's diplomatic representation. The government wanted its own consular service; King Oskar II refused.

The government then argued that, if it resigned and the king was unable to obtain an alternative government, his royal power would effectively have lapsed. It would then revert to the Storting, which would choose a new king. The Storting agreed to this plan, although a minority wanted specifically to exclude Swedes from the throne.

Oskar was hurt and the Swedish government outraged. Neither would have been placated by a plebiscite which showed 368,208 in favour of breaking away from Sweden and only 184 against. The two ad-

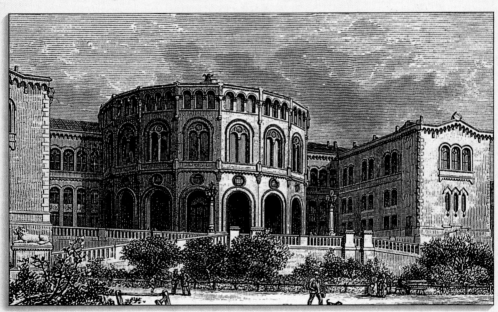

curious footnote, however, he once wrote to a friend in England saying "I have been revolving many things in my mind lately, and one of the conclusions to which I have come is that there are very strong traces in me of Scotch descent. But this is only a feeling— perhaps only a wish that it were so."

Battle of wills: Ibsen's strong sense of national identity was mirrored in the political events swirling around him. Problems within the union with Sweden came to a head in 1905 because of the long-running dispute

Left, King Oskar II. Right, an early picture of the Storting (parliament).

versaries—king versus half his country—played cat and mouse. The "compromise" reached in 1905 was in truth a surrender to Norwegian demands: Oskar's abdication and independence. The king's parting shot was that no member of his house would be allowed to accept the vacated throne even if it were offered. This was only in part petulance. Oskar was privately convinced that an independent Norway was bound to collapse and whoever was then king would thus be discredited. When (rather than if) that happened, an unsullied member of his house would of course be standing by to answer the call. That call was never heard.

The Prime Minister who led Norway to independence was Christian Michelsen, a Bergen solicitor who founded one of the biggest shipping companies in Norway and was by 1903 a member of the government. In the meantime, he had formed a breakaway group in Bergen of "liberals" from the Radical Left. At an early stage Michelsen's modest aim was to settle the consular issue (whether Norway should have its own consuls abroad) which finally destroyed the union with Sweden, but by 1904 he was

elsen quickly left the stormy waters of politics for a calmer and more profitable life in his shipping business in Bergen, though he remained an active elder statesman until his death in 1925. For their new king, the Norwegians had elected a member of the Danish royal house, who was also grandson of King Karl XV of Sweden. On his succession, he adopted the Norwegian name of Haakon.

In the long years of struggle, Bjørnstjerne Bjørnson had claimed that "the foreign policy of Norway should be to have no foreign

warning the Swedes not to assume that if negotiations failed this time, they would be easy to resume.

Michelsen had recognised the way Norwegian public opinion was running and the support the cause was getting from such famous Norwegians as the explorer Fridtjof Nansen (who later became Norwegian Ambassador in London) and the writer Bjørnstjerne Bjørnson. Soon Michelsen was heading a cabinet that included ministers from a wide range of parties and of many shades of opinion.

With independence established in 1905 and King Haakon VII on the throne, Mich-

policy," and immediately after independence, the aim of all parties was to avoid entanglement in the affairs of the Great Powers. But, despite its determined neutrality, within a decade newly independent Norway was faced with World War I.

The threat had the ironic effect of throwing Norway and Sweden back into one another's arms. "A new union, not of the old sort, but a union of heartfelt understanding" was the Swedish king's description of their concerted intention "to maintain the neutrality of the respective kingdoms in relation to all the belligerent powers".

Norway did well out of its neutrality, at

least for the first two years of the war. Germany was willing to pay top prices for all the fish Norway could supply, which attracted British attention and led to a secret agreement, hammered home by the threat to cut off supplies of British oil and coal, under which Britain would buy most of the fish itself. Norway, in return, would not export vital copper pyrites to Germany, but in other respects it was able to maintain lucrative trade with both sides.

Those lucky enough to get a share of this trade, and of the domestic black market, flaunted their overnight fortunes in such a way that workers on fixed wages, which were forever falling behind rampant inflation, became rebellious. Employers retaliated with lock-outs, and the government was forced to introduce compulsory arbitration.

Unlimited German submarine warfare put a damper on profiteering. Most of the Norwegian merchant fleet was under charter to Britain and by the end of the war half of it, together with 2,000 crew members, was lost. In absolute terms only Britain lost more of its shipping. The intervention of the United States also made matters worse for Norway because the Americans demanded big cuts in trade with Germany before agreeing to make supplies available to Norway.

At the end of the war the neutral countries had little say in deciding the terms of peace. Despite its heavy losses the Norwegian merchant navy received no compensation in the shape of ships from the confiscated German navy, and it was 10 years before injured seamen and the families of those who had died received voluntary compensation from the German government.

Nansen and the League: During the war the Scandinavian monarchs had met to discuss and set up committees to review the position of neutral countries when hostilities ceased. Under Nansen, Norway formed an Association for the League of Nations and drafted a potential constitution. But, as the war ended,

Preceding pages: manufacturing iron stairs in Kristiania (Oslo). Photo: Johan Lund, *circa* 1890–1900. **Left**, the Royal Family with their ski instructor. **Right**, King Haakon VII.

the great powers were not inclined to take much notice of mere neutrals. They themselves laid down the rules and allowed the neutral countries just two months after the League was founded to seek membership.

Norway, temperamentally against alliances, was fiercely divided and it was not until 1920 that the Storting finally voted in favour of membership of the League, Norway's first real move into internationalism. Nansen, who had been so influential in the struggle for Norwegian independence,

now had international links to America, the Soviet Union and elsewhere, and became active in the League, particularly in the slow repatriation of nearly half a million prisoners-of-war from Russia. He later donated his own Nobel Peace Prize money for similar work for Russian and Armenian refugees and devised the Nansen Passport which gave stateless people an identification document. He was still occupied with this work at the time of his death in 1930.

But in 1920, of the Storting's 20 votes against membership of the League of Nations, 16 came from the steadily growing Labour Party which, at the time, took most of its principles and goals from the ideas behind the Russian Revolution.

Briefly in credit: Although Norway was one of the creditor nations when the war ended, the cavalier business atmosphere of the war years carried over as financial recklessness, if not ignorance. In very short order the country was further into debt than it had so recently been in credit.

By 1921 conditions had deteriorated into a full-blown economic depression with more than a million tons of shipping laid up, free-spending local authorities in difficulty and—unthinkably awful in Norwegian eyes—one of the biggest banks going bankrupt in spite of secret state support.

unionists were already out of work when employers tried to reduce wages which, in spite of nearly a decade of economic turmoil, were still inordinately high by the standards of most European countries.

A lock-out at Norsk Hydro produced not only the most notorious incident in the history of Norwegian industrial relations (police and troops fighting demonstrators) but also the rise to public prominence of a figure as shameful in Norwegian memory as anyone since, say, Erik Bloodaxe. The defence minister who ordered the troops in was Vidkun Quisling, and he was soon accusing Labour of plotting an armed revolution.

Quisling was largely discredited in his

Storms and controversies over Prohibition caused the downfall of three different cabinets. The steadily growing Labour Party became more revolutionary in its beliefs, and passed a resolution reserving the right to use "revolutionary action in the struggle for the economic liberation of the working classes." The point having been made, militancy declined and by the end of the decade the Party had turned its attention back to parliamentary rule. In the 1927 elections, in spite of fragmentation, it became the biggest party in the Storting.

The Wall Street crash of 1929 compounded the misery. A third of all trade

own country by 1939. At that time he was in Berlin for reasons which were not clear then but soon became very obvious indeed.

By 1933, the economic crisis was so bad that the unlikely alliance of the Labour Party with the Agrarian (Farmers') Party put a Labour Prime Minister into power. He was Johan Nygaardsvold, with lengthy experience in the Storting. He was Prime Minister from 1935 with a direct responsibility for creating employment and, by 1939, the average day's wage had risen by 15 percent.

Precarious neutrality: When World War II broke out in September 1939 Norway immediately proclaimed neutrality, but had taken almost no precautions to defend itself if required to do so. Just 7,000 men were called up and the coastal defences were only half-manned. (Perhaps Nygaardsvold was too immersed in his economic renaissance. He remained Prime Minister until 1945 but in the recriminations and resultant inquiry that followed the end of World War II, he was deemed partly to blame for not making adequate preparations for Norway's defence before the start of the war.)

The first warning signs came from the Allied side, with Britain complaining that its ships were being sunk by Germany in Norwegian territorial waters. Furthermore, German ships were being given free access to

fjord to rescue the men while two small Norwegian vessels looked on, making vain protests. The Norwegian government complained to Britain about violation of neutrality, the British government asked why Norway had been unable to prevent German abuse of its waters, and Germany posed the same question the other way round.

Invasion by sea: Britain unilaterally began laying its own mines along the Norwegian coastline and, on the very day Norway lodged a protest—8 April 1940—German forces were on the high seas bound for Norway. Once the invasion was under way, the German minister in Oslo sent a note to say that Germany was only occupying a few

strategic iron-ore from the northern port of Narvik. The ancient Norwegian fleet was in no position to keep territorial waters neutral, so the British suggested mining them.

The dilemma was highlighted by the well-known *Altmark* affair. The *Altmark*, an auxiliary to the battleship *Graf Spee*, was on its way to Germany with 300 captured British seamen when it sought refuge in Norwegian waters near Egersund. The Royal Navy was alerted to its presence and charged into the

strategic points to keep the British out.

At last the Norwegian government woke up to what was going on. The German heavy cruiser *Blücher* was sunk by coastal batteries at the entrance to Oslo fjord, and two creaking Norwegian destroyers boldly took on a much larger German force at Narvik.

The Storting granted the government full powers "to take whatever decisions might be necessary to ensure the best interests of the country," the point on which many a debate would later hinge. On 10 April the Germans showed their hand. Quisling, whose National Unity party commanded all of 1.8 percent of the electorate, was their choice as new prime minister. The government, which had moved itself out of Oslo to Trysil, repeatedly refused to comply, and its defiance was repaid with a German bombing attack on the meeting place.

Norway's only hope against such lopsided odds lay in the Allies. From Britain's point of view, Narvik was the key because of the iron-ore traffic. The Royal Navy went into action against German naval units in the area and destroyed them. A combined force of Norwegians, British, French and Poles fought to regain control of the city itself and on 28 May succeeded in doing so.

Earlier, on 14 and 15 April, other Allied troops had landed on either side of Trond-

ing to Britain. On 7 June 1940 they boarded a British cruiser.

Reprisals begin: A hard Nazi, Josef Terboven, was despatched to Norway as Reichskommissar. Quisling was appalled; he had expected to be appointed Führer, in which capacity he would then conclude peace with Germany and mobilise on its side. Terboven had little time for Quisling, but the latter had friends in Berlin who arranged to have him appointed "Minister-President". As such, Quisling ordered all children between the ages of 10 and 18 to join his version of the Hitler Youth. His plans for the Nazification of the civil service, courts, all professional bodies and trade

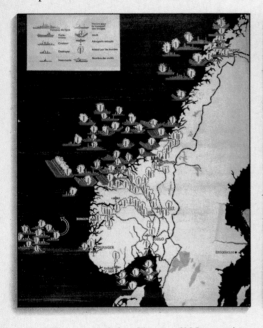

heim. They were joined by small Norwegian units. They put up a plucky fight but, practically without any air cover against the Luftwaffe, took a pasting from above. Towns where there was a British presence were bombed to ruin: Åndalsnes, Namsos, Steinkjer and Mosjøen. The fight for Norway was overshadowed, however, by the German steamroller in western Europe and, with what were seen to be greater needs there, the Allied forces were withdrawn, and Norway stood alone.

The king and government, evacuated to the north and ready to fight on, decided that the cause would be better served by decamp-

unions were in every instance fiercely rejected. Practically every lawyer, for example, refused to have anything to do with the organisation set up for them.

Resistance met with grim reprisals. Two trade union leaders, Viggo Hansteen and Rolf Wickstrøm, were shot; the rector of Oslo University was arrested. A steady flow of prisoners, including 1,300 uncooperative teachers, arrived at Grini, the concentration camp established outside Oslo. The most

Above left, strategic map from World War II. **Above right**, the struggle for Narvik, 1941. **Right**, Kirk Douglas in the film *The Heroes Of Telemark*.

THE HEROES OF TELEMARK

The most celebrated act of resistance in Norway during World War II was the sabotage of the Vemork heavy water plant at Rjukan, in Telemark, in February 1943. No visitor to Rjukan, dwarfed and darkened by mountains all round, could fail to be awed by the audacity of the saboteurs. More importantly, though, the production of heavy water in the plant was a race which, if it had not been stopped, could conceivably have given Hitler the atomic bomb.

The operation was originally planned for a joint force of Norwegian volunteers and British commandos in two towed gliders. It ended disastrously when both gliders and one of the aircraft towing them crashed 100 miles (160 km) from Rjukan. In spite of the commandos' army uniforms, the survivors were captured and shot.

The second attempt was an all-Norwegian affair. "Gunnerside", the code-name for six men who had been trained in Scotland, parachuted from 1,200 ft (360 metres) to a frozen lake where they were supposed to join up with "Swallow", an advance party on the ground. The first person they bumped into was a reindeer hunter. He was later released with food and money on the promise that he would say nothing about what he had seen.

Once the parties had linked up, they skied to the mountain ridge above Rjukan for the perilous descent on foot. They slithered down, up to their waists in snow. Just after midnight, the covering party took up positions while the six-man demolition team cut a chain on the gates and crept forward to the basement of the five-storey concrete building where the most vital equipment and the heavy water storage tanks were located. All wore British uniforms and were agreed that no lights would be carried; weapons would be unloaded to avoid the accidental discharge of arms and anyone captured would take his own life.

As the basement was locked, the best way in appeared to be a funnel carrying cables and piping. Two went through it. The solitary Norwegian guard was astonished but agreed to lead them to vital components and to mould explosive charges in the right shape. "I had placed half the charges in position when there was a crash of broken glass behind me," one of the pair wrote later.

The other members of the team, not realising that their leaders had managed to get in, had decided to smash in through a window. With the rest of the charges laid, the six began a rapid withdrawal. They were nonplussed by the co-operative guard who, understandably getting out as well while the going was good, implored to be let in again. He had forgotten his glasses! The request was granted, but the delay meant that the party had only gone a few yards when they heard "a cataclysmic explosion".

Five members of the parachute team reached Sweden "in excellent spirits and condition" after a 250-mile (400-km) journey on skis in indescribably difficult conditions; the sixth stayed on for another year. Of the Swallow party, an irrepressible character named Claus Helberg had the liveliest time. He was chased through the mountains by a German soldier who was very evidently an expert skier.

The pursuit ended in true Hollywood fashion. Both were exhausted. Helberg turned and fired one shot. He missed. The German panicked, emptied his magazine at Helberg without success and turned tail. Helberg took his time. "I sent a bullet after him, he staggered and finally stopped, hanging over his ski sticks."

Helberg was not out of trouble yet. Almost immediately he fell over a cliff and broke an arm. The next morning he walked into a German patrol but had a good enough story to be taken to a hotel to await treatment. Most of the hotel guests (but not the poor fellow with a broken arm) were turned out of their rooms to make way for Reichskommissar Terboven (the Nazi who ruled Norway) and his entourage.

Terboven was so enraged by a woman who refused to provide the amusement expected of her that he had the remaining guests, including Helberg, "bundled into a bus and sent off to the Grini concentration camp". Helberg jumped from the bus, ducked a volley of bullets and—broken arm or not—escaped. In due course he turned up in Britain, reporting for further duties.

summary reprisals were meted out to members of the military underground, Milorg, a nucleus of survivors of the 1940 fighting augmented by volunteers and armed by clandestine shipments from Britain under the auspices of the Special Operations Executive. It is not too fanciful to see the old Viking character revived in the small boats which opened up regular channels of communication with king and government in Britain.

But the "Shetland Bus", which carried volunteers between Shetland and Norway, was a perilous undertaking. Televåg, a village on an island near Bergen, was razed when it was discovered to be an assembly point for the "bus". The men were deported

Norway while their forces elsewhere capitulated—the army alone numbered 350,000. Fears that the whole country might be put to the torch like Finnmark were laid to rest only when they surrendered on 7 May 1945. The gates of Grini were thrown open and thousands streamed out to join what was undoubtedly the biggest street party ever held in Oslo. It was still going strong a week later when Crown Prince Olav returned. King Haakon's return was timed to coincide, to the day, with the fifth anniversary of his reluctant departure.

Cleaning up after the war concentrated on Quisling's prosecution. Charges were brought against 50,000, many for petty

to Germany, the women and children interned. A group of 18 men waiting in Ålesund for the trip to Britain were detected and shot. The most famous of the guerrilla operations was conducted against the heavy water factory at Rjukan in Telemark.

Celebration party: The final chapter of the Occupation was played out by German troops retreating from Finland through Finnmark in northern Norway. They adopted a scorched-earth policy which utterly destroyed many towns and villages. The inhabitants were herded into fishing boats to find their own way to the south.

The Germans were still very strong in

crimes rather than full-scale collaboration. The courts were not unduly harsh, perhaps sensing—and, if so, correctly—that participation in Quisling's so-called NS would remain a stigma. Only 25 were executed, including Quisling and two of his ministers.

After that necessary purging, Norway's greatest needs were to replace what had been destroyed during the war, and to modernise and expand industry and the economy. The whole of northern Norway had been so heavily devastated that in some cases traces of hasty rebuilding are only now being replaced, and many of the small northern towns still have an austere anonymity.

Against that, the terrible hardship and deaths of thousands of prisoners-of-war from Russia and many other countries has left a legacy of railway track and road systems that has certainly helped the north.

Fast economic expansion and many crash programmes led to large investment and over-employment, but it provided a rising standard of living that climbed faster and farther than most countries in Europe. By the early 1960s Norway used more electricity per head than any other country in the world and only three people in every thousand in remote areas had no supply. The mercantile marine had made good its wartime shipping losses by 1949 and tonnage tripled within 15

sion scheme, which aimed to give retired Norwegians a standard of living comparable with that of their working lives, was finally voted in in 1966 when the majority in the Storting was non-socialist.

In keeping with similar parties in Sweden and Denmark, post-war Norwegian socialism has been middle-of-the-road, led first by Einar Gerhardsen, who had been a prominent Resistance worker, Oscar Torp, and Trygve Bratteli (who, like Gerhardsen, had been Mayor of Oslo).

In later years, the best known Norwegian prime minister has been Gro Harlem Brundtland, who held office from 1986 for the remainder of the 1980s. Formerly Minis-

years. By the 1970s Norway was almost overwhelmed by the riches it was receiving from oil and its international industry.

All this went along with 20 years of Socialist government, which introduced comprehensive social welfare services, Scandinavian style, and much state control of industry. But this was no far-left Labour Party in the style of its post-World War I predecessors, and many shared its belief in an equal society and care for all. The People's Pen-

Left, Crown Prince Olav (now King) returns at the end of the war. **Above**, US naval ship enters Trondheimsfjord after a NATO exercise.

ter of the Environment, she was the first Norwegian woman prime minister, and became known on the international scene through her efforts to protect and improve the environment.

The attitude of King Olav V, who succeeded to the throne in 1957, also helped to keep Norway tranquil. King Olav took his father's motto of "All for Norway" and was a popular figure, made more so by his earlier prowess as a sailor and his continuing interest in that sport and in skiing.

International links: In 1945 Norway was one of the founding signatories of the United Nations, and a former Norwegian Foreign

Minister, Trygve Lie, became its first secretary-general from February 1946 until 1953. Lie held the office during the first hopeful years and continued to do so into the Korean War, in which United Nations troops took an active fighting role for the first and last time. Norway provided and staffed a field hospital in Korea.

Since then some 32,000 Norwegians have worn a United Nations blue beret. Norway has not since gone back on its commitment to internationalism and, like the other Scandinavian nations, has concentrated very much on human rights and humanitarian help in cash and kind for the poorer nations of the world.

Joining NATO, however, was more problematical. Norway saw its role as "bridge-building" across the divide of the emerging Cold War, and the country had no particular reason to feel paranoid about its Russian neighbour. Unlike neighbouring Sweden, Norway had never been at war with Russia. The Russians had recently acted as liberators in Finnmark, and the two countries were in fact negotiating joint occupation of Spitsbergen (or Svalbard).

Nevertheless, for most of the war years Trygve Lie had been advocating an alliance with the great Atlantic Powers for his "seafaring people", rather than with any power in Europe. The fate of Czechoslovakia, a country which also saw itself as a bridge-builder until the Iron Curtain clanked down behind it, convinced the doubters that Norway's security depended on more tangible Western links than would be afforded by Swedish-style neutrality.

As NATO's most northeasterly outpost, with a short 122-mile (196-km) border with the Soviet Union, Norway has inevitably walked a tightrope between the super powers. Soviet "merchant ships" visit the northern sea coast and unaccountably need lengthy, unspecified repairs which keep them in harbour for months. Ships of the Soviet Northern Fleet, based on the Kola peninsula, are a common sight in the North Atlantic when crossing to Iceland; but there have never been any major incidents and, long before *glasnost*, Norway turned a philosophical face to its massive neighbour.

The debate over whether to join the European Community aroused such passions, especially among farmers and fishermen who realised that membership would terminate their subsidies, that it is still talked about in terms of near-civil war. The Storting was generally in favour of applying for membership along with Denmark and Britain, partners in the European Free Trade Association, but the first approaches were rebuffed by an imperious General Charles de Gaulle.

Threat to identity: A referendum was organised in 1972 to gauge public opinion on whether another attempt ought to be made. There was never any doubting where the farmers and rural Norway as a whole would stand; it was less predictable that the issue should stir up the urban young, who thought they saw a threat to national identity and campaigned under such slogans as "Norway is not for sale". In the event, the country opposed joining by a vote of 52.5 percent.

At the end of the 1980s, the country braced itself for a reconsideration. Added to the arguments—which remained very much as before—was the twist which asked whether, on the evidence of what happened last time, the country ought to risk re-opening the debate at all.

Left, one of Norway's best known post-war prime ministers, Gro Harlem Brundtland, and her husband. **Right**, King Olav and Crown Prince Harald leave the Storting.

For the chronically under-employed off-shoots of European royalty, the rash of new states in the 19th and early 20th century brought blessed job opportunities. Their prospects were reduced by republican tendencies and other disappointments: Albania offered its throne to the England cricket captain, who declined, it but in 1905 Norway's criteria were less capricious.

Norway had a long royal pedigree, but it had died out during 500 years under Danish and Swedish rule. While Norwegians saw some advantages in a Scandinavian as king, there was the feeling that a Danish or Swedish monarch would amount to the despised *status ante quo*. In the event, the former considerations outweighed the latter, and an invitation went to Prince Carl, second son of the future King Christian IX of Denmark and grandson of Sweden's King Karl XV.

Prince Carl, then 33, was married to Maud, Princess of Wales, and was son-in-law to Edward VII of England. Most of his brothers and sisters married royalty, and one turned down the throne of Bulgaria. Prince Carl insisted first on a plebiscite. The result was favourable so on 25 November 1905, having assumed the title Haakon VII, he stepped ashore in Norway sheltering his two-year-old son, born Alexander Edward Christian Frederick but quickly renamed Olav, from driving snow. Haakon himself continued to sign letters to friends and relatives in England as "Charles".

As a cadet in the Danish navy, Haakon had received no special privileges. He was not allowed in restaurants without a chaperone nor to smoke in public. "His abilities and aptitude are not great," the principal of his naval college reported. "I have done wretchedly," the prince confirmed. He was relatively good at languages and dancing but weak in mathematics and sciences.

His earlier private education began with rising at seven for a walk and a spell of gymnastics followed by a breakfast of beer soup. Queen Maud's background was no more propitious. Her father, Edward VII, took no part in her upbringing because, he believed, that would make her shy and nervous. Unfortunately, she *was* frequently shy and nervous, never mastered Norwegian, and developed such poor eyesight that she could barely recognise anyone.

Republicanism survived in Norway. Politicians complained that the cost of the monarchy was "six or seven" times greater than for a presidency. The royal apartments in the palace were scarcely habitable to begin with and the government would only allow half of the estimated cost to put them right. Frugality was paramount, because of the fear that an ostentatious royalty would provoke a

countrywide epidemic of snobbery. By watching expenses as carefully as he observed constitutional niceties, Haakon gradually won over the sceptics. Left-wing doubts ceased in 1926 when he called on the Labour party to form a government.

The king worked hard at not being a foreigner. He travelled widely and impressed his subjects with a dignified modesty. The crown prince needed no encouragement to make up the perceived deficiency in the family tree. Although he was actually born in England, and attended Balliol College, Oxford, he felt at home and proved it by winning prizes on the Holmenkollen ski jump, as daunting a test of Norwegian authenticity as there could be, especially for one whose mingled Danish and English blood would not normally produce a skier. He also represented Norway as an Olympic sailor, another huge plus to his sea-minded subjects.

World War II was the supreme challenge. Implacably opposed to Hitler, King Haakon had to contend with the local clamour for neutrality. "I must be careful... not to say too much," he wrote to Queen Mary, his sister-in-law in London, "so that my ministers

years to the day after he had left the country.

Haakon died in 1957 at the age of 85 after a reign of 52 years. He was called the best king Norway had ever had—Haakon the Good. His son, who succeeded as Olav V, inherited the same unassuming manner, evident in his endearing discomfort while delivering the traditional New Year's Eve television broadcast, and the affection in which his father was held.

The present king is an only child. His mother died in 1938 and his wife, Crown

cannot say I am more English than Norwegian." He would abdicate rather than bow to German demands for recognition of the Quisling government. Running the gauntlet of the Luftwaffe, he escaped to the north and was spirited to England. His work, and that of the Crown Prince, with the Norwegian exile movement inspired dogged resistance at home and cemented a bond which gave the king a tumultuous reception on his eventual return to the steps of the Oslo city hall five

Left, King Olav is famous as a sailor, winning an Olympic title in the 1920s. **Above**, the king with Sami children in Karasjok.

Princess Martha, also died before he came to the throne, so Norway has not had a queen for more than half a century. The scarcity of Norwegian royals was compounded by Olav's daughters, Raghhild and Astrid, marrying commoners. Crown Prince Harald, born in 1937, also married one: Sonja Haraldsen. The birth of their daughter, Martha Louise, in 1971 meant there was still no succession because the constitution allows it only down the male line. The later birth of a son, Haakon Magnus, secured for at least another generation the future of what has been as successful as any off-the-shelf monarchy could be.

NATIONAL DAY

If you wish to find the soul of Norway, so they say, visit the country in May. It's a month when little gets done, much to the chagrin of foreigners who arrive on business. But it's the prime time for observing the patriotic emotions that lie not far below the surface of an otherwise taciturn people.

The month starts with the official 1 May public holiday which, like 1 May holidays in many countries, honours the declaration of the International Socialist Congress of 1889. The socialist thread dominates celebrations as left-wingers devote panegyrics to Marxist gurus and red flags adorn public buildings, but most Norwegians now regard it as an excuse to extend the nearest weekend. Flag Day on 8 May is dedicated to celebrating the surrender of the German occupying forces and hence the end of World War II in Norway. In most years, Whitsun is also in May, and is another official holiday, longer than many elsewhere, for it includes Whitsunday and the following Monday. Norwegians, like all Scandinavians make the most of stretching out their holidays.

The high point comes on the 17th, Norway's National Day. It is not an "Independence Day," as Norwegians politely point out if you use that term. It commemorates not independence, but the signing of the country's constitution and is called *Grunnlovsdag* (Constitution Day). Yet it is a day when a patriotic people outdo themselves in flying the flag, with the red, blue and white standard on virtually every pole, on city transport vehicles, and in the hands of the throngs that gather to watch parades in cities and towns.

No matter how small the village, it is sure to have a parade of its own. What makes things different is that Norway celebrates its National Day not with displays of military might but with long lines of happy children.

You hear the national anthem and other patriotic songs again and again and, from street stalls to elegant restaurants, everyone celebrates. Catering staff, taxi and transport workers and the police seem to be the only people at work that day.

It is the sort of celebration that erupts elsewhere only at the end of prolonged hostilities.

May is also a month for students. Throughout the country, exams over, senior school students waken their teachers at daybreak, join in the parades later in the day and then start a month-long spree that their elders are bound by tradition to condone. The students' collective name is *Russ* (which traces its roots to the Swedish Vikings who passed their name on to the country that became Russia) and they drive around in old cars and lorries, covered with insignia and slogans and painted red or blue to match the costume colours of their student owners, Blue indicates commercial students, red covers all the rest.

The cause of all this euphoria is one of the many accidents of European history, and has a powerful French connection. During the Napoleonic wars, Scandinavia was politically divided. Denmark, which then ruled Norway, was allied to Napoleon. Sweden had joined Great Britain and Russia in a coalition against Napoleon.

In Napoleon's ranks was Jean-Baptiste Bernadotte, a dashing military genius who rose to the rank of general by the time he was 31, and was promoted to marshall a decade later in 1804. He held the post just five years before he quarrelled with Napoleon and began to look elsewhere. He did not have long to wait before being "head-hunted". Sweden was on the look-out for a new heir to the throne and in 1810 Jean-Baptiste Bernadotte became Crown Prince Karl Johan of Sweden. At the peace negotiations in 1814 in Kiel, after Napoleon's defeat, Bernadotte acted boldly for his new fatherland and was successful in furthering measures which obliged Denmark to hand Norway over to Sweden, as part of the peace treaty.

The Norwegians, of course, baulked at terminating 434 years of Danish rule only to exchange it for Swedish rule. Church congregations throughout Norway swore to support their newly won independence and appointed 112 representatives to form a constituent assembly. On 11 April, the assembly convened in the headquarters of the Eidsvoll Iron Works, not far from Oslo, the only convenient large hall. While the great powers debated, the Eidsvoll 112 hammered out a complete constitution of 110 articles in slightly less than six weeks. On 17 May they finished their task and elected as king their former regent, Prince Christian Frederik of Denmark.

The new monarchy was short-lived. By late July, Sweden and Norway were at war and it was no surprise that Bernadotte's seasoned troops were easily the superior. They took just over a month to force the Norwegians to an armistice. Norway was united with Sweden and answered to Bernadotte, first as the emissary of King Karl XIII of Sweden and then, after Bernadotte's accession to the Swedish throne four years later, to him as King Karl XIV Johan, ruler of both Sweden and Norway.

Despite Karl Johan's ban, 17 May became a day of celebration and, in 1829, the exasperated

cessions in 1870. By 1900, the 17th was firmly established as the annual opportunity for Norwegians collectively to show their patriotism.

And show patriotism on the 17th, Norwegians certainly do, however old they may be, wherever they are in the world. Norwegian consulates, embassies, seamen's churches, and student groups abroad carry on the tradition. At home in Norway the festivities pervade all. If the day is close to Whitsunday, many Norwegians stretch the holiday to a long weekend and set off for cross-country ski treks in the mountains, where snow lies until June.

On the 17th, you will see them carrying flags, bright against the snow, often singing as is the custom of the day. Nowhere are the celebrations of the 17th as magnificent as those in the cities,

king resorted to force to uphold his decree. He dispatched infantry and cavalry to disperse a crowd that had congregated at the Stortorget market place in Christiania (now Oslo). Military might won the confrontation but the King lost the day. *Torvslaget* (the Market Place Battle) merely strengthened the legend that was to root the day in Norwegian consciousness.

Patriotism flourished. The national anthem, *"Ja, Vi Elsker"* (Yes, We Love) was first sung in public on 17 May 1864, some 20 years after Karl Johan died. Children first joined the public pro-

Left, the focus of National Day is the Royal Palace. Above, while most countries use National Days to parade their military might, in Norway it belongs to the children.

and each one has its own local flavour. In Bergen in the west, no 17 May would be complete without the *Buekorps* (Crossbow Corps) of marching boys.

The greatest festivities of all take place in Oslo. City centre streets are closed off and the parade marches up the main street—fittingly, or unfittingly named Karl Johansgate—waving a forest of flags. The review by the Royal Family takes hours yet, among the marching groups, you will see no military units. This is a parade for thousands of children, each carrying a flag and parents carrying children too small to walk. The songs they sing mention no past glories. It is a day, as the national anthem proclaims, for "a country of thousands of homes," and, as the marching children attest, the hope of children.

More than 20 years ago, as oil platforms appeared off the coast, Norway realised it was rich in oil, and the old port of Stavanger in the southwest found itself the latest international oil city.

Today, the shelves of busy food shops hold bulky packages of hominy grits, or just plain grits, alongside a connoisseur range of herbs and spices. The city owes the first to the American oil families; the herbs and spices are the travelling accessories of their French colleagues, which bring a new tang not just to expatriate cooking but to the blander flavours of the Norwegian kitchen. Around the markets and the harbour, many languages make up the vocal currency and there is a bigger range of restaurants than almost anywhere else in Norway.

High standards: Apart from these clear signs, the rush of wealth which followed the development of oil sharply raised the standard of living for most of Norway's 4.2 million population—64,000 now work in the oil services sector alone. It also transformed many areas of Norwegian life, and injected money into ailing industries that otherwise might not have survived. Cash in plenty led to a huge upgrading of roads, and the mountain and undersea tunnels that are so important in this fierce terrain, and gave a boost to research and education not just in oil industry theory and practice, in which foreign oil companies educated and trained a large number of Norway's new oil workers, but in many areas unrelated to oil.

Quite apart from its own oil income, foreign oil and gas operations have provided a massive revenue to successive Norwegian governments. Phillips Petroleum, for example, pays more Norwegian taxes than any other company in Norway, native or foreign.

Despite all the apparent benefits that followed the discovery in 1969 of the prolific Ekofisk oil and gas fields, however, this first major strike in the Norwegian North Sea has been a curse as well as a blessing. In the excitement of undreamt-of wealth, Norway's economy became hooked on oil,

Left, drilling rigs, like this one at Arendal, began to appear off the west coast in the early 1970s.

which worked well while crude oil prices remained high around the world. But attempts to set up a "petroleum fund" against the day when the oil flow began to diminish never materialised and Norway, even more than Britain, was sent reeling by the 1986 oil crisis when prices plummeted from around $40 to below $10 a barrel.

It was Norway's deepest depression since the 1930s, and unemployment rose to around 6 percent, astonishingly high in a Scandinavian country, and led to a record number of bankruptcies. The crisis also had painful, long-term effects on Norway's social welfare system, comprehensive as only a Scandinavian welfare system can be, which has suffered large cutbacks in an effort to get the Norwegian economy back on the rails.

The Norwegian government instituted a "queue" system for oil and gas development in an effort to keep annual investment in new fields at around Nkr 25 billion (£2.5 billion). At its peak, that investment figure reached Nkr 40 billion (£4 billion). The omission of a petroleum fund is now being rectified.

Where to sell: One of the greatest challenges facing the country is to find new outlets for the vast reserves of natural gas, which it has in far greater abundance than oil. Apart from the fact that the rest of the world prefers oil to gas, the irony is that Norway itself already has relatively cheap electricity from the thousands of waterfalls and watercourses that plunge down the mountains, and has little need of gas. Gas production is expected to last for the next 100 years but, until it can be sold profitably, the potential gas wealth is more apparent than real.

Norway is, however, now studying the possibility of itself using gas, which would preclude more damming of the country's numerous waterways, always unpopular with a local population. It is expected that the first gas-fired power station will be in action by the turn of the century.

But none of this has had much effect on the fjord cities of either Stavanger or Bergen. At first, Stavanger's new-found wealth was almost an embarrassment but, more recently, the city has completed much renovation and construction, including a new airport and concert hall—all raised on black gold. Stavanger has become a model city where petro-dollars have encouraged restoration of historical landmarks, such as the white wooden houses found in the cobblestone streets of Gamle Stavanger (Old Stavanger), which delight visitors and are the pride of the local "Siddis" (the colloquial name for a person from Stavanger).

Oil riches have improved the education systems; both Stavanger and Bergen have American, French and English schools as well as the native variety. The American School in Stavanger accepts Norwegian students and has a scholarship programme to US universities and an American-Norwegian student exchange programme. Another oil company, Amoco, has devoted money to looking after the city's beautiful park.

Many other oil companies offer a range of scholarships to both Norwegians and expatriates. Ruhrgas, for example, the big West German gas company that is also an important customer for Norway's natural gas, offers a grant system to bring Norwegian students to West German universities for energy-related courses.

Statoil ski-jumpers: Mobil has chosen to sponsor the visual arts, with an art competition to support and encourage up-and-coming Norwegian artists, and the company also brings painting exhibitions to Stavanger and Oslo. Sport is another popular investment: Mobil sponsors world track and field events held at the Bislett stadium in Oslo, and Norway's own oil company, Stavanger-based Statoil, sponsors some of Norway's principal athletes, including the entire Norwegian national ski-jumping team.

One result of all this investment is that the former Norwegian trainees of the foreign oil companies are now in a position to take over many senior management jobs. At the end of the 1980s, the departure of French, American and British families inevitably had an ill effect on house prices for the local Stavanager population. In the heady days at the start of oil, many in the city were able to rent homes to foreign incomers at three to five times their pre-oil value, particularly as there were, and are, constraints on foreigners who wish to buy land in Norway.

The cost of houses in general soared and, when foreign families leave these houses empty once more, inflated house prices

slump, and local people who want to move are unable to recoup the money they paid a few years ago. This has happened in many oil cities, the nearest example to Norway being Aberdeen in Scotland, on the other side of the North Sea, which faced a slump in the mid-1980s. Younger Norwegians, however, have the advantage of heavily subsidised first-time home loans which may help to minimise the difference when they sell.

Over the years, oil activities have moved gradually northwards up the west coast to include oil bases in coastal towns such as Harstad, Florø, Sandnessjøen and Kristiansund, to service drilling rigs and exploration rigs, which continue the search for oil. This

trend should continue as recent oil and gas finds have generally been made further north in the Norwegian Sea than the original fields, and the focus of oil activity may well move to Bergen.

For Norway today, sadder and wiser in the ways of oil, is pinning its hopes on a "second coming" of oil from areas as far north as the Barents Sea, but the country may have to wait with what patience it can muster for a time yet. So far, the exploration rigs have struck only the less profitable natural gas.

Above, at work on an oil platform. **Right**, conscripts undergo winter war training.

NORWAY AND ITS NEIGHBOURS

If you walked into a room and met three Scandinavians, it would be hard to tell which was the Norwegian, which the Dane and which the Swede. They look alike, have similar interests, and seem to speak the same language, even if the accent is different. The relationship is close because all three nations come from the same stock, have a shared history, and languages that descend from Old Norse.

The written languages are so similar they are easily understood by all, and Scandinavian Air Service, the airline shared by the three countries, solves communication problems by allowing its crews to use their own language. This works well when a crew is Norwegian, but less well with Danes and Swedes who sometimes find each other incomprehensible.

This Scandinavian family is often taken to include Finland, though the Finns are of a different race with a language related to Hungarian—and that only marginally. In any event, all four countries are part of the Nordic group, which includes Iceland, the autonomous territories of the Faroes and Greenland and the Åland Islands in the Gulf of Bothnia.

Like all families, Scandinavians have the usual squabbles, jealousies, misunderstandings and false images of one another that come out of close proximity and long-held ties. To other Scandinavians, Norwegians are "blue-eyed" or naive, often the butt of innocuous jokes, yet both Swedes and Danes are astonished to learn that similar jokes are told by Norwegians against them. The family analogy continues in that the Danes tend to look on Norway as a younger brother, with all that that implies.

Sweden, with which Norway shares a 1,000-mile (1,700-km) border, is often looked on by Norway (and to a lesser extent by Denmark) as an elder or even "big" brother, the sort of relationship that you find between Canadians and Americans, and Scots and English, with allegations of arrogance and insensitivity from the smaller countries and a tendency for the larger to think it "knows best". But since Norway discovered oil some 20 years ago, the big-brother attitude has taken a knock, and left Sweden looking at Norway with a degree of wonder and envy.

The image of Norway as the junior partner is partly due to the fact that, after 500 years, first under Denmark, then under Sweden, the present Norwegian state is less than a century old, though Norway has been a nation for as long as any other Scandinavian country. In the earliest centuries Norwegians were in the lead, as the explorers who colonised Iceland, Greenland and the Faroe Islands, and for many years Norway held territories in Scotland and its islands, and Ireland.

Norway's only non-Nordic neighbour is the Soviet Union. The two countries co-exist without much friction on Spitsbergen (Svalbard), the remote northern islands, best known for cruise ships, coal, bird and plant life, and the sealers and whalers of former days. But Norway and the Soviet Union have been at odds over their joint border on the continental shelf in the far northern Barents Sea, where the two countries are face to face on a dividing line more than 1,000 miles (1,700 km) long.

Norway favours a border on the median line equidistant between the two countries, but the Soviet Union prefers a sector principle. The area under dispute is as big as Belgium, Switzerland and Austria combined, and the Soviet preference would push the boundary west to give the Soviets control of larger fish stocks and oil reserves.

During World War II, when only Sweden was neutral, the Scandinavian countries did their best to help one another, although neither Norway nor Sweden has yet managed to forget that Sweden allowed German troops to pass through its country on their way to attack Norway. Many Finnish children left for homes in Sweden, and that country also became an escape route from Norway. At the end of the war, Norway, Denmark, and Iceland became members of NATO, Sweden continued to be non-aligned, and Finland (stuck in an uneasy position between the eastern and western blocs) declared itself neutral.

The European Community's intention to establish an internal trade market from 1992 has speeded action in the Nordic Council (formed in 1952) on European co-operation in general.

WHY DOES EVERYTHING COST SO MUCH?

Asked over lunch why everything in Norway except for electricity and second-hand skis was so expensive, a government critic stabbed his fork into a tomato and rotated it at eye level.

"Consider this piece of fruit," he began, "a home-grown Norwegian tomato. To eat, adequate; in every other respect, scandalous.

"This is a very fine country but it does not recommend itself to the cultivation of tomatoes or, really, of very many crops at all. Less than 3 percent of the land is fit for agriculture, and even that is not particularly good land. The German traders in Hansa times used to blackmail us by

fate a long time ago. We see things differently. Historically, Norway has always been a country of small farmers, and there are powerful political forces at work to keep it that way.

"Let us assume that this particular tomato was grown on one of these small, heavily subsidised farms in the back of beyond. How did it get to this table? Norway is not all that big in actual land area, about the same as the British Isles, but it is very long and very narrow. Pivot the country on Oslo and it would reach Rome. The weather forecasts on television, for example, have the map cut in half, placing the two sections side by side so that they can fit on the screen.

"Farmers who are paid to remain in isolated areas must have roads, and building them through the mountains is incredibly expensive. In winter

threatening to cut off our corn imports, and that is only one of the reasons which, taken together, have made us paranoid about the need to produce as much of our own food as we possibly can, regardless of cost.

"It has been the policy of one government after another to insist that every patch of land that could be used for farming *should* be—and, furthermore, that farmers are entitled to incomes at least equal to what they could earn in industry. That means huge subsidies: 10 percent of our national budget is spent on agricultural subsidies, a lot on tiny farms in remote places which, economically speaking, have no right to exist.

"Needless to say, the farmers are extremely satisfied with these arrangements. In Sweden, such farmers were abandoned to their economic

they must be cleared and even so the surfaces break up and must be relaid—more expense. What of the truck sent to fetch this tomato? Volvos are built just across the Swedish border in Gothenburg, but with our import duties a Volvo costs nearly three times as much in Oslo as it does in Los Angeles. A very expensive vehicle operating on a very expensive road.

"Who pays for the tomato's trip? The taxpayer, of course—another subsidy for the road haulier. But the tomato has not reached this restaurant yet. The truck cannot cross a fjord without a ferry. Who pays for the ferry? The taxpayer again—some ferries carry subsidies of 40 percent.

"When the tomato at last gets here, it is washed in the kitchen by someone earning not less than 120,000 kroner a year, the minimum wage, to which the employer must add another 30,000 kroner for national insurance. Try to find a porter in a Norwegian hotel; who can afford to employ one? The right to a job is written into our constitution, and while the North Sea oil money was still coming in we could maintain the illusion of full employment by padding the state payroll.

"The oil money's finished now—it's been spent twice over—so we have unemployment, whatever the constitution says. Can this restaurateur not then find someone who will wash tomatoes for less? No, he can't, because the unemployment benefits are equal to the minimum wage. The poor taxpayer who, having paid for this tomato at every stage of its unwanted life, is then presented with yet another exorbitant bill. A Spanish tomato could have occupied the same

expense of the banks. In the past, the banks were willing partners who lent money without asking very many questions. As long as interest rates stayed tolerably low, the system could be sustained: a new car in the garage, a flashy boat on the fjord, kitchens creaking with microwaves and every other gadget imaginable, a *hytte* in the country, and so on.

"The Norwegian mascot used to be the troll; suddenly it became the shopping centre. Wherever one looked, someone was building a new shopping centre. People arranged their social lives to accommodate a stroll around the latest.

"But wait! The splurge on shopping centres was indirectly the product of the North Sea agreement with Britain, which split the oil money 50-50. In Britain, the money had to be stretched

space on this plate for a fraction of the cost and wouldn't have cost the taxpayer a thing.

"Visitors to this country usually say 'Oh well, we expect earnings are very high'. For someone washing tomatoes, yes they are, but they quickly level out and, at a guess, I'd say an ordinary income is between 150,000 and 200,000 kroner a year gross. Most people ought to be paying tax at about 45 percent but, if they are doing better than average, it quickly rises to 70 percent or more.

"There would not be much left after tax to pay the sort of prices asked, so the solution is massive, personal debt. As it happens, almost all bank borrowing—not just house mortgages—is tax-deductible. The choice, therefore, is between paying taxes and having next to nothing left or enjoying our famous standard of living fully at the

among 60 million people, in Norway among only 4.5 million. Per head, that was money galore, like Saudi Arabia or Kuwait.

"When the oil money ran out, the show couldn't go on. Interest rates shot up and gradually the cars, boats, microwaves and shopping centres had to go back to where they really belonged: the banks. The banks were soon themselves in trouble, and resorted to the previously unthinkable course of laying off large numbers of staff and negotiating mergers.

"It could almost be said that the Norwegian economy has forever tottered between windfalls: the herrings which once miraculously appeared off the west coast, American money after World War II, North Sea oil. We are waiting now for the North Sea gas."

THE SAMI: PEOPLE OF FOUR NATIONS

The Lapps—or the Sami people, as they prefer to call themselves—have lived in Norway from time immemorial. One can find traces of them for more than 8,000 years, but in some areas today there is only a remnant of the old tribes. The area now regarded as "Samiland" (parts of north Sweden and Finland, and Sami people also live in the north of the Soviet Union) holds approximately 40,000 Sami. The greater number, something over 20,000, is assumed to live in Norway and particularly in the northernmost county of Finnmark.

Norwegian Sami divide roughly into three groups. The Mountain Sami are the most widespread, encountered from Varanger to Femunden. They live mainly by breeding reindeer. The River Sami live around the waterways in the interior of Finnmark and have turned more and more to agriculture and animal husbandry, though hunting, fishing and berry-picking still add to their income. The third group, the Sea Sami, is the largest, making a living from fishing and farming in a life that today differs little from that of Northern Norwegians as a whole.

Ancient culture: Remarkably enough, though they constitute a minority, the Sami people have been very successful in conserving their rich cultural heritage and many unique traditions. Not the least important is the Sami language which derives from Finno-Ugric and is closely linked to Finnish.

From ancient times, the sea has always been of great importance as an abundant source of fish, and of seal to provide them with valuable hides and skins. Once upon a time, there were walruses with their precious tusks which were highly prized, particularly by the craftspeople who produced the characteristic handicrafts.

It is a mighty land, Samiland, rich in lakes, rivers, small streams and not the least in grandiose mountains and boundless hills, which in some places reach as far as the Atlantic coast. Besides fishing, hunting was an important factor and there was much

game, big and small. Squirrels, martens, foxes, even bears lived there but the important animal was—and still is—the reindeer, which is the basis of the Sami household. The reindeer is the Sami's staple and his fortune. But never ask a Sami how many animals he has in his herd: it is considered to be an insult—like asking your neighbour how much money he has in his bank account.

Very few of the truly nomadic Sami people are left. They have largely settled down in the sense that they have a permanent

address but can move with their herds to the high ground in the summer. During late summer and in the autumn the reindeer are driven down to the woods near the foot of the summer mountains where the lichen pasture is rich. There they stay during winter, roaming in freedom until the spring when it is time once more to move up the mountain to the high slopes, now juicy, succulent and filled with nourishment.

Brilliant colour: Many visitors to Norway now come north to Samiland and to the *fjell* (the mountains), a beautiful sight for anyone who loves an untouched and clean nature. Mosses and lichens give a gentle splash of

Preceding pages: Kautokeino children ready for Confirmation. <u>Left</u>, Sami women loved their pipes. <u>Right</u>, Sami boy today.

colour to the vast land, and grasses, especially the sedges (*Carex*) are abundant here as in few other areas. In the beginning of summer the rare pale Pasque flower (*Pulsatilla vernalis*) is in blossom and the rosy cinnamon rose (*Rosa majalis*) gives colour to the rocky hillside and the edges of the bog. Carpets of mountain avons (*Dryas octopetala*) are characteristic of soil that is rich in calcium, as are many other species, often with names that begin with *fjell*.

It could be that the colours all around them have been a source of inspiration for the Sami costume. In days gone by, this dress was for daily use. Now it is kept for festivals, weddings, funerals and other serious occa-

reindeer hide, used on festive occasions.

The old religion: Like many other people living in close contact with nature, the Sami had, and still have, a religion related to Shamanism, where nature and its forces are of the greatest importance. The sun and the moon were the supreme gods, as they once were for the ancient Egyptians and Greeks and for people even further back in time. Next came a god connected with thunderstorms, one who ruled over fertility and over wild animals and the hunt, as well as over lakes and their fishes and other inhabitants.

In many areas this religion was related to the old Nordic mythology but it was even closer to nature. The gods had purely Sami

sions. Easter is the big feast, particularly in Kautokeino, with traditional reindeer-racing and other events. Then the richly ribboned skirts and frocks, with red their most outstanding colour, are fetched from drawers and chests. These generous ribbons are used as wristbands or cuffs and as "stockings".

There are no bounds to this richness and colour, which makes a magnificent sight. With these lavish dresses go jewellery in silver, exquisitely worked into chains for the neck and elegant pendants. Another speciality is pewter embroidery, in which very thin threads of pewter are sewn in ingenious patterns on fine bracelets or bags made of

names such as Peive, the Sun God, Horagalles, the God of Thunderstorms (corresponding to Thor in Nordic mythology). Under these "main gods" were many lesser gods or spiritual beings. There were evil spirits as well. One was Rota or Ruta, the demon of illness and death; another was the Devil himself, Fuadno.

Christianity did its best to combat and extinguish this popular belief and Swedish Laestadianism did much to destroy the Sami religion. Many of the "troll-drums" (part of the ancient religion) were burned and those which survived became very expensive articles scattered in different museums. The drumhead was painted in red and displayed figures with magical forces, of great importance in the Sami culture but anathema to the would-be missionaries.

The most effective advocate for the dissemination of Christianity among the Norwegian Sami was King Christian IV and Christianity became a very disruptive force in the Sami culture. King Christian travelled to Finnmark in the early 17th century and in 1609 introduced the death penalty for Sami who refused to give up their traditional faith. He followed that with an order to build the first Christian church in Varanger by the year 1650, and Finnmark also now has the only Greek Orthodox Church at Neiden where

Norwegianisation of the Sami people and, in any case, Sami culture had traditionally concentrated on the visual arts rather than literature. This led to the irony that one of the greatest writers of Sami descent, Mario Aikio from Karasjok, wrote only in Norwegian, though today a number of younger writers use the Sami language. In contrast, after the first great pictorial artist, John Savio, became famous for his woodcuts, several more artists of Sami descent have emerged, such as Iver Jåks, Åge Gaup and Hans Ragnar Mathisen.

As happened with many minority languages in recent times, Norway now pursues an aim of encouraging the Sami language. It

many Sami worship on the Sabbath.

To go to church was, nevertheless, impossible for many of the nomadic Sami, who had to travel over mountains and vast lakes. It was the great festivals which gathered the Sami together and so it is still: New Year, Easter, Lady Day, and the spring and autumn equinoxes. The Sami people count eight seasons, all of them related to their reindeer and these too must be celebrated.

Language revival: Before World War II, it was Norwegian policy to encourage the

is taught from the start of schooling and Sami people can pursue higher education in their own language in various establishments such as the Universities of Oslo and Tromsø and their own Teachers' Training College in Alta. Karasjok also has a secondary school where pupils can study the Sami language and history, and there is also a modern Sami Museum. In Kautokeino, where the great Easter celebrations take place, is the Nordic-Sami Institute.

When the Norwegian Broadcasting Corporation (NRK) planned a second radio channel in the early 1980s, it had the unusual idea of placing the first station in the remote

Left, Sami life a century ago. **Above**, Sami woman at the reindeer round-up.

north of Norway and starting broadcasts with the first Sami service, then gradually working its way south.

The Norwegian Sami have also fought for political control over their own affairs and for the preservation of their way of life which has continued to be eroded by the opening up of the northern areas. The establishment of national parks, for example, can lead to the protection of wild animals that prey on the reindeer herds and Sami people have been successful in gaining compensation for reindeer grazing areas and recognition of the right to hunt and fish. Sami have in some cases also succeeded in curtailing electricity development projects which would have

flooded whole districts and jeopardised the local Sami reindeer economy.

Home rule: Now, the Sami people have their own parliament (*Sametinget*), which was opened by King Olav in October 1989 with great ceremony and many festivities as the king met adults and children. The parliament is an elected body and to vote you must have a grandparent speaking the Sami language or, with typical Norwegian pragmatism, "feel that you are a Sami". In the early stages this parliament is no more than advisory but the intention is to transfer more and more responsibility for and control over Sami affairs from Oslo to Karasjok.

These changes have led to a growing interest in all things Sami—language, music, art and song—by young people. Of great importance in getting inside the world of the Sami people is to understand their unique form of "song" or *joik*, a kind of primitive music comparable with unaccompanied humming or melodic scanning. *Joiking* is a sort of communication that has grown out of the small society to give a fellow-feeling from one Sami to another. This custom is not to be compared with our own songs and ballads, nor can outsiders understand the words in the Sami language. Words can be isolated or can often be subordinated to melody and rhythm, followed by a long row of soft, meaningless syllables—*voia-voia*, *ala-ala*, *lu-lu-lu* and so on, strange to untuned ears.

Especially in Finnmark, this form of "singing" has grown strong and each Sami has his own melody. A young boy will compose his own *joik* for the girl he is courting and, today, *joiks* can be composed to order—an innovation that has followed the tracks of the snow-scooter and radio.

It probably grew out of the fact that, in Samiland, man is often alone in the mountains or down in the scrub and brush woods. The sound of the *joik* keeps the reindeer herd quiet and at the same time frightens wild animals away. But the *joik* is also used as entertainment when people gather together as well as when they are alone.

Decent hymns: Like many other traditions, the *joik* was forbidden by the Christians. At a time when the only decent song was a hymn, it was seen as sinful. But the *joik* could not be burnt like the troll-drum. Many of the old melodies are still alive, handed on from one generation to the next. At the beginning of this century, around a thousand older compositions were written down from Norwegian and Finnish Sami and later from Swedish, and the modern Sami composer John Persen has turned to the *joik* as a source of inspiration for his compositions.

Perhaps because it is not accompanied by instruments, the *joik* has often been regarded as unmusical. Nothing could be further from the truth. The *joik* bears witness to a great musicality that, like the Sami people themselves, has survived from century to century.

Left, a character from the Sami theatre. **Right**, old Sami woman at her tent.

Although exploration is most often associated in modern times with rocket journeys into space, the names of at least two Norwegian explorers are as evocative now as at the time of their epic achievements. Roald Amundsen, a medical student, is forever remembered as the man who raced and beat Captain Robert Falcon Scott to the South Pole; Thor Heyerdahl for the Kontiki expedition, which produced a book subsequently translated into more than 36 languages.

Their fame steals some of the limelight which ought to be apportioned to a much larger cast of intrepid Norwegians, beginning with Bjarni Herjolfsson who, in 986, lost his way while sailing from Iceland to Greenland and ended up, according to an ancient saga, as the first European to sight the American continent. On Bjarni's return, Leif Eriksson borrowed his boat to investigate the mysterious sighting and it was he and his Viking companions who, in roughly the year 1000, were the first Europeans to set foot on the American continent.

Early migration: A 19th-century Norwegian explorer, Fridtjof Nansen, set the pattern for the investigation of human migration. He had established his reputation in 1888 with a hazardous crossing of Greenland from east to west, a journey recounted in his *First Crossing of Greenland*. A few years later he was excited by the discovery near the southern extremity of Greenland of some wreckage whose origins were traced to the New Siberian Islands. How had it got there?

Nansen determined to find out. His vessel, *Fram*, was specially designed to lift herself under the crushing pressure of the drift-ice in the Arctic Ocean. She was set adrift off the New Siberian Islands in September 1893 and after two years emerged near Spitsbergen, the island no-man's land about 400 miles (650 km) north of Norway—but without Nansen. He had left the ship in charge of his second-in-command in a heroic but vain attempt to reach the North Pole with dog-drawn sledges. He and his companion survived a winter in Franz Josef land, living in an ice hut and eating whatever they could shoot. They reached safety on practically the same day as *Fram*, and Nansen's six volumes of findings are the basis of the science of oceanography.

Such was Nansen's fame that, when war threatened between Norway and Sweden over the dissolution of their union, he was sent to London and Copenhagen to win support for the Norwegian cause. He later

won the Nobel Peace Prize.

The purpose of the 1947 Kontiki expedition was to test a theory about the origins of the Polynesian people and culture. Heyerdahl demonstrated that a balsa-wood raft set adrift off the coast of Peru could eventually—it took him more than four months—reach the Tuamotu archipelago 5,000 miles (8,000 km) away. In the 1960s he successfully conducted a similar experiment, in this instance to discover whether West African voyagers using their traditional rafts might have reached the West Indies before Colombus. (*Kontiki* and *Ra* are on view in Oslo.)

Although Heyerdahl proved the excep-

Preceding pages: Nansen's ship *Fram* stuck fast in the Arctic ice. <u>Left</u>, Amundsen expedition member Hanssen beside the flag, newly-planted at the South Pole 1911. <u>Right</u>, Roald Amundsen.

tion, the rule for Norwegian explorers was normally to capitalise on their experience of ice and snow to explore the Polar regions. They were also, out of necessity, superb seafarers. Travel along the west coast, with the deep indentations made by the fjords, was far easier by boat than overland. Mastery of the open seas meant that, for practical purposes, a port like Stavanger was closer to Scotland than eastern Norway and, in particular, to what later became known as Oslo. From the end of the 8th century, the North Sea crossing to the British Isles was in their backyard; they made the journey regularly.

The father of Norwegian exploration, or at least the earliest recorded explorer, is Erik

replacements from Iceland and to persuade others to join his return. Erik trumpeted his new-found land with the zeal of an unprincipled estate agent. It was so wonderful, he told his audiences, that he had decided to call it Greenland. By 985 he had acquired animals and enticed enough colonisers to fill 25 ships, of which 14 reached the destination.

It was in one of the settlements founded by Erik the Red that his son, Leif, having heard Bjarni Herjolfsson's strange tale, prepared to find out for himself what it was all about. He was "big and strong, of striking appearance, shrewd, and in every respect a temperate, fair-dealing man," which would seem to set him apart from his father. His 35-man

the Red, a man who seems to have had a liking for slaughter. In the 10th century he was banished from Norway to Iceland for murder. Then he was banished for three years from Iceland as well, for several more killings. Unwelcome anywhere, he sailed west with a shipload of livestock and discovered the world's largest island—a lump of ice, more than 2 miles (3 km) thick in places.

Obviously a keen angler, Erik was so engrossed by the excellent catches to be had in summer that he neglected to collect enough animal fodder for the winter. His livestock starved to death. He resolved to risk violation of his ostracism to collect

expedition left Greenland about the year 1000. They landed first at "Markland", a wooded region on the coast of Labrador, and then continued south to "Vinland".

An inscription on a map probably drawn by a monk in Basel in 1440—about half a century before Columbus sailed to the New World—describes Leif Eriksson's discovery of "a new land, extremely fertile, and even having vines… a truly vast and very rich land". Attempts to settle the land were defeated by the hostility of the natives.

American proof: Certainly the existence of "Vinland" was known to Adam of Bremen, a chronicler in the 1070s, and to writers of the sagas, but it was through a typically bizarre quirk of archaeology that Eriksson's discovery of America is put virtually beyond doubt. Excavations on the site of a Greenland farm which belonged to a member of the "Vinland" expedition produced a lump of coal which proved to be anthracite, a material unobtainable in Greenland but plentiful on the surface in Rhode Island.

The case was strengthened in 1960 by Helge Ingstad, who thought about the likely landing place on the American continent of an expedition from Greenland. Working like a detective, he backed a hunch and at L'anse aux Meadows, on the northern tip of Newfoundland, came up with a winner. Six

hunting boat, *Gjøa*, and applied his time to studying the Eskimo inhabitants and making reckonings on the magnetic pole. After a third winter in the ice, Amundsen forced a passage through the Beaufort Sea and reached the Bering Strait in August 1906.

Amundsen knew about Captain Scott's ambitions to reach the South Pole but he himself was more concerned in reaching the North. Nevertheless, faced with the shattering disappointment of the news that Peary had pipped him to the post, he secretly went south instead in Nansen's old ship, *Fram*. But not until he reached Madeira did he let anyone know what his intentions were.

Amundsen decided to dispense with all

buildings had once stood on the site and carbon-dating proved they were medieval. The archaeological remains left no doubt that the occupants had been Norsemen.

Amundsen had served a rigorous apprenticeship for his famous assault on the South Pole, which came about as a last-minute change of plans. Although he had taken part in a Belgian expedition to Antarctica his first interest was the Arctic. He was stuck for two years off King William Island in a seal-

Left, Thor Heyerdahl supervises *Ra's* construction at the foot of the Giza pyramids. Right, *Ra II* leaves port at Safi.

scientific work in his sprint to the South Pole. Scott had a head start but discovered too late that his Siberian ponies were useless in the conditions. He and his team had to pull their sledges. Amundsen took a shorter, rougher route and had the benefit of dog-teams. In the event, he beat Scott by a month.

The dispirited English team perished on their return, and this unlucky fate, together with the pathos of Scott's diary, took some of the lustre off Amundsen's feat. At last, though, the director of London's Royal Geographical Society, which had backed Scott, paid tribute to Amundsen's effort as "the most successful polar journey on record".

BOAT BUILDERS AND ENGINEERS

Norway is 1,000 miles (1,600 km) long and has a coastline like jagged teeth, numerous islands and more than its fair share of mountains. As a result it is a nightmare for those who plan road and rail transport. Added to such geographical difficulties are a rugged winter climate and a population of just over four million scattered over this long, thin country. It is not surprising that Norway has traditionally relied on the sea as its basic means of transport, or that most towns and villages lie along the coast and fjords and have harbours big or small.

When roads were still primitive tracks and railways in the early stages of construction, shipping routes for passengers and cargo were already established. This was the main reason that early tours of Norway seldom penetrated inland but kept to towns and villages along the coast and the fjords. A guide book published in 1911 confirmed this: "A good deal of travelling in Norway must be done by water and steamers ply on almost all the fjords and on many inland lakes."

The backbone of the domestic sea transport was—and still is—the famous Hurtigrute, the coastal express steamers which have linked north and south and the numerous communities along the coast for many years. These ships followed the route of the Vikings and were originally a series of unconnected independent services. Many operated only during the summer, anchored at dusk, and did not sail through the night.

It was the Vesteraalens Dampskibsselskab that established the first year-round express service in 1893, which sailed between Trondheim and Hammerfest—without overnight stops. Later, other lines joined in and the Hurtigrute assumed a major role, carrying mail, cargo and passengers, including tourists, from Bergen in the southwest to Kirkenes in the northeast.

Today, in spite of the development of other forms of transport, coastal shipping continues to play an important part in the

Preceding pages: snow in the mountains as late as May. **Left,** Tjeldsund Bridge, Tromsø, in a high wind. **Right,** safe landing at a wintry northern airport.

Norwegian communications network. The 11 vessels belonging to the four companies of the Hurtigrute maintain their unique year-round passenger and cargo service which is used by the local inhabitants as a floating bus route. It also provides visitors with the opportunity of travelling on a working ship as opposed to a cruise liner and, even today, as the express coastal ship comes gently into one of the 34 small harbours along its route, the local onlookers come on to the quayside. In days gone by, the arrival of the Hurtigrute

brought out the whole population.

As new roads and bridges have been built and new tunnels bored, the number of smaller ferry services has steadily declined; but Norway still has around 100 active routes. The car ferry provides an essential service, carrying cars, trucks, buses and passengers, and provides a short cut across a fjord, which would otherwise call for a 40 to 50-mile (65 to 80-km) drive.

The ferries are workaday vessels, often careworn in appearance with minimal facilities, although on routes over half an hour there is usually a small cafeteria. But go up on deck to take a photograph or watch the land slip by and the view of the fjord and coastline make the journey worthwhile.

Ferry berths are simple: a few marked-out parking lanes for vehicles, perhaps a kiosk, and the ramp. Tickets may be sold on board or while waiting in line in the parking area. Ferry crews are adept at squeezing every vehicle they can on board.

Advance reservations are rare, so one must join the queue. On key routes at peak summer weekends you may have to wait for a long time, although the black spots are being eliminated. The old Kvanndal-Kinsarvik ferry, which carried Bergen-Oslo traffic, used to develop vast queues, with motorists waiting all day to make the crossing. This

seated two persons. An alternative, a *kalesjevogn*, seated a maximum of six passengers. It is fascinating to read in a guide book published as late as 1925 that: "the normal method of progress along the country roads from posting station to posting station is the native cart, the *stolkjaerre*". This same book made no reference to touring by car.

When the car made its first appearance there was little to encourage it; gradually roads improved, although it was not until after World War II that the Norwegians made major progress. In the past 15 years a surge of activity has gained increasing momentum. Even now, it is not possible to travel as fast as in many other European

has now been replaced by the 7½-mile (12-km) Vallvik tunnel and the much shorter shuttle crossing from Bruravik to Brimnes—and even this crossing is due to be eliminated by a bridge.

Until a couple of decades ago, many quite important roads were still unsurfaced. Road building has never been an easy option in Norway and a lot of highways were narrow and rough, while those which crossed the higher mountains and *fjells* were closed in winter and damaged by weather.

Before the car, the principal form of transport was the *stolkjaerre*, a two-wheeled horse-drawn cart without springs which

countries; there are mountains to cross, fjords to circumnavigate and many stretches of main road remain narrow and twisting. There are only a few short sections of motorway and Norway has its own types of hazard, ranging from animals on the road to narrow bridges, blind corners and steep gradients on the mountainous secondary routes.

Minor roads, particularly in the mountains, are frequently unsurfaced while some of those covered with asphalt—especially in the north—suffer from frost heave. But Norway's civil engineers are among the best in the world. They have achieved wonders, creating new highways with good surfaces, building superb bridges and blasting numerous and lengthy tunnels.

The Norwegian skill at tunnelling through the solid rock that forms their mountains creates the biggest impression on visitors. Tunnels can be up to 8 miles (13 km) long, with new ones constantly planned or under construction. They are rarely flat or straight, but wind up and down the mountains with gradients, curves and probably spirals as well to make for adventurous driving.

The more dramatic examples can gain 1,000 ft (300 metres) in a few minutes' effortless driving. They have replaced roads that once clung to the mountainside in a succession of hairpin bends and steep gradients

ously Fjærland was isolated, reached only by ferry. The only hazards now are sheep, which have learned to appreciate the comfort of lying in entrances to tunnels where it is cool in summer and warm in winter. Tunnels are also free from snow in winter, which keeps roads open all year round.

Having mastered the skill of tunnelling on land, the Norwegian engineers have now turned their attention to the seabed and undersea tunnels. One of the most spectacular burrows out from the mainland to Vardø, which lies on a small island off the north Finnmark coast. It is 1¾ miles (2.8 km) long and at its deepest point lies 288 ft (88 metres) below the cold waters of the Arctic Ocean.

that were closed by snow all winter long. Such roads may involve up to 30 hairpins and a 3,000-ft (910-metre) difference in height between top and bottom.

Nothing has stopped Norwegian engineers from tackling the incredibly difficult to the near impossible—such as the tunnel on the road between Skei and Fjærland which lies beneath an arm of the mighty Jostedal glacier. The entire road is 19 miles (31 km) long and nearly a quarter is in tunnels. Previ-

At Ålesund on the west coast two undersea tunnels, totalling 4¾ miles (7.7 km) now link the main town to the island of Vigra, where the airport is, and have cut out a ferry crossing. With an economical turn of mind, the Norwegians used the rock drilled out of the tunnels to extend the airport's runway. One of the ferry bottlenecks which affects everyone driving to North Cape is the crossing from Kåfjord, on the mainland, to Honningsvåg on the island of Magerøya; even here, an undersea tunnel is now to be built.

The cost of these projects is enormous and the pace of the work has made it impossible for the government to contain them within its

Left, an early train at Voss on what became the magnificent Oslo–Bergen line. **Above**, a modern train near Voss today.

budget limits. So more and more of these improvements are now paid for by tolls.

Public transport makes good use of Norway's road system to reach outlying towns and villages. The bus station in the centre of any town is busy from morning to night—a revelation to those for whom a bus is almost an extinct species. What is more, Norwegian public transport has done a marvellous job of integrating road, rail, ferry and even airline schedules. The ferry waits for the train, and the smaller planes owned by Braathens and others, which carry most of the internal passengers, hop neatly from small airfield to small airfield. Particularly in the north, Widerøe aircraft bring remote communities closer to their neighbours.

There are also long-distance buses, the most outstanding being Express 2000 which runs between Oslo and Hammerfest. It takes 25 hours, also travels through Sweden and Finland, and claims to be the longest service of its kind in Europe.

Norwegian mountain ranges, fjords, rivers and lakes, heavy winter snowfalls and severe frosts all made life just as difficult for the railway engineer, so much so that a technical article published in 1850 considered that "the use of the locomotive is impossible or impracticable." But the engineers proved the writer wrong, although it was slow going. The first railway line from Christiania (now Oslo) to Eidsvoll opened in 1854, principally for the transport of timber from the Lake Mjøsa region to the harbour at Christiania for export overseas.

Losing track: This was typical of how the railways developed piecemeal, with unconnected segments serving a particular industry. The tracks were not even the same width and, although the question of the gauge was resolved in 1894, it was 1949 before the last line of importance converted to European standard gauge.

The most important rail route in Norway, from Oslo to Bergen—now one of Europe's great railway journeys—was also one of the most difficult to build, and its 295 miles (471 km) did not open until 1909. Before that time, the steamer was the accepted mode of transport between the two cities and Bergensere claimed that it was easier to get to England or Germany from their native city than to reach the Norwegian capital.

The Oslo–Bergen line, now electrified, is still regarded as one of the most sensational railway routes in the world. It includes a 4¾-mile (7.6-km) tunnel at Ulriken, a long climb over the great massif of the Hardangervidda, the long light flickering against the windows as the train winds in and out of the snow sheds that protect the line, and an unbroken gradient which lifts the line 2,500 ft (762 metres) between Voss and Myrdal.

Untroubled lakes: At the summit at Taugevatn—4,267 ft (1,230 metres) above sea level, the snow drifts are deep even at midsummer. The entire route includes 50 miles (80 km) of tunnel and snow sheds (to shelter the train), and the views past untroubled lakes and up to mountain peaks make this one of the finest scenic journeys anywhere. Despite the fierce winter weather on these heights, the train rarely misses more than a couple of days in a season.

At Myrdal there is a spectacular branch line to Flåm, on the Aurland fjord, which descends from 2,845 ft (867 metres) to just 6 ft (1.8 metres) above sea level in 12 miles (20 km). It is one of the major tourist attractions of western Norway. The trains pause midway on the journey so that passengers can see and photograph the spectacular Kjosfossen waterfall.

The Oslo–Stavanger line is less spectacular but it was also extremely difficult to build, with numerous bridges and tunnels—two over 5 miles (8 km) long. By 1938 it had only reached from Oslo to Kristiansand and it was 1944 before the last section to Stavanger was finished. Trondheim, on the other hand, was linked to the capital by a roundabout route via Røros in 1880 but the more direct connection across the Dovrefjell was not opened until 1921.

North of Trondheim the railway extends 454 miles (730 km) to Bodø. During World War II, Russian and other prisoners toiled to push this line north, and the occasional Norwegian can still remember slipping a few slices of bread to an emaciated figure, wrapped in layers of rags against the bitter winter weather. The final link was not completed until 1962, and it is unlikely that the railway will ever go north to Narvik, at the narrowest part of Norway. It already has a railway line to Riksgränsen on the Swedish side of the frontier, which links south by the Swedish State Railways.

This isolated 28-mile (45-km) section of

the Norwegian State Railways is one end of the spectacular Ofotbanen which was built for the transport of iron ore from the Swedish mines, principally at Kiruna, to the ice-free port of Narvik. Opened in 1903, it had to overcome many natural obstacles, including the steep ascent from sea level at Narvik to 1,700 ft (518 metres) at the Swedish frontier.

All over Norway, the many gradients and curves on virtually every line, plus the fact that much of the system is single track, mean that train speeds, even today, are not high. A limit on the volume of traffic, because the railways link comparatively small centres of population, also mean infrequent services. However, new coaches, including dining

Norwegians have brought to aviation much of the same spirit that they brought to the development of shipping.

The major international carrier is Scandinavian Airlines System (SAS), a joint operation of Norway, Sweden and Denmark, but the dominant domestic airline is Braathens. It began flying internal routes in 1954 and today its modern fleet carries an astonishing three million passengers every year. The jets serve 15 centres with a total of up to 200 departures a day.

Flying the "thinner" routes are Widerøe, Norsk Air, and Norving. Widerøe, founded in 1934, has a remarkable network linking 36 airports, many of them serving small com-

and sleeping cars, are very comfortable.

Just as Norway's natural conditions encouraged the development of coastal shipping, so the same conditions have proved to be made-to-measure for air transport. The thin spread of the population has not inhibited the development of an extensive domestic network with 50 airports. These services are used by 5.5 million passengers a year—a ratio of passengers to population claimed to be a world record. The domestic and international network is long established and the spur of long distances has meant that the

Above, selling wild flowers at the roadside.

munities, particularly in the north of the country. The small twin-engined aircraft provide a regular and efficient service, even during the harsh winters.

Most of the airports which serve these small towns are tiny and are carved out of what appears to be quite unsuitable terrain. The airlines provide a bread-and-butter service, carrying not only passengers and mail but also newspapers and cargo of all kinds. They are, in many respects, the successor to the steamer services of years gone by, while skilled airmanship has, in turn, replaced—or at least complemented—the Norwegians' outstanding ability as sailors.

AN OUTDOOR LIFE, ALL YEAR ROUND

"The Norwegians, both men and women, seem to go a good deal on walking tours, and probably know infinitely more of their fatherland than does the average Briton of his island, the superiority of which he seldom fails to impress on the long-suffering foreigner." So reads the entry for 20 July in the classic travelogue *Three in Norway By Two of Them*, first published in Britain in 1882. In a fascinating account, authors J.A. Lees and W.J. Clutterbuck describe timeless traits of the country and its people that are as entertaining to read today as they were over a century ago, "in the glorious era when the savage country of Norway was being discovered by English adventure-seekers," according to the reprint's preface. Now, as then, the common denominator is the great outdoors of a land long remote.

As a race, Norwegians are quite at home in their wild, unspoilt country, and have a great feeling for its mountains and high uplands. Composer Edvard Grieg, who did much to capture the Norwegian landscape in his music, wrote with passion of the Jotunheimen range in Central Norway: "When I contemplate the possibility of a future visit to the mountains, I shudder with joy and expectation, as if it were a matter of hearing Beethoven's Tenth Symphony." There are higher, more remote, more exotically named countries with more photographically stunning landscapes, yet few can claim a population so attuned to its great outdoors.

One Norwegian in four counts outdoor recreation as a first pastime, and Norwegians excel at sports evolved from self-propelled outdoor pursuits such as cross-country running, orienteering (a combination of cross-country running and map reading), cross-country ski racing and cycling. Everyone, from all walks of life, takes part: blue-collar and white-collar, urbanite and ruralist, commoner and King tramp the terrain, year round. Foreign visitors, unaware of the penchant, often find this mass migration to the open-air unnerving, especially if they arrive

on business at Easter or during the month of July, the prime times of the year for moor and mountain, sea and shore.

Centuries of that view evolved into a common law that first became a statute 50 years ago. One of the shortest laws, the latest version of the appropriate paragraph of *Lov om friluftslivet* ("Outdoor Life Law") states succinctly that "At any time of the year, outlying property may be crossed on foot, with consideration and due caution." The lack of a concept of trespass means that the

wilderness is a giant common, there for everyone's use no matter who owns it. The few restraints imposed are for environmental or safety reasons. Camping isn't permitted in the immediate watersheds of drinking-water reservoirs, and bonfires are forbidden during summer dry spells that can turn the taiga to tinder and a spark causes a conflagration that lasts for days.

This liking for untethered roaming seems an integral part of the national character. Among the country's real-life heroes are Fridtjof Nansen and Roald Amundsen, towering figures of the Golden Age of Polar exploration around the turn of the century.

Preceding pages: Norway's vast forests provide wonderful walking. **Left**, end of a perfect day. **Right**, glacier climbing in Jotunheimen.

Ethnographic explorer Thor Heyerdahl is today perhaps the most widely known Norwegian abroad. Glaciologist Monica Kristensen's recent scientific expedition in Antarctica and her attempt to reach the South Pole on skis catapulted her to a national prominence rivalling that of entertainers and sports stars.

Though on a smaller scale, close encounters with nature thread the fabric of everyday life. A family returning from an autumn hike to pluck wild mushrooms will drop into a public mushroom check station to verify the edibility of their harvest. In the winter, city dwellers heading for a ski tour in a nearby forest dial the same snow report number that

gians are much likelier to meet nature on its own terms and seek or make their own comfort wherever they go.

In a country where winter days are short and nasty weather can crop up any time of the year, comfort translates to secure shelter, often your own. Fully a quarter of the country's households also own a holiday home, or *hytte*. By accident of etymology, *hytte* translates to *hut*, but there the similarity stops. A *hytte* is by no means a rough structure; most are well-appointed small wooden houses, and many are larger than their owners' permanent homes, especially for those living in cramped urban flats.

Those without a *hytte* of their own are

they dialled last summer to learn the water temperatures at local bathing areas.

Early starts: Norwegian kindergartens and day-care centres are usually small buildings attached to extensive outdoor playgrounds, designed for day-long activity. Only in extreme weather, defined in most places as temperatures below −10° C (5° F), do the kids stay indoors or at home. Coddling in Norway does not include separation from the wrath of the elements.

Yet Norwegians see no valour in doing battle with nature. As the British Polar exploration chronicler Roland Huntford points out, that's more the British psyche: Norwe-

frequently related to, or are close friends of, *hytte* owners. Otherwise, there are many channels to the comforts of a *hytte*. Clubs and associations often own one, and one of the standard business "perks" is liberal use of the company *hytte*, popular as a non-taxable privilege. Holiday flats and time-share apartments are cropping up in vacation towns, but the *hytte* still reigns supreme in fulfilling its original intent: to supply comfort in remoter places where it is otherwise unavailable.

Supreme on that scale are the *hytter* run by Den Norske Turistforeningen, literally "The Norwegian Tourist Association," with

Tourist implying "on foot". Now well into its second century of housing and otherwise providing for walkers, skiers and climbers, DNT and its sibling local tourist associations own *hytter* throughout the Norwegian wilderness. Even the simplest put to rest any thought of a "hut", while the larger make the title ludicrous.

Pay as you leave: Consider a "hut" with 114 bunk beds in two and four-person rooms, hot showers, a staffed dining room serving three meals a day, a snack bar and three lounges. It's Finsehytta, is one of the largest *hytter* in Norway, a few hundred metres from the Finse railway station, about halfway between Oslo and Bergen. Other DNT lodges

Well-marked walking trails connect the lodges, which stand at crossroads on networks so extensive that DNT's trail marker, a red painted letter "T" on cairns, has become synonymous with serious walking. When winter snows cover the cairns, poles in the snow serve the same purpose. The bulk of the trails and lodges are conveniently in the middle of the "bump" that forms the southerly part of the country, within a triangle with its corners at the three major cities, Oslo, Bergen and Trondheim. That makes the remote reaches of the wilderness accessible. A central entry point is Finse, once no more than a railway-workers' hamlet above the timber line at a height of over 4,000 ft (1,200

(the better translation of *hytter*) are still larger. Gjendesheim in the Jotunheimen mountains has 129 bunks, and Glitterheim has 120. Rondvassbu in the Rondane range has 102 bunks, and seven other DNT lodges have more than 50. There is also unstaffed self-service accommodation with 8 to 32 bunks. Here you can prepare your own food or purchase from a pantry. You pay upon leaving, by putting money in a box on the wall. The honour system works well.

Left, glaciologist Monika Kristiansen after her expedition to the South Pole. **Above**, quick winter skinny-dip.

metres), midway on the railway line between Oslo and Bergen.

Finse's main street is the station platform; there are no cars because there are no roads. Life pulses with the arrival and departure of trains. When a train has gone and the last passengers have left, Finse returns to normal, a speck in a seemingly infinite expanse of rock, ice and snow. So ethereal yet so accessible is this place that it was chosen for the filming of sequences in *The Empire Strikes Back*, the sequel to *Star Wars*.

Giants' country: To the north lie the Jotunheimen mountains, the range that took its name from Norse mythology, literally

"Home of the Giants". The name is appropriate: peaks jut a kilometre and more skywards from lake-studded, moraine-strewn flats, all above the timber line. Nonetheless, even the loftiest, Galdhøpiggen and Glittertind, with summits over 7,900 ft (2,400 metres) the highest in Northern Europe, rank low on the international scale where sheer altitude, not challenge, is the criterion.

Though that physical fact has led to anonymity—few Norwegian peaks are mentioned in the classic literature of mountaineering—it is yet another boost to the popularity of wilderness recreation. Most trails meander from around 3,000–4,000 ft (900–1,200 metres) above sea level and

ice that shaped their land is currently the Norwegians' fastest growing wilderness recreation and many centres have begun to organise specialist courses.

Outdoor recreation: In travelling time, even the remote wilderness areas are close to the bulk of the population: the wilderness itself is still closer. Oslo is bounded on its landward side by Oslomarka, a vast open area of seven adjoining forests set aside for outdoor recreation, larger than greater London. Fully two-thirds of the city of Oslo is literally in the woods, and the geographic centre of town is in a stand of sturdy conifers.

Likewise, Bergen is bounded on two sides by seven stony ramparts, which are known

there are few or no acclimatisation problems at that height. Nor do you need to be a trained mountaineer to sample the magic of these mountains. Norwegian mountaineers can ascend the equivalent of the Matterhorn or Mont Blanc—the vertical scales are the same—without having to cope with the problems of altitude.

Some of the glaciers that hewed the landscape left offspring. One, Jostedalsbreen (Jostedal Glacier), is the largest on the mainland of Europe. Jostedalsbreen and its siblings throughout the country are the places to see crampon-shod parties wielding ice axes from spring until autumn. Contact with the

locally as Vidden, "the Mesa". Here each weekend a cable car takes hundreds of Bergen families from town to the top station some 1,150 ft (350 metres) to the timber line, on the edge of the coastal mountain plateau.

Trondheim has its Bymarka, Tromsø its Tromsdalen. No Norwegian city is without nearby natural, unspoiled surprises. But to Norwegians, who are as likely to shoulder rucksacks as to tote briefcases on city transport, that's no surprise.

Above, one of hundreds of small harbours along Norway's long coastline. **Right**, patriotic crowd at Holmenkollen.

THE GREAT SKI JUMP

The Holmenkollen Ski Festival is the oldest in the world and one million people leave the centre of Oslo for Holmenkollen during the 11 days of the festival in March each year. At the climax on Holmenkollen Sunday, more than 100,000 people gather at this famous ski-jump hill inside the Oslo city boundary, to watch ski-jumping in the country that invented it. But though the Nordic skiing competitions (cross-country and ski-jumping) and the newer events attract top competitors eager for World Cup points, Holmenkollen is much more than yet another international winter competition. This is very much a citizens' festival, a chance for ordinary Norwegians and visitors to take part in cross-country skiing and other events.

The idea of sitting or strolling as a spectator all day in the middle of a Norwegian winter might sound like the best way of catching a cold but the excitement is high. Wrapped in boots, anoraks, gloves and hat, with the necessary extra of a warm cushion to sit on, everything is happening and you need no more than a regular quick coffee, best laced with aquavit, to keep out the cold.

Norway was the first country to introduce ski competitions when Norwegian soldiers began to compete as early as 1767 and the first civilian event took place in 1843 at Tromsø, in the far north. A little later, Sondre Norheim from Morgedal skied to Christiania (Oslo) with his farmer friends from Telemark, to demonstrate the success of his new style of skiing. The men from Morgedal opened the world's first ski school in the capital. By the 1880s, the Norwegian Society for the Promotion of Skiing already held a winter competition and in 1892, this transferred to Holmenkollen. That year, the longest ski-jump was 72.17 ft (22 metres). Today, it is more than 364.17 ft (111 metres).

In the very first days the competitors were all Norwegian but even by 1903 Swedes had arrived, joined in the next few years by French and German skiers and, since World War II, foreign skiers from most of the skiing countries have taken part—and won.

Norway's King Olav V, a first-class sportsman, made his debut on the Holmenkollen jump in 1922, and is a faithful spectator more than 60 years later. He takes a keen interest in the events, spending his time by the finishing line for the big cross-country touring race, and leaving the Royal box to other members of the Royal Family.

Women first competed in 1947 when Alpine skiing events were introduced but they had to wait until 1954 to be admitted to the cross-country race; now the programme has been expanded to include cross-country for disabled skiers and a military cross-country race including shooting.

The fortnight begins with the Handicap Ski Race; next comes the Guards' Race, followed by the Norwegian Members of Parliament—fitter perhaps than their counterparts elsewhere—and local politicians, and cross-country skiing at all levels. On Children's Day more than 5,000 children swarm into the arena, for events to mark the end of the season at the children's ski school, and on Holmenkollen Sunday itself, the Holmenkollen March attracts around 7,000 to 8,000, many just ordinary skiers, to ski either 13 or 26 miles (21 or 42 km) through the Nordmarka forest and finish right under the jump.

The atmosphere of Holmenkollen Sunday is electric. They call it Norway's second national day, after Constitution Day on 17 May, and most spectators set off early for Frognerseteren, the nearest stop to the ski-jump. There is then time for a large breakfast-cum-brunch at one of the hotels to keep out the minus-zero cold, before they find their seats. First come the children's events, demonstrations of skills such as Telemark skiing and parachute jumping, the exciting finish of the Holmenkollen March as the skiers arrive at the hill, and singing and dancing competitions, which lead up to the climax, the great ski-jump.

The huge crowd packed into the arena hushes as the first skier appears. Up there on the top platform, he looks like a being from another world. The silence lasts until the tiny, bright figure takes off and, in a second, is flying through space with an ease that makes it look simple. Then as skier follows skier in graceful arcs, a roar loud enough to disturb the snow fills Holmenkollen.

Were you to poll Norwegians on the famous of their country, the result would invariably be a list peppered with the names of sports stars. In everyday awareness, sports names loom large, and, to the outside world, they personify the country.

As elsewhere in this age of instantaneous electronic media, sports have allied themselves with the entertainment industry, and top sports names are common currency in conversations. Most top names are both seasonal and transitory: when snow blankets the country, summer sports are upstaged by winter sports, and vice versa in summer. A national, European or World Champion is in the limelight until the next year, when most often a new name ascends the throne. But in Norway there is also a more permanent component in the picture: there are sports names that endure to become legends.

Charisma on ice: Among them is an uncrowned, yet unquestioned queen: Sonja Henie, the legendary figure skater and film star. Born in Oslo in 1912, she grew up skating. Her talent soon outstripped the sport, and she set new standards of performance, so dazzling that she won Winter Olympic Gold medals while still in her teens and twenties in 1928, 1932 and 1936, and dominated the World Championships from 1927 until 1936. In 1936, she turned professional and starred in ice shows throughout the world. Her charisma on ice led her to Hollywood and to a career as a film actress.

She became a consummate collector and, with her husband, Niels Onstad, also a patron of the arts. The couple donated their extensive collections to, and financed the building of, the Henie-Onstad Art Centre at Høvikodden, just west of Oslo. Opened in 1968, the Centre is now looked on as one of the leading museums of modern art in Europe. It houses the Henie-Onstad memorial collections (Henie died in 1969, Onstad in 1978) and Henie's sports medals and trophies.

Birger Ruud, a contemporary of Henie's, excelled in his sport of ski jumping as she

Left, Sonja Henie, Norway's greatest skater. **Right**, Grete Waitz, a founder of Norway's Marathon successes.

excelled in figure skating. Born the second of four boys in Kongsberg, Ruud early took to all-round skiing and then to ski-jumping, following in the ski tracks, so to speak, of his elder brother Sigmund. In the 1928 Winter Olympics in St Moritz, Switzerland, Sigmund won a silver medal in the ski-jumping event. Birger was to improve on that performance: he won Olympic Gold in 1932 in Lake Placid, New York, and in 1936 in Garmisch-Partenkirchen, Germany. In the 1936 Olympics he also won the downhill

ski-racing event, which made him the world's first and, as yet, only ski competitor to win in both the Nordic and Alpine skiing events.

He held his skills long: in 1948, at the age of 37, he replicated Sigmund's feat and won a silver medal in jumping in the Winter Olympics, again held in St Moritz.

As Ruud brought his competitive career to its startling close, another Norwegian ski star was rising. In Oslo, young Stein Eriksen was literally leaping up the ladder of success in Alpine ski racing. Like Ruud, Eriksen was an all-round skier. He recklessly pushed his equipment and challenged the techniques of the times. His approach both worked and helped change the sport. In the 1952 Winter Olympics, held in Oslo, Eriksen blazed to a gold medal in the Giant Slalom event by leaning far out from his skis to make his spectacular turns.

Ski-racer or runner: As Eriksen was at the height of his professional skiing career, Ingrid Christensen was growing up in Trondheim, a windblown city where the winters are long and the skiing is excellent. Ingrid took up skiing and, like many others from that part of Norway, excelled at it. In 1977, when she was 20, she was in the national A team, the pool of racers from which Norway draws the teams it sends to major

international events. But she was not just a skier. She was also a capable runner, good enough to be on Norwegian international teams from 1971 on.

Running finally won. Ingrid dropped ski racing, married Arve Kristiansen, became a mother and a full-time runner. Her achievements substantiate the choice: she currently holds the world records in 5,000 metres (14.37.33 min., set 1986 in Stockholm) and 10,000 metres (30.13.74 min., set 1986 in Oslo) and the unofficial world record in the marathon (2 hours, 21 min., 6 sec, in 1985 in London). She has won five of the six major world marathons, in London, Stockholm,

Boston, Chicago and Houston. She is a World Champion many times over, in cross-country running (Auckland, 1988) and in urban 15 km events (1987 in Monte Carlo, 1988 in Australia).

Early in her running career, Ingrid Kristiansen followed in the footsteps of another runner, Grete Waitz, whose record of firsts is unequalled in women's running. Born in Oslo, Grete began to win when she was 12, and by 1974 she was world class, with a bronze medal in the European Championships 1,500-metre event. Win after win followed, as Grete set records and pushed the limits of women's distance running.

From 1978 to 1983, she won five World Championships in cross-country running. Starting in 1978, she won the New York marathon nine times, itself a world record. She has held the world records in the 3,000 and 5,000-metre events, and she was the first woman in the world to run the marathon in less than two and a half hours.

In addition to running, her current tasks continue to build upon her astonishing career: she is a member of the Norwegian Olympic Committee; she lectures on women's sports with the skill of a teacher, the calling for which she is trained; and she is involved in campaigns to promote fitness for the general public.

Into the woods: Throughout the sports spectrum in Norway, the criterion is performance first, popularity thereafter. The memorable stars endure, even in the less flashy sports. On the modern scene, orienteering—the sport where competitors run cross-country, finding their way by use of map and compass—is one of the least flashy. People who run through woods at irregular intervals on unpredictable courses are not the easiest targets for a television camera, but, as all Scandinavians know (orienteering is Scandinavia's leading participation sport), it's a tough sport and the competition is keen.

In that sphere, two names stand out: Åge and Ingrid Hadler, a couple who met while competing. Their record as a couple—Åge was twice World Champion, in 1966 and 1972, and Ingrid was once World Champion, in 1970—still stands, whatever the sport.

Left, Ingrid Kristiansen wins the London Marathon. Right, disabled and blind skiers fearlessly tackle the slopes at Beitestølen.

Put the question "Are you a skier?" at almost any social gathering anywhere in Europe, and you could expect a few positive responses and perhaps a lecture or two on the virtues of the sport. Put the same question to someone you meet of a Sunday afternoon at one of the ski trail lodges in Norway, which you can only reach on skis, and the answers will be quite different—"No, I'm a bank clerk"; "Heavens no, I am just a housewife"; "Who me? Never dream of it!"

Why the disparity? Why does someone sitting in a pub in England, far from snow, profess to be a skier, while someone out for a day's skiing in Norway apparently declines all interest in the sport? The answer lies in a tradition that has woven sport deeply into the fabric of Norwegian life.

It is reflected in the language. While English has just one word, "sport", Norwegian has two: "*sport*" and "*idrett*". Both translate to sport in English but in Norwegian each denotes a distinct aspect. The Norwegian *sport* is the umbrella word which covers all sporting events, so that a sports journalist in Norway plies exactly the same trade as his or her English equivalent.

The word *idrett* is reserved for events in which the ultimates in performances are determined by the capabilities of the human body. Horse riding is not *idrett*, while scuba diving is. There is a further nuance: *aktiv* (active) means a person currently competing in a sport classified as *idrett*.

This explains why, when you ask skiing Norwegians "are you a skier?", you have asked if they currently compete in the sport. Ask often enough, and you unearth the astonishing statistics of just how many Norwegians take part or have taken part in sports based on human capabilities. In total, for all sports classified as *idrett,* one Norwegian in three is currently active.

That amazing fraction is reflected in the high priority Norwegians give to sport. Oslo has two statues of living Norwegians, both in sporting poses: a statue of King Olav V

skiing, near the Holmenkollen Ski Jump, and a statue of marathon runner Grete Waitz, running, of course, at the marathon gate of Bislett Stadium. The architects of high-rise flats are obliged by law to include "sports gear storage rooms" in their plans. Norges Idrettshøgskole, the modern, well-equipped Norwegian College of Physical Education and Sport in Oslo, is the envy of physical educators elsewhere. One of the departments of the Ministry of Church and Education is dedicated to "Youth and *Idrett*". Nearly

every municipality has its own "consultant for sport and *idrett*," and all large cities have a Department of Parks and Facilities for *Idrett*. City newspapers vie with each other in sales on the strengths of their sports sections, and from 12 to 14 percent of the Norwegian Broadcasting Corporation's (NRK) annual television broadcast hours are devoted to sports.

Pinnacles and plateaux: So pervasive are sports that, to the unknowing eye, the sports spectrum may seem dull. "Where is the flash, the excitement?" visitors sometimes ask. The answer is that the pinnacles are there, as high and sometimes higher than elsewhere,

Left, Norwegians, they say, are born ski-jumpers. Right, Prince Haakon Magnus shows his skill as a water-skier

MORGEDAL AND THE TELEMARK REVIVAL

For jazz fans, New Orleans is the ultimate magnet, just as Wimbledon is for tennis players. For skiers, the start of it all is Morgedal, in the southern county of Telemark, a hamlet that long remained an entry only found in history books pored over by scholars of the sport of skiing. Today, that has all changed because of a worldwide reawakening of interest in the style of skiing called Telemark, which evolved in Morgedal in the 19th century.

More than a hundred years ago, when the story starts, there were even fewer people than the 200,000 who live in Telemark today—a hardy breed of woodsmen, small farmers, hunters, and traders, who fashioned their own implements including the skis they needed to get about on winter snows.

Morgedal is in the mountains, so the ski makers there sought designs that would perform well in the surrounding rugged terrain, both in everyday winter skiing and for impromptu sporting meetings. Among the best in the mid-1800s was Sondre Norheim, a young tenant farmer. He excelled not only in village ski meetings but also in ski-making skills. Norheim's innovations and the manoeuvres they made possible changed skiing forever.

He devised bindings (devices that hold feet in boots to skis) that were firm and were the first to give the feet control over the skis. He also gave the skis what is known as sidecut, the slight "hourglass" profile of a ski seen from above. Sidecut is what enables skis to run true and turn easily and his sidecut principle remains a cornerstone of basic ski design.

Norheim and his fellow Morgedal skiers used the new designs to perfect new skiing manoeuvres, including ways of turning and stopping on snow, and ways of landing from airborne flights off snow-covered rooftops and natural outcrops. Their fame spread and, by 1868, Sondre Norheim and his farmers from Telemark were ready to show off their new skills. Norheim led them on skis for the 112-mile (180-km) journey from Morgedal to Christiania (now Oslo), where

the city crowds turned out to greet and applaud the peasant skiers and their miraculous new techniques. This led to the start of the big ski jumping contest at Husaby near Oslo in 1879, where 10,000 spectators led by the king cheered the skiing pioneers from Telemark. Around the same time, the Telemark skiers established the world's first ski school in Oslo, and in 1892 the Husaby competition moved to Holmenkollen, where the great ski jump is still held today.

In 1902, the first ski-jumping rules committee met to compile criteria for judging the style of competitors at the annual Holmenkollen ski-jump meetings. They honoured the origins of the two most skilful groups by affixing their names to the two turns then executed by ski jumpers to come to a stop after landing from flight.

The turn in which the skis are held parallel throughout was named the Christiania, while the bent-knee stance with one ski trailing became the Telemark.

Few modern skiers know the meaning of "Christiania"; it is a casualty of time, and in 1925 the city for which it was named became Oslo. But Telemark, the skiing manoeuvre and the county for which it was named, are both part of the present scene.

In modern Telemark skiing, the heel is free to lift up from the ski, and turns are steered, with one ski trailing and at an angle to the other. From the side, the manoeuvre looks like a genuflection in motion. Although competitive Telemark ski races are now held on packed slopes, as are Alpine ski races, true Telemark skiing is a throwback to the skiing of Sondre Norheim's time, to mastering deep snows with skill and strength. The rebirth of the Telemark turn has revived another skiing skill of the past, skiathlon. Competitors must ski jump, ski through a slalom course, and run a cross-country ski race, all on the same pair of skis. The name is new, but the combination of manoeuvres dates back to the times when the men from Morgedal first mastered the ski-jumping meets in Christiania some 130 years ago. But a ski jumping performance then required the competitor to jump through the air, come to a stop after landing, ski back uphill to the top of the ski jump, and jump again before finishing.

but the surrounding plateaux are so high that they make the peak less prominent. Norges Idrettsforbund (the Norwegian Confederation of Sports), the umbrella organisation for 45 separate sports associations, in total more than 1.6 million members, spotlights that fact in its stated goals. The overall objective is wrapped up in the motto "Sport for All", and the pinnacles are grouped and designated "elite". So, for the Confederation and its member associations, competitive sport is both egalitarian and elitist. From the broad base of people for whom sport is a major leisure time activity come the elite, competitors who enter the many national championships and represent Norway in international

gold medals in the 1988 Olympic Games were not in the gruelling endurance events in which they have long excelled, but rather in wrestling and in rifle marksmanship.

Pervasiveness and prowess have their price. The annual turnover in sports, excluding the sports equipment sector, is over £100 million (1,000 million Nkr), and sports are supported through many channels. The government gives 55 percent of the surplus from the state-run football (soccer) pools. The 5,000-odd clubs use extra-curricular activities, such as bingo and lotteries, as their largest single source of income, close to 40 percent of the totals. Wherever you go, you are besieged by young people selling lottery

sports meetings. The results speak for themselves. For a country with a small population, Norway has always been disproportionately strong in sports. There's hardly one in which Norwegians have not won Olympic or international championship medals. The competitive prowess of the sub-Arctic country with a long coastline has understandably long been in winter sports and in sailing, but has also filled out to include as diverse disciplines as marathon running, cycling, and ballroom dancing. The Norwegians' two

Left, Telemark skiing uses one stick only. **Right**, speed-skating at Bislett Stadium in Oslo.

tickets to support the local sports club.

Football figures first: As elsewhere in Europe, in figures, football (soccer) is Norway's number one sport, with some 1,800 clubs and a total of over 280,000 players. It is also the best supported by the football pool funds, at about £64 million (Nkr 640 million) per year.

Number two in the statistics and, its supporters contend, spiritually number one, is the country's traditional stalwart, skiing, with over 1,500 clubs and a total membership of over 200,000. Together the four skiing disciplines—cross-country, alpine, ski-jumping and biathlon (cross-country skiing and rifle shooting)—are funded as well and sometimes better than football. Third is gymnastics, with over 500 clubs and over 100,000 members. Then follow handball, track and field athletics, orienteering, shooting, swimming, sailing and volleyball to fill out the top 10 sports as measured by the numbers participating.

Of these top 10, only three, football, handball and volleyball, are team sports. The other seven are individual events. The balance is almost the complete reverse of most countries, where team sports dominate the overall picture. The cause and effect is a chicken-and-egg question: does the predominance of individual sports reflect Norwegian mentality, or is it the converse?

Whatever the cause, individual sports are the country's international showpiece. Albeit earned on the strength of an early dominance that has waned, Norway can claim more winter sports Olympic medals than any other country, and winter sportsmen and women are among the country's heroes.

Orienteering, the sport in which participants run over terrain, using a map and compass to chart their own course between checkpoints and to the finish, is not surprisingly a Norwegian strength. It's also the only sport in which a Norwegian couple, husband and wife Åge and Ingrid Hadler, have both been World Champions.

More recently, Norwegian women distance runners have consistently ranked among the world's best; two have set world records and have virtually monopolised marathons and terrain events. Gymnastics has been a Norwegian strength ever since its team won this event in the 1912 Olympics.

Giant iceberg: The backbone of Norwegian sports capabilities is, of course, Norwegian involvement. Accurate statistics are notoriously hard to come by, but estimates indicate that of the country's 1.4 million families with children, almost half are involved in sports in some way other than direct participation. *Papa* is an official of the local club, and *Mama* helps on the stalls at the annual club flea market. The older children sell club lottery tickets; in fact the whole family helps to run the annual club meets.

Most families have one member who is either a certified coach or is training to become one. All these services are voluntary and form the true underpinnings of the giant iceberg that keeps sport so visibly afloat.

One persistent reminder of that effort is the seeming ubiquity of sports facilities and sports instruction. Most suburban and rural schools have ample adjoining playing fields. Multi-purpose sports grounds are common in residential areas. In summer and autumn, they are hatcheries for future football and track and field athletic talents. In winter, their iced surfaces swarm with figure and speed skaters and serve as mini-arenas for ice hockey and bandy, a related sport played with a ball instead of a puck, to rules more closely resembling those of field hockey.

Ski museum: It is the clubs that further sports. The country's largest club in Oslo, the most populous area, incorporates that purpose in its name: Foreningen til Skiidrettens Fremme, the Society for the Furtherance of Ski Sports, or Skiforeningen in short. Skiforeningen owns and operates the Holmenkollen Hill, with its famous skijump, site of the annual ski meetings that predate the modern Olympic Games. It also owns and maintains the Ski Museum, renowned as one of the world's most complete; publishes a major snow sports magazine; and arranges hundreds of courses a year.

This high involvement has some drawbacks. In the more popular sports, competition has become so fierce that the criteria for doing well have been elevated to seemingly unattainable heights, which dissuade neophytes. Youngsters pushed into competition by overzealous parents can burn out prematurely, and this has become a recognised problem in almost all sports.

Television coverage has robbed events of spectators, a trend that most hurts the less important, least well-off sports. The escalating demand for high-quality facilities—tracks to run on, halls to play in, courses to ski on—has concentrated sports in larger population centres. One indirect problem is that the preoccupation with sports can eclipse other endeavours.

Internationally renowned violinist Arve Tellefsen's prime lament is that his infrequent sports ventures—his boyhood skills of ski-racing and football—invariably rate more media coverage than his violin virtuosity. But that doesn't prevent him from putting on a pair of skis or kicking a football.

Right, water footballer all at sea.

To Norwegians, fish is the standby staple. Even in modest markets, the varieties of fish and fish products are amazing, and Norwegians look on a proper fresh fish shop as an asset to a community. Fish is both humble fare and holiday cuisine. Fish balls in white sauce are the Norwegian dining-table stalwart, and steamed cod is a favourite for Sunday dinners. On festive tables, herring in myriad forms takes its place with other delicacies such as *gravlaks* (cured salmon), *rakørret* (half-fermented trout), and *lutefisk* (dried codfish marinated in a lye solution, a dish few foreigners appreciate).

It is not surprising that Norway is a country of fishermen of all kinds. The language differentiates accordingly: *fisker* means "fisherman", one who lives by commercial fishing, while *sportsfisker* is the amateur variety, an "angler". But there the similarity stops. Angling in Norway is done both for the sport itself and as part of other outdoor pursuits. Fishing tackle is among the paraphernalia of camping trips, just as it is the prime equipment for avid anglers.

The long coastline is a mecca for saltwater angling, yet freshwater angling is the more popular variety, and there are a quarter of a million fishable inland lakes and ponds. The most common of around 40 freshwater species are trout and char; in the northernmost parts, and in lakes and ponds at higher elevations, they are the only fish. Grayling and pike are more common in larger lakes and rivers in eastern and central areas. Local legends about lakes rich in pike hold that the fish are descended from stocks set out in the late 18th century by the ruling Danes.

Bream, whitefish, perch and carp are found in most lower lakes in the southern part of the country, as well as in Eastern Finnmark in the far north. Reliable varieties in saltwater include cod, coalfish, haddock, whiting, halibut, herring, and mackerel.

The stars on the angling scene are Atlantic salmon and sea trout, related varieties which are both popular game and commercial fish. The commercial varieties now come largely from commercial fish farms, but the game fish still swim the rivers until they are two to six years old, migrate to the sea, and then return to spawn in some 400 rivers.

Norwegians argue about the best rivers, but five in the northern part of the country stand out—the Alta and Tana rivers in Finnmark, and the Gaula, Namsen and Orkla rivers in Trøndelag, all of which draw anglers from around the world. There, the sport is so popular that you have to apply for licences as much as a year in advance.

You need two types of angling licence to keep within the law. The first and most easily acquired is the *Fisketrygdeavgiften* (fishing

insurance fee), a national fee that helps to offset the costs of overseeing fishing. Valid for one calendar year, it can be obtained by postal giro order on forms available at all post offices, at Nkr 60 for fresh water fish, and Nkr 100 for freshwater fish and salmon, sea trout, and sea bream.

Saltwater fishing is otherwise free of licences and fees, but freshwater fishing is by licence only. Freshwater fishing licences come from the owners of the fishing rights, usually the property owners along the banks of a river or the shores of a lake, whether private persons or communities. These licences vary in price, and are valid for specific dates and durations, ranging from one day to several weeks. You usually buy them from hotels, sports shops, or tourist offices near the waters to which they apply.

Fly fishing is popular, so much so that Norwegians compete in the sport, including the world championships in fly casting, held annually since 1981. Other countries do better in fly-casting competition, but the Norwegians pride themselves on their versatility. Lure fishing leads, and spoon-hook fishing and trolling are also widespread.

fish, water, or wet fishing boats or other equipment from one watercourse to another.

Norwegian angling records are respectable: 71.6 lb (32.5 kg) for freshwater salmon and 82.6 lb (37.5 kg) for cod caught in the sea. Trout average 1 lb (0.5 kg) but the freshwater trout record stands at 33.7 lb (15.3 kg). The minimum permissible sizes for keeping fish caught are 9.8 inches (25 cm) in length for salmon, sea trout and sea char, and 11.8 inches (30 cm) for all other fish.

Just as winter does not deter Norwegians

Even youngsters start fishing using artificial bait, and early learn the skills of outsmarting fish. Theories abound as to why this is so, but the most plausible ascribes the situation to Norway's location and topography. In the north, there are few insects large enough to use as bait, and worms are hard to find on rocky shores. Minnows and other live fish are prohibited as bait, primarily to curtail the spread of parasites and diseases that affect fish. For the same reasons, the fishing statutes prohibit the transfer of live

from walking (they switch to cross-country skis), frozen lakes do not halt fishing. Ice fishing is a prime wintertime hobby, a simple and straightforward form of angling, which requires only a baited hand line or short pole and line, warm clothing, and lots of patience. Ice anglers must hew holes in the ice by hand as motor augers are prohibited.

It's a sport for the hardy, and ice angling contests are for the *very* hardy. One of the more popular has been the Ice Fishing Festival at Vangsvatnet in Voss, a town of about 8,000 people a quarter of the way between Bergen and Oslo, on one of Norway's best angling lakes for char, trout and cod.

Left, the strange fascination of ice-fishing. **Above**, cleaning the catch at the family *hytte*.

Culture in Norway? Well, certainly it exists—in its own fashion. Just take a look at your fellow travellers in the Oslo Central Station. Half of them trudge around in boots and a backpack; the other half have only the backpack. They are all heading for isolated cabins—Norway's holy *hytter*—far away from the city and its urban pleasures.

The Munch Museum, National Theatre, art galleries and some of the best food in Europe all take second place to trekking the Norwegian highlands, searching hidden mountain valleys for *rosemaling*, the indigenous folk art. Frankly, a chinchilla stole and an alligator bag would be very out of place in the Oslo station. Norwegian culture sets great store by protecting animal species.

That is all culture certainly, though not of the grand, *haute* culture sort. But who is to say that evening dress and stiletto heels are the top of the society ladder? Although Norway does not foster diamond tiaras and glittering opera soirées—though galas do, of course, occur, a notable example being the awarding of the Nobel Prize for Peace each December.

But, however well done, such parties are really just the icing on the cultural cake and ever so slightly foreign, imported glamour (Nobel, after all, was a Swede). Real Norwegian culture is something more fundamental—folksy, a reaction to foreign domination of the national identities.

As a political entity, Norway is a child of the 20th century, established in 1905 after centuries of Danish and Swedish rule. Exploitation by the second sons of Danish nobles robbed the nation of its political and social initiative. These foreigners administered (patriots say plundered) hugely rich silver and iron deposits, vast timber forests and "the unruly mass of native labourers, speaking barbarian dialects." All Norwegian "dialects" were forbidden by the Danes for official documents and communications. The new national constitution of Norway was drawn up at Eidsvoll in 1814—in Danish. Ludvig Holberg, the Samuel Johnson of Norway, had to seek his education and his fortune in Copenhagen, wrote in Danish and is actually claimed by Danes for their very own. Such cultural imperialism was crushing to Norwegian self-esteem and it nearly abolished the national identity.

Ordinary Norwegians were driven away from the centres of power to subsistence farms hanging spectacularly from fjord cliffs. Traditions, folk costume, the old ways became a cultural refuge and eventually the

treasuries of Norway's national personality. Culture with a capital "C" was something the overlords brought with them from foreign capitals. And it was something they took away with them when they left. Norway today has no noble families excepting the king and his household.

While politicians could elect a king and parliament, it fell to cultural workers, especially writers and painters, to revive the national identity. They turned for inspiration to the traditions of those isolated valleys with their ancient farmsteads and their equally ancient verbal traditions, telling heroic sagas about an expansive Norway of earlier days

Preceding pages: National Day, the heart of Norwegian culture. <u>Left</u>, jewellery on a national costume for traditional occasions (<u>above</u>).

with settlements across the seas and of the greatness of native Viking lords.

Henrik Wergeland, a richly talented poet and prose writer, became an early and passionate propagandist of this sort of Norwegian nationalism. Following the same call, artist J.C. Dahl left his studio for the wilds of Norway's hinterland, becoming the country's first and best nature painter. His shimmering, majestic views of the mountains are major attractions at the National Gallery which he helped to found in 1836.

On the dark side, the epoch's fears of isolation and rampant anxiety of the future inspired the violent, emotionally charged style of painter Edvard Munch. Death and

desolation are his recurring themes most strongly expressed in his shocking works, *The Scream* (1893), *The Kiss* and *The Vampire* (both 1895). Munch's fears of enslavement come so close to the national heart that his works have been enshrined in their own Oslo museum as well as on an entire floor of the National Gallery.

Equally loud cries for freedom came from Henrik Ibsen whose poetic drama *Brand* was a spirited indictment of Norwegian authority at home. It put Ibsen on the cultural map for the first time even outside Norway.

At the same time, the close of the 19th century, other authors turned homewards for inspiration. Alexander Kielland abandoned a promising international career to write about old Norway. Nobel laureate Knut Hamsen's chilling novel *Hunger* (1890) is an exposé of the abuses of bourgeois Swedish rule. His masterpiece, *The Growth of the Soil* (1917), reflects a deep love of nature and concern for the effects of material conditions on the individual spirit, themes that still dominate Norwegian writing.

Even architects abandoned continental idioms to embrace a native "Viking Romanticism". They began building in heavy timber and turfed roofs. Eaves and gables sprouted carved and polychromed dragon heads. Sitting rooms suddenly became imitations of chieftains' halls. An excellent example of the style is Troldhaugen, the last home of composer Edvard Grieg. Just outside Bergen, in fjord country, the house fits perfectly into Grieg's unabashed folkloric, wildly romantic style. He titled his creations after national heroes such as the *Cantata Olaf Trygvasson* (1873) and the much loved *Peer Gynt Suite* (1876, words by Ibsen). National romanticism became the midwife of Norwegian cultural independence.

A century ago, new plays by national playwright Henrik Ibsen, works by major authors such as Amalie Skram and Kielland were front-page news in Oslo, Bergen and Trondheim. Critics and politicians publicly debated new works; plays became issues, even national causes. Literature became the smithy where the new nation's identity, its culture, was being forged.

Dramatist Bjørnstjerne Bjørnson, championed the Norwegian cause, working his entire life to free the Norwegian theatre from Danish influence. While director of Bergen's Ole Bull Theatre (1857–59) and the Oslo Theatre a few years later, he commissioned new, sagalike dramas drawing on Norway's epic past, such as the *Sigurd Slembe Trilogy*. His efforts helped to revive Norwegian as a literary language. He became poet laureate and his poem, *Yes, We Love this Land of Ours* became a rallying point in the struggle for political independence from Sweden. The poem is now the national anthem of Norway.

Even today this tradition of didacticism and political engagement has a strong hold on Norwegian literature—occasionally in the extreme. This long, thin country of just over 4 million souls boasts three languages. Sami is smallest, used almost exclusively by the Lapp minority and in official communications with their representatives. Then there are *bokmål* (book language) and *nynorsk* (new Norwegian), two variations on a theme. Each has developed from the spoken Norwegian of the Oslo area enhanced with (some people contend the correct term is infected by) dialectical variations. Norwegian spelling is meant to be phonetic but tends to be surprising: check = *sjekk*. After 400 years of foreign rule, a logical, if not purely linguistic, method of recreating the Norwegian language had to be charted out.

Pragmatic Norwegians went about this by also called *riksmål* in its more Danish form.

New Norse, that is *nynorsk* to the initiated, is only used by about 15 percent of Norwegian primary school children—the direct heirs of last century's linguistic and social national didacticism. This new language draws heavily on the archaic Old Norse of the central-western dialects. "True Viking language" as one zealot gushed. Since this is a language based on rural culture, *nynorsk* has suffered by 20th-century urbanisation, losing ground to *bokmål*, though to complicate things, around 15 percent of the country's fiction writers still use *nynorsk*. They live mostly in the western districts and call themselves regional authors.

gradually exchanging Danish loan words for words discovered in native dialects, by substituting Danish syntaxes with Norwegian, soft Danish consonants became hard Norwegian ones. And so *bokmål* became the official language, used today by about 80 percent of the towns and throughout the entire northern districts. It is the language tourists and businessmen will most likely encounter as 90 percent of all industrial, business and communications publications are in *bokmål*,

Left, a corner of the Munch Museum, Oslo. **Above**, "the artist and his brain children" by the sculptor Gustav Vigeland in Frogner Park, Oslo.

Among these writers is one author who recently published an essay on his own works in a sumptuous limited edition. It is available exclusively through direct contact with the author or his publisher. As one critic describes it, "a work of literature in Norwegian—this peculiar language spoken and written by only 4 million people—is a precious thing, the arduous work of one person only, meant for another individual, who must labour equally arduously, when the work is submitted to her scrutiny." That is certainly a different standpoint from the position of international media moguls who pour cascades of suave commercial culture over the heads of stubborn Norwegians. There seems to be a native "save the language campaign" among publishers, educators, writers and even politicians to protect the tongue from such internationalism.

Poetry is no more read in Norway than in other western European countries; an average of 40 or so volumes appear annually in editions of less than 2,000—most of which go unsold. Still, there seems to be a nearly Nietzschian determination to keep the genre alive despite the economic odds. One rainy June recently, large crowds gathered in the Oslo harbour area to hear the works of poet Olaf Angell and novelist Axel Jensen, keynote speakers and initiators of the Oslo Inter-

misery; just the sort of woe-wrought exposés found everywhere in 1970s Scandinavia and not the stuff for minting literary coinage.

However, the 1980s produced a sort of realistic novel, written in sociology textbook style, directly opposed to the older, bourgeois psychology novels, "a die-hard heritage from Hamsun, Cora Sandel and Torborg Nedreaas." Most readable among these "revolution" works are Dag Solstad's Trilogy about World War II, *Svik* (Betrayal), *Krig* (War) and *Brød og Våpen* (Bread and Arms). More existentialist is Espen Haavardsholm's *Store Fri* (The Big Break). This revival of social realism allowed an author such as Asbjørn Elden to produce

national Festival of Poetry. The 40 international speakers drew not just academics and publishers into the bad weather but politicians, industrialists and even diplomats. As one reviewer put it, "poetry is dead, but poets are alive and kicking." Or was this another manifestation of pride in things Norwegian?

Author Einar Økland placed an article in London's *Times Literary Supplement* in 1971 heralding "a new Golden Age of Norwegian literature," which turned out to be a simple, but highly successful, chronicling of the Norwegian working class against capitalism. The literary agenda contained works on strikes, working conditions and general

essentially modern yet "back to our roots" sagas about the inconspicuous lives of ordinary people such as his autobiographical *Rundt Neste Sving* (Around the Next Bend).

Women have come to the fore of Norwegian writing. Cecilie Løveid and Kari Bøge crashed on to the literary scene in the late 1970s with audacious, even shocking works. Ignoring male-dominated social realism, they picked apart purely female problems using "street language" and spoken modes of expression. Løvied's lyrically erotic *Sug* (Suck) rocked the staid Oslo critics but has brought her international recognition. Suddenly Norway was reading female authors writing about female interests. Liv Køltzow's third novel, *The Story of Eli*, and Gerd Brantenberg's *The Daughters of Egalia* explore the female mystic and sex roles in society.

More recently, there has been a renewal of the experimental novel by the best of the new Norwegian writers. They have had a hard time getting their strange new works to sprout in utilitarian Norwegian soil despite worldwide recognition of storytellers such as Tarjei Vesaas. Much as Ibsen did a century ago, these writers try both to capture and to dismantle the realities of their age. That means delving into the jargon of the media, using, physics, micro-biology, ecology and

All this experimentation, despite its solid Norwegian roots, has not caught on with the general public at home—the people in the boots and backpacks. Of course, they will pick up a copy of the latest hit novel, read a chapter or two, then put it away "for my retirement reading."

Like most other Scandinavians, Norwegians love going to art galleries and auction showings. But here again they flock to the romantics of the 1880s and 1890s not the moderns scooped up by *avant gardist* Swedes or the 18th-century artists idolised by Danes. But for a Norwegian to show deep abiding interest, lead him to an ancient timbered house from the mountain valleys.

other modern sciences as dictionaries.

Seeking to turn foreign trends into Norwegian literature, the new writers mix genre. They have opened the museum of archaic styles bringing turn-of-the-century names back to life. Authors to look out for are Kim Småge (whose first novel *Night Dive* introduces a female crime solver and earned her the coveted Riverton Prize), Jon Michelet, another detective story writer, Tor Åke Bringsværd and Jan Kjærstad.

Left, writer and nationalist Bjørnsterne Bjørnson at the dinner table. **Above**, Live Køltzow (left) and Kari Bøge (right).

"Collecting old houses is something of a family mania," says one shipowner—the nearest Norway comes to an aristocracy. "My father, brother and I have been combing the back country for 40 years for handcrafted dwellings and objects, homesteads, barns, cabins and huts complete with their country beds, chests, baskets and cupboards. Each must be unique to its own valley and period. Passing tourists often mistake our jumble of sod roofs and agricultural paraphernalia for a folklore museum and inquire where they should pay the admission. They always look very confused when we explain that this is our home."

Typical of the national mania for folk art, this family's collection began simply by bartering with valley farmers for small country items, such as handcrafted butter and porridge *tine*. These colourful, wooden caskets, often a first gift to a betrothed, form an unbroken tradition from Viking times to the present. Always highly decorated, the *tine* are still used by country lads to show off their carving and *rosemaling* painting skills.

This rose painting first appeared on the walls of parish churches in the 18th century, bright, naive distillations of baroque marbling, rococo tendrils, medieval meanders of acanthus leaves and Empire-style portraiture. Too conservative to borrow directly

from outsiders, Norwegian farmers carefully extracted only those aspects of those major European art movements that fitted their own sense of colour and decoration. Each remote valley became its own art centre for a particular style of *rosemaling* and architecture. Hallingdal farmers were partial to delicate S-curves applied to everything from walls to spoons and bowls. In affluent Gudbrandsdal, the locals carved their decorations into built-in benches and box beds. The most isolated districts such as Setesdal have a very simplified *rosemaling* tradition.

Part of the attraction of trekking in Norway is learning to recognise and appreciate the country's thriving rustic art heritage; a way of returning to the national roots. A 250-year-old *stabbur* (storage barn built on stilts) is a powerful clan totem for a Norwegian; something to be revered.

This becomes most obvious at the outdoor Folk Museum near Oslo, opened by the national romantics a century or so ago, "to honour and preserve the traditions that have held our land together." Here are collected dozens of old buildings, barns and farmsteads from every corner of the country. Even regional costumes are collected here to serve as patterns for new outfits. Many Norwegian brides and grooms choose their home village's own special costume for their wedding-day apparel. The Nobel festivities also bring out the colourful outfits, side by side with the white ties and tiaras. This fascination with the past is more than just folklore, it is simply the national profile.

Still, all this heritage can be a bit somnolent for casual visitors. Refer to any tourist guide book of the past 20 years for confirmation: "Oslo is the most beautiful and deadest city in Europe." Another travel writer says kindly: "The emphasis is on the number of nature trails and the outstanding views from various points, usually a good hike well above sea level. All that fresh air and exercise is so exhausting that any thought of activity after dark, beyond a quick meal, a good book and a comfortable bed, is out of the question."

But times do change. "Was the deadest capital" comes closer to the truth about Oslo. Norway, despite all its interest in the past, has come alive to the attractions of city fun. Perhaps this is a result of growing self-confidence or the result of the vast flocks of Norwegians who travel abroad each winter.

"Lots of champagne gets drunk here," says one habitué of a baroque watering hole for Norway's beautiful people (mostly those shippers again and the bankers and stockbrokers who serve them during the working day). Humla, the surrounding entertainment complex—you never have to go outside into the cold and drizzle—offers dancing, live and disco, a nightclub and theatre and even artists such as Eartha Kitt and the Swedish drag show cabaret "After Dark".

The capital makes a speciality of these entertainment palaces—offering "everything" under one roof. Most impressive is

Møller, perched on an old industrial waterfall on the Aker River. Take the taxi ride that drops you in Møller's tropical bar, or in the lounge with its live entertainment and banks of tables à la 1935. The piano bar is for a bit later in the evening for quiet chats. But food is usually an afterthought—and expensive—at these Oslo fun emporiums.

In this town, bad food is expensive and good fare does not cost more. Most of the nice restaurants are within walking distance of the centre of Oslo. Best of them is Bagatelle in the Bygdøy Allé, complete with Michelin star and a good collection of works by contemporary Norwegian artists decorating the dining rooms. Chef-owner Eyvind

long and the food is good, even excellent, and generously spiced with Norwegian produce and game.

Despite all the fun of doing Oslo till the last bars close at 6 a.m., natives still pull on their boots and head for the hills. Love of nature and folklore are inbred in today's Norwegians. This is most obvious and moving on the National Day, 17 May, something of a national carnival, everyone dressed up to the nines, most women in their regional costumes. Even the bus-loads of visiting Swedes and Danes put on ties and jackets. Everybody not on their death bed—and even a few of those—floods the streets surrounding the Royal Palace. Brass bands

Hallstrøm specialises in Scandinavian modern dishes and a generous dash of French tradition. Another devotee of Nordic fare is young Lars Barman at Kastanjen. Two of his specialities are smoked lamb with a parsley root sauce and cod on a bed of multi-coloured beans. There are other equally interesting restaurants all over Oslo, such as Theas, Feinschmecker, Årstidene and Brasseriet at the SAS hotel, La Mer. The list is

Left, pop and rock any night of the week. <u>Above left</u>, the mood for modern sculpture is everywhere. <u>Above right</u>, Oslo Museum of Contemporary Art.

stream by, flags wave, fiddles squeak.

Slowly, order comes to the chaos and Norway marches towards the palace to meet its king. First in line are the school children come especially for the event from Lindeness to distant North Cape. The much-loved Olav V and his family appear on the balcony and the people make their homage by singing Bjørnsons's National Anthem, then the King's Song. And here on the lawns below a palace built for a foreign monarch is the distillation of all things Norwegian: an abiding love of nature, of tradition, of pride in a stubborn conviction that "things Norwegian are the best of things."

FILM INDUSTRY? *WHAT* FILM INDUSTRY?

To the new city-poor who had streamed into Christiania (Oslo) in the last decade of the 19th century, the first Bioscope show at the Tivoli Gardens was a sensation. The generation that first migrated from the farms of rural Norway to work long hours in the factories of the new industrial revolution lived drab lives in crowded slums. The flickering images of a kangaroo boxing or of acrobats leaping seemed magical.

This first public projection of a "motion picture" came from the German inventor brothers Max and Emil Skladarowsky, only a few months after the Lumière brothers' Paris exhibition in December 1895. Eight years later, Christiania had its own film theatre.

The first Norwegian pioneer was Hugo Hermansen, director of Norsk Kinematograf, a Norwegian branch of a Swedish film company. In those days, cinematographers owned film theatres as well as making films and Hermansen quickly opened 26 establishments on the east and west coasts. His greatest coup was to persuade the new king and queen to visit a cinema. He filmed the occasion and subsequently screened it.

Perils of a Fisherman, in 1907, was the first attempt at film drama. This improvised story, without a script, was filmed in a few hours on the Norwegian fjord by a young Swede, Julius Jaenzon, who worked in Norway for many years before returning to Sweden to become one of that country's cinematographers.

Though *Perils* was the start of a native industry, it is now lost, along with almost every other Norwegian film made between 1907 and 1920. This may have been due to Hermansen's sudden death only a year later, which destroyed his cinema empire and left the fledgling industry stranded. By the start of World War I, Norway had produced only nine films.

The cinema was popular. By the end of the war Christiania had 26 cinemas and around 1.8 million adults and 800,000 children visited annually, bringing in Nkr 1 million. It was a working-class audience from the "wrong" side of the town, and children made up 45 percent of the audience.

Always ready to spoil people's fun—a characteristic not confined to Norway—the moralists, organised into "moral societies", determined to act against what they dismissed as "the demoralising influence of the higher-class tivoli."

By 1913, when the industry was still profitable, a long, ardent, nationwide debate with strong moral overtones led to the cinemas coming under municipal administration. The private cinema owners gradually disappeared but Norwegian film-making benefited little, as profits now went direct to the local authorities and film production was still left wanting. Around the same time Norway set up a censorship authority.

Towards the end of World War I, two film-makers emerged. The author Peter Lykke-Seest became director of the Christiania Film Company which produced nine out of the 10 Norwegian films made between 1916 and 1919. His masterpiece, *The Orphans*, starred his 12-year-old son but his productions suffered because he spread himself too thinly by insisting on taking on all the jobs needed for a film.

Around the same time, Ottar Gladtvet made *Daughters of the Revolution*, based on the political unrest of the time. Though Gladtvet attempted to speak to the audiences against what he saw as the danger of growing radicalisation of the workers' movement in Norway, his message was too often drowned in commercial romance.

When the film industry in neighbouring Sweden began to draw on the writings of Norwegian authors such as Ibsen and Bjørnson for their own cinema, the status of the native Norwegian film industry began to grow. It began to be regarded as a worthwhile and acceptable evocation of traditional Norwegian life rather than subversive, popular entertainment for the masses. *Fante-Anne* by Rasmus Breistein was an example of a style which came to dominate Norwegian productions until the advent of sound—a national romanticism with yearnings for an idealised peasant past.

But though the cinemas of the 1920s were paying 10 percent of their box office receipts as a luxury ticket tax, prosperity did not last. By 1926, the craving for cinema romance was saturated and this led to low ticket prices, low film rental and high distribution fees. The local authorities which had begun to act as though cinema profits could be used against any municipal crisis, had to realise that the celluloid goose was dead.

Nevertheless, the national production company, Norsk Film, opened in 1932 and Norway's first studio was built in 1936. Just before World War II, Helge Lund made the first internationally recognised film, *Aitaga* (The Bastard), shown at the 1941 Venice Film Festival.

By that time, Norway had been overrun and its German occupiers had applied the principle of *Bleichshaltung* to Norwegian films as German officials entrenched themselves firmly in all aspects of the industry. They also established a film production fund with money from the old "ticket tax".

Although Norway is still struggling to impress its personality on the international film scene, this fund has formed the basis of Norway's state support for a film industry, again hit hard by the arrival of television in the 1960s. Today, operational costs in Norway are high, though there is little of the "star" and "star director" system that operates elsewhere. Norwegian film-makers seek their rewards at Scandinavian and other film festivals rather than in their bank balances.

The Government scheme subsidises productions to 55 percent of box-office receipts for Norwegian-language films of 75 minutes or more, backed by Norwegian capital, and using a "preponderance" of Norwegian technicians. Outside Scandinavia, this insistence on the Norwegian language is itself a hurdle in selling films, but the success of the first Scandinavian Film Festival in Rouen in 1988 and its second event in 1990 indicates that selling Scandinavian films as a whole could be successful.

At the beginning of the 1990s, various schemes guaranteed Nkr 36 million in loans to the industry and Nkr 20 million in subsidies for television and cinema, but the policy is slowly to phase out subsidies and the government is encouraging commercial loans and private investment.

Left, *The Pathfinder.* <u>Above</u>, **Liv Ullman.**

The first modern international success came in 1987 with *Pathfinder*, directed by Nils Gaup and produced by John M. Jacobsen. This film for children was nominated the following year for an Oscar for the best foreign film by the American Film Academy. Jacobsen and Gaup had the commercial acumen to sell *Pathfinder* to a London distributor, which has played a major part in the film's international success, and earned around Nkr 40 million.

The success is all the more surprising because *Pathfinder* relies heavily on a cast of Norwegian Lapps (Sami) from the North and was the first Norwegian feature film to be shot in the Sami language. But this suspense film makes much use of Norway's dramatic scenery and the Sami language may add to its exotic appeal. The next project from the same team is *Håkon Håkonson*, based on a classic Norwegian adventure, written in 1862, about a 13-year-old working on a sailing vessel. It was shot in Fiji, England, Spain and Norway, also in an English-language version.

Among the newer directors and producers are Harald Ohvik, formerly with Norsk Film, whose films include *A Handful of Time*, and *Karachi*, a box-office success about drug smuggling. Vibeke Løkkberg is a director/actress whose *Sea Gulls* was made for Norsk Film, and Svend Wam and Petter Vinnerød followed *Hotel St Pauli* with *The Wedding Festivities*, first shown at the 1990 Berlin Film Festival.

Many Norwegians actors and directors have had to make a career outside their native country. Not all have returned. Although she has made many of her best-known films with Ingmar Bergman in Sweden, Liv Ullman is an exception and has kept close ties with the native industry. Today, she is honorary president of Norway's main film event, the Haugesund Film Festival.

Each year at Haugesund Norway's film-makers hope for recognition at home by winning one of the "Amanda Awards" for television and film in various categories, and show their work to the rest of the world. Norwegian film-makers know full well that their maximum home audience will never be much above the 4 million mark, and that leaves them with the need to look outwards for the only possible future.

"In this year, dire portents appeared over Northumbria and sorely frightened the people. They consisted of immense whirl-winds and flashes of lightning, and fiery dragons were seen flying in the air. A great famine immediately followed those signs, and a little after that in the same year, on 8 June, the ravages of heathen men miserably destroyed God's church on Lindisfarne, with plunder and slaughter."

So the *Anglo-Saxon Chronicle* for the year AD 793 documented the destruction of the monastery at Lindisfarne, now Holy Island, just south of Berwick upon Tweed in North-umberland in the north of England. It was the first major impact on Christendom by the Vikings, the pagan men of the North who were to set their mark on European culture for the next three centuries. But in the end, it was a reciprocal cultural exchange. An early Viking king, Olav Haraldson converted to Christianity, was baptised in Normandy, and returned to his homeland, Norway, to intro-duce the faith. By the year 1030, when he fell in battle, he had firmly rooted Christianity in most areas as the country's future religion.

The components of those three centuries, the Vikings, the swiftness of their attacks being likened to those of dragons from the air, the mixing of cultures and the gradual transition to a Christian society, set an indel-ible stamp on the traditions of the country. Today that stamp is neither blurred nor bur-ied, but still highly visible in a myriad of forms, collectively termed the folk arts. Wood carving, rustic painting, colourful national costumes, and decorative painting are the most obvious forms.

Wood carving: The Viking Age owed its very being to superior sea power. The Viking craft, or long ships as they became known, were at once extremely seaworthy and boldly beautiful. They were clinker built (overlapping planks held together with iron rivets) on long keel planks that swept up to a stem at either end. The Vikings carved elaborate decorations on the prows down to

the waterline, often with dragon heads and figures. They also carved elaborate designs on everyday items, from the handles of implements to the lever of the aft-right mounted *styrbord*, or "steering board" (hence the word "starboard" in English for the right-hand side of a vessel). On land, the details of buildings were similarly enhanced. Pillars were carved, not just at their capitals, but over their body surfaces. There were ornate friezes, interior mouldings were decorated and gable ends became display points. Wood carving was a highly deve-loped art, executed primarily for, and partly by, the aristocracy.

By the 12th century, Christianity had supplanted the Viking aristocracy as the prime patron of the arts, and the *stavkirke* (stave church—built of upright timber) be-came the major outlet of wood carving as an art form. About 750 of these magnificent structures were built, most in a hundred-year period from 1150 to 1250, and 32 survive to this day, making them among the world's oldest buildings of wood. Their ornately carved portals serve the same purpose as old book illumination in England. They are one of the country's manuscripts. First, there are the animal heads of Nordic mythology, documenting the remnants of the Viking Age. Then the classical tendril of Christian art appears, springing from the jaws of a beast. Finally, tendrils and flowers assert themselves, sometimes solo and sometimes interwoven with other motifs, partly but not completely replacing the beasts. Aside from the stave churches and their various arte-facts, these early people decorated chairs, beds, tables, ladles, bowls, chests and other household items with ornate carving. Some of the best-preserved examples of the work of Norwegian medieval artisans are the carved portals, window surrounds and other details of farm buildings.

The traditions survive to the present day. The timber *hytter*—even the ultra-modern *hytter* built in the 20th century—must have some exterior carving and the Frogn-erseteren Restaurant, built in 1891 and re-modelled in 1909 on a hillside overlooking Oslo is one of the best examples of the more

Preceding pages: traditional rose-painting. Left, part of Tidemand's painting *The Grandmother's Bridal Crown*.

modern dragon style of decorated wooden buildings. Today's nostalgia in home furnishings is not for the lavish designs of the courts of the past, but rather for peasant pieces of native spruce or pine, the more ornately carved the better.

Rose painting: Much as wood carving evolved from the urge to decorate functional items, the art Norwegians call *rosemaling* or "rose painting" sprang from humble surroundings. The two were often used together: carved building details and household furnishings and implements were frequently painted, both as enhancement of, and in contrast to, the carved wood. The name misleads: roses appear only in a few of

the paints, were first available in rural districts. Theories on its origins abound. One school of thought holds that the original mission of rose painting was simply to add colour to drab interiors. From medieval times on, the typical rural dwelling was an *årestue* ("hearth house"), a windowless room with an opening in the roof to permit the smoke from the open fire in the centre to escape. Rose painting could have been the peasants' reaction to their otherwise gray interior environments. Another line of thought, with some substantiation in contemporary historical records, is that the peasants emulated the ornate decorations of churches, which were then also the major

the traditional patterns; it would be more correct to term it "rustic painting," which denotes its agrarian roots, far removed from the cities. True rose painting is not limited to flowery designs, although variations of the tendril motif are its strongest themes. It also includes geometric figures, portraits, and an occasional landscape.

The earliest painted decorations on buildings and household items have survived less well than the carvings on the wood of which they were made, so the beginnings of rose painting remain an enigma. The oldest surviving examples of the art date from around 1700, centuries after the wherewithal for it,

civic buildings in rural areas.

Whatever its origins, rose painting evolved and, in its own right, became a record of its times. The earlier rose paintings of interiors and household articles clearly show that the art of the Renaissance reached as far as the Norwegian countryside. The colours are the peasant stalwarts, blue, green, red, and yellow, but the patterns are delicately those from afar.

The prosperity of the late 18th century brought more clerics and more functionaries to rural districts and with the new professionals came their belongings, decorated household furnishings and implements. What the peasants saw they replicated as best they could in their own style.

Most were untutored and the commonest way of learning the skills was either from travelling artists or from local practitioners. The relative isolation of the valleys, cut off from their neighbours by the high mountain ranges, meant that every valley had its own fresh style. Chests, beds, cupboards, dressers, chairs, tables, implements, mouldings, doors and walls were the most commonly decorated items and, so truly individual were the styles, today's experts in rose painting can identify the age and origin of almost any item with uncanny accuracy. Their knowledge is currently in much demand in the antique business, as rose-painted period furniture now commands the highest of prices for Norwegian antiques.

Rose painting survives today, like wood carving, as a nostalgic link with the past and throughout the country amateur rose painters keep that link alive. For most it is a hobby with the occasional spin off of small profits from sales to local handicraft shops. But for some it has become a slightly shady affair. One of the antique business scandals of 1989

concerned cleverly faked, rose-painted "antique" peasant furniture.

The national costume: Norway's *bunad* is as colourful as the national costumes of any country and, in one respect, it is unique. It is not just worn by folk dancers or for fancy-dress parties but is in regular use as formal attire at weddings and official ceremonies, and at gatherings on national holidays. Many claim that the *bunad* is Europe's most often worn national costume.

Like the habits of religious orders, the *bunad* is a throwback to the everyday clothing of times past, and the word itself means simply "clothes". But unlike habits, *bunads* have developed, varying in style, cut, colouring and accessories, according to locality and the skills and tastes of their makers. There were costumes for men, women and children, everyday *bunads* and dress *bunads*. As with rose painting, every area of the country had its own style.

Historical record: Despite the differences between areas, the *bunad* has common characteristics that identify the dress as Norwegian. Women's costumes characteristically have skirts or dresses of double-shuttle woven wool and bodices or jackets of similar or contrasting material worn over blouses with scarves. Sashes, purses, the beautiful silver accessories and traditional shoes and

Left, national costume is still worn for festive occasions. **Above**, Einar Holte at work on one of his famous miniature wooden boats.

stockings complete the costume. Men's *bunads* are essentially three-piece knicker-bocker suits, with matching or contrasting waistcoats, white shirts, long socks and traditional shoes. Many of the variations of cut, colour, materials, embroidery and embellishments that distinguish the various styles can be traced to differences in the ease of communication in days gone by. Like wood carving and rose painting, the design of a *bunad* is in itself a historical record. For example, the *bunads* from coastal areas often show more Continental influence than those from the remote valleys, where housewives spun, dyed and wove their own woollens to local patterns.

In the mid-19th century, factory-made cloth and garments began to replace homespun products. As people moved from farm to town, the *bunad* seemed to be heading for extinction. It was rescued single-handed by Hulda Garborg, a prominent author who saw a need to preserve the rural traditions which found it hard to survive in the growing towns. Shortly before the turn of the century, she founded a *leikarring,* or folk dance group, in the capital. Folk dances should, she maintained, be performed in folk costumes which led her to compile the first anthology of *bunads*, published in 1903. It was a best seller and Garborg and one of her dancers,

Klara Semb, achieved the start of the folk dance movement and a *bunad* renaissance which continues to the present day.

Today, Norwegian dress varies, like most in Europe, from trendy to conventional. Yet a romantic undercurrent still runs strong. Although *bunads* are no longer daily wear, the numbers of known types and varieties are greater than ever. Some, like the *bunads* from Setesdal, until recently one of the more isolated valleys of Norway, date back 300 years or more. Others, like the costume from Bærum, a western suburb of Oslo, have been designed in the last 40 years. Although there were once as many styles for men as for women, women wearers now far outnumber men. Part of the reason, experts agree, may be the greater female flair for the embroidery detail of the *bunad*, plus the elaborate silver accessories often used to decorate it.

But there is also a practical side to the matter. While the standard dark suit remains the bastion of the Norwegian male wardrobe, women still face the dilemma of what to wear for formal occasions. In Norway, a *bunad* is always correct. It is timeless and may be passed on from generation to generation, while the silver belt is often a gift from a father and mother to their son's wife.

Arguments persist: The design varies considerably today. *Norwegian Bunads,* a compendium published in 1982, pictures and describes fully 50 women's and half as many men's *bunads*, and its widespread appeal is now matched only by the range of opinions about its wear.

Traditionalists contend that a *bunad* from a particular district should be worn only by a person born and bred there and that, in any gathering, the costumes should match the dialects of the wearers. Moderates maintain that correct style outweighs the circumstances of the wearer's birth and upbringing, and the radicals view the *bunad* as a style to be copied piecemeal in modern clothes. Some dare to go so far as to joke about this *bunad* affray. In Oslo, the commonplace wear for male office workers consists of grey trousers, a dark blue or black blazer, a white or blue shirt and a tie with just a trace of red. They call it an *Oslo Bunad.*

Left, Hulda Garborg (left) in an **1899** *bunad*. **Right**, Borgund Stave Church, from around AD **1150**, near Flåm.

TO DRINK OR NOT TO DRINK?

As weariness sets in, many Norwegians feel obliged to explain why they are drinking. It is, they will say, because they are exceptionally happy or, as the case may be, wretchedly sad. They may equally be feeling lonely and neglected, or unable to remember when they were last in such excellent company. Before a dark cloud of Nordic gloom settles on the proceedings, there will be a discourse, particularly if visitors are present, on why Norwegians drink so much. Or, of course, why they don't drink much at all.

Alcohol and its corollary, teetotalism, have long been burning issues in Norway. The strident minority in favour of total prohibition saw World War I, in which Norway remained neutral, as an opportunity to press their case. The excuse was to conserve the raw materials that went into the making of beer and spirits. When the war ended the restrictions were not lifted. On the contrary, they were extended by prohibitionists to cover all alcoholic drinks except wines below a certain, modest strength.

Unfortunately for the prohibitionists, France, Spain and Portugal were among the largest customers for Norway's important fishing industry, and they paid for the fish with wine, none of which qualified under the new regulations for sale or consumption in Norway. Under pressure from the fishing industry, the limit was lifted just enough to admit the French wine, but the country was also saddled with 88,000 gallons (400,000 litres) of French brandy for which it had no possible use, having given an undertaking not to re-export it.

The government immediately declared prohibition permanent, a signal to Spain and Portugal that it would not be hoodwinked in similar fashion again. Two years later, the Norwegian negotiators in Spain let it be known that 110,000 gallons (500,000 litres) of fortified Spanish wine were nevertheless on their way, shortly to be followed by 185,000 gallons (850,000 litres) of Portuguese. The government resigned rather than face a country awash in untouchable drink.

The new government lifted the ban on wine,

and in so doing put the skids under national prohibition. Since 1923 the import and sale of wines and spirits has been a state monopoly, so that government buyers decide what is made available (and the price) in the chain of Vinmonopolet shops, as well as in most hotels and restaurants. It is said that by this act the Norwegian state has made itself the biggest single buyer of alcoholic drinks in the world, a painful irony for the considerable number of prohibitionists who are still beating the drum. The Vinmonopolet shops, it must also be said, are as uninviting as a dentist's waiting-room, with no concession to the notion of alcohol as a human pleasure.

One of the results, as present-day visitors find out, is that drinks are freely available in major cities, albeit at numbing prices (typically Nkr 40 for a half-litre of beer, Nkr 120 for the cheapest bottle of wine in a bar). Indeed, it is now easier to be served a drink in Oslo at 2 a.m. than it is, say, in London. Laws affecting the sale of alcohol, however, are decided at the *kommune* level (i.e. by town and rural councils), so outside the cities, and especially on the west coast Bible-belt, it is a matter of luck whether a particular place is completely dry and without a legal drink within 60 miles (100 km). Some restaurants may be limited to serving no more than two beers per hot meal, and even hotels in some resort areas may refuse to serve non-residents. The ban on Sunday drinking is widespread, and so is a law that decrees that orders for beer, sold only by the case, must be placed at least two days before collection. The intention, apparently, is to discourage spontaneous drinking, whenever humanly possible.

The alcohol question is discussed everywhere so keenly that visitors, who are bound to become involved, might like to familiarise themselves with the background.

Statistics prove, it is said defensively, that Norwegians actually consume less alcohol than almost any other European nation. The average Frenchman consumes 32 pints (17.9 litres) of pure alcohol (in various forms) per year, the West German 14 (8), the Briton 8 (5), and so on... until one triumphantly reaches the Norwegian, near the bottom of the scale, at a trifling 4.7 (2.7). Statistics of this sort, however, refer only to business conducted through the state monopoly. More interesting statistics would encompass the consumption of sugar and potatoes, ingredients in the national pastime of illicit home-distilling.

It would be unrealistic to seek reliable information about smuggling along Norway's long coastline, although there may be a clue in the fact that, when a strike closed the Vinmonopolet shops for months on end a few years ago, there were no apparent shortages—and, as soon as the suppliers had geared up for the unexpected windfall, the price of alcohol went down to levels unknown before or since.

The first attempt to curb drinking in Norway—possibly in the world—was made by King Sverre in Bergen in the 12th century. He was the leader of a rapacious bunch of ruffians called the Birkebeiner, who might have won the Battle of Fimreite for him against the rival Magnus Erlingsson and his nobles, accept that they were too drunk to fight on his behalf. Sverre's attempt failed.

The teetotalism issue in this century, which is to say since Norway gained its independence in 1905, has brought down three governments—notably in 1923 over the previously mentioned proposal to import the 185,000 gallons (850,000 litres) per year of fortified Portuguese wine; and in 1924, when the government of Abraham Berge attempted to repeal prohibition in order to be able to tax alcohol sales.

During prohibition in the 1920s, doctors were allowed to prescribe alcohol for medicinal purposes. One doctor alone was found to be writing out prescriptions at the rate of 48,000 a year.

Hoteliers' and restaurateurs' mark-up on wine, which they themselves must buy from the state at prices that would have a Frenchman or Italian begging for mercy, is customarily about 400 percent. Beer and spirit prices are fixed at low profit margins, so poor wine-drinkers are effectively subsidising all the others.

The climate is often blamed for Norwegian drinking. There may be some truth in this, because long winters used to put a premium on the art of preserving and storing food. Salt was the key, and it was therefore consumed in such enormous quantities that great thirst necessarily

followed. The "normal" consumption of beer and mead was between 10 and 18 pints (6 and 10 litres) per day.

The aristocracy drank wine from the earliest times; the distilling of spirits, invented by the Arabs and passed on to the Italians as a remedy against plague, was introduced to Scandinavia at the end of the Middle Ages—but in this instance as a means of making gunpowder!

The 19th century produced a rash of travel books about Norway, and all of them drew attention to a weakness for drink or, as the French traveller Lamothe put it, "adoration of Bacchus". Even boys of 12 and 14 years, according to the Rev. R. Everest, indulged in the "odious vice", drinking quantities of brandy "that would have astonished an English coalman." Samuel Laing, whose assessment of the Norwegian character generally was a raving panegyric, confines himself to saying that he never saw a drunk Norwegian "in the morning".

Pontoppidan, whose *Natural History of Norway* was published in 1755, admired the Norwegians as much as Samuel Laing did later: "so hospitable... liberal... willing to serve and oblige strangers". Not, however, when they drank: "When a peasant with his family was invited to a wedding, the wife generally took her husband's (funeral) shroud with her; on these occasions they seldom parted before they were intoxicated with liquor, the consequences of which was fighting, and those battles seldom ended without murder."

Norwegians are extremely hospitable and at home are apt to offer their guests "anything"—that is, a choice of whisky, gin, vodka and so on. In reality, very few people will pay Nkr 300 (£30) a bottle or more to stock a bar. The various drinks are almost certainly the same basic wood-alcohol, a by-product of the wood pulp industry, differentiated in colour—though barely in taste—by little bottles of essence, on sale everywhere.

Visitors offered the traditional Viking drink of mead out of curved horn should remember to hold the point of the horn downwards. This is not etiquette but gravity: liquids find their own level, and holding the point upwards will deposit the contents all over the drinker's face.

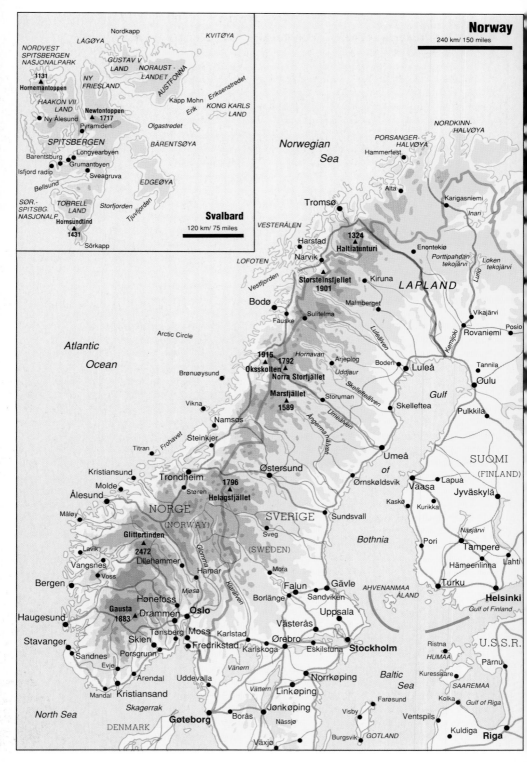

Norway

240 km/ 150 miles

Svalbard

120 km/ 75 miles

Nordkapp

KVITØYA

LÅGØYA

NORDVEST
SPITSBERGEN
NASJONALPARK

GUSTAV V
LAND

NORAUST-
LANDET

1131
Hornemantoppen

NY
FRIESLAND

AUSTFONNA

HAAKON VII
LAND

Kapp Mohn

Newtontoppen
1717

Erik

KONG KARLS
LAND

Ny Ålesund

Olgastredet

Pyramiden

SPITSBERGEN

BARENTSØYA

Longyearbyen

Barentsburg

Grumantbyen

Isfjord radio

Sveagruva

EDGEØYA

Bellsund

SØR.-
SPITSBG.
NASJONALP.

TORRELL
LAND

Storfjorden

Tjuvfjorden

Hornsundtind
1431

Sörkapp

Erik senstredet

*Norwegian
Sea*

NORDKINN-
HALVØYA

PORSANGER-
HALVØYA

Hammerfest

Alta

Karigasniemi

Inari

Tromsø

Enontekiø

Porttipahdan
tekojärvi

Loken
tekojärvi

VESTERÅLEN

Harstad

1324
Haltiatunturi

LAPLAND

Narvik

Enontekiø

Lurio

LOFOTEN

Storsteinsfjellet
1901

Kiruna

Vestfjorden

Bodø

Malmberget

Vikajärvi

Posio

Fauske

Sulitelma

*Atlantic
Ocean*

Arctic Circle

Brønnøysund

1915
Oksskolten

Hornavan

Arjeplog

Boden

Rovaniemi

Kemijoki

Tannila

1792
Norra Storfjället

Uddjaur

Luleå

Oulu

Vikna

Marsfjället
1589

Storuman

Skellefteälven

Skelleftea

Gulf

Pulkkila

Namsos

Umeälven

Titran

Frohavet

Steinkjer

Ångermanälven

Umeå

of

SUOMI

(FINLAND)

Kristiansund

Trondheim

Østersund

Ørnsköldsvik

Lapua

Molde

Støren

1796
Helagsfjället

Vaasa

Jyväskylä

Ålesund

Kaskø

Kurikka

Måløy

NORGE

(NORWAY)

SVERIGE

Sundsvall

Bothnia

Näsjärvi

Glittertinden

2472

Lillehammer

Sveg

(SWEDEN)

Pori

Tampere

Vangsnes

Voss

Hamar

Mora

Hämeenlinna

Lahti

Bergen

Hønefoss

Mjøsa

Falun

Gävle

AHVENANMAA
ÅLAND

Turku

Gausta
1883

Drammen

Oslo

Borlänge

Sandviken

Helsinki

Gulf of Finland

Haugesund

Skien

Tønsberg

Moss

Karlstad

Uppsala

U.S.S.R.

Stavanger

Porsgrunn

Fredrikstad

Karlskoga

Ørebro

Stockholm

Ristna

HUMAA

Pärnu

Sandnes

Evje

Karlstad

Eskilstuna

Västerås

Kuressaare

SAAREMAA

Arendal

Uddevalla

Vänern

Norrköping

*Baltic
Sea*

Kolka

Gulf of Riga

Mandal

Kristiansand

Linköping

Farøsund

Visby

Ventspils

Kuldiga

Riga

Skagerrak

Gøteborg

Borås

Jönköping

Nässjö

GOTLAND

North Sea

DENMARK

Växjö

Burgsvik

PLACES

Norway is a long narrow strip of a country, stretching north from mainland Europe far into the Arctic. In the ancient capital of Trondheim, you are 350 miles (500 km) from the modern capital of Oslo, yet only a quarter of the way up the country's long coast. Oslo is as far from Monaco as it is from North Cape, with Norway's northernmost outpost, the islands of Spitsbergen (Svalbard) hundreds of miles further on. With a population of only 4.2 million, Norway has, above all else, space.

Yet travel is not difficult. From early times, the Norwegians – the first Vikings – were magnificent sailors, and this old way of travel continues today through the ferries and cargo ships that link the coastal communities. Networks of aircraft bring similar links. In addition, in the past 100 years, the Norwegians have achieved the seemingly impossible by building railways, roads, bridges across their fjords, tunnels through the mountains and, more recently, under the sea.

This is one of Europe's most beautiful countries. The scenery is dramatic and the land changes constantly, from mountain to sea, fjord to forest. Oslo, Bergen, Stavanger and Trondheim are small manageable cities that fit into the countryside. Neither the Norwegian climate nor the people are as chilly as the northern latitudes might suggest. The Gulf Stream warms the west so that the seas are ice-free all the year round, and the great distances and long journeys between villages, towns and farms have encouraged an age-old tradition of hospitality.

Norwegians are an outdoor people, and Norway a country where inhabitants and visitors alike can make the most of limitless space for walking, skiing, touring and just breathing in the clear air. In the 1970s, oil brought wealth to Norway and now, as a post-industrial society, these stubborn, self-sufficient, deeply patriotic people enjoy one of the highest standards of living in the world.

Preceding pages: summer lasts forever; the E6, the long road north in Finnmark; Borgundfjord.

OSLO, NORDIC CITY OF LIGHT

In the 1880s and 1890s, Edvard Munch drew and painted an Oslo seemingly inhabited by spectres. Men and women were dressed all in black, their hat brims pulled down low, their faces chalk. To him they were like "the living dead who wend their tortuous way down the road that leads to the grave."

This is the Oslo that was, a dour city lacking the vitality of Copenhagen or Stockholm; Munch left it to live in Berlin and Paris. Nearly 100 years later, into the mid-1980s, many of Oslo's cultural attractions were still imported, while native talent left for the lights of brighter cities. The only real cultural diversions were a few museums based around explorers and skiers.

Expensive and remote, Oslo also bore another black mark. Nights were once meanly trimmed of their fun by laws that severely curbed drinking hours, a testament to the influence of that side of Norwegian Lutheranism which brings the mentality of the small village to the big city (as Ibsen has shown so clearly in his plays). And so travellers to Norway used to give Oslo no more than a passing nod as they steamed through on their way to Bergen and the more spectacular scenery of the west coast fjords.

To call Oslo the Nordic City of Light would be too pat a way of saying that Oslo has come of age. But in a short space of time it has, and Oslo today bears little resemblance to the dim place that Munch so hated—or even to the Oslo of the early 1980s.

Its birth as a cosmopolis in the late 1980s has been in part conscious, in part a natural outcome of infusions of money in the right places. If the talent were to be lured back home, things would have to change dramatically. They did. On the back of the oil boom came more and more money for the arts. A lot of artists still used their stipends to work abroad, but suddenly there was sufficient going on at home to make them curious enough to return. (One famous Norwegian who stayed faithful

to Oslo during her artistic career was actress Liv Ullman, who came back again and again to play in Ibsen here.)

Best by boat: Oslo is at the head of a fjord shaped like a swan's neck; it is surrounded by low hills. Your initial impression will depend entirely on how you arrive. The ideal way is by boat, for then you get the most integrated picture. Most boats dock on the Pipervika inlet, which is lined with busy quays and puts you directly at Oslo's doorstep.

There are very few tall buildings in this capital so your view will be dominated by the **Rådhus**, or City Hall. It is a large, mud-coloured building topped by two square towers—not a favourite building among Oslonians, but useful to get a sight on as it houses the tourist information centre by the harbour. Oslo was officially established in 1048 and the Rådhus's opening commemorated the city's 900th anniversary. The building improves on closer inspection. The courtyard is adorned with fantastic figures and symbols from Norwegian mythology; see the **Yggdrasill Frieze**.

eceding ges: orting arliament) d Oslo on ational Day. ft, onoliten (the onolith) at e centre of geland rk. **Right,** lo's Aker ygge.

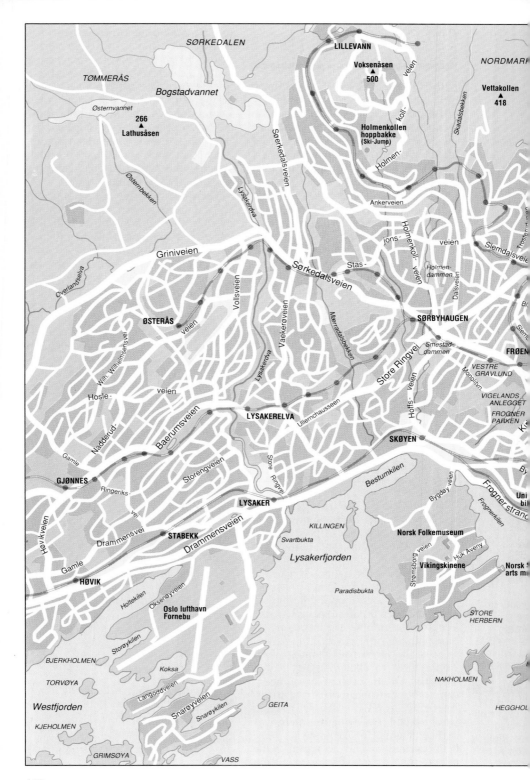

158

Sogns-
Svartkulp
MARIDALEN
Maridals-
vannet
vannet
LILLOMARKEN
Breisjø
Svartkulp

Kringle-
vann
KRINGLEFJELL
Lange-
vann
379
▲
Linderudseter-
høgdene

Sognsveien
Carl
SOGNSVANN
Sognsveien
Kjelsens
Vei
Nordbergveien
KJELSÅS
veien
379
▲
Grefsenåsen
Trollvann
Alnsjøen
Lilletjern

Store
Ringvei
Maridalsveien
Kjelsåsveien
Kjelsåskoll-
Akerselva
Kapelveien
Storoveien
STORO
Grefsenkoll-
Kjelsåsveien
Lofthusveien
Årvollveien
Trondheimsveien
RØDTVET
VEITVET
Nedre

Tåsenveien
veien
LINDERUD
Vei
Brobekkveien
Aker
Kalbakvei

veien
Griffenfeldts G.
Uelandsgate
Colletts Gate
Akerselva
Chr Michelseus Gate
VOLLEBEKK
Økernveien
RISLØKKA
ALNA
Strømsveien

Pilestredet
Ullevålsveien
Akerselva
Sars Gate
Trondheims-
CARL
BERNER
Økernveien
Store
Ringvei
ØKERN
Østre
HASLE
Ulvensplitten
HAUGERUD
Ringvei

Trefoldig
hetskiken
Stortinget
JERNBANE-
TORGET
BOTAN.
HAGE
Finnmarkgata
TØYEN
Grønsveien
TØYEN
ENSJØ
Strømsveien
Ole Deviks Vei
Løelva (Alna)
TVEITA
 Vei

Rådhuset
Dømkirken
Lakkegata
GRØNLAND
HELSFYR
Østensjø-
Tvetenveien
HELLERUD

Radhusgata
Dokkvn.
Bispegata
BRYNSENG
BRYN
GODLIA
kershus
lott og Festning
Bispevika
Dyvekes
Vei
HØYENHALL
Hedins veien

HOVEDØYA
BLEIKØYA
Bleikøysundet
SJØMANNSSKOLEN
EKKEBERG-
SLETTA
Ekebergveien
MANGLERUD
RYEN
Adolf
SKØYENÅSEN
Haakon Tveters
OPPSAL
Vei
General Ruges Vei

ESSHOLMEN
RGØYA
ORMOYA
Mosseveien
HOLTET
BRANN-
FJELL
Sandstuveien
KARLSRUD
Raschs Vei
BRATTIKOLLEN
Europaveien
Østensjø-
vannet
Ulsrudveien
ULSRUD
Østensjøveien
BØLER
BOGERUD

Oslo

1300 m / 0.8 miles

The mosaics inside are based around more modern themes.

To the right, abutting the fjord, is medieval **Akershus Fortress**. Built originally in 1308, it helped protect Christiania (as Oslo was called until 1905) from marauders throughout the periods of Danish and Swedish dominance. The Nazis took over Akershus during the occupation of Norway (1940–45). They shot several Resistance fighters by the old magazine. When the war was over, the traitorous Norwegian chancellor, Quisling, was shot on the same spot. The **Hjemmefrontmuseum** (Resistance Museum) in the grounds illustrates the intense story of occupied Norway.

Thrusting up on the opposite side of the Pipervika inlet are the glass, chrome and neon traceries of the **Aker Brygge** complex, an urban mall containing arcades full of shops, bars, restaurants, food stalls, theatres, and galleries. There is an open-air sculpture court at its heart.

Fiery fates: Away from the harbour the streets are lined with neoclassical buildings dating mainly from the 19th century, mixed with groupings of newer concrete and glass buildings. Oslo's many fires are to blame for the fact that there are so few authentic wooden buildings left. Remnants of the old city or **Gamle Byen** (east of the centre), under excavation for some time, are barely discernible.

The city's main reference points are **Jernbanetorget** to the east, the location of Oslo-S (Sentral) train station, and **Slottet** (the Royal Palace) to the west. They are connected by Karl Johansgate, for much of its length a pedestrian street and a busy central artery for shoppers. At its western limit it becomes part of the broad avenue leading to the doors of the palace. On National Day (17 May), a parade of thousands of children marches here to be greeted by the king.

Parallel to Karl Johansgate is Grensen, another busy, shop-lined street. Oslo's **Domkirke** (main cathedral, 1697) dominates **Stortorvet** (big market square) at the east end of

Akershus Fortress.

Grensen. Its exterior is of darkened brown brick. Inside is an organ five storeys high. Artists of the 18th, 19th, and 20th centuries have contributed to the cathedral's adornment, making an eclectic but nonetheless important display of Norwegian church architecture and interior design. Behind Domkirke is a round, colonnaded market with food and handicraft stalls.

Student area: Grensen becomes Christian IV's gate as it passes the Storting (Parliament) and Eidsvollplass then runs alongside the old university. **Studenterlunden**, the small park around the university, contains the main university building, **Universitetets Aula**, which faces the street. It is decorated with murals by Edvard Munch.

The **University Library** is on Drammenveien, and the **National Theatre** is just opposite Studenterlunden; and **Slottsparken** (the palace garden) immediately west.

In summer, greenery encroaches on Oslo from every side. From the fjord approach you'll see the tops of the trees of Slottsparken, and several parks stretching north beyond it to the wooded hills at Oslo's back. There your eye will inevitably be drawn to the giant white curlicue of the **Holmenkollen** ski jump arched against one of the city's highest hills.

From anywhere on the harbour, you will see how much Norwegians love and use their boats. The fjord is filled with skerries and islands, some inhabited, some not. Tiny boat harbours line the mainland and islands, and ferries and the larger passenger ships ply back and forth throughout the year.

Even if you don't arrive in Oslo by boat, you'll appreciate that the harbour is a pivotal point. Oslo hugs the fjord, and the city limits travel quite far down its sides. Just west of the harbour is the **Bygdøy peninsula**, where the old **Viking ships** and the explorer ships *Fram*, *Kontiki* and *Ra* are kept. East is Ekebergsletta, a hilly park suburb with extensive paths and wonderful broad views over Oslo and the fjord. Large tidy homes are set up high on the hill;

Oslo's waterfront by night.

wind-bent apple trees grow in many of the gardens.

The feel of Oslo: While there have been a lot of ringing successes in the new Oslo, there have been failures, too, mainly as a result of overzealous planning. Bankruptcy is common. New clubs sometimes last only a few weeks before financial collapse. New buildings often remain empty; during their construction it can look as though they'll never be built at all. Giant cranes at a huge site just north of the **Storting** (Parliament) stood motionless for months while the project awaited refinancing. But most of the projects are enlightened ones, such as the sinking of Oslo's three main trunk roads underground to leave the centre freer and cleaner for pedestrians.

Progress has been in the forward direction and the pulse of the city has quickened palpably. Norwegians, with a seagoing past, have always had a fine awareness of faraway cultures. It has always been hard to entice the foreigners they admired—not just their work—to their own shores. Norway was too remote, the population too small.

Riotously enthusiastic reception can make up for a lot, however, and that's how Oslo now gets its favourites back year after year. The Philharmonic, whose home is the **Konserthus** on Munkedamsveien, performs with a dazzling sequence of guest conductors and soloists. Every August there is an international jazz festival, and in September it's the *Gjøglerne kommer* (The Clowns Are Coming), a performing arts festival with venues throughout Oslo; participants come from many countries.

Music making: The variety of music to be heard at Oslo's clubs and concert halls is vast, from South American to punk rock. Jazz man Miles Davis comes twice a year. Frank Zappa, Bruce Springsteen, and Leonard Cohen also put in stock appearances. Large shows are held at **Drammen Stadium** outside Oslo, but a new **Forum** near Oslo-S will seat tens of thousands and be convertible into an arena for concerts, festivals, conferences and sports events.

A modern monument to massive rebuilding.

Statue of
Camille
Collett, one
of Norway's
earliest
women
writers, in
Slottsparken.

The simple need for space to accommodate all these artistic ventures has also played a role in reviving neglected parts of Oslo. It has helped breathe life back into Christian IV's town, an historic area characterized by old customs and shipping houses, and grand open plazas; its southern reaches are at Akershus fortress and its northern limit along the heavily trafficked Rådhusgate.

Until recently, Christian IV's town was frequented only by streetwalkers and their pursuers, who could be assured of empty streets to use as pick-up points. Christian IV town's history as a redoubtable part of Oslo is reflected in its former nickname, "Little Algerie"— see the painting in **Engebret Café** on Bankplassen, an artists' haunt since the early 1900s.

But the **Gamle Logen** on Grev Wedels Plass is a now a dance and concert venue and there's also the **Cinemathèque** (repertory film theatre). The **Modern Art Museum** is housed in the just-restored Norges Bank, on Bankplassen. Galleries across the city are abloom with art in every medium, and established museums have opened their doors to the works of contemporary, living artists.

In the long run, buildings can go up and museums be opened, but only a city that is really lived in can have any permanent sparkle to it. There are only 450,000 in Oslo and, until recently, the vast majority lived in its far-flung suburban parts.

City dwelling revival: For two years in the late 1980s a nationwide salary freeze was instituted in order to curb inflation. An after effect was a depression in housing and property prices. It was a buyer's market then, and properties in the centre sold the fastest. Meanwhile, younger Norwegians were moving into former working class eastern Oslo—its architecture is far more interesting than the boxy concrete and glass communities that appeared in 1960s and 1970s. Re-population revived interest in the area, which led to its restoration. Once restored, its appeal became much wider.

The city feels tangibly alive these days, especially in summer, when everything is happening in Oslo. Festivals come fast and furious, opening hours are greatly extended, and the crowds at restaurants and cafés brim over on to the pavement.

Oslo's growth as a night-time kind of place owes much to the lifting of restrictions on licensing hours. The city used to shut down at midnight. Now beer and wine are served until 6 a.m. So alcohol is more widely available, even if still brutally expensive. The number of new bars and clubs that have sprung up in order to take advantage of late-night traffic is astounding. Even more astounding is that they draw people seven nights a week. Meals and snacks are served into the small hours, with a few 24-hour cafeterias also on the scene.

Advertisements placed in Swedish newspapers for short stay packages in Oslo now mockingly beckon Swedes to "Scandinavia's Weekend Capital". The contention is not idle. Oslo has increased her magnetism tenfold, and

music lovers, art worshippers, bar crawlers, and any combination thereof, will revel.

How to stay solvent: Oslo is a small, easily walkable city. It claims to be one of the 10 largest cities in the world in area, yet much of this area is farmland and forest. Bewildered bears and wolves—very occasionally—have wandered into town.

The city centre is encapsulated in an area roughly twenty blocks square, with some permutations to allow for parks and slightly out of the way museums. The public transport system makes most points accessible within about 20 minutes. If you invest in the Oslo Card (Oslokortet), which works both as a travel pass and parking and museum discount ticket, you won't be counting your krone every minute. (Also pick up the *Oslo Guide*, an invaluable source of city information.) In summer, hotel rates are deeply discounted to make up for the lack of business and conference traffic. In winter, you can sometimes do fairly well with weekend rates, but watch out for school and ski holiday weeks when hotels are crowded and rates higher again. Pensions, mission churches, and youth hostels are usually reasonably priced. Then there's camping—the site at Ekebergsletta is just over 1½ miles (3 km) from town.

Another significant way to save is to avoid eating a large evening meal in a restaurant. Norwegian hotel breakfasts usually offer a large, help-yourself selection. The better assortments are likely to include toast and crispbreads, cheese, marinated and smoked salmon, herring, cereals, fruit, eggs, juice, tea, and coffee. (The *Koldtbord*, which is the lunchtime variation, will have some hot dishes added.) If you can make a hearty breakfast your main meal, you'll manage to keep to a reasonable budget.

The most common street snack is the *pølser*—a long, skinny hot dog served either with *brød* (bread) or rolled in a *lompe* (potato pancake). But there are now a lot of cafés, brasseries, and pizzerias where you can get small to medium-sized meals that won't break the bank. Full meals can be reasonable, too, as

Norwegians are generous in a good cause.

long as you don't order a lot of alcohol.

Alas, the high cost of liquor is unbeatable. Bringing in your maximum duty-free allowance helps, but you can't really tote your own bottle around the streets or in restaurants, so that provides a limited solution. A half-litre of beer is just larger than a British pint and is sold for about Nkr30 (just under £3). So your drinking costs are high enough even if you stick to beer. If you choose wine or spirits, they'll skyrocket. In some restaurants, the cheapest half bottle of wine available may cost what you'd expect to pay for a decent full bottle in London.

Ibsen in Norwegian: Tickets to the cinema—book early for Sunday evening, Oslo's favourite time to go to the movies—are reasonable at around Nkr50 a seat. The cinemas show films in their original language with Norwegian subtitles. There is no English language theatre but Norwegians are devoted theatre-goers, and companies perform everything in Norwegian, from Eugene O'Neill to Andrew Lloyd Webber. You will find international drama festivals

across Norway in summer, which would be your only chance to see something in English. However, if there's an Ibsen play on that you know well, it might be worth seeing it in Norwegian—the emotiveness of Ibsen should get through any language barrier. Tickets to the Philharmonic start at Nkr95. Opera and ballet tickets start at Nkr50.

Combining a museum visit with a stroll is a relaxing and usually a cheap way of spending part of a day or evening. Once you leave behind the bigger hotels and restaurants where business people wine and dine, food and drink prices drop significantly. The exploring suggestions below focus on sights outside the very heart of Oslo; the sights within the basic 20 block square area are easily found and no special planning is needed to reach them.

From Munch to minorities: One of Norway's best-known museums is **Munchmuseet** at Tøyen (T-bane stop of the same name). A tremendous collection of Munch's work is housed there, all donated by the artist. The

building is a plain piece of modern architecture with a lecture hall. Edvard Munch (born 1863, died 1944) was a doctor's son. As a child he often accompanied his father on calls, a time of his life reflected in numerous paintings of the sick and dying. Festive renderings of gypsy families and blazing autumn landscapes counteract these gloomier works. The famous "Scream" (*Skrik*) is darkly riveting, as is the "Death of Marat" series (1907) in which Munch portrays himself bleeding from gunshot wounds inflicted by an angry mistress.

After a series of breakdowns, Munch returned to Norway, having spent most of his adult, artistic life in Paris and Berlin. He sought peace, but continued working, in his cottage at Åsgårdstrand, Vestfold. Munch's early works had been greeted with "shocked" reactions; his own country was probably the slowest to accept him, until at last he was hailed as one of the fathers of Expressionism. He died aged 80 in 1944, in occupied Norway.

The Munch museum is flanked by parks. The one to the east contains the **Tøyenbad** (baths), for swimming and saunas. To the west is the **Botanisk Hage** (Botanical Park) with the **Zoological**, **Mineralogical**, **Geological**, and **Palaeontological Museums** at its north end. In September, this is the site of Norway's largest circus.

A few streets northwest of Munch-museet, across Trondheimsveien, is the **Grünerløkka** district. It is a former working class neighbourhood, now densely populated with artists and writers. At the intersection of Trondheimsveien and Thorvald Meyersgate is the **Schous Bryggeri**, a brewery that has been in business since 1821. At Thv. Meyersgate 49 is the **Oslo Kunstersenter** for contemporary and applied art.

The most interesting street in Grünerløkka is **Markveien**, painted in muted pastel colours and lined with galleries and boutiques. In the courtyard near Markveien 42 is a brick building housing various artists' studios. Continuing north on Markveien, you'll find a cross street called Grünersgate.

Immigrant communities are not very obvious...

From here up to Schleppergrellsgate are some magnificent residential courtyards. The gates are usually open. Peer inside for a look at how tranquil urban living in Oslo can be.

Kampen, whose northern limit is Kampenspark (southeast side of Munchmuseet, also near Tøyen T-bane), is a district of gorgeous wooden houses brilliantly painted in siennas, golds, pastels, and vibrant blues. Some of the streets in lower Kampen are overhung by trees and are supremely quiet; look up, too, at the dormer windows above the street corners, hung with macramé and lace curtains.

Directly west of Kampen is Oslo's largest Pakistani neighbourhood. It is an interesting sidelight on to a largely mono-ethnic city, but in truth there is not much to do or see here unless you are hankering for a Pakistani meal. There are a few good, cheap grill restaurants, and local grocers sell fresh market produce. A second generation of Pakistanis has been born here; most of their parents came in the late 1960s.

...but dark-eyed children are starting to appear among the blue-eyed in an Oslo play area.

Oslo is not as ethnically diverse as Copenhagen and Stockholm. Yet there are small groups of Vietnamese, Eritreans, Jews (only 5 percent of the pre-war population survived the Nazis), student Africans (particularly African women, who get help from the Norwegian government to study administration and law for the developing world), Iranians, Somalians, Namibians, and people from the Ivory Coast scattered throughout Oslo.

Large numbers of Poles come in the summer months for seasonal work, many living in their cars on campsites. While Sweden and Finland have fairly prominent populations of Romany gypsies, and of Turks who came in the 19th century as fur and skin dealers, Norway's most noticeable older ethnic group is the Tartars. They have been in Norway for centuries. With Mongolian origins, they are smaller of stature and darker than the pure Scandinavian.

Sculpture and skiing: West of the city centre is **Frogner Park**, which lies in the same direction as the Holmenkollen

ski park. Frogner, a famous sculpture park containing the works of Gustav Vigeland, would be a long walk from the centre—about 40 minutes. However the route there, Bogstadveien, is a long, lively street of art galleries and enticing shops. You could easily walk up it by following from the Slottet on Hegdenhaugsveien, which becomes Bogstadsveien, or pick up a bus or tram (number 2) in the direction of Frogner. The wooden T-bane 15 from Nationaltheateret to Frognerseteren stops at Majorstuen, the end of Bogstadveien and the beginning of the park; it also stops at Slemdal, nearer the Vigeland museum. (For Majorstuen only, take T-bane 13, 14, 15, 16.)

Once inside Frogner, you'll come across **Vigelandsbroen** (bridge), bedecked with 58 copper figures of men, women, and newborn infants. Next is **Monoliten**, a great spire of figures made of a whitish granite and measuring 55 ft (17 metres) in height. The last of the sculptures, the **Wheel of Life**, is a continuum of human figures in a kind of airborne ring dance. When the sculpture catches the last rays of sun, they are supposed to appear to rotate. The museum at the foot of the park contains the rest of Vigeland's art.

Some Norwegians love the park, others despise it. Vigeland lived from 1869 to 1943; his work on the park spanned 40 years. Taxpayers' money went to support the park and Vigeland over that entire period, which Munch found reprehensible, and proved it by donating all his own work. The Vigeland museum in the grounds contains more sculpture; the **City Museum** (Bymuseet) nearby has a fine interior and a lot of photographs of old Oslo, but not much English text to go with them.

For **Holmenkollen** and the **Ski Museum**, take T-bane 15 and get off at Holmenkollen. The jump is only actively used in February and March. The crowning event in the jumping season is the competition on the second Sunday in March. Built in 1892, Holmenkollen is the world's oldest jump, and a Norwegian national symbol. There is seating

The rich patterns of Vigeland's Monolit.

for 120,000 spectators, and room for 30,000 more standing.

The adjoining Ski Museum is a small but fascinating monument to "One Thousand Years of Skiing." Very old skis and snowshoes are on display, as well as the trail-worn paraphernalia carried by such intrepid Norwegian explorers as Fridtjof Nansen, who crossed Greenland on skis. For the observation tower (**Tryvannstårnet**), take the T-bane one more stop to its end destination, Frognerseteren. The area is thickly forested, and popular for Sunday walks. If you choose to go back to Holmenkollen on foot (signposted), the walk takes 15 to 20 minutes.

Other exploring possibilities are provided by the islands and peninsulas of the Oslofjord, most of which are accessible by ferry from Aker Brygge quay. **Nesodden** is at the tip of a hilly, wooded peninsula jutting from the east side of the fjord. Local artists exhibit at **Hellviktangen Manor**, where they serve coffee and waffles on Sundays. The house is surrounded by apple trees and daisies, and gives directly on to the fjord. Further down the same peninsula is **Drøbak**, a handsome old fishermen's town, and another artists' haunt; you reach it by hydrofoil in summer, or by suburban bus.

Hovedøya and **Lindøya** islands have beaches, but the best are reputedly on the western edge of **Bygdøy**. **Gressholmen** and **Langøyene** have good beaches and free camping. **Kalvøya**, on the western side of the fjord in Sandvika, is the site of big outdoor rock concerts in summer; access from Sandvika is by footbridge.

A multitude of museums: The assortment of museums is wide, so refer to the Oslo Guide from the tourist office which gives descriptions and detailed schedules for each one.

The **Henie Onstad Art Centre** at suburban Høvikodden (Bærum) serves as both a museum of contemporary art and a cultural centre. Apart from the art display, there is a room devoted to the late Sonja Henie, the museum's benefactor; mementos of her phenomenal

Sculpture and echo in the Vigeland Museum.

NOBEL'S PEACE PRIZE

One of the great ironies is that the Swedish armaments manufacturer Alfred Nobel should have been the founder of the world's most prestigious prize for peace. Was it the realisation that his invention of nitro-glycerine could and had been easily turned from peaceful rock tunnelling to war that led him to include the peace category alongside prizes for physics, chemistry, medicine and literature? Or was his conscience troubled by the thought that his huge business empire and great riches were built on weapons of war? It could have been no more than a tribute to the Norwegian reputation as workers for peace. Nobody knows what went on in the mind of this introspective, isolated man.

Almost as strange is that, when he set up his trust fund, Nobel should chose the Norwegian Storting (Parliament) to make the peace award. It was a time when the near century-old union between Sweden and Norway was collapsing. Perhaps Nobel hoped that, by giving the Peace Prize into Norwegian jurisdiction, he might help to keep the two countries together. If so, he failed. The Union was dissolved only four years after his death in 1901 and Norway was already a year-old sovereign state at the first ceremonies in 1906.

Except for the Peace Prize, the other five categories are judged in Sweden and presented in Stockholm to those who, in Nobel's words, "shall have conferred the greatest benefit on mankind." In Oslo, the Nobel Peace Prize ceremony is held in the Great Hall of Oslo University, against a wall of murals, called *The Sun*, by one of Norway's finest painters, Edvard Munch.

Scientists, writers, doctors and more have been honoured by Nobel Prizes in the five subject categories, but somehow none of the five confers such honour as the Nobel Prize for Peace. Nobel's early instructions were that the Peace Prize should be used to award efforts to reduce the size of military forces and standing armies but the Prize broadened its remit to the promotion of peace in general. This vague brief can lead to controversy, as it did when the Israeli and Egyp-

tian Prime Ministers, Menachem Begin and Anwar Sadat, received the Peace Prize jointly for their 1978 efforts to open up talks and communication between their two countries. Dr Henry Kissinger's award in 1972 also aroused controversy, particularly when his Vietnamese co-recipient, Le Duc Tho, turned down his own award for their joint efforts in ending the Vietnam war.

There were no dissenters when the Red Cross received the prize in 1917 for its work amid the battlefield carnage of World War I. The explorer Fridtjof Nansen regarded the Nobel Peace Prize as the greatest of the tributes to his years as internationalist, humanitarian and head of the Norwegian delegation at the League of Nations, though he donated his prize to his work with Russian refugees and the task of giving them identification documents.

When the Russian physicist Andrei Sakharov won the Prize in 1975, the Soviet Union refused to allow him to travel. Lech Walesa faced the same problem in 1983 from the Polish government, though his wife came to Oslo to accept the Peace Prize on her husband's behalf. Saddest of all of those who could not come in person was Carl von Ossietzky, the German pacifist: in 1935, when he gained the award, he was already in a concentration camp, where he died three years later.

Many winners have received acclaim: Martin Luther King and Dr Albert Schweitzer; George Marshall in 1953 for the imaginative Marshall Plan which helped to save and rebuild Europe after the devastation of World War II; organisations such as Amnesty International for its work with political prisoners; and the little known Norwegian-American scientist Norman Borlaug in 1970 for combating hunger by raising the productive capacity of new strains of wheat and rice. Borlaug's parents were among the farming emigrants from Norway to Iowa and no doubt Borlaug had heard much of poor harvests on thin soil.

But most popular of all was Mother Teresa in December 1979. In the cold of a Norwegian winter, she appeared in her customary habit and sandals, standing out as a tiny figure of a woman in white against the guests' sombre suits and the rich colours of Munch's great mural.

skating career include Olympic trophies and early photographs. Niels Onstad was her husband. The centre sits on Blommenholm harbour, an inlet of the Oslofjord with a marina and small beach. Adjoining it is the **Veritas** centre with forest and paths where you can walk after your visit to the centre. Take buses 32, 36, or 37 from Universitetet, and ask the driver to call the stop—the museum is not visible from the road.

Kunstindustrimuseet (Applied Art) is at St Olavsgate 1. It is graced by two earthen urns at its entrance, and has superb displays of Norwegian textile, fashion, and furniture design. The most famous tapestry in its possession is the Baldishol, dating from 1180, and one of the most popular exhibits is the royal costumes. On the uppermost floor is a collection of Scandinavian design for the home ranging from bentwood chairs to streamlined kitchen gadgets.

Bygdøy peninsula, mentioned earlier, is a centre for Norwegian maritime history. It is home to the **Viking Ship Museum** and the separate museums housing the Polar sailing ship *Fram,* and Thor Heyerdahl's raft, *Kontiki*. In the **Kontiki Museum** are the *Ra II*, a fragile-looking reed barque on which Heyerdahl travelled to Egypt, and the *Kontiki* raft on which he travelled to Polynesia. There is also a fine collection of his Easter Island artefacts. The **Sjøfartsmuseum** (maritime museum) concentrates on the history of the craft of boat building.

Also on Bygdøy is the **Folkemuseum**, an indoor/outdoor museum devoted largely to Norwegian rural culture. The collection of outdoor buildings, mainly from farms, gives a good idea of what old villages and agricultural settlements looked like. Other exhibits include Ibsen's studio, Lapp ethnography, and a pharmacy museum. A summer ferry runs from Aker Brygge quay to the Kontiki, Fram, and Maritime museums. From this group, there is a bus (summer only) to the Viking and Folk Museums, or you can walk to them in about 25 minutes. Alternatively, take bus 30 from Universitetet.

<u>Left</u>, the Dalai Lama receives the Nobel Prize for Peace. <u>Below</u>, Karl Johansgate.

Nationalgalleriet is for anyone who has never heard of any Norwegian artist apart from Edvard Munch. The sheer size, if not the content, of the forest and fjord paintings of the Romantic artist J. C. Dahl will impress you. You'll also see the work of his prolific contemporaries, Tidemand and Gude. There is a wonderful series of etchings depicting barn dances and village scenes and festivities. Representation in the international display, especially Impressionists, is also excellent. And don't forget the Munch room.

The **Norwegian Museum of Architecture** was founded in 1975. It is set in Oslo's first garden suburb, which dates from the 1850s; the address is Josefinesgate 32–34, Oslo 3 (request best directions from Tourist Information). The changing exhibits focus on 20th-century architecture, and the library is open to all.

Weekends out of doors: A typical city dweller from Oslo spends huge amounts of time outdoors. On workdays, many take their *matpakke* from

home—a basic lunch bag stuffed with sandwiches and fruit—and sit outside, weather allowing, between 11.30 a.m. and 12.30 p.m. to eat it. (Lunch is eaten later in restaurants, from 12–2 p.m.) The number of outdoor and pavement establishments has grown astronomically of late, so those without *matpakke* can also lunch out of doors.

The Oslo area gets very, very warm in summer—in 1989, the temperature reached nearly 38° C (100° F)—and very cold and snowy in the winter. So if it's summer, people are likely to plan outdoor activities after work, anything from swimming, berry-picking, walking, jogging, or cycling at home in the suburbs in the light of the evening sun. Norwegians treasure their space and contact with nature, and many people who work in Oslo live a fair distance from the city. In winter, this means they can get quickly on to the floodlit slopes and cross-country ski trails after work.

Come the weekend, there is a widely followed pattern for the 48 hours. Friday night is usually a night out on the town. This may begin after dinner and a change of clothes at home, especially for younger people, who don't start to fill the bars until well after 10 p.m. Saturday morning is given over to shopping—stores close early on Saturday—and Saturday evening tends to be dinner or a party at someone's home.

No matter how wild or calm the Saturday night, Sunday is *tur* day. The *tur* is a walk or ski-tour, and a formidable tradition. Depending on a person's age, physical condition, and the number of accompanying children, the *tur* can be anything from a one to six-hour affair. The *matpakke* provides lunch in the forest. Some walks will include café stops in one of the 70-odd cabin lodges in the **Nordmarka** area of Oslo; if not, coffee and hot chocolate come along in a thermos.

There is a great swathe of forest due north of the city centre. Larch, birch, pine, aspen, and several deciduous species dominate; the colour contrast in autumn is fantastic. Den Norske Turistforening (Touring Association) at Stortingsgate 28 has free sketch maps of

From the top of Tryvanns-tårnet, Oslo's radio tower, the view stretches to Sweden.

most routes in these areas; maps 1 to 12, the *Oslo og Omegn Turistforening* series, cover the Oslo region; they also sell survey maps. Access to these routes from the centre is easy and cheap via public transport.

For **Grorud** and the **Lillomarka** area (northeast), take either T-bane 5, destination Vestli, or bus 30 from Jernbanetorget. Trails begin just west of the Grorud T-bane. Due north is **Grefsen**, along a suburban train line (information from Trafikanten at Oslo S) or tram 11 (Grefsen/Kjelsås) or 27C to Grefsenkollen. For walks in the Holmenkollen area and northwest—part of the Nordmarka—take T-bane 15 to Frognerseteren (not to be confused with Frogner Park) and stay on until the end of the line. The Touring Association can recommend trails or, even better, ask a Norwegian to recommend a favourite *tur*. Refer to maps for bus and train routes, roads, and parking areas. The trails are signposted, but if you get lost, seek help from other walkers. (Also, see the *Oslo Guide* under "Outdoor Activi-

ties: Summer—Hiking/Bicycling in the Nordmarka Forest" for other suggested and easy-to-follow routes.)

Many of the forest trails circumnavigate lakes, so a swimming break might be included if it's hot. Come winter, there's skiing, skating and sledging to add to the general flurry of activity on a Sunday (also see *Oslo Guide* or *Winter in Oslo Guide* for ski trails, centres, and competitions, both cross country and slalom style). If a good snow cover has been established, walking trails double as cross country skiing trails. The more daring head for Holmenkollen to practise their jumping and the best prepare for the annual jumping competition in March. Home then to change for an early dinner, then it's off to the cinema. And thereby hangs a weekend.

Sliding on into the night: Norwegians are serious coffee drinkers and nowhere in the city should you find yourself far from a café to take respite in. There are cafés that are simply cafés (sometimes spelled *kafé*). Then there are *gjæst-giveris*, *kros*, *bistros*, *spiseris*, and

Sunday in the Oslofjord.

kafeterias which all tend to be a bit more casual than restaurants; in other words, they are likely to serve smallish meals plus snacks all day and into the night.

Most eating and drinking places start to fill slowly after working hours and turn more boisterous after supper. If you're allergic to smoke, be forewarned that Norwegians are heavy smokers; come the shuttered windows of winter, you may find some places unbearable.

Café de Stijl (address Rådhusgate 5, entrance Skippergata) is darkish inside, with black and white tiled floors and a definite Parisian bistro kind of feel. Fresh food is available, the tea, coffee, and cocoa come in gargantuan cups. There is a large vaulted room downstairs where a lot of dancing goes on; the crowd is mixed straight and gay. As the evening wears on, the music slides from Piaf to post-punk.

Nearby at Rådhusgate 19 is **Kafé Celsius**; it adjoins the Young Artists' Association. The building has an open courtyard, draped with Virginia creeper. Inside are tables in two rooms split by a long, hooded fireplace; the floors are slate. Lunch and small dinners are served. The mood remains mellow: half the crowd drinking wine or beer, the other half coffee. It is a spartan, brightly lit place with photographs and movie stills on the walls.

In another part of town, at the back of Studenterlunden is **Café Nordraak** (address St Olavsgate 12, entrance from Christian IV's gate where it runs along the Royal Park). While the Café de Stijl and Café Celsius attract a mixed city-centre/artistic crowd, Nordraak is distinctly a painters' haunt—but a very homely one. Snacks are served cafeteria style. Buy a coffee in a thick white mug, and you can sit reading newspapers and magazines for hours. The tapes range from jazz to salsa. Nordraak is open until 3 a.m. most nights.

As the evening progresses, you might feel like moving on to places with more of a nighttime feel, or places with live music. **Rosenkranzgate** is a good street for bar-crawling. Bars and clubs are spread throughout the city, and range

Henrikke, "outdoor" café in the centre of Oslo.

from underground to upmarket—consult the *Oslo Guide* and *What's On in Oslo* (from tourist information), or consult someone who knows Oslo. **Blitz** is punkish, **Joys** is gay.

Smuget (Kirkegate 34, through courtyard) is considered by some to be more of an after-hours place, though doors usually open at 8 p.m. It is multi-level, and multi-mood. On the ground floor is a more carefully dressed café crowd. Upstairs is a series of rooms. One contains a music stage for live performance, where blues, salsa, reggae, and rock groups are headlined. The other room features a dance floor.

Rockefeller Club in the old Torggata baths (Torggate 16, entrance on street west from Marieboesgate) has a great setting and tremendous amount of space. It offers a very mixed menu of music and entertainment, spotlighting both local and international talent. They also stage parties here for almost any reason, like the Bat party in 1989 the night before the colossally hyped *Batman* film came to town. Local figures

like Morten Jorgensen, a man to whom many muses have spoken (he is a novelist, poet, and also leads in his own homegrown band) perform here.

Shopping scene: Handicrafts, textiles, woollens, and pewter are favourites for most visitors in Oslo. **Basarhallene**, one of the few "older" shopping areas at the back of the Domkirke, has a wonderful jeweller's, Elias Sollberg, and a hatshop. Glasmagasinet across the way (Stortorvet 9) and Steen & Strøm at Kongensgate 23 are full-blown department stores. Aker Brygge on the waterfront and Oslo City, next to Oslo S, are two major malls.

Grensen is the street to shop for bargains, while Lille (little) Grensen has outdoor stalls selling everything from sausages to skateboards. Hennes & Mauritz, the Swedish clothing chain, has a bargain basement on Kirkeristen. Off-the-beaten-track shopping—tiny galleries, clothes boutiques, ceramics shops (and a fur and leather shop!)—can be found on Markveien in Grünerløkka.

Friday and Saturday evenings stretch into the wee small hours.

AROUND OSLO AND ITS FJORD

At dusk the islands of the **Oslofjord** look like hunched prehistoric animals about to sink into a subaquatic sleep. In the colder months, the sky at sunset grows from lavender to purple while the islands turn slate-grey, then ominous and black. Summer sunsets bring twisted pink clouds underlit by a huge red sun that drops only briefly behind the fjord's western cliffs before journeying east to rise again.

Daytime along the 60-mile (100-km) long fjord reveals a high concentration of industry down both the eastern and western sides. Oslo, at its head, receives most long-distance ships' passengers but only a fraction of its total traffic. The rest of the fjord is Oslo's workhorse, its roads travelled by juggernauts with cargoes of lumber and oil, its ports and waterways busy with yachts and barges. Oslofjord is home to more than a third of the nation's population.

Sprinkled liberally with islands, skerries, natural marinas and swimming beaches, the fjord is wildly popular with Oslo residents in summer. Norway's longest river, **Glomma**, which reaches nearly to Trondheim, flows into it. Outside its working ports, Oslofjord is a magnificent expanse of water stretching into the Skagerrak.

Akershus, **Vestfold** and **Østfold**, the three main counties to touch Oslofjord, claim the country's most important defence points—and archaeological finds. Some of Scandinavia's oldest ruling families were found buried in Vestfold along with several sunken Viking ships loaded with booty. Østfold is rich with rock paintings and stone circles thousands of years old.

Akershus county contains the Oslo conurbation plus a broad swathe of agricultural and forest land reaching to Sweden, its total area about 1,930 sq. miles (5,000 sq. km). At Akershus's northern reach is the Mjøsa lake town of **Eidsvoll**, where the Norwegian Constitution was signed and the modern state born in 1814.

Østfold (east) and Vestfold (west) spread down from Oslo like a pair of lungs. In each of these counties are provincial cities of major historic significance: **Fredrikstad** in Østfold, a magnificent fortress town, and **Tønsberg** in Vestfold, the oldest extant Scandinavian city, founded in 872. Remains of **Kaupang** just over a mile (2 km) from Tønsberg, the oldest Nordic town yet discovered, are in Oslo's Historical Museum. Corroboration of its early existence appeared in a world history by England's 9th-century monarch King Alfred the Great.

Despite its rich history and good travel links (not to mention its seafood festivals), the Oslofjord area gets few tourists from outside Scandinavia. The scenery isn't as dramatic as the west coast's; the rise from fjord to mountain is not so swift, nor are the fjord's depths so black. There are however more habitable islands than in any other fjord, many with sports centres and hotels offering everything from tennis to windsurfing and swimming.

Cycling country: Inland is sloping countryside punctuated by forests, orchards, and tilled fields. Vestfold's mountains range up to 1900 ft (600 metres), but the Oslofjord area appeals more to cyclists than climbers, and to people on short journeys or with children who want to avoid overland hauls.

Larger towns usually have an old section closely packed with superbly crafted wooden houses. **Halden**, at the Swedish border, in Østfold and **Larvik** in Vestfold are the southernmost points on the fjord, each accessible in 90 minutes by car or about two hours by train. And don't be surprised to observe a lot of souped up old Chevrolets cruising by or parked under the apple trees, country and western music blaring out.

The Akershus area: There are fantastic walks in the **Nordmarka** (the Oslo woods) accessible by bus, train, or tram. Much of the Nordmarka is privately owned by lumber barons who have kept it open to the public and, in any case, Norway's democratic "Outdoor Life Law" allows people to cross outlying property on foot. (For Akershus county tourist information, tel: 02-20 80 55.)

Oslo og Omegn sketch maps 1–12 (free from Den Norske Turistforeningen at Stortingsgate 28, Oslo, weekdays only) cover the Nordmarka's network of cleared trails. Around **Grefsen**, south of Maridalsvatnet, is a luxuriant parkland (tram or T-bane destinations Grefsen, Grefsenkollen, Kjelsås). **Maridalsvatnet** is a tremendous lake fed by a series of charming clearwater brooks. **Sognsvann**, the lake west of Maridalsvatnet is also on the T-bane. One Sognsvann trail leads past an old staging post, the lake, and the two-storey **Løkka farm**.

By car you can explore further. If you're a fan of Norwegian rural and barn architecture you'll have your fill in outer Akershus. One scenic route is E68 from Drammen north until Sundvollen; turn right and follow the toll road (15 krone) into the **Krokkleiva** district. The paths cross wooded hills 1300–1600 ft (400–500 metres) high. **Kongens Utsikt** (lookout) gives stupendous views

across **Steinsfjorden** and **Tyrifjorden**. A vegetarian mountain-hut hotel called Kleivstua is set 1250 ft (380 metres) up.

Afterwards, rejoin the E68 northbound, direction Hønefoss. Leave it before Hønefoss to pick up road 241 northeast from Bråk, and then strike east on to road 242. South of this road is a wilderness of pine swamps, hidden lakes, oak forests, and stream-bordered fields (survey map *Oslo Nordmark— Nordre Del*). There are some 10 krone (10 krone coins *only*) tolls but when you see how wild the area is, you'll appreciate the fact that there are any roads here at all. Highway 4 south returns you to Oslo; northbound it leads to Gjøvik on Lake Mjøsa.

At the bottom of Mjøsa is **Eidsvoll**, on the E6 from Oslo some 40 miles (65 km) north. It is a lake town of old wooden houses and churches, and a national landmark: the **Eidsvoll Building** is a mini-museum to the Norwegian constitution. Then tour Lake Mjøsa on the old paddle steamer *Skibladner*. The round trip is 12 hours, with the halfway point at Lillehammer, site of the 1994 Winter Olympics. Try riding the narrow-gauge **Tertitten Railway** from Sørumsand, on summer Sundays. South of Eidsvoll, near Gardermoen, is the tremendous **Raknehaugen Viking** burial site.

The fetching artists' village of **Drøbak**, southeast of Oslo, was once a fishermen's settlement. **Galleri Finsrud**, a one-artist operation, is on the fjord between **Mammastrand** and **Pappastrand**—neighbouring beaches where women and men split up, with children urged over to Pappastrand. Knut Hamsun, the Nobel prize-winning novelist, lived at the handsome **Reenskaug Hotel**—still extant and very friendly—in **Drøbak** early in the 19th century. The town was a rich source for his 1920 novel, *Konene ved Vannposten* (Women at the Pump).

Another point of pride is the cross-timbered church (1776). It has an elaborately carved model of a ship inside, a common piece of church decoration in seafaring towns. Rococo touches in-

clude wooden busts of Moses and Aaron. The church has gospel and jazz concerts in summer; a small waterside park surrounds it. Other favourite walking areas in Drøbak are the hills above the town and **Follo** with 5½ miles (9 km) of walking and skiing trails, and a wonderful folk museum. Its farm buildings and school have their interior trappings intact. If you're in a Christmassy mood, visit **Jul** *(Yule)* **Hus** in the old meeting house, stacked to the rafters with handicrafts and toys.

East of Drøbak is an area of outstanding wild beauty: **Lake Øyeren** and its nature reserve. In the woods the ground is padded with mosses and lichens, and in late summer there are edible mushrooms and berries. Many migratory bird species are sighted here annually.

Open-air activities: Østfold is a long funnel through which tourists from Sweden pour. Despite its industrial towns, Østfold is not an unhealthy place; it buzzes with outdoor pursuits. Canoeing and cycling are popular here, and the area is dotted with hiking and skiing centres. There are also golf courses, and the **Mysen race track**.

Then there's the draw of the fjord. **Jeløy** peninsula is the site of **Galleri F Manor** at Jeløy, which has fjordside trails and stupendous lawns. Exhibitions are laid out through a light-filled house. Its cafeteria is a beloved coffee pit-stop. Down the coast, the King's Ship is docked at **Hankø**, Norway's regatta centre. And the **Hvaler** archipelago (chalet rental centre on Hvaler island) is ideal for water sports.

History and pre-history figure largely in Østfold's attractions. **The Ancient Highway**, Route 110 between Skjeberg and Fredrikstad, has runic paintings 3,000 to 4,000 years old and burial sites like **Hunn**, covered with stone circles. The area once had links with ancient Tuscany. (Get the tourist board's *Highway of the Ancients* brochure.)

Fredrikstad is a gem among Østfold towns. It is Scandinavia's only totally preserved fortress town, dating from 1567. **Gamle Byen**'s cobbled streets were laid by prisoners; wooden stocks

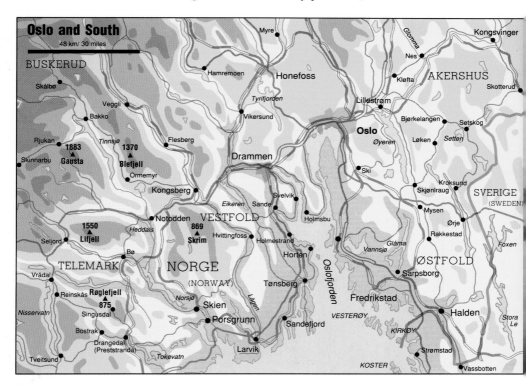

face the former prison, now a bank (prisoners' room preserved). Its restaurants and galleries keep their old facades. The **Domkirke** (1880) is Østfold's head church; Fredrikstad's stately town hall was planned by the architect who designed Oslo's Storting. For a trip out, hop aboard the Hvaler ferry over the fjord.

Halden, close by the Swedish border, is dominated by **Fredriksten Fortress**, a largely intact ruin with many of its buildings serving as small theme museums. The streets below were laid out along the cannons' blast lines to give the fortress's defenders freedom to fire. Halden's hosting of the 1991 International Amateur Drama Festival was the excuse for the opening of a new open-air theatre in the fortress grounds. In summer, a passenger boat travels the inland waterway system, navigating through tremendous locks.

Song and dance: Throughout Østfold, St Olav's day (29 July) is celebrated with a great show of folkloric costume, music and dance. One of the best displays is at the **Borgarsyssel Museum** in **Sarpsborg**; it also features a children's farm in summer. Sarpsborg is the site of one of Østfold's two youth hostels, on Tune lake; the other is at Moss. Sarpsborg has brewery tours and trips on the jazz boat *Krabben*.

Two old-style hotels in Østfold which serve superb meals—especially their wild game dishes—are the Grand in Halden and the Victoria in Fredrikstad. For area tourist information, contact the Svinesund office, tel: 09-19 51 52. You can travel around Østfold by car, rail, or bus.

Across to Vestfold: The Moss-Horten car ferry connects Østfold and Vestfold; it crosses in under an hour. There is much shared history between the two counties. Both have played crucial roles in Norway's defence. It was the fast action of troops on both sides of the fjord that sank the first Nazi warship, the *Blücher*, scuppering Hitler's plans for an easy invasion.

The **Maritime Museum** at Horten documents this event and hundreds of

View of Halden from Fredriksten.

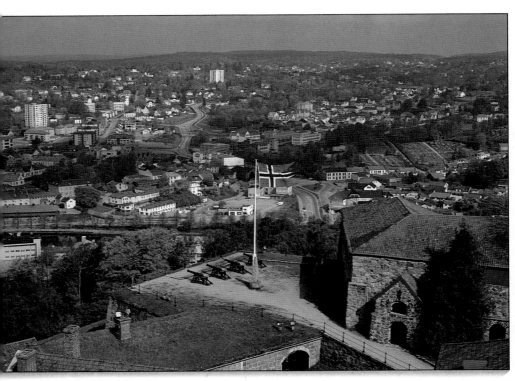

others in displays bulging with weird, wonderful artefacts. Multiply the experience a hundredfold if you meet retired Kontre Admiral and Destroyer Commander Owren here. Still trim despite a "religious" habit of half-litres at the pub, he left Norway in 1940 and fought with the Allies in nearly every major battle of the war. Note the Armagnac dedicated to him by a thankful maquis upon France's liberation.

There are museums of **Photography** and **Veteran Cars** in Horten. Tranquil **Løvøy** island has a solemn medieval stone church. This was Viking country, and **Borre Park**, en route to Tønsberg, contains enormous turf-covered humps concealing Viking kings' graves. Overlooking them is **Prestegård**, which was once the parish priest's manor and is now a tremendous working farm. Borre is Norway's oldest national park, with an extensive network of trails.

Åsgårdstrand is where Edvard Munch lived when he returned to Norway from abroad, and he used it as a setting for many of his paintings. This tranquil village's white wood houses merge into the sky on misty mornings; set back from the harbour are a huge old meeting hall and public baths on a square at its centre. The finest Åsgårdstrand garden is the tiny one behind the antique watch museum. In summer, local artists have crafts stalls here.

Near the promontory where Munch painted *Three Girls on a Bridge* is **Åsgårdstrand Hotell**, the town's only hotel. In summer a great gush of activity emanates from here: boat trips, barbecues, and Åsgårdstrand Days, when there are dance and piano concerts—and a great Wiener schnitzel cook-up.

You can spurn these organised activities to cycle (hire from the hotel), swim in the fjord, fish in Borre's lake, or watch the fishermen come in each afternoon with the fresh catch. Summer ferries and a bus travel here from Horten; information from the hotel.

Between Tønsberg and Åsgårdstrand is **Oseberg**, the most important Viking site yet discovered. Oslo's **Viking Ship Museum** contains the finds, including

A young girl tries out a *lur*, a traditional Norwegian instrument.

184

the 65 ft (20 metre) arch-ended wooden ship that often appears as an emblem of Norway. The woman buried here was grandmother to the murderer Erik Bloodaxe, and of Harald Hårfagre, who unified Norway at the Battle of Hafrsfjord. These early bluebloods formed the Ynglinge clan of Nordic saga fame. They founded Dublin 1,000 years ago and set up a slave market there. Only the mound itself, near Slagen's church, remains, but as a symbol Oseberghaugen (*haugen*, hill or mound) has a subtle, magnetic power.

Just south is history-rich Tønsberg, established in the 9th century. On Slottsfjellet, 190 ft (65 metre) high are the fortress remains and tower. The main street, Storgata, is flanked by Viking graves. These were excavated and incorporated, under glass, into the ground floor of the new library. Across the street are the old walls of the **Church of the Order of White Monks**, one of only two medieval round churches in Scandinavia. The most renowned king to hold court in

Tønsberg was Håkon Håkonsson IV, the absolute monarch of Norway for half of the 13th century.

A more recent native son is Roald Amundsen, the polar explorer. Less known outside Norway is Svend Foyn, the Tønsberg whaling captain who invented the explosive-powered harpoon.

Island tours: The steamship *Kysten* (built 1909), moored on **Byfjorden** near the old customs house, does a 3½-hour islands tour. North of the *Kysten*, pick up **Nordbyen**, a street with old wooden houses hunched along it. Across the water is a birdwatcher's tower; enquire from tourist information about kayak rentals. Follow Nordbyen back into town to see the ruins of Håkon Håkonson IV's court. The **Domkirke**, on Storgata, replaces a church on this site from 1100. Adjacent is Hotel Klubben, renowned for its bars, summer festivities, and cabaret shows.

Nøtterøy, **Tjøme**, and the skerries are fantastic summer hangouts. Rica Havna (all grades accommodation: deluxe hotel rooms; cabins; camping) is

Berry picking is always popular—in the forest or garden.

on a gorgeous natural haven carved from rock. "Verdens Ende" (World's End) is at the end—but for a few boulders—of the chain. The old lighthouse here is a beautifully simple structure made of stone and a suspended brazier. In bad weather, see it from the café.

Sandefjord is a famed whaling town and its whaling museum is excellent. The sea still dominates life here. One of the main industries is marine paint production. Trans-Scandinavian ferries leave from the bowl-shaped harbour. The town centre is compact, and the cosy old Kong Carl Hotel is one of its handsomer buildings.

Near **Badeparken** are the former spa and the old town, along **Thaulowsgate**. **Preståsen** is the hilly park above it. Just outside Sandefjord are the **Gokstad Viking grave site** and Vesterøy peninsula, ideal for walking, biking, and boating. Vesterøy farmers sell fresh produce from their homes. It's a supremely peaceful place—Liv Ullman's summer house is in the vicinity.

Larvik was home to two legendary boat lovers: Thor Heyerdahl, and Scotsman Colin Archer, designer of the polar ship *Fram* and Norway's modern rescue vessels. Archer's first house was at **Tollerodden**, on the fjord. At Larvik's back is the huge lake **Farris**.

There are many fine waterside spots around Larvik, such as **Mølland** beach, stacked with sea-rounded pebbles, and **Nevlunghavn**, an exquisite fishing cove tucked around the bay west of **Stavern**. The fish and shellfish festivals in the Larvik area are renowned. Hotels often host them; the Grand in Larvik has both excellent seafood and a superb "wild" menu including pheasant, ptarmigan, and elk in their seasons.

Inner Vestfold's rivers run with salmon and trout. **Brufoss** is a favourite anglers' haunt (accommodation and day licences available). In winter, this is a popular downhill ski district, particularly now that **Svarstad's Ski Centre**, off route 8 near the Lågen river, is fully operational. You will find a lot of ceramic works which offer tours in outer and inner Vestfold and, in common with

Left, Runic inscription at Skjeberg (near Halden). Right, The Whaling Monument at Sandefjord.

Østfold, every little hamlet seems to have an art gallery. Travel is easy in Vestfold whether by car, rail, or bus. The area tourist board office is at Tønsberg, tel: 033-14 819.

Modern pride: People who live along Oslofjord have a strange modesty-pride complex. They are the first to point out the area's shortcomings (smallish mountains, the stink of the pulp and paper plants). But once these are out of the way, the superlatives begin to flow. The birthplaces of the most intrepid explorers are here, as are the greatest sailing races, the warmest summers, the finest archaeological discoveries, the best drinking water, the greatest summer resorts... the list goes on.

Neither the modesty nor the pride is false. Oslofjord's charms may need some searching out, but this is no wasteland. Oslo is the area's—as well as the country's—vibrant heart, and the whole of the fjord area surrounding it echoes its pulse. The close juxtaposition of active city centres and serene rural outposts exist nowhere else in Norway in such intense concentration. Oslofjord is the country's main communication point with the rest of Europe. Hence, Norway's involvement in affairs beyond its own borders can be measured from here.

Fierce aggressors: The Vikings, enshrined in their fjordside burial mounds, were its most famous inhabitants, but they were fierce aggressors. It is strange to see that their descendants are diplomats and peacekeepers, though the world has seen what cunning, capable warriors they can be if pushed to fight for what they love and against what they hate.

The people of Oslofjord are sophisticated yet unpretentious. The area they live in has more cultivated charms than natural ones, perhaps. But if this region was in any country other than Norway, heralded as a kind of last frontier of wild European beauty, one would not for a moment hesitate to rave over its natural charms, its peacefulness, and the resourcefulness and kindness of its undemanding people.

Cold beer in Tønsberg.

TELEMARK AND THE SOUTH

As they are proverbially advised to do "when in Rome", visitors to Oslo—or, equally, to Stavanger and Kristiansand—could usefully do what the locals do for recreation. The fundamental choice is either mountains and lakes, in which case they steer a course for Telemark, or the sea, which draws them to Aust and Vest Agder, jointly known as Sørlandet (the south country).

Locals would usually travel in their own cars, a definite advantage in trying to make the most out of Telemark but not so necessary on the coast, along which it is possible to leap-frog from port to port on ferries which are sufficiently frequent to permit an improvised itinerary.

Oslo, Kristiansand and Stavanger, the principal cities along the southern rim of Norway, have good inter-connections, including flights, so they all serve as practical starting or finishing points for a tour, and you can combine Telemark and Sørlandet on one of several coach excursions. One from Oslo, for example, covers nearly 750 miles (1,200 km) by road and ferry and lasts five days. Norwegian tourist offices at home and abroad have details.

Vest and Aust Agder: In 1639 King Christian IV of Denmark-Norway had the sort of whim which is the privilege of kings and very few others. He wanted to found a town and name it after himself. In the event, the choice of the site where **Kristiansand** now stands was not entirely capricious. It was an admirable base from which to control the approaches to both the North Sea and the Baltic. The town had to be fortified, and much survives of the first of many forts to be built, **Christiansholm**. Through nearly three turbulent centuries, however, none of the forts ever fired a gun in anger (not until 9 April 1940), and gradually Kristiansand changed from being a military town to a trading and administrative centre.

Kristiansand has had its problems: with witches, one of whom confessed (1670) to having flown to Copenhagen to pour poison into the mayor's ear, fire (1734), syphilis (1782) and a "privateer" period (1807–14) marked by such wholesale swindling, bribery and corruption that it caused "violent upheavals in the economic life of the country."

Sunny strolling: Present-day Kristiansand has managed to put all that behind it. It is a pleasant city, laid out in squares according to Christian IV's directive, and the sort of place which invites visitors simply to stroll about. The weather is more reliably sunny than anywhere else in Norway, the port and central market are always busy, the **Kvadraturen** is a picturesque quarter of old wooden houses, and one never has to look far for a spot to sit down and spectate. "A total of more than 10,000 seats in cafés and restaurants" is the city's proud claim.

Sightseeing boats leave daily for two-hour cruises among the hundreds of islets and skerries in surrounding waters. The city's zoo is "the most visited family park in Norway" while just north

of the centre the **Ravnedalen Nature Park** is set in attractive, hilly grounds.

The **Gimle Mansion** across the Otra River is a magnificent symbol of 19th-century Norwegian capitalism. It was built by a shipping and trading tycoon, Bernt Holm, and passed down the family (with a five-year interruption while it was occupied by the German army) until bequeathed to the city and opened to the public in 1985. The **Setesdal Railway Museum** with its narrow-gauge steam railway is a short way north of the city.

About 28 miles (45 km) west of Kristiansand is **Mandal**. A busy port long before Christian IV felt the urge to build Kristiansand, it suffered from the competition afterwards. A 1799 traveller remarked that "the houses are jammed together so tightly that a careless pipesmoker at any open window could spit into his neighbour's parlour".

The slightly incongruous appearance of some of the old houses is attributable to the nostalgia of foreign residents: Dutch who were there to trade and Scots who, while also traders, showed a keen interest in the local salmon. The point known as **Kastellet** is where a wealthy Dane, who once reached into his trousers to make a personal loan to the notoriously empty-pocketed King Frederik IV, installed cannon to keep pirates away from his estate.

The nearby lighthouse at **Lindesnes** marks the southernmost point of Norway, and the small islands about 3 miles (5 km) offshore are frequently mentioned in the ancient sagas as a refuge for Vikings ships waiting for better weather before turning the corner into or out of the Skagerak.

Farsund, a little further up the coast and once a privateer centre, has suffered the misfortune of being destroyed by fire so often that there is hardly a building left pre-dating the present century. Nevertheless, the relatively modern houses are painted white and present a pleasing spectacle.

Tunnels and waterfalls: The region is rich in **rock carvings** and **ancient sites** including, near Vanse, the remains of nine Iron Age homes surrounded by 350

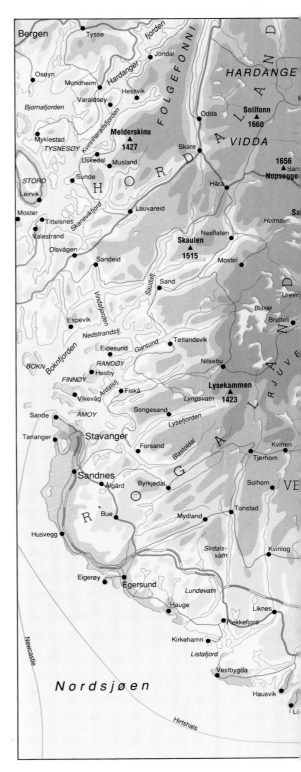

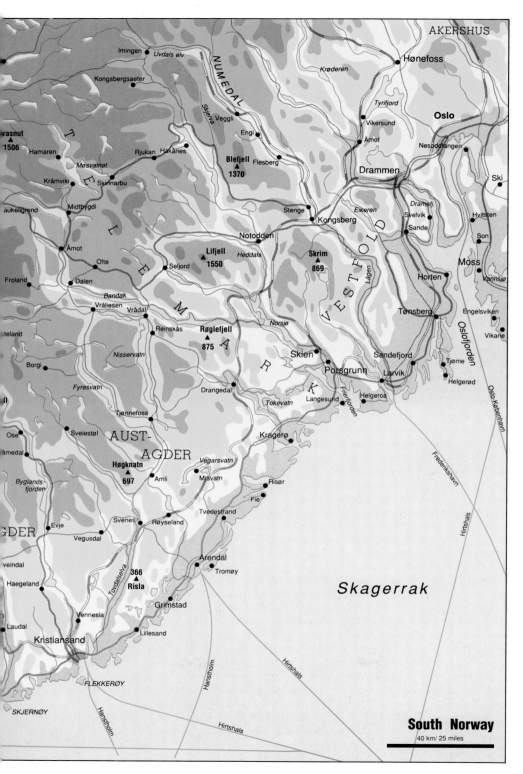

South Norway

40 km/ 25 miles

burial mounds. **Lomsesanden**, a popular beach on the Lista peninsula, is all of 6 miles (10 km) of white sand. The last town before Vest Agder rises to meet Rogaland is **Flekkefjord**. This is mountainous country which, apart from necessitating the construction of some of Norway's longest railway tunnels (there are 46 between Flekkefjord and Egersund), has created several waterfalls, especially around **Kvinesdal**.

The principal centres along the coast east from Kristiansand are, in order, Lillesand, Grimstad, Arendal and Risør. **Lillesand** has a special place in Norwegian history as the centre of an 18th-century revolt led by a farmer named Lofthus, a Robin Hood figure who travelled to Copenhagen to confront the Crown Prince with a long list of grievances. On his return he collected a force of 2,000 irregulars and caused panic among the Danish "establishment" in the coastal towns. The house where he was arrested still stands; he spent the rest of his life in chains.

Grimstad is indelibly associated with Ibsen. It was there that he served his apprenticeship to a chemist. Ibsen was an unhappy young man and Grimstad, though a pretty place, must have contributed (together with Skien, where he was born) to his searing exposure of goings-on in small Norwegian towns. His works caused a scandal at the time, but years have healed the wounds and he is commemorated in the town's **Ibsen Museum**.

Arendal is full of character, every ounce of which was needed to thwart King Christian's plan to close it down and transfer the inhabitants to his pet project, Kristiansand. One of his successors, Frederik IV, visited Arendal in 1704 and was puzzled about dinner with the local priest who "went to great trouble to explain in detail how the rite of circumcision was performed by the Jews". Arendal prospered as a conduit for timber shipments abroad, including much of the timber used for rebuilding of London after the 1666 Great Fire.

House on stilts: Arendal itself lost to fire (in 1863) the houses on stilts which

Lindesnes lighthouse.

had earlier given it the nickname **Little Venice** but, overflowing on to a number of small islands, it retains its lovely setting. An unusual and recent addition to its attractions is a museum meticulously created by unpaid volunteers out of the contents of a pottery factory that went out of business a few years ago. The enthusiasm of the staff is infectious. The **Town Hall** in Arendal, previously the home of a merchant, is said to be one of the largest wooden buildings ever constructed in Norway.

Risør, the last town in Aust Agder, was also threatened by the creation of Kristiansand. Its traders were forced to maintain residences in the new city but they kept their links with Risør. Mary Wollstonecraft, an English visitor in 1795, noted an addiction to tobacco. The men never took their pipes out of their mouths and absolutely refused to open a window. The women, she decided, dressed like tarts or, as she put it, "sailor girls in Hull or Portsmouth".

Many of these women were probably Dutch because it was fashionable among young seamen to bring wives back from the Netherlands, the main trading partner. In Risør, as in other parts of Sørlandet, children may still be given distinctly Dutch names.

On to Telemark: The E12 running from Kristiansand to Telemark climbs sharply up the **Otra Valley** and runs north along the **Byglandsfjord** to **Setesdal**. Until modern times this area was extraordinarily remote. The inhabitants sent their timber down to Arendal by pushing it into a river which plunged 2,300 ft (700 metres) over a distance of about 90 miles (145 km). Otherwise, contacts were few and Setesdal preserved its own almost medieval way of life, including a distinct dialect, dress and cuisine, right into the 20th century.

The most famous dwelling in Setesdal is at **Rygnestad**, a windowless tower of three storeys with an amazing collection of relics, such as leather hangings depicting St George's battle with the dragon. The tower was built about 400 years ago by Vond-Asmund who, on discovering that his fiancée

The popular bathing beach at Mandal.

was about to marry someone else, snatched her away from the wedding procession. From the upper floor of his fortress, he fired off arrows at anyone who approached and in so doing killed at least four people. His descendants still farm in the area.

Although a finger of Telemark reaches the sea at **Kragerø**, not far from the mouth of the Oslofjord, the province is associated in most minds with the inland terrain which inspired an eccentric farmer named Sondre Norheim to turn the pedestrian business of plodding about in snow on two planks into the sport of skiing. His discovery of the delights that could be achieved with planks that were properly shaped and had heel bindings made him overlook his domestic chores. It is apparently true that, when he ran out of firewood in winter, he simply hacked off another piece of his house and put that on the fire (*see also page 118*).

Morgedal, where Norheim lived (he later emigrated to America) deserves to be called the cradle of skiing but it is now only one of dozens of skiing centres in the province, many of which have ski-lifts to complement the traditional cross-country courses which do not need mechanical contraptions.

Ibsen's birthplace: The capital is **Skien**, Ibsen's birthplace, which originally came into existence on the back of an industry producing stone projectiles for military slingshots, even stranger than another industry which prospered in Ulefoss until the close of the 19th century, namely the production of ice. Ice was easily transported along Telemark's natural waterways which were rationalised this century into a canal system.

Visitors with their own transport in Telemark can hardly go wrong: pick any of the winding roads and the scenery is bound to be breath-taking. The waterways are a wonderful alternative for those who do not have a car. Skien is on a main line from Oslo and a good place to pick up boats going north through **Sauherad** to **Notodden** or, branching off at **Ulefoss**, west to **Dalen**.

Left, Ibsen's statue in his birthplace, Skien. **Right**, beekeeper.

Schedules change according to season—in some parts the boats press on with the help of a small ice-breaker—so it is advisable to make specific enquiries of the tourist information services.

The stretch between **Rjukan** and **Rauland** is particularly lovely and can be covered by public bus. Keep an eye open for highly decorative wooden houses and double-storey barns, sometimes bigger than the house itself, with a ramp leading to the upper floor. The obvious attraction of Rjukan itself is the heavy water plant, now partially an industrial museum but in 1943 the target of a daring sabotage attack by the Norwegian resistance (see *The Heroes of Telemark*, page 67, for full story). The town library, incidentally, has a good collection of literature about the operation, including some books written by those who participated. A few of these are in English and the charming librarian could not be more helpful.

Rjukan is generally rather gloomy because the sun is nearly always blocked off by surrounding mountains.

On top of those mountains, though, another world of vast vistas opens up, and it said that on a good day it is possible to see one sixth of Norway. Take the road leading to the **Gaustablikk Hotel** which shares its magnificent surroundings with a smaller hotel which has a total ban on smoking and some traditional cottages for rent. It is not necessary to double back through Rjukan; to do so would in fact be to miss the exceptional scenery which stretches for miles on the other side.

Throughout Telemark one senses an older Norway lurking just beneath the surface. The upper districts were, until recently, impenetrable except on skis, travel in winter being easier than in summer. Isolated communities were not inclined to take orders from interfering outsiders, although a lot of water has passed under the bridge since the people were described (in 1580) as "shameless bodies of the Devil whose chief delight is to kill bishops, priests, bailiffs and superiors—and who possess a large share of all original sin."

A small goat farm.

THE HEART OF NORWAY

The heart of Norway is characterised by three features: **Lake Mjøsa**, the country's largest lake, the great massif of the **Dovrefjell** to the north, and the long slanting valleys of the east. In this widest part of Norway, they lie straight and narrow from southeast to northwest, their rivers like veins cutting between the mountain ranges. Alongside the rivers are fertile farms, which climb up the valley sides to forests. Then, above the treeline come the bare slopes of tussocky grass and rocks, a playground for skiers and walkers.

Despite Norway's busy network of rural buses, it could be difficult to get into some of the remoter corners. But this region of mountains and valleys makes wonderful country for touring by car. Each new vista is more magnificent than the last as the road climbs and dips and circles. Nevertheless, for some of the higher plateaux, it can be simpler and quicker to push further into the wilderness by train, which stops at many small stations along the magnificent line between Oslo and Trondheim—almost as spectacular as the famous route between Oslo and Bergen in the west, which is Europe's highest conventional railway line.

Paddle steamer: Lake Mjøsa also lies southeast to northwest some 100 miles (160 km) north of Oslo and has an area of 142 sq. miles (368 sq. km). One of the best ways to enjoy the lake and its surroundings is a trip on the old paddle steamer *Skibladner*. Built in 1856, she is based in **Hamar** on the east of the lake, a highlight of any visit to Norway.

Around Mjøsa lies some of the most fertile agricultural land in Norway and throughout the gently undulating countryside are large farms, encircled by thickly forested hills. Where Mjøsa is at its widest, some 10 miles (16.5 km) across, is the attractive island of Helgøya. At its southern tip, the island has a burial mound, part of the historic Hovinsholm estate—a Royal estate from Viking times until 1723.

Three main towns lie along the lake: **Hamar** and **Lillehammer** are on the eastern shore and **Gjøvik** on the west. A bridge across Lake Mjøsa, 15 miles (25 km) south of Lillehammer which opened in 1985, links the municipalities and, in a commercial sense, has combined the area into what has been christened Mjøsabyen (Mjøsa City). All three backed Lillehammer's successful bid for the 1994 Winter Olympics.

With a population of 16,000, Hamar has a long history. In the Middle Ages, as the centre of Roman Catholicism and the seat of the bishop, it enjoyed great prosperity and had an impressive cathedral. Hamar's downfall came in 1537 when the Danes carried off the bishop, and 30 years later when the Swedes burned the town to the ground. Now all that remains from that era are the cathedral ruins on a spit of land by the lake.

Railways and opera: Not until the 19th century and the coming of the railway did Hamar regain a measure of importance, as a railway junction with a locomotive building works. It was not sur-

Preceding pages: Linnehammer. **Left**, a well-decorated *stabbur* (food store) from 1863, on an old bailiff's farm at Erlien, near Røros. **Right**, Hafjell, outside Linnehammer, site of the 1994 Winter Olympics.

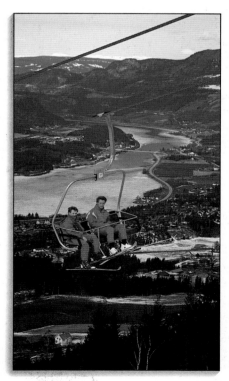

prising, therefore, that it became the site of the **Railway Museum**, established in 1896, and the oldest technical museum in Norway. It moved to its present lakeside site in 1956. Among the large collection of locomotives and rolling stock is the early steam engine *Caroline*, built by Robert Stephenson in 1861.

Also impressive is one of the massive Dovregubben (Dovre giant) locomotives built in 1940 to haul heavy trains over the Dovrefjell, and later on the Oslo-Bergen line. These, and many other items, make the museum an essential call for all railway buffs. Those interested in opera may prefer the memorial collection of the singer Kirsten Flagstad, and not far away is the **Klevfors Industrial Museum** in a former cellulose and paper works.

By comparison, **Gjøvik** is basically industrial in spite of its name of "the white town of Mjøsa." There is a glass collection in the town hall from the former glassworks and the **Eiktunet Museum of Cultural History**.

The third and largest town is **Lillehammer** (population 22,000) at the northern end of the lake where it narrows to become the river Lågen and the start of **Gudbrandsdalen**. Here both the main railway line between Oslo and Trondheim and the E6 road wind through some of the most beautiful country in Norway. Lillehammer is called the capital of the Gudbrandsdal valley and its success in gaining the 1994 Winter Olympics confirms its popularity for winter sports. No fewer than 310 miles (500 km) of well-prepared tracks for cross country skiing criss-cross mountain and valley and the prospect of the Winter Olympics led to the opening of a whole new downhill skiing area on nearby **Hafjell**.

Good health: For summer visitors, the biggest attraction is **Maihaugen Open-Air Museum**, remarkable even in a country of many open-air museums. Maihaugen has some 120 old buildings brought into the 100-acre (40-hectare) site from all over Gudbrandsdalen, to show life as it once was. The museum was the life work of Anders Sandvig. A

Odalen man's best friend, a *dølahest* (eastern Norwegian horse).

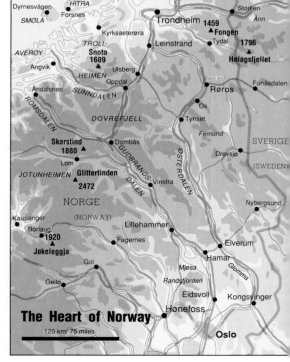

The Heart of Norway

120 km/ 75 miles

dentist by profession, he came to Lillehammer in 1885 suffering from tuberculosis and with a life expectancy of a mere two years. Whether it was the interest of the museum he founded in 1887 which kept him alive or not, Sandvig achieved another 65 years and died only in 1950.

He is the town's only honorary citizen with his statue prominent in the market place. Apart from the buildings, which range from the medieval to the 19th century, Maihaugen has some 30,000 artefacts, all collected by Sandvig, and the many demonstrations of old skills and crafts give the museum a real sense of being alive.

If Hamar attracts the railway fan, then Lillehammer, not to be outdone, has something for the motoring enthusiast. It is the only **Museum of Road Vehicles** in Norway and includes everything from horse-drawn sleighs, gigs, and carioles to motor cars. There are some unusual examples, including steam and electric vehicles, a strange six-wheeled Mustad and a 1922 Bjer-ing, which seated two people in tandem and could have its front wheels replaced by skis in winter. There is also the Troll, the last car to be manufactured in Norway, which ended its production run of 16 vehicles in 1956.

The quality of light in Lillehammer and its surroundings has attracted numerous artists to the area, including Fredrik Collett, Lars Jorde, Alf Lundeby, Einar Sandberg, Kirsten Holbø, Erik Werenskiold and Henrik Sørensen. As a result, the town has an impressive art gallery which includes works by Jacob Weidemann, and Norway's most famous artist, Edvard Munch. One of Lillehammer's most revered names is Danish-born Sigrid Undset, winner of the 1928 Nobel prize for Literature, who took up residence at nearby **Bjerkbæk** in 1921. Among other works, she made her name by writing historical chronicles set in medieval Norway and her most celebrated work is her trilogy *Kristin Lavransdatter* which ends at the time of the Black Death.

Lake Mjøsa at sunset.

Aulestad, some 6½ miles (11 km) from Lillehammer is the home of another famous Norwegian writer, Bjørnsterne Bjørnson, who wrote the national anthem and was one of the writers who inspired the nationalist movement in the 19th century, along with musicians such as Edvard Greig and the violinist Ole Bull. Bjørnson too became a Nobel prize winner and his house today is exactly as it was when he died in 1910.

Miniature Lillehammer: Alongside these literary attractions, Lillehammer has not neglected its younger visitors. On the outskirts of the town, at Øyer, is **Lilleputhammer** with its quarter scale version of the centre of Lillehammer as it was in 1900. You walk down the main street, peer in the shop windows and find some are open to the public. It also has a variety of activities for children. At **Hundefossen** 6½ miles (11 km) north of the town is **Lekeland** or Playland, also for children, with a whole range of things to do and, in glass fibre, the world's largest specimen of a troll; Norway's figure of fable is said to have an evil disposition and a face as gnarled as the mountains and rocks where trolls have their homes.

To the east of Lake Mjøsa lies **Østerdalen**, which cuts through the mountains on a line roughly parallel to Gudbrandsdalen. At times the valley is narrow, with seemingly endless forests on either side, broken only occasionally by patches of farmland. It starts at Elverum in the south and continues northwards for 155 miles (250 km) and becomes broader and more open the further north it goes. Throughout its length flows Norway's longest river, the Glomma, kept company by the railway and road 3.

Elverum is one of the essential crossroads of Norway, and lies at the junction of many valleys, with routes to Hamar to the west, Kongsvinger to the south and Trysil to the northeast. It has the well-preserved **Terningen bastion** built in 1673, and a climb to the top of the water tower provides a good view. The town's most famous episode is commemorated in a monument to the fierce battle fought in April 1940, which delayed the German army for long enough to allow the king and members of the government to escape to Britain.

By far the most important of the town's attractions are two major museums. The **Glomdal** is the third largest traditional museum in Norway and was opened in 1911. On a large natural site, it has 88 old buildings of many kinds, brought in from Østerdalen and Solør. The museum's main building, opened in 1973, includes an exhibition hall with 30,000 catalogued items, an auditorium and library. The indoor area is divided into three sections: the farming year, transport and communication, and handwork and crafts; there is also a collection of antiquities from the Neolithic age and Viking era. An open-air theatre is another feature, while the exhibits are intended to show what life was like in the Glomma valley from 1870 to 1900.

The second museum is devoted to Norwegian forestry (**Norsk Skogsbruk Museum**) and encompasses forestry, hunting and fishing. The main building also has exhibits devoted to

On the summit.

geology and wildlife and children will head for the aquarium. The outdoor collection is extensive and is mainly situated on the 12-acre (5-hectare) island of **Prestøya** in the middle of the Glomma river.

Oldest skiing: To the northeast, **Trysil**, in Hedmark near the Swedish border, is a popular winter sports area. It has the distinction of being home to the world's oldest ski club, the Trysil Shooting and Skiing Club founded in 1861. In summer, Trysil is a centre for paragliding, rafting, canoe tours and mountain tours with pack dogs to carry the luggage. But it goes without saying that almost anywhere in the heart of Norway, you only need to go a short way for the sort of outdoor recreation that mountain, river and lake can provide.

North from Elverum there are few places of any size or importance. At Koppang, about halfway along the length of Østerdalen a road goes east to a long thin lake, the **Storsjøen**, which also lies parallel to Østerdalen. If you take this detour, you can rejoin the origi-

nal road (3) at Tynset. Northwest of Tynset, you come to Kvikne and near it the rectory at **Bjørgan**, the birthplace of Bjørnsterne Bjørnson.

The whole of this area is well off the tourist track and ideal for exploration. Try route number 27 which turns west at Atna, some 20 miles (30 km) north of Koppang, for a drive into the foothills of a wild and mountainous region of the Rondane, where the peaks rise up to 6,000 ft (1,800 metres) high. At **Enden**, it is joined by an equally enjoyable road, which has taken the parallel route north from Ringebu, north of Lillehammer up the Gudbrandsdal valley. Called the **Rondevegen**, the road climbs steeply from **Ringebu** to some superb views of the Rondane mountains.

After coming this far, it is well worth continuing from Enden to **Folldall**, past the great peaks that include **Rondeslottet** at over 7,000 ft (2,177 metres) high, with the **Rondane National Park** to the west. The road rises to nearly 3,000 ft (914 metres). Folldal itself is one of the highest permanently inhab-

Rich pastures in the lowlying land near Lake Mjøsa.

RØROS AND THE OLD COPPER COUNTRY

Røros was the archetypal company town with life and society revolving around the mining of copper. Isolated, exposed, nearly 2,000 ft (610 metres) above sea level and surrounded by mountains and enduring winter cold, it was far from other centres of population and close to the Swedish border. Its existence was entirely due to the discovery of copper, which was first mined there over 300 years ago and was worked until 1972. The town was hardly beautiful, and slag heaps and the smelter provided the backdrop to the miners' houses. These were usually small and overcrowded but many workers also possessed a small patch of land and one or two animals as a source of food.

Further away from smelter and slag lived those higher up the company pecking order—in the executive area. By some miracle Røros survived without any of the devastating fires which have so often laid waste the wooden buildings of Norwegian towns.

Today Røros has a unique townscape and the authorities have wisely placed preservation orders on over 1,000 buildings—in effect, the entire older part of the town. Doors, windows and colour schemes all have to conform, buildings have to be lived in and there is strict control of advertising signs and notices. As a result, Røros is in a time warp, retaining much of its mining town atmosphere to put it on UNESCO's World Heritage list.

The most noticeable feature in Røros is the stone church—"the pride of the mining town"—which was dedicated in 1784 and replaced a wooden one built in 1650. The interior reflects the mining society, with paintings of clergymen and mining officials, while prayers were said every Sunday for the company and its directors.

The smelter was the heart of the copper mining company and the focal point of the town. Its bell was rung at the start and end of each shift and is still there today. Smelting ended in 1953 and the company went bankrupt in 1977. The smelter stood abandoned, damaged by fire after activities ceased, surrounded by artefacts of the industry.

The government bought the ground and part of the estate and plans were drawn up for an imaginative museum which would provide the visitor with a picture of mining and the development of the town and the surrounding area. The old smelting plant was restored. The exterior still resembles the building in 1889 but the interior is now given over to a series of four primary exhibitions. These cover mining in Røros, mining techniques in Europe in the 18th and 19th centuries, cultural features of the southern Lapp society and aspects of Røros society and its environs.

One of the most interesting elements in the museum is the series of working models to one-tenth scale which demonstrate the arduous methods called for when the only power available was water, horses and human muscle. In the past it was usual to make one-tenth scale models to see if a particular technique or piece of equipment would work so today's replicas are following an old tradition. The museum was opened in 1987 by Queen Margrethe II of Denmark.

Eight miles (13 km) from Røros is Olavs-gruva (the Olav mine) which was opened as a mining museum in 1979. A guided tour takes visitors 1640 ft (500 metres) into the mine workings at a depth of 164 ft (50 metres) below ground. The tour starts in Nyberget, the oldest mine, which was opened in 1560 and has light and sound effects to add to the atmosphere. It ends in the Olav mine which was worked from 1936 until 1972. Here there are machines and tools as if ready for use by the next shift. Within the mine are impressive galleries and chambers, some of considerable size.

The technique originally used for mining was called *fyrsetning* and involved setting fire to wood piled against the rock face. The fire's heat cracked the rock and, after it had cooled, the miners set to with hammers and chisels. Immense quantities of timber were needed. Dynamite, invented in 1680, was not used until 1880.

In the surface museum of the mine are displays which show mining activities in the region from 1644 until 1970s, but the bare and bleak scenery surrounding the mine, even in the summer sun, is the most telling way to emphasise the wretched existence of those early miners.

ited communities in Norway, which started when copper was discovered in the area in the 18th century.

Although the mine is no longer worked, the mining company still has its administrative offices and maintenance workshops at Folldal, to serve a new mine at **Hjerkinn** some 20 miles (30 km) away. The old Folldal mine, and some of its buildings, now form a museum with guided tours in summer. At **Streitlien-Uppigård**, also nearby, is a rural museum of typical local buildings, which was established by Dr. Anton Rabe and his wife, a Norwegian actress, Tore Dyveke Segelcke.

Instead of driving west from this isolated mining town to the newer mine at Hjerkinn, if you turn east (road 29) you return to the Glomma river valley, all connected to and part of the system of valleys and rivers that spread out from Østerdalen. Along the way, numerous abandoned mine works indicate how important minerals were and, to some extent, still are to this area. North of Alvdal is the grey cone-shaped summit

of the **Tronfjell**, another of the peaks in these wild mountains that rises more than 5,000 ft (1,500 metres). Rail, road and Glomma river now strike out northeast, through Tolga and Os (the start of **Kopperveien**—the copper road—which takes you east to Femund lake) and to Røros, one of the most interesting towns in Norway with a long history of copper-mining, many preserved buildings and an impressive church *(see facing page)*.

In the wild: Røros is also a junction for roads which lead through an eastern wilderness with little habitation: the first to the Swedish frontier, only 29 miles (46 km) away to the east, past several lakes, some artificial, dug to provide water for mining operations; another to Ålen which has a small open-air museum, then through the fast-flowing gorge of the Gaula river until the valley broadens out near Støren; yet another is an alternative route to **Femund lake**, Norway's third largest, which gives good fishing.

After Østerdalen, Gudbrandsdalen is

Left, the preserved mining village of Røros. Below, as this selection shows, each area has its own national costume.

the second longest valley in Norway. The Lågen river runs its full length and the valley stretches for 87 miles (140 km) northwest from **Lillehammer** to **Dombås**, where it merges into the upland fjells of the Dovre plateau, 3,000 ft (914 m) high. Trails and huts cater for hill and mountain walkers, who can wander at will in this huge empty area and in the surrounding peaks, which tower twice as high as Dovrefjell itself. Gudbrandsdalen has long been the traditional route for travellers from eastern Norway to Trøndelag and Trondheim; today, railway and the E6 highway run alongside the river.

Perhaps because it was surrounded by mountains, which emphasised its sense of identity, the Gudbrandsdal valley has a long tradition of folk dancing and folk music; it is famous for its woodcarving and rose painting, and you can find good craftwork to take home.

North of Lillehammer at **Ringebu**, you can visit one of Norway's old stave churches, built of enormous upright timbers in the early Middle Ages. It has a statue of St Laurentius, and crucifixes and a baptismal font from medieval times. **Hundorp**, not far away, has a monolith to King Olav, who became Saint Olav. It was also the seat of the great Viking chieftain Dale Gudbrand who was baptised by Olav in 1021.

Real Per Gynt: Vinstra is the heart of Per Gynt country and his farm, **Hågå**, now privately owned, is only a mile or two away. One of the Gynt cottages serves as the information office in Vinstra, another has gone to the Maihaugen Open-Air Museum at Lillehammer, and the third remains above the farm. In the cemetery at **Sødorp**, a mile from Vinstra, is a monument to this strange, legendary Norwegian figure.

Though Per Gynt is legendary to many, he is real enough to Norwegians as a marksman, ski-runner and something of a braggart who was often "economical with the truth." Yet he inspired the poet and dramatist Henrik Ibsen to write the play which he called *Peer Gynt* and the music of Edvard Grieg's *Peer Gynt Suite*.

The special pattern devised by the Dale Knitwear Company for Norway's Olympic team has become popular ski wear.

Today Per (or Peer) Gynt is a handy legend to use in the promotion of tourism, hence the creation of the **Peer Gynt Way**, a minor road which goes round in a huge semicircle through Golå and returns to the E6 at Tretten. It reaches an altitude of over 3,000 ft (915 metres) and presents a near continuous panorama of desolate mountains and lakes—stark but appealing. There are a number of mountain hotels (*fjellhotell*) in this area which are popular in both winter and summer. If scenic indigestion has not yet set in, an alternative cornucopia of mountain scenery is provided by a second road (255) which makes an even wider sweep along the waters of the **Espedalsvatnet**, through Forset and Follebu, to emerge north of Lillehammer at Fåberg.

Scottish visitors should make a point of stopping at **Kringen** to see the memorial to a battle of 1612, when an army of Scottish mercenaries was defeated by local farmers. Despite their defeat, the Scots (said to be Sinclairs) have another memorial in the checked cloth used in one local costume, which looks remarkably like Sinclair tartan. At Otta the river of the same name and an offshoot road go west via Lom until they eventually reach the western fjords and form the northeast boundary to the great peaks of the **Jotunheimen**—the home of the giants.

Further north, road, rail and river climb up and over the Dovrefjell, where the train stops at small stations such as Fokstua, Hjerkinn, Kongsvoll and Drivstua to disgorge walkers with boots and backpacks.

On the far side is Dombås, another junction, where road 69 and railway follow the Lågen river on its long course to Åndalsnes on the Romsdalsfjord away to the west. The summit of Dovrefjell is at **Hjerkinn**, with its modern mine, which is reputed to be the driest place in Norway. For the rest of way, it is all down hill across the **Dovre National Park**, en route to **Oppdal**, a mountain centre for winter skiing and summer outdoor pursuits.

With the Dovrefjell to the south,

Oppdal sits looking up towards this great plateau, and to Trollheimen to the northwest. Trollheimen has most things that make a mountaineer happy, arduous peaks and plateaux, and wonderful views from jagged rocks falling sheer to the fjord. The mountains are also famous for their rich mountain flora. As early as 1756 Professor Oeder from Copenhagen University discovered the flora of Upper Drivdalen and botanists have been visiting ever since.

Such variety means that there is space for everyone. Skiers need not damage the flora, and noisy snow scooters can be kept away from people who want silence. The new Hovden gondola cable car takes skiers 3,750 ft (1125 metres) above the village and in summer it is a way up for walkers. Oppdal is fine country for fishing, rafting and riding.

Dovrefjell is one of the three places in the world where you find musk ox in the wild and Snøhetta (at some 7,500 ft/ 2,289 metres, the highest mountain) has many wild reindeer, which migrate in an endless quest for good pasture. Not far from Oppdal, off road 16, a small path leads to a peaceful place with trees and uneven mounds which are Viking graves. This is Vang, once the centre of the community until the railway brought Oppdal to life. Many graves were desecrated in the 19th century but now Oppdal plans a Viking centre.

A track branches off to Gjevils-vassdalen and its lake through some of the most beautiful land in Norway. Here Anders Rambech, an 18th-century country attorney and one of the negotiators of the 1814 Constitution, built Tingstua. Today the wooden building in its lovely setting is a popular upland inn. Small and simple though it is, the inn has been favoured by Crown Princess Sonja who made it her base for mountain walking into Dovrefjell.

To many Norwegians, these mountains of the Dovrefjell represent the strength of their country, something that brings their nation together. With admirable brevity, they sum it up in the old phrase *"Enig og tro til Dovre faller"*—"United we stand until the Dovre mountains fall."

FJORDS

To create a fjord, take a mountain and a river, and mix in an Ice Age many thousands of years ago. To describe the fjords is to find yourself running out of superlatives. The deepest water, the highest mountains, the narrowest, the most beautiful, the stillest, the most peaceful... each fjord has its own special characteristic, from the Sognfjord (the longest) to the Geiranger, which many people think the most beautiful. But who would argue? With so many fjords, everybody is entitled to their own opinion.

The fjords gave Norway its great seafaring tradition. From the early Vikings who found Scotland, Iceland and the rest of Europe easier to reach than their own southeast area around Oslo, to the modern traveller who chooses a ship as the most comfortable way to travel this magnificent coastline, the sea has provided the link.

The fjords begin at Stavanger in the south, now Norway's oil capital, not far from Prekestolen, the great slab of rock standing a dizzy 2,000 ft (600 metres) above the Lysefjord. They stretch north to the Hardanger, an early favourite where the old traditions of music and story influenced travellers such as the composer Edvard Grieg. On the way, they encompass Bergen, the fjord capital, Sognfjord and Nordfjord, in an area of glaciers, lakes and mountains massifs, Storfjord, with its branches biting far into the land, and, finally, the quiet calm of Geirganger.

From their high mountain sides, waterfalls cascade into the fjord, and small farms cling to every ledge and acre of green. The fjords are beautiful, timeless, and everyone's idea of the soul of Norway.

Preceding pages: blossom time on the fjord; the coastal town of Ålesund seems to float on water. **Left**, small coastal freighter at Femrissundet (sound) in the north.

ROGALAND AND THE SOUTHERN FJORDS

Many people believe that Norway's fjord country begins at the Hardangerfjord and the city of Bergen, and stretches north. If so, they are missing all the southern fjords and islands, where Norway first became a nation. Today this area of Rogaland is centred on Stavanger, the focus of Norway's highly successful oil industry, and of some of the fjord country's most spectacular natural sights. What a pity to miss **Prekestolen** ("the pulpit,") a flat slab of rock swooping some 2,000 ft (600 metres) up from the **Lysefjord**, which offers a 180° horizon over fjell and fjord.

Rogaland has the mildest climate in Norway and the beauty of the coast is unsurpassed. These coastal and outer fjord areas have the highest average temperature in Norway but pay the penalty for their closeness to the sea in unexpected showers and a higher rainfall. In winter, thanks to the Gulf Stream, there is little snow and the fertile fields are green for most of the year.

Getting there: By air, the way in is Stavanger's international airport at **Sola**, or you might come by express boat from Bergen in just under three hours, and Norway Line sails into Stavanger from Britain for nine months of the year. From the south, the main road north is the E18, which crosses into the county south of the old town of **Egersund**. There is also a coastal route (road 44), which is never far from the sea, and which goes all the way north to Stavanger. At the southern corner of this route, small fjords bite into a rough, rocky coast, which leads to green valleys and a myriad of shining lakes. North of Egersund, the land becomes much flatter.

The best view of Egersund's sheltered harbour, with its dozens of yachts both big and small, is from the top of the lighthouse. The town itself has the **Faience Museum**, which displays painted earthenware crockery, once the town's main industry. Inland is the waterfall, **Fotlandfossen**, and further north on the E18 you come to the southern end of **Ørsdalsvatn**. From here, Rogaland's last remaining inland waterway boat, *Ørsdølen*, sails the 13 miles (20 km) to **Vassbø** at the far end of the narrow lake. Near there you can have a simple homemade meal before the boat returns. A few miles further on the is **Vikeså**; from here, road 503 to **Byrkjedal** runs past lakes and **Gloppedals Scree**, where the boulders are as big as houses.

The flat and fertile country above Egersund is the biggest producer of meat, dairy products, poultry and eggs in Norway but it was not always as peaceful as it is today. In AD 872, it was the scene of the **Battle of Hafrsfjord**, where King Harald Hårfagre (Fairhair) won his final and most important battle to unite the warring Norwegian kinglings. That battle is marked at the edge of Hafrsfjorden, the near circular fjord to the southwest of Stavanger, where three huge sculptured swords, point downward into the ground.

In 1977, by royal decree, a narrow

strip some 43 miles (70 km) long, from Raumen island at the southern end to Tungnes Lighthouse (north-west of Stavanger) became **Jærstrendene Protected Landscape Area**, which includes offshore islands. **Raumen** itself is one of eight bird sanctuaries where, at different times of the year, you can find northern birds such as turnstones, ringed plovers, knots and more, taking a brief rest on the long flight south to winter in southern Europe or Africa; offshore are wintering eider and long-tailed ducks, and the islands provide nesting places for seabirds, often in protected areas which no-one can enter during the breeding season.

In the eight botanical reserves you find such delights as the Spear-leaved fat hen saltbush, and the rare Marsh Orchid grows at Ogna Botanical Reserve. There are also four geological sites and no less than 150 monuments listed and protected. But this does not mean that Jærstrendene is given over solely to flora and fauna. Beaches with white-gold sand are popular picnic spots and,

though the water can be chilly, this does not deter swimmers.

Bicycle land: Sandnes on Sandfjorden, is Norway's "bicycle town," where the famous DBS bicycles are made and, whether this is the reason or not, pleasure cycling is popular all over the flatter areas, with bikes for hire. Another delight for youngsters is **Kongeparken**, Scandinavia's biggest leisure park, not far from Sandnes at the little town of **Ålgård** on Edlandsvatnet (lake)

At 260 ft (80 metres) long, Kongeparken's Gulliver sign is hard to miss. Inside, Gulliver's body is full of unusual playthings and the park has Scandinavia's longest bob-sleigh ride.

In many of the mountain areas around the fjords, waterfalls cascade hundreds of feet below. One of the most famous is **Månafoss** on the Frafjord, the innermost finger of the Høgsfjord, reached by road 45 south from Sandnes to Gilja. At **Gilja**, turn down the steep road to Frafjord, which gives a fantastic view of the fjord. The car park at the mountain foot gives directions to Månafoss.

Enterprising young buskers at Haugesund Film Festival

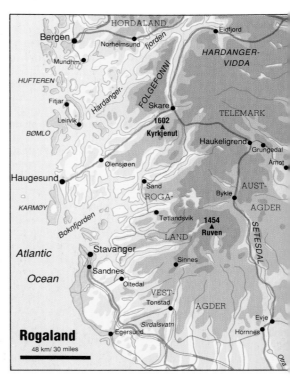

Fjords once more: The **Ryfylke** area northeast of Stavanger is true fjord country, one of the least known parts of Norway despite the drama of its scenery. In the south, due east of Stavanger, Ryfylke starts with **Lysefjord** and stretches north past long narrow lakes that once were open fjords, until it reaches **Vindafjord**, **Saudafjord** and **Suldalsvatn**.

Although he never saw it, Victor Hugo described Lysefjord in *The Toilers of the Sea* as "the most terrible of all the corridor rocks in the sea." Hugo probably meant "awesome" and that the fjord still is. Every visitor to Norway should walk out through heather moor and scrubland to stand on the top of **Prekestolen** (Pulpit Rock) this strange platform high above the fjord, and 25,000 do so each year. On the way are golden eagles, willow grouse, ptarmigan and other birds of the tops as well as reindeer and the angular shape of an elk.

The great height of Prekestolen gives a view towards Stavanger and the fjords to the west, and upwards to the treeline and the rocky heights above. Everywhere there are lakes, waterfalls and rushing torrents. The walk to Prekestolen takes two hours each way and the Prekestolhytte (a Touring Club cabin) has overnight accommodation.

From the village of **Forsand** at its mouth, Lysefjord is 25 miles (40 km) long and, at its innermost end, has one of Europe's most remarkable feats of civil engineering: the road to the hydro-electric power station at **Lysebotn**. Opened as part of a new hydro-electric project, the road, which seems to defy gravity, snakes up or down more than 2,500 ft (750 metres) with 27 hairpin bends and connects Lysebotn to Sirdal and Setersdal along the Lyseveien. If you dare to keep your eyes open as the bus takes its near perpendicular route down, the view is magnificent. Many hundreds of feet inside the mountain, you can tour the hydro-electric plant.

Even this road is not the highest viewpoint. Near the end of the fjord on the south side towers **Kjeragfjell**, an enormous granite mountain around

3,550 ft (1,084 metres) high. Lie on your front and look down through the wedge cut out of the mountain plateau to the fjord around 3,000 ft (900 metres) of vertical rock below. To reach Kjerag takes about two hours walking from several spots along the Lyseveien.

Inshore islands: The sheltered bay north of Stavanger, and the outer islands such as Karmøy, protect Ryfylke's inshore islands from the North Sea. Christianity flourished early here under the protection of the bishops of Stavanger and the islands have many churches. In summer, the 12th-century **Utstein Cloister** on Mosterøy makes a beautiful setting for concerts which are mostly classical, though the season may end with a burst of jazz. The cloister's setting, accoustics and the sense of history give these concerts a very special atmosphere.

The many lighthouses are not only landmarks for islanders and seafarers but make excellent birdwatching sites, with the hunched outlines of cormorants and other seabirds on wave-washed rocks. The waters around these peaceful islands are a sea kingdom for sailors of all kinds with enough coastline to give every boat a bay to itself and many yacht harbours. Most of the island grocers also provide boat services and it is easy to hire rowing boats and small craft with outboard engines.

Northeast highlands: Here fjords, lakes and rivers are rich in fish and fine for sailing and canoeing, and all these inland, eastern areas of Rogaland have good cross-country skiing tracks in winter, and some fine alpine slopes.

Among the best holiday areas is the **Suldal** district, stretching from **Sand** on the Sandsfjord, along the Suldalslågen (river)—where the rushing waters have produced huge salmon (the largest so far weighed almost 75 lb/34 kg)—to the long narrow **Suldalvatn.** At the Sand end of the Suldalslågen is **Laksestudioet**, an observation studio, built under Sandfossen (waterfall) where visitors look through a large window at the salmon resting before their next leap up the fish ladder on the way to their **Avdalsnes Church.**

spawning grounds. Where river meets lake is **Kolbeinstveit Museum** with the old **Guggedalsloftet Bygdetun** (farm) which dates back to the 13th century.

Sudalen is the site of Norway's largest hydro-electric scheme; here five power stations in the giant complex of the **Ulla Førre** plant make use of 13 dams on the enormous **Blåsjø** (lake) on the eastern border with the adjoining county of Aust-Agder.

From Sand, a bus follows the line of the river to the giant **Kvilldal** station, opened in 1982 by King Olav, who chiselled his signature into the mountainside, a popular royal tradition in Scandinavia. On the way to this cavernous power station the bus stops at the **Salmon Castle** at Lindum, built by Lord Sibthorp in 1885, when the British "salmon lords" looked on a few weeks in Norway as part of the fishing season. River and lake still draw anglers from many countries and the castle is a popular guest house and seminar centre.

From Stavanger and Jæren, ferries and express boats reach this fjord country and its islands, and it is easy to combine bus and ferry. **Vindafjord**, **Saudafjord** and **Suldalsvatn** look up to 5,000-ft (1,500-metre) peaks that lead the way to the great mountain massif of the **Hardangervidda**, in the next county of Hordaland. In summer you can take the exciting old mountain road north from Sauda to **Røldal**; the new road now has long tunnels to keep it open all year. At Røldal, and on the road from Suldalsvatn you pick up the **Discovery Route** (E76), which has come all the way over the Haukeli mountains from Telemark and eastern Norway, and you can continue to its end at **Odda**, a remote industrial town at the head of the **Sørfjord**.

The sea route north to Bergen is one of the most popular ways to see the northern coast. By taking an express boat (a cross between a catamaran and a hydrofoil) you can drop off at any of the harbour stops and stay a night or a week according to your whim. **Karmøy**, the island at the south of the outer islands chain, is big enough to merit its own

boat service, which goes to **Skudeneshavn** in the south, an idyllic old port with white, wooden houses along narrow streets. The north of the island is linked to the mainland just south of Haugesund, the first sizeable coastal town north of Stavanger, fast becoming prosperous through oil and the last mainland town in the county.

Day of Judgement: Karmøy's known history dates back to saga times, when it was the "North-way" shipping lane that gave Norway its name. Harald Hårfagre made his home at **Avaldsnes** after the battle at Hafrsfjord. Also here is **St Olaf's Church**, built between 1248 and 1263 by King Håkon Håkonson, and restored in 1922 as the parish church. Near its north walls stands **St Mary's Sewing Needle**, a strange 21-ft (6.5-metre) high stone pillar leaning towards the church wall. Legend tells that the Day of Judgement will come when the pillar touches the wall; many priests are said to have climbed the pillar at dead of night, to pare away the top to make sure that the Day was not yet nigh.

Near the east coast town of Kopervik are burial hills and mounds and stone pillars. The largest burial mound, Doøa Hill, was restored in 1978 and, though it has not yet been fully excavated, it dates back to the Bronze Age. Further north, on the mainland side of the bridge to Haugesund are the "Five Bad Virgins," stone monuments some 8 ft (2.5 metres) high, where excavations in 1901 revealed a Roman bowl dating from AD 300-400. On the west coast, outside Åkrehamn Town Hall stand two stone pillars from the Iron Age which came from Åkretunet nearby, once the council meeting place.

Further south at Ferkingstad are historic boathouses with walls made of stone blocks 5 ft (1.5 metres) thick.

Fish and festivals: Haugesund has long been a centre for fishing, shipping and farming. Today its harbour is filled with pleasure boats; the town has also become a festival and congress centre and has played host to the Norwegian Film Festival for many years. Numerous fjords and lakes cut into the roughly shaped peninsula—like a piece of well nibbled cheese—ideal for fishing, sailing, rowing, canoeing, sports diving and walking.

Further out to sea a boat trip to the idyllic group of islands of Røvær, around 6 miles (10 km) to the west, occupies a half or whole day and offers shore fishing, interesting flora and fauna and, in summer, a wharfside café.

For the adventurous, *MS Utsira* provides a daily service to the island of the same name, familiar from European shipping forecasts and Norway's western outpost. The 90-minute journey out makes a wonderful tour for birdwatchers, as does the island itself. Fishing is also excellent and Norwegian salt water fishing is free to holders of a national licence (*see page 122*). Day licences for lakes in Rogaland and for salmon and sea trout in the many rivers vary from around Nkr20 to Nkr150.

From Haugesund, it is just a few hours to Bergen, the fjord capital, but the short stay in Rogaland is certain to convince any visitor that this southern county is where the fjords begin.

Left, this fearsome road to Lysebotn has 21 bends. **Right**, fish market on the island of Utsira.

STAVANGER

Strange though it may seem in a city which has devoted nearly 1,000 years to the sea, the best way to arrive in **Stavanger** is by overnight train from Oslo. As the dark night grows lighter, the train slips along the side of the fjord with black mountain peaks outlined on either side, past the huge latticework of oil rigs and drilling towers which have made Stavanger Norway's oil capital. Enormous though they are, somehow they do not intrude on the landscape because the size and grandeur of mountain and fjord dwarfs even these industrial giants, growing clearer as the sky turns from grey to pink.

Stavanger has been lucky because the sea has always been good to the city. As one source of prosperity disappeared, another arose. Shipping, fishing and trading have taken the city's ships and people all over the world, and brought seamen to Stavanger, to give it an easy-going relationship with other nations.

Today, the city is as international as ever, not just the headquarters of Statoil (the Norwegian state oil company) and the Norwegian Petroleum Directorate, but also the Norwegian headquarters of 10 foreign oil companies and home to an international community; 8 percent of its 97,000 inhabitants are foreigners.

International eating: This cosmopolitan community has demanded high standards and Stavanger has good restaurants, hotels, food, entertainment and a cosmopolitan atmosphere out of all proportion to its size. Eating out in particular has changed a great deal since the arrival of oil money. As well as the traditional restaurants which specialise in good Norwegian food, there are many new gourmet and international restaurants, with a choice of Indian, Italian, Greek, Portuguese, Mexican and Japanese restaurants, and at least half a dozen Chinese, the latter a popular cuisine in most Norwegian cities.

Restaurants, and particularly alcohol, are expensive in Norway, but a great many cafés, bars, and pubs (unknown until recently) have sprung up, sometimes with a piano or small group, plus a handful of youthful discos, which do not necessarily serve alcohol. In the fish market, where fresh crabs eaten on the spot are the favourite buy, and the next-door fruit and flower market, you will hear the sound of many languages, and in the heart of Stavanger's shopping streets behind the market almost all the assistants speak English.

Apart from the prosperity and development brought by oil and its ancillary industries, Stavanger is also the principal town, and the seat of local government, in Rogaland *fylke* (county), the most southerly of the fjord countries of West Norway.

The past: The Stavanger *Siddis* (the colloquial name for a Stavangerian person) claims to be the oldest true Norwegian; that dates from the Battle of Hafrsfjord in 872 when King Harald Hårfagre won his final battle to unite the kingdom. The battle is marked at the edge of Hafrsfjorden, which cuts far into the land to the southwest of the city,

Left, Stavanger's past prosperity was based on sardines. Right, winter city street scene.

by three huge sculptured swords pointing downwards into the ground.

When work began on the cathedral in 1125, Stavanger was simply a cluster of small wooden houses at the end of the narrow inlet called **Vågen**. It was chosen as the heart of the bishopric, nevertheless, because it was the only recognisable settlement along this southwestern coast. From then on Stavanger was the most important town in the area. It grew slowly; the population was only 2,000 at the start of the 19th century, but jumped to 30,000 by 1900. Now it has something under 100,000 inhabitants.

In the 18th and 19th centuries, the city depended on fishing and maritime trade and faced the world with an unbroken row of wharves and warehouses dedicated to these industries. Around the 1870s, at a time when fishing and shipping were beginning to face decline, the fishermen turned their attention to brisling, which were cured and canned in the towns and sent as Norwegian "sardines" all over the world. At one time Stavanger had as many as 70 canneries

and 70 percent of the population worked in the industry. In the first half of this century, the smell of oily fish hung over the town, permeating every breath. But Stavanger was never in doubt about the value of that smell. When, on a particularly odiferous day, a cheeky youngster wrinkled a disdainful nose, a mother would say: "Don't scorn it, that's the smell of money."

It was, and Stavanger thrived on sardines until, after World War II, that all-pervasive tang began to fade along with the demand for sardines. For nearly 20 years, Stavanger knew difficult times. Then, in the 1960s, came oil—once again the sea had provided.

Present-day reminders: Many traces remain of these fluctuations in the city's fortunes. From the late 17th and early 18th century is **Gamle Stavanger** (Old Stavanger) more than 150 white wooden houses looking down towards Vågen, with cobbled streets lit by old-fashioned street lamps. But this is no museum. There may be a preservation order on the exteriors, and the owners

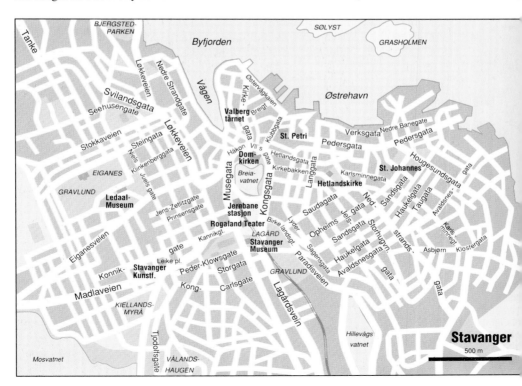

take a pride in keeping them in character, but the interiors have every comfort and gadget that modern Norwegians expect, and Old Stavanger is one of the most coveted areas to live in.

Nor have the canning factories been lost. Many are converted into modern offices, without destroying their scale and shape, and buildings that once canned sardines may now be the headquarters of an international oil company. One factory at Øvre Strandgaten, near the harbour, has been preserved as the **Canning Museum**. In the big open room with its curing ovens, the guides explain the life of the men and women who worked long hours in the intricate process of threading the sardines on to long rods, smoking, then packing them, almost all of it being done by hand.

Even nearer the harbour and the centre of the town is the **Maritime Museum** in one of the old mercantile houses on Nedre Strandgaten, with its warehouses towards the sea. It traces the history of Stavanger's maritime links over the past 150 years, from wood to steel and concrete, from sailing ships to oil platforms. Today, large windows have replaced the warehouse doors and you turn your head from the history behind you to the modern town today.

On the Nedre Strandgate side, away from the harbour, is the general store, full of the provisions and supplies that it would have held before World War II. On the upstairs floor, where the owner lived "over the shop", is an office just as it might have been when a young crewman called in during the 1930s in search of a berth, or the skipper came to pay his respects. The owner's flat shows the comfortable life of a shipowner in the late 19th century, with much of its furniture and ornaments in a style that has returned to popularity today.

Centre of worship: The heart of modern Stavanger is the area around **Breivatnet**, the small lake in the middle of the city, near the oldest and biggest building, the beautiful 12th-century **Domkirken** (Cathedral). Built in the Anglo-Norman style, it can claim with justification to be among the best-

preserved medieval cathedrals in Europe. Alongside the main building is a **Cathedral School** built in 1758 on the 12th-century foundations of the Bishop's Residence, destroyed in one of the inevitable town fires in 1272.

Inside, this stone cathedral has a feeling of austere strength in the massive pillars which contrast with the elegant arches of the chancel and a remarkable tapestry (made by Frida Hansen in 1927) in the vestibule. Both chancel and vestibule were rebuilt after 1272 in a style similar to the Scottish Gothic of the times, a reminder of the links Stavanger had with other countries even in those early days. One of the finest pieces in the cathedral is Andrew Smith's ornate 16th-century pulpit.

Even earlier is the Iron Age farm at **Ullandhaug**, about a mile or so (2 km) to the southwest of the centre. Here archaeologists unearthed and then reconstructed part of the farm to show three houses, parts of a cattle track and the original stone wall which encircled the whole farmstead between AD 350 and 550. This was a Golden Age in Norway, and the city's **Archaeological Museum** is gradually furnishing the houses to show how people lived then.

From Ullandhaug, it is well worth visiting the nearby **Stavanger Botanical Garden**, which has a herb and perennial garden with more than 1,500 species from all over the world. Rogaland is rich in birds and fauna from coast to mountains and the **Stavanger Museum** has an excellent exhibition, not only of Rogaland wildlife but also displays of cultural history and the history of fishing, which covers the industry and its creatures, including whales and seals. The countryside south of Stavanger is an area of rich farming. Because cliffs and beaches lined the coast rather than harbours, the sea was not as helpful as in some parts of the west and the early people began to clear their stony acres, turning them into sheltering walls around good soil.

Nature area: Stavanger is right on the doorstep of the **Jærstrendene Protected Landscape Area**, which stretches 43 miles (70 km) down the southern coast and its offshore islands, with nature reserves and wonderful silver beaches, ideal for swimming and picnicking. In winter you can have the best of both worlds. Thanks to the Gulf Stream, Stavanger remains mild and the fields around the city are rarely covered by snow, yet it is not much more than an hour from good ski slopes.

Sport at any time of the year is good: indoor and outdoor swimming, sub aqua diving, sailing, wind-surfing and fishing, but there is also an active hiking club plus archery, tennis and horse riding in Jærstrendene. There are so many miles of coast on sea and fjords that you are never far from a good, quiet beach.

The sea-going Siddis jump on to a boat as unconcernedly as most of us jump on a bus. There are tours to the islands and fjords and fast ferries northwards as far as Bergen, where business travellers sit in their city garb alongside holidaymakers' picnic boxes and fishing gear. For business or pleasure, Stavanger is the gateway to an enticing variety of seaborne pursuits.

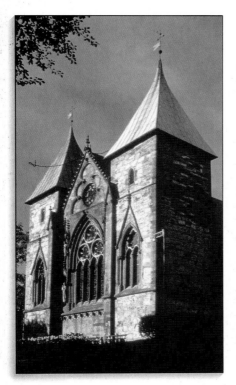

Left, Stavanger Domkirke. **Right,** much of Norway's food comes from the area south of Stavanger.

HORDALAND: ISLAND AND FJORD

Nobody knows how many hundreds of islands lie off the coast of Hordaland. Deserted skerries, green islets, prosperous small harbours and busy communities, they stretch out along the coast like a knotted skein, from the southern islands of Bømlo and Stord, to the beautiful small island of Fedje not far from the mouth of the Sognefjord.

Many of the inner islands around the fjord capital, Bergen, are linked by bridges and causeways in a pattern of islands and sea that seems all of a piece with the many branched fjords. Inland, the further east the higher the ground becomes until it reaches the Hardangervidda, the great mountain plateau which stands above 4,500 ft (1,300 metres).

Water, water: The southwest district of **Sunnhordland** has islands, skerries, sound and straits, good harbours and sheltered bays. Though the North Sea is its neighbour, the climate is surprisingly mild, ideal for watersports and boat enthusiasts in particular.

The three main islands are **Bømlo**, **Stord**, and **Tysnesøy** and even so close to the sea they have a variety of scenery. An upland ridge on Stord reaches nearly 2,500 ft (750 metres) and the view stretches east to the Hardangerfjord and the white sheet of the Folgefonn Glacier, and south towards Haugesund. Everywhere are sails of all colours, the white wake of an express boat from Stavanger to Bergen, and the smaller trails of pleasure craft.

Stord also makes a good paddling-off point for sea canoeing, either from island to island, or into the mouth of the Hardangerfjord. It is an "oil island" too, where the gigantic outlines of the most advanced oil platforms take shape, some of them nearly 1,250 ft (380 metres) high.

The sagas tell that in 1024 St Olav first introduced Christianity to Norway in these islands. Since 1984, an annual outdoor performance of the historical play *Mostraspelet*, held at Mosterhamn on Bømlo, has dramatised this ancient saga. Nearby is a **stone cross** erected in 1924, the 900th anniversary of the arrival of Christianity, and Mosterhamn has the oldest stone church in Norway.

Gateway to Hardanger: Where the cold waters of the **Hardangerfjord** begin to seep into the warmer tides from the west is the lovely **Rosendal Barony**, the only one of its kind in Norway, which largely lost its aristocracy with the departure of the Danes. Though the connection is said to go back to Håkon Håkonson, the manor house was built in 1665 by Ludvig Rosenkrantz. He is buried in the nearby medieval **Kvinnherad Church**, snuggled into the shelter of a rock face and once owned by the Barony. The Barony today has a peaceful park and a large carefully tended rose garden and is held in trust by Oslo University, which uses the land as an experimental farm. During the summer, there are lunch time concerts in the Yellow Room, and a Musical Festival during May and June.

This seabound peninsula at the mouth of the Hardanger is as beautiful as any-

where in the fjord itself but the irony is that Sunnhordaland as a whole tends to be overshadowed by the fame and drama of the Hardangerfjord, so that too many visitors travel through quickly on their way to other places. The discriminating know it deserves a longer look!

The **Hardangerfjord** is part of the Norwegian legend, the fjord that gave its name to Norway's national musical instrument, the eight-stringed Hardanger fiddle, and provided inspiration for the composer Edvard Grieg, the musician Ole Bull and, indirectly, for the 19th-century nationalist movement that led to Norway's independence. Among these mountains and fjords, Grieg and Bull travelled on foot and horse, learning old melodies and dipping into centuries-old cultural traditions and customs.

Tourism came to the Hardanger district as long ago as the 1830s when the poet Henrik Wergeland wrote about "wonderful Hardanger," and foreign as well as Norwegian artists, scientists, and other travellers began to arrive; first

in a trickle, then in a flood when, 30 years later, the steamers began to run regularly from Bergen or Stavanger.

Like the visitors of today, they came to Hardanger for its waterfalls, for the secret beauty of smaller fjords that lead almost to the massif of the Hardangervidda and for glaciers and mountains that rarely lose their snowcaps, contrasted with orchards lining the fjordside. Nearly half a million fruit trees grow here, turning the fjord pink and white in spring as the blossom reflects in the deep, still water. At blossom time, the waterfalls shoot over the sides of the mountains and Hardanger has two of Norway's highest and best known: **Skykkjedalsfoss**, which falls 1,000 ft (300 metres), and **Vøringfoss**, lower but famous for its beauty.

As well as the cruise ships, many day or longer excursions leave from Bergen by boat or road. Coming by the E68 route, the first stopping point is the **Kvam** district, with the fjord villages, **Strandebarm**, **Norheimsund** and **Øystese** on the sunny side of the fjord.

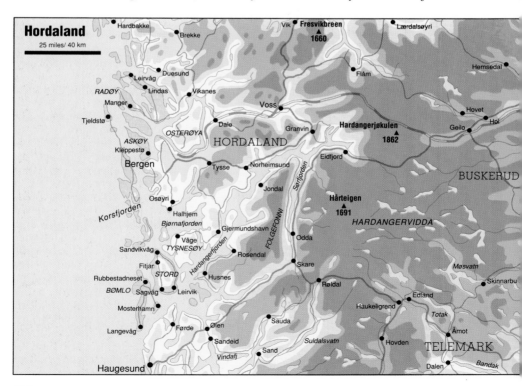

All three offer excellent trips for exploring the fjords by car and ferry, and marked paths here and at Kvamskogen further inland make for safe walking at all standards.

Wooden boats: Not to be passed by is the **Hardanger Ship Conservation Centre** at Norheimsund where conservationists are patiently restoring the wooden craft that made Norwegian boat-building famous. They range from small rowing boats to the centre's most prestigious restoration, the *S/Y Mathilde*, a 73-ft (22-metre) Hardanger yacht launched in 1884. This superb yacht has regained her former splendour under the guidance of Kristian Djupevåg (who also restored Roald Amundsen's yacht, *Gjøa*) and it has the world's largest authentic yacht rigging. The *Mathilde* sleeps 25 passengers in bunk benches or hammocks and is available for cruises and also day excursions, when she can take 50 people to sail fjord and sea as they might have in days past.

Jondal, on the other side of the fjord, is the entrance to the Folgefonn glacier,

and the **Folgefonn Summer Ski-centre**. The safe but exciting road to the new ski-centre opened in June 1989, and is clear from June to September. With permanent snow, there are three mobile ski lifts, alpine or cross-country skiing tracks, ski hire, a cafeteria and guided walks on the glacier.

Jondal itself has a country museum, in the old **Sheriff's House**, and **Hardanger Cathedral**, (the largest church in the Hardanger region). Not far away at **Herand** you will find Bronze Age rock carvings and, at **Herandsholmen**, Hardanger's first guest house opened in 1754. By now, into the inner fjords, the road suddenly turns sharply southeast along the short straight sides of the Utnefjord to **Utne** village, part of Ullensvang *kommune*, which also includes both sides of the Sørfjord.

Five generations: When the fjords were West Norway's main "roads", Utne was an important junction between east and west and had the first post and telegraph offices in Hardanger, in 1836 and 1876 respectively. Two es-

Rosendal, Norway's only Barony, near the mouth of the Hardanger-fjord.

tablishments in Utne which sum up Hardanger life over the past centuries are the **Hardanger Folk Museum**, and the **Utne Hotel**, founded in 1722, the oldest hotel in Norway still in operation. Since 1787, five generations of the same family have owned the Utne Hotel and it first became famous internationally during the time of Torbjørg Utne (1812–1903), known with affection as Mor (Mother) Utne.

Her picture hangs on the sitting-room wall and the family is represented today by her great granddaughter, Hildegun Aga Blokhus. It has always been a favourite spot for artists who have donated many paintings and the hotel also holds exhibitions of national costumes and characteristic embroidery.

Since it opened in 1911, the **Hardanger Folk Museum** has collected old houses and farm buildings for its outdoor museum, formed into a "cluster farm" as it would have been before the Norwegian agricultural reforms in the middle of the 19th century. Along the shore are old boathouses and a merchant's shop which was in use in Utne not all that long ago, and an orchard preserves many old varieties of fruit which have now disappeared from other parts of the Hardangerfjord.

Inside, the museum has a modern exhibition, other rooms showing old crafts and folk-art and the famous Hardanger fiddle, and changing exhibitions on special fjord themes.

Middle Ages: Past Utne, the fjordside road turns due south into the **Sørfjord**. Alternatively you can take the narrow road from Utne through Aga on the west of Sørfjorden to **Agatunet**, the farm of a 13th-century local sheriff. From the Middle Ages to the immediate past, it grew into a nine-family village with a cluster of some 30 buildings. Today, the families no longer live there and the buildings are preserved by law.

On the eastern side of the Sørfjord is the area's main amusement park, **Ferieparken** at **Kinsarvik**. A favourite with children, it has a water chute, trampoline, a miniature zoo, a boating lake, and lends out surf-boards, water

The old fjord village of Utne.

mopeds and water skis. Kinsarvik was also part of the east-west route and its market place attracted merchants from both sides of the Hardangervidda to exchange bog-iron and furs for sea salt. The **old stone church** is said to have been built by Scottish builders around 1200, and has a 17th-century pulpit painted by Peter Reimers.

Until Utne Church was consecrated in 1896, Kinsarvik had for centuries drawn its congregation from all around the fjords, and many worshippers arrived in church boats. At Sørfjord's southern end is **Odda**, favourite of the early travellers, with its **Hotell Hardanger**, then the biggest and best known in Hardanger. Today, Odda is an important industrial town on the main Bergen/Oslo road, the E76, which connects it to Rogaland and the south as firmly as it does to the fjord country.

Farm and forest: Back to Kinsarvik at the mouth of the Sørfjord, the choice is an irregular "V" either northwest or northeast. West through Utnefjord you come to **Granvinfjorden**; to the

northeast is one of the area's most beautiful stretches of water, the **Eidfjord**.

Granvin is at the heart of a farming and forestry district, which includes Ulvik, some 9 miles (14 km) away on an offshoot of the Eidfjord. Both have good fishing, camping, walking, mountain walking on the **Osafjell** and up towards the Hardangervidda and, for the sturdy, outdoor swimming. The bell in **Granvin church** is Norway's oldest and still in use.

From Granvin, the main E68 road north runs past **Skjervefossen** (waterfall) and, for the energetic, a longer walking route on the old Post road takes you to **Ulvik**. Artists and other visitors have been coming to Ulvik for longer than almost any other place in Hardanger and the village has permanent exhibitions by artists such as Tit Mohr and Sigurd Undeland. No one should miss the fine examples of rose painting in Ulvik's **19th-century church**, painted in 1923 by Lars Osa.

The Eidfjord cuts far into the dramatic area which holds the **Hardanger**

Traditional wedding at Voss led by the fiddler and toastmaster.

Glacier, and below it **Skykkjedalsfossen**, Norway's highest waterfall, and **Vøringfoss**, not the highest but the most famous waterfall, high over the wilds of Måbødalen. You can walk down to view this great outpouring from below, and fitness fanatics might welcome the challenge of the age-old packhorse track up **Måbøfjell**, with 1,500 steps and 125 bends. Above tiny Simadalsfjord is **Kjeåsen**, a mountain farm which claims to be the world's most isolated settlement. It lies like an eagle's nest 2,000 ft (623 metres) on near vertical rock above the distant water. Those feeling strong and brave can tackle the old path to the top and marvel that this was how the villagers struggled up with their every need. For frailer spirits it is possible to reach Kjeåsen through a magnificent new tunnel. Inside the mountain is the **Sima hydro-electric power station** which arranges public tours.

Back in the city, Bergen's islands are linked so closely that sometimes it is hard to realise that you have crossed water, but islands such as **Askøy** and **Osterøy** to the north have their own character, and the area round the **Bjørnefjord** (the Bear fjord) to the south is particularly mild and green, and full of boats of all sorts. After an hour's drive to the long narrow island of **Sotra** which shelters the city from the North Sea, there is no doubt that this is a different world. Sotra is a good base for safe sea canoeing in and out of its small offshore islands and rocks and, in good weather, as far as the open sea to combine canoeing with ocean fishing. In any case, shelter is never far away.

Wild tranquillity: North of Bergen is a second island district, **Nordhordland** stretching to the Sognefjord. At weekends, it is a favourite area for Bergensere who go sailing, swimming and fishing. Largely still unconnected by road and bridge, it gives visitors the chance to use the old ferry network which was once Bergen's only route to other parts of Norway.

In Nordhordland the sea can be at its wildest, smashing against the western coast, yet the area has been inhabited for some 8,000 years. Håkon den Gode (the Good) is buried at **Seim**, near Knarvik (around half an hour from Bergen by express boat). Another rare reminder of the Vikings is a **beech wood**, also at Seim, 1,000 years old and the northernmost beech wood in Europe.

Today, fish-farming is important to Nordhordland, which exports vast quantities of salmon and trout, and the fish-farmers are now attempting to rear cod, halibut and other species. Some fish farms are open to the public. Oil is a modern, though not conflicting industry in this widespread area with the night gleam of the light from Mongstad one of the few reminders of this large refinery. There is good sea fishing for cod and coalfish, and special rosy coloured trout inhabit many of the lakes. Diving and sub-aqua fishing, as well as treasure-hunting, are easy in these transparent waters.

Most remote of all, and a target for both sailing picnics and holidays, is **Fedje**, an important navigation point for many centuries with two 19th-cen-

Snowman outside Voss Church.

tury lighthouses still in use today. In these ever-changing waters, Norwegian sea laws insist that all ships must carry a Norwegian pilot, and Fedje has a busy pilot station. Accommodation on Fedje is limited, a *pension* with a former fishing warehouse, and a big *hytte*, but the island remains an idyll of birds, flowers and a community of wild rabbits.

Hang-gliding to skiing: At **Voss**, in the middle of rich farmland, the contrast from the sea is complete, and the Voss *kommune* (district) makes full use of its surroundings to attract visitors twice a year. In summer they come for touring, fjord excursions, mountain walking, parachuting, hang-gliding and paragliding from **Hangurfjell**, and fishing and watersports on **Vangsvatnet**, the lake near the centre of the small town. In winter, everything changes and Voss becomes one of the best centres for alpine and for cross-country skiing of the more energetic touring variety.

The top station of the cable car up Hangurfjell gives one of the best prospects of Voss in its bowl-shaped valley.

As the ground drops away below, the two gondolas, "Dinglo" and "Danglo" take only four minutes or so from the centre for the exciting journey up 2,000 ft (610 metres). On a sunny day, a coffee on the platform outside the cafeteria is magnificent, with the occasional excitement of a paraglider soaring into the sun and over Vagnsvatnet, spread out below. At the beginning of World War II, Voss was badly damaged by German bombing and not much remains of the old town centre except the **church**, which dates back to 1277. Two centuries earlier the proselytising King Olav Haraldson visited Voss and, tradition has it, raised the great **stone cross** standing in a field south of the church. The church walls are 7½ ft (2 metres) thick and the wooden octagonal steeple is unique in Norway.

Below Hangurfjell, about half an hour's walk above the town, is **Voss Folk Museum**, a collection of 16 old wooden buildings standing in traditional form around a central courtyard. The houses date from 1600 to 1870 and

The long climb to the glacier.

contain implements and furniture in use until 1927, incredible though it may seem. Yet somehow, despite the heavy farm work and meagre evening light, farm people like these managed to produce some of the beautiful embroidery, wood and other craft work in the new museum building. One of the most delightful is a traditional wood carving of a Voss bridal party riding to church, with the bride's horse led firmly by her father as though he feared she might gallop away. The carving is by Gudleik Brekkhus, a local sculptor, and is based on a bronze relief in the little park below Voss Railway Station by Nils Bergslien, in which the main figure, the bridal fiddler, is the legendary Ola Mosafinn who died in 1912.

Voss has long been a centre for artists and musicians, and their monuments are scattered around. The 1957 **Sivle monument** marks the centenary of the birth of the author and poet Per Sivle, who grew up on the mountain farm of Sivle, in the great Stalheim Gorge; the **Bergslien monument** by Magnus

Dagestad behind Voss Church commemorates three Bergslien artist brothers, Brynjulf, Nils and Knut; near Voss Fine Arts Society is a memorial to actor **Lars Tvinde** born and bred on the farm of Tvinde, which lies below the Tvindefossen (a waterfall to the north of Voss) and on the same road the 1958 **Sjur Helgeland** memorial commemorates another local fiddler and composer.

Costumes and fiddles: This artistic tradition continues and Voss is one of the best places to hear the Hardanger fiddle and see the old dances performed in beautiful costumes. On the High Street is a wonderful shop where you can see—or even buy—the ornate silver belts and jewellery that go with the Norwegian costume.

Voss is a good centre for mountain touring and sport fishing in the 500-or-so lakes and innumerable mountain rivers and streams, with the **Vosso** river famous for the size of its salmon. Even in summer the high mountains call for boots or very strong shoes and plenty of extra clothes. Temperatures drop quickly; this applies in all upland areas.

Touring is by car, tour bus, or on day excursions, such as the "Norway in a Nutshell" tour which leaves Voss by bus for **Gudvangen**, with a stop at the Stalheim Hotel. The hotel parapet looks down over the great depths of the **Stalheim Gorge**, scene of one of the fiercest battles of World War II. A hairpin descent leads to the fjord and Gudvangen. From Gudvangen, the ferry travels through Norway's narrowest fjord, **Nærøyfjord**, (part of the Sognefjord) where the fjordsides are twice as high as the width of the water. Next comes the pretty fjord village of **Flåm** for lunch and afterwards the 40-minute panoramic journey up 2,800 ft (845 metres) of steep mountain gorge to **Myrdal**, stopping on the way to photograph the torrent of **Kjosfossen** and to pick up passengers and rucksacks at one or two of the tiny stations before reaching the main line train at Myrdal and thence back to Voss. But for the lack of an island or two, that day tour might well have the alternative title of "Hordaland in a Nutshell".

Left, midday snack at the Hangur ski centre. **Right**, Stallheim Gorge, scene of a fierce action during World War II.

BERGEN

There's always a sense of symmetry and order about a city built on hills. If it also stands on a peninsula and has a harbour at its heart, it is bound to be beautiful. **Bergen**, the capital of West Norway, has all these things. Built on seven hills, the city grew outwards from the coast and harbour in the quaintly-named Puddefjord and spread across the steep slopes and over the bridges that link islands and headlands.

The best place to get a feel of this natural shape is to take the funicular that climbs more than 1,000 ft (300 metres) in just eight minutes from the centre to **Fløyen**, high above the town. On the down journey, you seem to be tipping headfirst into the city—but Fløybanen, Scandinavia's first cable railway, has been running in perfect safety since 1918. At the top is the lovely old-fashioned building that houses **Fløyen Restaurant**, built in 1925, and the start of eight marked walking routes, the longest no more than around 2½ miles (4.2 km), though this does not mean they do not contain steep hills through woods and open moor.

A leisurely coffee or lunch on the verandah of Fløyen Restaurant gives a chance also to drink in the superb view over hundreds of islands, many with the small *hytter* (wooden cottages) and a couple of boats tied up to a landing stage that sums up a Norwegian's ideal summer. All around are mountains and hills that cradle the city— Damsgårdfjellet, Løvstakken, Sandviksfjellet, Rundemanen, Blåmanen, and the highest of the seven, Ulriken at around 2,000 ft (600 metres) where the cable car climbs slowly and carefully up its cable like a big red spider.

Trade and contact have made this city the most outgoing in Norway and given the Bergensere a jauntiness in their walk that hints at generations of sailors, quick wits, worldliness and a sense of their own worth. Bergensere are certain they are the best, secure in the knowledge that, although Oslo may now be the capital, it is historically a mere toddler compared with Bergen.

Olav Kyrre's city: King Olav Kyrre is credited with founding Bergen in 1070 at Torget, now the site of the daily fish, fruit and flower market. But it would be naive to believe that, long before, the perfect harbour and sheltered fjords were not a home for people who depended on the sea. During the 13th century, Bergen became the first capital of a united Norway, and a great ecclesiastical centre, with a cathedral, 20 churches and chapels, five monasteries and two hospitals for the poor—more ecclesiastical institutions than any Norwegian town of the time. Today it is the main city of Hordaland *kommune*.

Bergen lost its capital status to Oslo during the Middle Ages, but still dwarfed the new capital. In medieval times, it was the biggest city in the Nordic countries and, until 1830, the largest in Norway. Today, with a population exceeding 200,000, it is roughly half the size of Oslo.

Much of this early size and success

Preceding pages: Bergen harbour. Left, "Jacob" from Jacobsgården, a necessary identification when people could not read. Right, Fløibanen clambers up to Fløien, one of Bergen's seven hills.

came when Bergen was chosen as the hub of the medieval German Hanseatic League in the north. Their trading base on the north side of Vågen became the power house of all trade on the north-west Norwegian coast. But the Hansa began to grow too powerful all over Scandinavia and, at last, Norway broke the tie that kept the west in thraldom.

As in all wooden cities, fire has swept through Bergen on many occasions, often devastating it. The result is that the oldest surviving buildings are noticeably built of stone, and the present streets of Bergen, following the last dreadful fire in 1916 when a gale fanned the flames to an inferno, are wide and designed as fire breaks.

Resistance movement: During World War II, Bergen was a centre of the Resistance movement and many young people from the town took the perilous route out through the islands to Scotland. There they trained for resistance work and then smuggled themselves back to West Norway to become members of sabotage groups. The city still has an active Linge Club, survivors of the men who trained under Colonel Linge. The Theta Museum on Bryggen commemorates their exploits.

Yet the major disaster of this unhappy period came not directly from war but through accident caused by war. In 1944 a Dutch ammunition ship in the harbour blew up, damaging many of the oldest buildings on the northern promontory, including Håkonshallen and Rosenkrantztårnet. Anti-German feelings ran high at that time and, letting down his hair, an occasional Bergenser will still mutter that it was a pity it did not destroy the Tyskebryggen (German quay) of the Hansa, now tactfully abbreviated to Bryggen, and one of Bergen's historical gems.

Starting with the past: The earliest archaeological remains are in **Bryggens Museum**, past the Hansa houses on the north side of the harbour towards the end of the **Holmen** promontory, now extended by the quay for North Sea ferries. The museum is also the Erling Dekker Næss Institute for Medieval

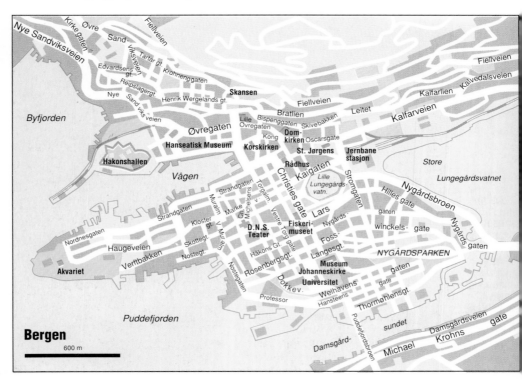

Archaeology and care has been taken to show the authentic remains uncovered by the archaeologists between 1955 and 1972. There are also many artefacts, and some sensitive recreations of medieval rooms, which made use of written sources to ensure accuracy. It all gives a picture of the time when Bergen was a small fishing and sailing community that clung to the shallow slopes above the shore.

Nearby is the oldest building still in use, **Mariakirken** (St Mary's Church) built in the early years of the 12th century and justly proud of its rich baroque pulpit. The only other medieval churches to survive periodic fires are the present **Domkirken** (Cathedral), once St Olav's but now a blend of many different periods, and **Korskirken** (Holy Cross), most of it now in the Renaissance style of the 17th century. The latter two are relatively close to the harbour and all three merit a visit.

Holmen was the site of **Bergenshus**, the old timber-built royal palace used when Bergen first became a capital. At a time of much building in the 13th century, it was converted to a fortified stronghold of stone, and the restored remains are close to where the original cathedral and bishop's residence stood. There are two particularly notable buildings. **Håkonshallen**, built by King Håkon Håkonsson between 1247 and 1261, was used for the wedding of King Magnus Lagabøte (the Lawmaker), who was Håkon's son and co-ruler. **Rosenkrantztårnet** was the work of a Danish governor of Bergenhus, Erik Rosenkrantz, who grafted it on to Håkon's original "Keep of the Sea".

Håkonshallen is the largest secular medieval building still standing in Norway. When both it and Rosenkrantztårnet were extensively damaged in the 1944 explosion, Norwegian historians took the opportunity to reconstruct them as closely to the originals as possible. Today, Håkonshallen makes a magnificent concert hall, with gallery and restaurant on the floor below, so that you can still see the massive pillars that hold the Great Hall, with its beauti-

Left, policemen patrolling Bryggen. Right, trolls guard the entrance to a souvenir shop.

ful modern tapestries. Rosenkrantz-tårnet is now a museum, with both permanent and special exhibitions. In both buildings, the remnants of different periods make it possible to trace something of the history in stone.

The Hansa: Guides from Bryggen Museum, often students, also conduct the tours through the row of Hansa houses that line **Bryggen**. These Hansa homes and warehouses were all built after the great Bergen fire of 1702, which destroyed many buildings, and are on the UNESCO World Heritage list. The Norwegians living in the early tenement communities had long been traders with many parts of the world and in summer Vågen was packed with ships of different nationalities. But, from the 14th century, the German merchants steadily moved in to monopolise trade in Bergen and the north.

One key to understanding the Hansa way of life is a visit to the **Hanseatic Museum**, furnished in the style of the time when the merchant had his accounting room within the main office on the first floor. This small room enabled him to keep an eye on the liquor room next door. The adjoining room, decorated with a Royal Cod, distinguished by a bump on its head and said to bring luck, served as dining and sitting room for merchants and apprentices. On the floor above are the apprentices' tiny box beds, one above the other. Although apprentices were merchants' sons, sent to learn their business with a colleague, they were locked into their tiny "prisons" each night.

Beer jugs and bibles: As a fire precaution—all too often in vain—no heating was allowed in these Hansa houses and the Germans must have suffered torments of cold in the biting damp of a Bergen winter. No wonder that **Schøtstuene**, the assembly rooms nearby, were so popular during winter when trade was slack and few ships in the harbour. The long central table held both beer jugs and the Bible, exemplifying the two religions of the Hansa. In a drawer was the cane used to discipline the apprentices who had their schooling

Boats line up at Bergen's busy harbour.

there. On one wall, written in German, are the "rules of the club". The names of offenders were listed on a blackboard until a demonstration of good behaviour merited their erasure.

Here was the centre of the privileged Hansa life. In the end, however, privilege led to its downfall because of local resentment that the Germans did not have to join the army and evaded some Norwegian taxes. More important for Norway was the stranglehold that the Hansa merchants kept on trade. On present-day festive occasions, Schøtstuene are still used for their original purpose as a meeting place.

At Elsesro, further out along the coast road, past Bergenshus and the North Sea quay, is **Gamle Bergen** (Old Bergen), the obligatory open-air museum beloved of Scandinavia. Here there are a collection of 35 wooden buildings which date from Bergen in the 18th and 19th centuries, the interiors decorated to show different styles. Along the cobbled streets, guides in traditional red calf-length costumes and black shawls lead tours which range from the French Empire splendour of the official's drawing room to the tiny house, just living-room and kitchen, where the seamstress plied her diligent needle in the 1860s. Nearby is **Sandvik Sjøbad**, a popular sea-bathing area, which looks out over Byfjorden to the city. You can reach Gamle Bergen by buses 1 or 9 from the centre.

Tall ship: Back along Vågen, a short ferry trip from below Rosenkrantztårnet to the **Nordnes** peninsula gives a good opportunity to view the beautiful lines of the sailing ship *Lehmkuhl*, which trains youngsters in sailing techniques and gleams with polished brass. A short walk towards Nordnes point reveals another castle, **Fredriksborg**, and further on is the popular **Nordnes Sjøbad** (bathing place) which includes a heated outdoor pool.

If the weather is unkind, you are within easy reach of the **Bergen Aquarium**, one of Europe's best collections. Seals and penguins swim and dive, or lounge on rocks around outdoor

pools, and the main hall has nine tanks, some 5 ft (1.5 metres) deep, which gives the feeling of having dipped below the surface of the sea. (From Bergen centre take bus 4.)

Morning must: Bergen's fish market is bright with flowers, house plants and fruits early each weekday morning. Middle-aged women, elegant even at that time, engage the fishermen in serious conversation about the day's catch, watched by an interested circle, and the stalls sell *gravlaks* (cured salmon) and other delights to take home. This busy scene is the heart of Bergen, where there is always something going on and where people linger to watch the transactions or peer into the boats tied up at the quay after a night's fishing. Nearby are a couple of good fish restaurants, one where those with the stomach for it can select their own supper from the fish swimming peacefully in a tank.

Not far up the hill from the fish market in another old part of the city is **Gamle Rådhuset**, the **Old Town Hall**. Built as a private house in 1558, it was presented to the town in 1562 and served the city for several centuries until, in 1974, it was replaced by the inelegant highrise modern block not far away. Another attractive old building in the area is the **Hotel Victoria**, once an old inn and now a smallish, comfortable city hotel that costs a little less than some of the bigger ones.

Also not far away from the fish market is another square where people like to linger, **Torgalmenningen**, with many of the best shops in the city. The square also holds the **Sailors' Monument**. Carved figures march round the base of this memorial dedicated to all Norwegian sailors who lost their lives at sea. Important also for visitors is the town's main tourist information centre, which has leaflets with details of places and events in and around the city, an accommodation service, booking facilities for activities and tours, and a helpful staff to answer queries. From the square you board Bergen's latest innovation, the **Bergen Express**, a road train which tours the centre, the Fish Market and along Bryggen.

Tour buses offer another quick overview of the town as a guide to what to return to later. They leave from beside the Hotel Norge, one of Bergen's oldest and best-loved hotels just across from Torgalmenningen. Another introduction to this city of the sea is a harbour cruise on the motor cruiser *White Lady*, which also provides fjord tours.

Museum cluster: Bergen is also a good walking city and, if you fix your eye on the tall steeple of **Johanneskirken**, a two-minute walk up Vest Torggate from Torgalmenningen takes you to the top of **Sydneshaugen**, near the university area and a clutch of museums— the **Naturhistorisk Museum** (Natural History) standing in a fine botanic garden, the **Historisk Museum**, and the **Bergen Sjøfartsmuseum** (Maritime) which traces the history of this seafaring area from the Old Norse period to the present day.

Not far from these, near the Student Centre, is **Bergen Teatermuseum**. This was once the university area, though today much of the university has

Carnival in Bergen.

moved to the northern part of the city at Helleveien. Nevertheless, the old building which housed the Bergen Museum remains and is now part of the university. Here the famous northern explorer Fridtjof Nansen spent his early career, and it was also a base for the father of weather forecasting, Vilhelm Bjerknes.

Famous names: It is not surprising that this lively city, with its close European links, should have been the birthplace of many famous people. It was also a strong base for 19th-century nationalism which culminated in 1905 in Norway's separation from Sweden and its complete independence for the first time in 500 years. The Prime Minister who led Norway then was Christian Michelsen, whose home at **Gamlehaugen** at Fjøsanger (near the happily titled southern suburb of Paradis) is now the residence of the King when he is in Bergen.

Nationalism had strong roots in the 19th-century revival of Norwegian culture, led by the playwright Henrik Ibsen, the violinist Ole Bull, the com-

poser Edvard Grieg, and writers like Bjørnstjerne Bjørnson. Though Ibsen and Bjørnson were not natives of West Norway, Bjørnson was for a time director of Bergen's **Den Nationale Scene** (The National Theatre) founded by Ole Bull in 1850, and Bjørnson's statue stands on the steps of the theatre.

The virtuoso violinist Ole Bull made his debut with the Paris Opera Orchestra at the age of 25 and continued to tour Europe and the United States for the next 45 years. His contribution to Norwegian culture also came through his wanderings in the villages of West Norway and the great Jotunheim mountain plateau east of the fjord country. Here he collected many old folk melodies which were played on the Hardanger fiddle, the area's traditional instrument. Later, Grieg transcribed some of these folk tunes for piano, saving them from being lost.

Musical homes: Every year, thousands of visitors come to Grieg's summer home at **Troldhaugen**, on a high point above the fjord. Here Grieg also had a

hytte where he could find peace to compose. The house is just as Grieg left it; his manuscripts are scattered around and even his piano is in working order in the comfortable drawing room. In the past, this room was the venue for many musical evenings; today, if you are lucky, the curator will play some Grieg music on it. The size of the room inevitably limited the possibilities and in 1985 Troldhaugen opened a special **Chamber Music Hall**, seating 200, built into the hillside so that it is barely visible among the tall trees. The villa is still used for more intimate recitals.

Troldhaugen is a wonderful setting for a concert and a continuation of the summer evening tradition when Grieg and his wife, Nina Hagerup, a Danish singer, would entertain their friends in the quiet garden outside the drawing room. (Any bus for the Fana district goes to Hopsbroen, then a 15-minute walk leads to Troldhaugen; many city excursions also include Troldhaugen.)

Ole Bull built his home on the island of **Lysøen** in 1873, when his fame had long spread throughout and beyond Norway. Bull turned the whole island into a park with woodland and walking routes and the house itself is unlike any other in the country. Made of traditional Norwegian wood, the decorated and screened balcony and the pointed arches of the windows on the front of this timber building have an almost Moorish flavour, and the tower topped by a minaret is reminiscent of St Basil's in Moscow's Red Square. His American descendants long preserved the property and have now donated it to the Society of Ancient Norwegian Monuments. By bus from Bergen takes around 50 minutes (gate 20 at the bus station on the bus marked Lysefjordruta). It is a good idea to combine the visit to Lysøen with a stop on the way at **Lysekloster**, the ruins of a 12th-century Cistercian abbey, which was a daughter monastery of Fountains Abbey in Yorkshire, England.

Artistic legacy: Whether as a result of the fame of people such as Bull, Grieg and the painter J.C. Dahl or not, Bergen

The long view from Fløien.

has a lively artistic and cultural life. The **Bergen International Festival of Music**, held each May and early June, attracts international artistes and thousands of visitors. At the end of the 1970s, the Festival led to the building of a new concert hall, **Grieghallen**, with marvellous acoustics which may or may not owe their quality to its strange architecture. For the outside of the building is remarkably like that of a concert grand piano, perhaps as a tribute to the composer whose name it bears. This is the heart of the 12-day festival but the whole city is involved, with events in Håkonshallen, Troldhaugen, Lysøen, and the old Mariakirken.

Bergen also has several strong art collections, mostly centred on **Lille Lungegårdsvann**, the octagonal lake in the middle of the park, not far from the statues of Edvard Grieg, and of Ole Bull playing his violin, and near Grieghallen. Here are the **Municipal Art Gallery**, with a large collection of Norwegian painting over the past 150 years, the **Rasmus Meyer's Collection** which also specialises in Norwegian paintings with many by Edvard Munch, and the **Stenersen's Collection**, which has some marvellous works by Munch and also by Picasso and Klee. Bergen, like many Scandinavian cities, is also strong in private galleries, many of which specialise in modern painting.

Shops often offer opportunities to see examples of more homely objects by specialising in traditional and modern crafts. Best known is Husfliden, which has examples of the richly decorated Norwegian costumes (different for each area), handknitting and woven textiles, brass and woodwork, including the famous and decorative rose painting on bowls and plates. Norwegian glass is also beautiful and **Irgens** in Markveien and **Bergens Glasmagasin** are good stockists. The jeweller Magnus Aase specialises in silver and gold and beautiful enamelled silverwork. Bergen's biggest department store, **Sundt**, in Torgalmenningen offers almost everything and the three newest shopping malls, **Bystasjonen**, **Kløverhuset** and

A concert in the ornate music hall of Ole Bull's house on Lysøen.

Galleriet, are happy hunting grounds for gifts to take home, with places to rest your feet over a coffee.

To show Norwegian traditions in action, Bergen has summer displays mid-June to late August. The Bryggens Museum makes an appropriate background for the **Bjørgvin Regional Folk-dancing Group** with traditional folk dances and music from rural Norway. A pleasant way to spend a Sunday evening is the **Hotel Norge's** folklore entertainment but the nearest to the real thing is **Fana Folklore**, in the district of Fana to the south. This is designed as a country wedding with typical Norwegian food, such as *rømmegraut*, a rich celebration "porridge" which bears little resemblance to the breakfast variety, cured mutton and sausage, flat bread and other dishes of the past.

By bus, you travel first to **Fana Kirken**, the 800-year-old church, worth a day visit in its own right, for a short recital of old hymns and old melodies by the organist; then on to **Rambergstunet**, and a traditional welcome

by the *lur*, a folk instrument something like a coaching horn, and then to the long trestle tables for the wedding fare, accompanied by folk dancing displays where the dancers weave and jump in the prescribed steps that almost died out during the 19th century. Later, guests get a chance to join in and there are also displays by children and songs accompanied by one of Norway's most haunting musical instruments, the *langleik*, a one-string zither traditionally used to accompany songs. You return to Bergen full of good food and memories of colour and music.

Outdoor city: Naturally the most popular pastime in this city of the sea and fjord is sailing. Next come sea-fishing and swimming. There are plenty of opportunities to be active in all three, or you could simply take a fjord cruise, sometimes lasting more than a day. The hills above Bergen, just 10 minutes away from the centre by the Fløyenbane, are ideal for walking, and **Sandviken Ridesenter**, not far from the Gamle Bergen museum, has riding tours both long and short. There is tennis, both indoor and out. For something different, try an evening at the trotting course at **Bergen Travpark**, at Åsane, around 10 miles (16 km) from the city. This is a peculiarly Scandinavian sport and excitement is electric as the horses and their drivers race round the track.

Apart from the gardens at Troldhaugen and Lysøen, the **Norwegian Arboretum** at Milde, founded in 1971, is busily planting up shrubs and trees from many parts of the world, and this pretty area along the shore has rocky gorges, hills, and a small lake. The Fanafjord also provides good swimming. (By bus to Mildevågen, then a 15-minute walk in an area that looks out to islands and sea.)

Too many people make the mistake of allowing only a day or even half a day for Bergen at the start and end of a visit to the western fjords, which doesn't give the city a chance. Much better to use it as a base for a fjord holiday and combine the delights of cosmopolitan, outgoing, outdoor Bergen with the splendid scenery of the fjords.

Left, Ole Bull nicknamed his house "The Little Alhambra". **Right**, old houses in the maze of narrow lanes behind Bryggen.

THE WORLD'S MOST BEAUTIFUL VOYAGE

The ship slips out of Bergen's hill-ringed harbour at 10 p.m., day in, day out, all year round. In winter, it has been dark for hours and passengers linger no longer than to wave good-bye to the lights of the city before they scuttle below for the warmth of saloon and cabin. In summer, it is a different matter: the deck is crowded as the big steamer sweeps out towards the fjord, leaving behind Håkonshallen, and Rosenkrantztårnet and the small German houses where the Hansa merchants once lived and traded.

The coastal express heads north through Byfjorden and Hjeltefjorden, past the islands of Askøy and Holsnøy for the open sea, at the start of a trip of 1,250 nautical miles round North Cape to Kirkenes near the Soviet border, crossing the Arctic Circle.

Nowadays, this coastal voyage has become one of the most popular journeys for visitors, but it is much more to the Norwegians themselves. From earliest days, this long and beautiful coast has been the easiest link in Norway for communication and trade so that ties between communities hundreds of miles apart could be close; the Western and Northern Norwegians once regarded Scotland and Iceland as being easier to reach than their own southeast region around present-day Oslo.

In winter it was the only way to travel because the Gulf Stream kept, and still keeps, the seaways open—even when the temperature is minus $1\,^{\circ}$C (30° F) on shore. Even today, when the mountains are impassable and the fjords frozen, villages can be completely isolated except by air or on skis.

The swift route: The first steamship, the *Prinds Gustav*, set out from Trondheim to Tromsø in 1838. In time, other steamers also began to ply between the coastal towns and in 1893 a local steamship company, Vesteraalens Dampskibsselskab, opened the Hurtigrute (literally "swift route") between Trondheim and Hammerfest, in the far north-west and still a main stop for the ships today. As the line extended to Bergen and Kirkenes, several ship-owners became involved and five companies now run 11 ships for a round-trip that takes 12 days from Bergen to Bergen.

The Hurtigrute makes 36 stops at ports along this ever-changing coast, some at places no bigger than a handful of houses around the harbour, with local people waiting on the quayside to collect a car or a container, to greet friends who have hopped a short distance between small towns where the alternative is a long difficult drive, or just as a social occasion where locals wave to the passengers looking down from the rails when the stop is too short to go ashore.

Part of the charm is watching a working ship going about its business: the efficient mooring as the crew shout down to the dockers, the crane winching over a tractor which has been chained fast to the deck during the voyage, and the nervous face of its owner as a car is winched up.

The first stop for going ashore is

Ålesund, one of the three Møre towns. It has all the natural design of a town built round a harbour and, because of a disastrous fire in 1904 when 10,000 lost their homes, it was rebuilt all of a piece, with the wooden houses in an Art Nouveau style, carefully preserved and painted in brilliant colours.

The next main stop is Trondheim, further up a magnificent coast which boasts 87 peaks, snow-capped for much of the year. When it was the ancient capital, Trondheim was called Nidaros, and Nidaros Cathedral is a national shrine; it holds the Royal regalia and a memorial to King Olav Haraldson, killed at the battle of Stiklestad, north of Trondheim, who became St Olav the Holy. The Trondheim stop is long enough for a morning tour of this historic city, with its busy harbours and bays and wide streets lined with small wooden houses and old warehouses, which have now become much sought-after dwelling houses.

Early next morning, as the ship steams north again, it crosses the Arctic Circle and sails into "the land of the midnight sun".

This used to be Norway's great tourist slogan until an inconvenient honesty forced Norwegians to drop it because not all Norway enjoys midnight sun! But, as far north as this, in summer there is no doubt about the title or the fact that you can stand on deck at midnight and admire the coast running alongside the ship. On the way south, at the Arctic Circle crossing, King Neptune joins the celebrations on deck to award Arctic Circle certificates.

Hamsun's Nordland: Into the Lofoten Islands, the ship is now in Nordland, the territory of one of Norway's most famous writers, Knut Hamsun. Hamsun named the old trading centre of Kjerringø "Sirilund" in his novels, which describe the surprisingly outward-looking lives of these northern fishing and trading families around the turn of the century. A Hamsun novel (particularly *The Wayfarers*) is a good accompaniment to a voyage that illuminates his own characters and their thinking, and

The ship hug the dramatic northern coastline.

gives an insight into life in these northern lands today.

On deck, as the coastal steamer weaves in and out of the islands, bird-watchers find it difficult to go below even to eat or sleep, in case they miss one of the numerous sea-bird colonies, the congregations of colourful exotic ducks in winter harbours and, particularly, the comical little puffins in their hundreds of thousands.

The ship makes a brief summer detour into the Trollfjord, something no big cruise liner could do because the sheer faces of rock and scree press close in this narrow fjord. This, too, calls for a celebration and the ship's chef serves a special Trollfjord soup to the accompaniment of Grieg's most troll-like music and the arrival of a troll to delight the passengers.

Fancy dress party in summer, when the Hurtigrute takes on a cruising air.

In winter, ice makes entry impossible, but against that is the endless fascination of the ever-changing Northern Lights—sometimes white spears, at others a brilliant blue-green aura across the sky, or a multi-coloured spectacular that gleams and sparkles. The high mountains of the fjord country further south have disappeared by now but, during the brief light of a winter day, the low slanting sun picks out the white cones of snow-covered hills, like raspberry sauce topping an ice cream.

Through the seasons: In spring and autumn, the 12-day journey feel like a voyage through the seasons. Leave Bergen in May, when the fjord valleys are brilliant with blossom, and the hills and mountains of the north will still be white as snow flurries scurry across the fjords and mountains.

The return journey is the reverse. Just as the north is beginning to slip out of its winter grip, the swift Norwegian summer marches north and will have already reached Bergen and the mountains around it, and it could be warm enough to lie out in a sheltered corner of the deck as the ship nears the end of its long journey.

The northern city of Tromsø, set on an island in a rugged landscape, has the world's northernmost university, and

gets the nickname the "Paris of the North" because of its numerous restaurants and cafés. The city is a base for scientists at a Polar institute, who study the Polar regions and also as a centre for the Arctic fleets and expeditions.

Returning south to Tromsø in summer, there is time for a midnight excursion by cable car to the summit of Mount Stornsteinen. At 1,350 ft (410 metres) above the sea below, there is a wonderful view of coast and country.

Into Finnmark the ship sails past a coast of scoured hills and watercourses with forests along the valleys, to Hammerfest, Norway's most northerly town. In summer, the coastal express, working ship or not, makes a concession here and slips through the Margerøy Sound to Honningsvåg and the start of an excursion by coach to Nordkapp, North Cape. This is one of the highlights of any visit to Norway.

North Cape also marks a change of direction to the east across the very top of Norway on the way to Kirkenes, 3 miles (5 km) from the Soviet border, a coast where the place names begin to show Sami and Finnish origins. Kirkenes itself is a mining town by the river Pasvikelva, in a strange no-man's land between East and West, which is also influenced by the Sami culture. There is a coach expedition to the border, and long before *glasnost* and the revolutionary changes in Eastern Europe, the two cultures met here with cross-border contacts and visits.

Nowhere missed: On the way south again, the ship stops by day at the places it visited when northbound passengers were fast asleep below decks, so nowhere is missed. Nor is it generally a rough voyage: the steamer mostly hugs the coast or weaves in and out of islands that shelter the ship from the excesses of the Atlantic Ocean and the Norwegian Sea, even in the far north.

In the most popular summer months the ship takes on some of the trimmings of a cruise ship with dancing, film shows, and cruise guides to point out the sights in good time and organise excursions ashore. But this coastal steamer is always a working ship and part of the charm out of season is that it reverts to its traditional role of carrying westcoast Norwegians, who treat it as a bus, for business and pleasure. As they come on board, they pile their rucksacks on to the luggage racks near the gangway entrance, spend a few hours on board, play cards or music, talk among themselves and to the crew as people they already know, and step off with no more than a casual wave.

Although the network of small aircraft linking scattered communities has done much to reduce this traffic, the coastal steamer is still there when airports are closed and roads blocked. For supplies and deliveries to distant industries and traders, ships are invaluable and can carry things too big for the plane. Whether one sits quietly in the saloon in winter, or stands at the rails protected against the cold by boots, gloves, hat and duvet coat, to watch all this activity is to feel close to a way of life that, for all its modern equipment and swift communications, still retains much of the past.

Left, passengers leave a winter steamer at Tromsø. Right, sunbathing even further north in the Arctic Sea near Vadsø.

FROM SOGN TO NORDFJORD

From a seat in one of the small planes that somehow contrive to land on the narrow strips along the fjords or the tiny green patches between the mountains, it looks an impossible territory. Yet the land that runs from Sognefjorden in the south to Nordfjorden to the north has all the features that made Norway famous: the world's longest and deepest fjord, Europe's largest glacier and its deepest lake, and Jotunheimen, Scandinavia's greatest mountain massif.

The large *fylke* (county) of Sogn and Fjordane lies between a zigzag coastline drawn by the waters of the North Sea and the start of Jotunheimen's heights. Narrow fingers of water push inland from the main fjords to reach far into the mountains, and waterfalls tumble hundreds of feet into the fjord below. The force of all this water feeds powerful hydro-electric power stations, tucked away inside the mountains, which send electricity as far as Oslo and West Germany. Aluminium plants also make use of the spouting waterfalls to generate power and, among other things, produce the road barriers for most of Europe's mountain roads.

In the past, fjord, mountain and valley could be near impassable in winter. Today, though journeys often take longer than elsewhere, travel is made easier by a web of ferries and boats, and by roads with tunnels and bridges that climb up and down to many of the highest summits and remotest valleys. From Bergen, an express boat (a catamaran with water jet engine) reaches the furthest point of the fjord at Årdal, half way to Sweden, and many people come to Sogn as part of a fjord cruise.

Deepest and longest: At 120 miles (200 km) and 4,260 ft (1,300 metres) the **Sognefjord** is unmatched anywhere in the world. After British visitors discovered it in the 19th century, royalty too endorsed the fjord's delights, As Crown Prince, Edward VII came over from Britain as early as 1898, and the German Kaiser Wilhelm II was on summer holiday in Sogn when he learned of the assassination of the Archduke at Sarajevo which triggered World War I.

In spring, the fjord is pink and white when this apparently ungrateful soil puts up umbrellas of fruit blossom in orchards and gardens. In the warm summer days, far above the fjord, cattle and sheep cling to the small grass plateaux, the mountain farms or *seter* where once women and young girls spent the summer to milk their cows and make cheese, a time of ease and enjoyment. The majority of the 100,000 people in the county still make their living by farming or fishing, forestry and fruit growing.

On both sides of the fjord small villages cling to every square foot of land, each with its own atmosphere. **Balestrand** has been a favourite since the 19th century and has an English church, **St Olav's**, founded towards the end of the 19th century by one of those fearless Victorian Englishwomen who travelled the world.

German artists from the Düsseldorf

Academy were also quick to appreciate the beauty of Sognefjord and built Swiss-style houses, decorated with dragon heads in deference to their hosts' Viking past, to add to the charm of this picturesque village. The area is renowned for a mild climate and across a small neck of water at **Dragsvik**, a local pastor-botanist planted exotic trees which thrive in the sheltered bay.

A narrow side-fjord leads to the little community of **Fjærland**, reached by ferry or car, a dairy farming centre near the two southernmost offshoots of the great Jostedal glacier. In summer, local guides lead tours and glacier exploration courses from here and many other villages to different offshoots of the glacier. The **Gaular mountains** towards Sunnfjord in the north offer wonderful mountain walking in an area filled with interesting plants and birds.

The ferry from Dragsvik runs to **Vangsnes** on the south side and, from there, go a few miles south to admire **Vik** and the 12th-century **Hopperstad Stave Church**, with dragon heads on the outside and rich decorations within. Vik also has the oldest Norwegian stone church, **Hove Church**, only 20 years younger than Hopperstad. On the way back, stop at the statue of the Norwegian Viking hero, **Fridtjof**, a gift from Kaiser Wilhelm II in 1913.

Going east from Balestrand, a short crossing takes you to **Hella** and past the glistening arc of **Kvinnfoss** (Lady's Waterfall) close to the main road. At the head of the fjord, **Sogndal** is the centre for trade and administration in an area of forestry and farming. The pretty little town has a population of around 6,000, which swells considerably during term time because it is also a centre for education, with colleges at university level and Norway's oldest folk high school. To the north, 500 people live in farms strung out along Sognadalen's narrow lake; it is a popular walking spot in summer and for skiing in winter.

Kaupanger Stave Church is the biggest in Sogn. Built towards the end of the 12th century, its plain dark wood exterior has been restored to its early

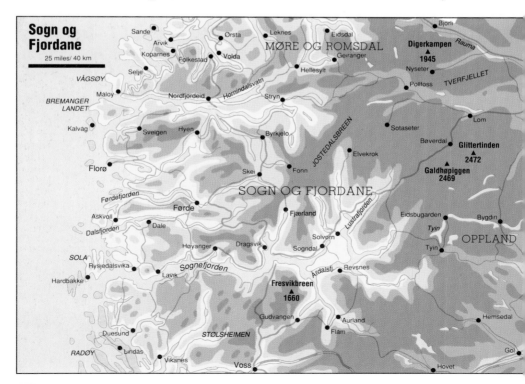

form, and it is a lovely place to listen to the organist's summer recitals. **Sogn Folk Museum** (the Heibergske Collection) is one of Norway's oldest and biggest folk museums, founded in 1909 by the then landowner Gert F. Heiberg as a living museum with animals, plus 32 houses and farm buildings to show how people lived in Sogn from around 1500 right up to the present. Best of all, the museum is used as a setting for folk music and dancing.

Standing tall beside the fjord at **Nordnes** is a stone to mark the **Battle of Fimreite** in June 1184. That was when King Sverre and his peasant Birkebeiner (called Birchlegs from their birch-bark boots) defeated King Magnus Erlingsson and the nobility, a turning point in Norwegian democracy.

Cool, green waters: In **Luster**, behind Sogndal, is another of Sogn's bumper crop of stave churches: **Urnes** is thought to be the oldest in Norway and is linked with the coming of Christianity. Also within easy reach is yet another icy tongue from Josterdal glacier, called **Nigardsbreen**, where one of the delights is a boat trip over the ice-cold, green waters of a glacier lake. South of Sogndal, Sognefjord ends in the two most easterly fjords leading to **Årdal** and **Lærdal**, lovely valleys with mountain farms, walking and climbing, or fishing in high-level lakes and streams.

Aurland, **Flåm**, and **Gudvangen** lie along the inmost recesses of the fjord, which stretch south from the main fjord like an upside-down letter "Y". **Nærøyfjord** to the west is the narrowest in Europe, and both provide the most dramatic fjord cruise in West Norway, the mountains pressing so close that you wonder if the boat will squeeze through.

The 6-mile (10-km) mountain railway from **Flåm** up to **Myrdal** (on the main line between Oslo and Bergen) is Norway's most remarkable, spiralling up the steep mountain gorge, sometimes disappearing under the snow covers that protect the line in winter, or stopping to admire or photograph a waterfall. (See *page 242*.)

The coast: The best way to get a view

Children brave the water of the Sognfjord.

of **Sunnfjord's** hundreds of islands, the bulk of the county's chain, is from the high peaks in the east, though the coast itself is by no means all flat. **Bleia** rises straight from the side of the Førdefjord to more than 4,300 ft (1,310 metres), the summit of the **Sunnfjord Alps**, and many of the islands have high peaks. These islands stretch the length of the coast, from Fensfjord and the island of **Sandøy**, north to **Vestkapp** (West Cape) where the Hurtigrute (coastal steamer) turns northeast to its next stop at Ålesund.

It's an odd thought that **Florø**, the only community in this large county big enough to be called a town, should lie on the remote edge of the sea, but not so strange when you remember that Norway has always depended on the sea for food, trade and transport. This most westerly town had its birth in the herring industry which flourished in the middle of the 19th century. Since then, its prosperity has swung up and down like the waves, but still depends on the sea for fish—nowadays often fish-farming—

and fish processing. Oil and gas fields away to the west have, nevertheless, turned Florø into an oil centre, and visitors can see both industries at work.

All along the coast, people own boats. Over 1,000 pleasure craft are registered in Florø, enough to carry the whole population. Every family has a favourite bathing place or small island for fishing and picnicking, and midsummer is a time of great celebration. The sea eagle breeds in this area, probably the furthest coastal point south where this magnificent predator builds its nest.

Offshore sights: There are many places to see—rock carvings at **Ausevik**, southeast of Florø; the nearby island of **Svanøy** has the ancient stone cross of Saint Olav, covered in runic inscriptions, a manor with an old garden and magnificent trees; there is a Romanesque medieval church on **Kinnøy**, where a special play, *The Song from the Deep*, is performed by the county theatre group and local people, and draws thousands to the island each June.

Further south, in the mouth of the Sognfjord, are the islands of **Sula** and **Ytre Sula**, surrounded by hundreds of islets, with so many bays, inlets and promontories that it is impossible for anywhere to be crowded.

At the opposite end on the island of **Bremanger** at the Nordfjord's mouth, the **Vingen carvings** are even older than Ausvika's, and show the lives of the fishing-settlers of Nordfjord. To the north, the village of **Måløy** on **Vågsøy** is one of Norway's largest fishing and trading ports, and **Raudeberg** salts and dries fish of all kinds. But size is relative, and industry does nothing to detract from the rural quietness of this hilly island which rises up some 2,000 ft (610 metres) at **Brurahornet**.

North of Vågsøy and Raudeberg is **Silda**, a tiny island for sea-anglers, sports divers and birdwatchers. A good anchorage for setting off to the waters of Stadhavet to the west, Silda has only 80 inhabitants, and no cars. On an islet in the middle of the harbour, a restored fish salting works serves a feast of seafoods.

Windy West Cape: The island of **Selje** nearby holds the medieval ruins of St

The Viking *knarr* (freighter) *Saga Siglar* in Sognefjord just before it left for a two-year round-the-world voyage.

Sunniva Monastery. On the northernmost peninsula is **Vestkapp** (West Cape) where winds blow fierce in your face and the nearest land is the Shetland Isles off the north of Scotland. With good binoculars, the locals say you can see the oil rigs to the west and the Shetland boathouses standing open; but more often the headland is wild and the waves stormy.

Away from Sunnfjord's coast, smaller fjords splay out into farm and moorland so that you are never far from the sea. They lead to narrow lakes between the mountains, and penetrate the foothills of the high tops in the east. Rivers such as the **Gaula** and **Nausta** are excellent for salmon and trout, and after leaving **Jølstravatnet** (lake) underneath **Grovebreen** (glacier) the **Jølstra**, said to be one of the best salmon rivers, drops hundreds of feet by the time it reaches **Førde** at the fjord mouth. Here you find the main **Sunnfjord Museum**, a collection of 17 old buildings, some reconstructed as a farmstead from around 1850.

On the south side of Jølstravatnet, you come to **Astruptunet** (the Astrup farm), home of Nikolai Astrup, who lived from 1880 to 1928 and was considered the most typical of all West-Norwegian painters because he found themes in his own surroundings. Astruptunet is just as it was during the painter's life, though the barn has been replaced by a new art gallery with a permanent exhibition. A couple of miles to the west is another farm, **Midttunet**, a typical old collection of 12 protected buildings, which depict life 200 years ago in this still largely rural community.

From Jølstravatnet, it is easy to reach **Grovebreen** (glacier), some 5,400 ft (1,650 metres) high, and **Haukedalsvatn** to the south is quite close to the far side of the glacier. Walkers can reach the great icefields of the Josterdal Glacier. A series of valleys, lakes and fjords links these high plateaux into the Nordfjord system to the north.

North to Nordfjord: The **Nordfjord** is 60 miles (100 km) shorter than the

By stolkjærrer to visit the Briksdal Glacier.

Sognefjord, but with so many side fjords, lakes and valleys, that it is easy to get into the mountains where reindeer roam, or make the journey up the **Briksdal Glacier**, one of the most beautiful in the fjord country. Even better is that you can climb up to the base of the glacier in the two-wheeled farm carriages, *stolkjerrer*, pulled by small sturdy, cream-coloured Norwegian horses (*fjording*).

The traditional home of the *fjording* is the **Eid** district, centred around **Nordfjordeid**, where the Nordfjord proper has already divided itself into **Eidsfjorden** and **Isefjorden**. Eid is also famous for **Firdariket**, the seat of the last Viking chief, and the town has traditional white-painted buildings. The church, from 1849, is decorated with beautiful rose painting. Around the 1780s, the rural chief magistrate lived in a large farm nearby, which now holds the **Leikvin Gallery** and a museum.

Eight miles (12 km) to the east, the road reaches **Hornindalsvatnet**, formed thousands of years ago when water flooded the valleys. The Ice Age retreated to make it the deepest lake in Europe (1,680 ft/514 metres). The lake valley leads to the biggest community, **Grodås**, where the ground begins to climb. This was the traditional inland tourist route to Nordfjord.

Hornindal has long traditions in handicrafts and folk music, and musicians wear the black breeches, or the long black skirt and green bodice of the area. The most famous artist was Anders Svor, first a wood carver and then, after a time at the Copenhagen Academy of Art, a sculptor who won the gold medal in Berlin in 1891. The **Anders Svor Museum**, opened in 1953, holds 450 sculptures. Others appear all over Norway and abroad.

Fur-breeding: To the south, **Gloppenfjorden** ends at **Sandane**, the main town of Gloppen, the biggest farming district in the whole county and also a large fur-breeding centre. The **Nordfjord Folk Museum** started in 1920 with five turf-roofed houses. It now has 32, including several different

Sunset lights up the slopes of Sognefjell.

types, and barns, cowsheds and a mountain *seter*. At the fjordside is a 100-year-old sailing barge, *Holvik-jekta*, the last of the traditional freighters that served coast and fjord.

There is also a fine adventure centre, **Gloppen Adventure**, which offers a week's programme of riding, canoeing, windsurfing, mountain and glacier walking, mountain cycling, special canoe and glacier tours, and sight-seeing to various beauty spots. Several similar centres offer adventure and activity holidays in Nordfjord.

But to ski in summer you need to go to the Inner Nordfjord, where the fjord system ends at **Stryn**, **Loen** and **Olden**, the start of three spectacular valleys stretching up to the northwest edges of the Jostedal Glacier. Nowadays, three tunnels out of the Stryn valley cut right through the mountain to the renowned Geirangerfjord to the north.

Stryn is famous for summer-skiing on the northeast of **Strynsvatn**, where the ground rises to the **Tystigbreen** (glacier). Until you watch, it is hard to imagine skiers in swimsuits or shorts and teeshirts with Caribbean deep tans, but there they are enjoying every moment. The ski centre has a slalom ski school which also teaches the Telemark technique, lifts, restaurant, ski hire, and **Snowland**, a play centre for children. It is open from June to September.

Oldendalen is the route to the Briksdal Glacier, from the Briksdalsbreen Fjellstove by horse-carriage or foot and then a half-hour walk to the great cascade of ice which hangs above the ice flows and the green waters of the glacier lake. Small birds flutter over the water and, in olden times, farmers from eastern Norway drove their cattle over these great icefields down into the kindlier valleys of the west.

The county of Sogn og Fjordane offers fresh air and freedom and, whether it be island, coast, fjord, upland or mountain, the outdoor life is superb. In every area, *hytter* and campsites or the mountain huts of **Den Norske Turistforeningen** make fine holiday homes for independent travellers.

The sturdy fjord horse, the *fjording*, typical of the area.

MØRE AND ROMSDAL

For nearly a century the coastal steamers of the Hurtigrute have called at Ålesund, Molde and Kristiansund along the sea route that leads to Trondheim and the north. This jagged coastline is 3,750 miles (6,000 km) long and more than 10 percent of the *fylke's* (county's) population lives on islands. It's scarcely surprising then to learn that, even today, the sea is still the great provider for Møre and Romsdal. Apart from fish, prospecting and providing for the oil industry are important activities and North Sea oil and gas are likely to become even more significant as Norway seeks new fields.

Looking at the jumble of coastline, islands and fjord mouths on a map, it is sometimes hard to distinguish where sea and islands end and fjord and mainland begin. Yet move inland and half the area lies above 1,800 ft (600 metres). In the southeast the highest peaks reach over 6,000 ft (1,800–1,900 metres). The county is divided into three *kommuner* (regions): Sunnmøre, Romsdal, and Nordmøre of which the main centres are Ålesund, Molde and Kristiansund.

Sea trade has always been important and, from the Middle Ages, the accolade for a settlement was to be given market (*kaupang*) status. At that time there were two: Borgundkaupangen, only 3 miles (5 km) from the centre of Ålesund, in Sunnmøre; and Veøykaupangen, in Romsdal. Both provided trading centres for north-south and east-west routes on sea and land.

Rare harmony: Ålesund is Norway's largest fishing town but best known for its Art Nouveau architecture, built in 1904 after the Great Fire which destroyed the centre. First to the rescue came the Norvegophile, Kaiser Wilhelm II of Germany, who sent four ships laden with supplies and building materials. With help and donations from all over Europe, the people off Ålesund completed the rebuilding of their town by 1907 in the now carefully preserved Art Nouveau style. Towers,

turrets and medieval-romantic front-ages, often with more than a trace of Nordic mythology, give the town a harmony which extends to the painted wooden warehouses along Brosundet, the deep inlet of the inner harbour.

Until the 1950s, Ålesund, was a veri-table Klondyke for fish, fishermen and their boats, and *klippfisk* (traditional Norwegian split, dried cod). But as fish-ing changed so did Ålesund, which added fish-processing and fish-farm-ing. Many of the earlier warehouses are now offices and restaurants, pleasant places to try out one of this coast's more unlikely specialties such as *bacalao*, made from boneless klippfish. A more traditional dish is *brennsnute*, a potato and meat stew.

From the top of the 418 steps up **Aksla hill** in the centre of the town, the wider community stretches over several islands, now all linked by 8 miles (12 km) of deep underground tunnels. With great practicality, the builders used the rock from the tunnels to extend the airport on the island of **Vigra**.

Every book and brochure that de-scribes the county's thousands of is-lands shows similar happy pictures of people in, on, or under the sea, and anglers with magnificent catches. There are sea caves, tunnels, and bird cliffs, little harbours, campsites, clean, white beaches and *hytter* to rent. Some have relics of the Vikings, many have summer festivals. What these sea is-lands have to offer is almost unlimited: the difficulty is which to choose.

Bird island: Near Ålesund is one island not to miss. **Runde** attracts professional and amateur naturalists from all over the world. More than 200 bird species have been recorded but this small island is best known for breeding birds, which line the cliffs in their hundreds of thou-sands. When they fly, it looks as if a gigantic swarm of insects has darkened the sky. As a bonus, the waters round the island close over interesting wrecks; not so long ago divers found a cache of gold from a Dutch ship, *Ackerendam*.

South from Ålesund between the Vartdalsfjord and the Hjørundfjord, the

Preceding pages: peaceful countryside around Olden; the Geiranger-fjord from Flydalsjuvet.

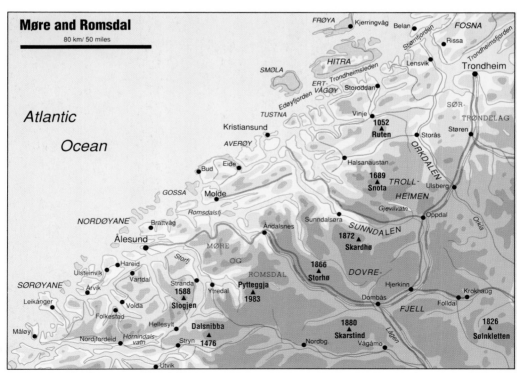

Møre and Romsdal

80 km/ 50 miles

Atlantic

Ocean

FRØYA · Kjerringvåg · Belan · FOSNA
Stjørnfjorden · Rissa · Trondheimsfjorden
HITRA · Lensvik · Trondheim
SMØLA
ERT- · Trondheimsleden · Storoddan
Edøyfjorden VÅGØY · SØR-
TUSTNA · Vinje · TRØNDELAG
Kristiansund · 1052 ▲ Ruten · Storås · Støren
AVERØY
Halsanaustan · ORKDALEN
Bud · Eide · 1689 ▲ Snota · TROLL- · Ulsberg
GOSSA · Molde · HEIMEN
Romsdalsfj. · Gjevilvatn
NORDØYANE · Brattvåg · Sunndalsøra · SUNNDALEN · Oppdal
Åndalsnes · 1872 ▲ Skardhø · Orkla
Ålesund · MØRE · 1866 ▲ Storhø · DOVRE-
Storfj. · OG · Hjerkinn
Hareid · ROMSDAL · Pytteggja · Dombås · Krokhaug
Ulsteinvik · Vartdal · Stranda · 1983 · Folldal
SØRØYANE · Arvik · 1588 ▲ Slogjen · Ytredal · FJELL
Leikanger · Volda · Hellesylt · Dalsnibba · 1880 ▲ Skarstind · 1826 ▲ Sølnkletten
Folkestad · Hornindals- · Stryn ▲ 1476 · Nordbg. · Vågåmo · Lågen
Måløy · Nordfjordeid · vatn
Utvik

280

Sunnmøre Mountains plunge straight into the fjord in the district of Ørsta, one of the early targets for the many British climbers who first made Norway's mountains known. Ålesund is also the main entrance to the Storfjord, where the cruise ships turn in to reach their goal of the **Geirangerfjord**, claimed by many to be Norway's most beautiful fjord. One road to Geiranger goes through **Stranda**, main town of inner Storfjord, or Ørsta to **Hellesylt**. From there you can travel to the inner end of the Geirangerfjord by boat or, in summer, there is a path along the fjord's high southern wall.

In this most secret of fjords far from the sea, great waterfalls tumble hundreds of feet in such delicate cascades that they are given names—the Seven Sisters and the Bridal Veil. Lofty mountains reflected in the mirror-still water give the fjord a gentle grandeur and, in some places, little farms cling to unlikely pockets of green. A small landing stage or two indicate that people climb up and down to these distant farms, to make use of every last inch of ground.

It is much too beautiful to miss and everyone stays on deck until the boat reaches Geiranger village, where the houses and hotels huddle under the half circle of mountains. Half-way up the winding road behind the village is the appropriately named **Hotel Utsikten Bellevue** (Outlook) which must have one of the best views in Norway. The road was opened in 1939 to make a new inland route from south to north. **Dalsnibba**, at 4,600 ft (1,495 metres) the highest point, is just off this road and below it, Geiranger and the countryside spreads out like a carpet.

North like an eagle: Heading north once more for Åndalsnes, the first 15 miles (25 km) to **Eidsdal** on the Norddalsfjord becomes **Ørneveien** (Eagle's Road) and it is not difficult to see why as it winds ahead to **Ørnesvingen**, another vantage point. Over the fjord is the start of an even more spectacular road across the **Gudbrandsjuvet** (gorge). Mountains rise into the distance of the west, until you reach

Ålesund, the Art Nouveau town.

Trollstigen, the top of the "trolls' ladder", or "trolls' causeway". This is the heart of inner Romsdal.

To the east is **Trolltindane**, around 6,000 ft (1,787 metres) and everywhere, fold upon fold of mountains stand like regiments on parade. At Trollstigen the snow is usually good enough for skiing well into July, then the route zigzags down through 11 gigantic bends hewn out of solid rock, to Åndalsnes.

Åndalsnes has the nickname "the village between the fjell and the fjord." It sits on a promontory in a circle of fjord and mountain, looking up to tops that challenge climbers of every nationality. They arrive by the score to tackle Trollveggen (the Troll Wall) part of craggy Trolltindane, which rises almost vertically from Romsdalen in the east, to its summit bowl of permanent snow.

Trollveggen itself has over 3,300 ft (1,000 metres) of vertical and overhanging rock, first climbed in 1965. New routes are still being discovered. By less hazardous paths, the climb up Trolltindane takes around four hours and calls for boots and strong clothing.

Åndalsnes is the terminus for the train from Oslo through Romsdalen which brings thousands of visitors to double and treble the population. A 19th-century British traveller, Lady Beauclerk, described **Romsdalen** as "precipitous, grey rocks ending in points apparently as sharp as needles... emerging into the sunniest, and the most lovely little spot... sheltered from every wind by the snowcapped mountains that surrounded it, while a most tempting river ran through the dale." It is as true today.

Famous climbers: The pleasant valley was the base camp for early climbers such as William Slingsby and Johannes Vigdal who, in 1881, made the first ascent of **Store Vengetind**. In the same year, another early pioneer, Carl Hall, made the second ascent with two local climbers to the sharp point of **Romdalshornet**. It had first been conquered 50 years before by two local farmers.

To cater for all this early interest, a local police sergeant, Anders Landmark, opened a simple wooden inn at

Left, Art Nouveau detail on a door in Ålesund. **Right**, Molde, the city of roses.

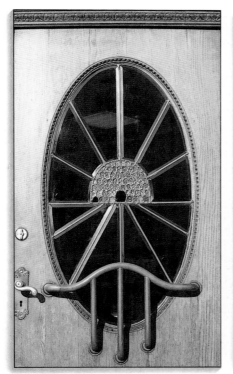

Aak, regarded as Norway's first tourist hotel, and many of Europe's mountain addicts stayed there. Some 3 miles (5 km) into the valley from Åndalsnes, it has recently reopened as a mountain sports centre, with summer courses in climbing and scrambling and, in winter, instruction in ice climbing and mountain (or Telemark) skiing.

Rafting and canoeing are also good possibilities on the **Rauma** river, one of Norway's well-known fishing rivers, which runs through the valley. But it is not necessary to be a rock climber to get high into these mountains. Most have easy alternative routes, and roads reach over 2,500 ft (850 metres).

Proceeding back towards the coast and Molde, detour into Langfjord until you reach **Nesset** on Eresfjord, deep into the mountains. Norway's prominent 19th-century writer and patriot Bjørnstjerne Bjørnson, who had a summer home in the area, described the Nesset mountains: "some standing white, others standing blue, with jagged, competing, agitating peaks, some marching along in ranking row."

The view today from the ferry along the **Eikesdalsvatnet** shows you what he meant. The mountain peaks rise abruptly out of the fjord sides, and you get a glimpse of Northern Europe's biggest waterfall, **Mardalsfossen**, over 2,000 ft (655 metres) high. In the 1970s, hundreds of people chained themselves together near the waterfall, to prevent the building of a hydro-electric power station. It became a hot political issue and, though they did not win the final battle, the protesters ensured that the summer falls still exist. The struggle also brought the unexpected gift of making Nesset famous and encouraging climbers and other visitors.

Molde is part of a collection of islands and peninsulas sheltered from the Norwegian Sea; its mild climate, green vegetation and rose gardens earn it the title "the Town of Roses". The statue of the **Little Rose Seller** stands in the market place, which has stalls selling everything from fruit and flowers to clothes and, of course, roses. This

Tovik,
Averøya,
south of
Kristiansund.

pretty, easy-going town makes an excellent base for touring on fjord or road.

From **Varden**, Molde's best vantage point, you look over fjord and island to the snowcaps of the **Sunnmøre Mountains**—townspeople claim you can see 87 peaks—and half an hour away to the north are small fishing villages which brave the worst of the west winds.

Molde has the inevitable outdoor museum in a particularly beautiful spot where the timber houses, national costumes, and folk dancing seem to fit in with the landscape. The museum's collection of *bunads* (national costumes), showing the fine details of shawl, headdress, bodice, jewellery, and embroidered purse, is one of the most appealing. The **Fisheries Museum**, 10 minutes by boat from the market place, illustrates the life of local fishing families over the last 100 years.

Yet there is little that is traditional about Molde's entertainment. The modern stadium is well used, with an all-year football ground (Norway largely plays football in the summer) and the streets are often full of musicians, particularly each year during the famous Molde Jazz Festival.

North by car: Molde is also a good start for the Geirangerfjord. Another fine route, this time north by car, is by roads 67 and 664 from Molde to the 16th-century village of **Bud**, right on the west coast. Here a boat trip goes to the old fishing-station of **Bjørnsund**, now only inhabited in the summer. Before Bud, a walk from road 67, reveals **Trollkirka**, the Troll church—a cave, some 235 ft (70 metres) long, divided into three sections, with a great waterfall tumbling down from the upper opening into a white marble basin in the mountains. From Bud a small coastal road leads to the "Atlantic Road" to Kristiansund, over **Averøy**, the biggest island in the area. As this road heads north across the rim of the ocean, it's a bit like driving on the sea itself.

Averøy deserves more than the view from a car window. Archaeologists believe that this was one of the first places to be settled after the last Ice Age,

Transporting hay on a mountain farm.

and their finds in 1909 are unique remnants of the early **Fosna Culture** around 7,000 BC. (Fosna was the original name of Kristiansund, Nordmøre's principal town.) One of the best ways to get around is a 32-mile (50-km) tour which varies from seaward skerries and small islands linked by bridge or causeway, to hills around 2,500 ft (502 metres) in the centre, and there is a fine stave church at Kvernes on the east.

Near **Bremsnes** is the **Viking Stone of Horg**, where the victor of Hafrsfjord, Harald Hårfagre, had his famous hair cut and washed, having fulfilled his vow not to touch it until Norway was united. It is just 15 minutes by ferry from Bremnes to Kristiansund.

Many influences: Unlike Ålesund and Molde, **Kristiansund** has little protection from the worst the North Atlantic can do. It is right on the coast, with weather-beaten rocks pounded by the sea, yet not far inland are grass and small woods. This is the *klippfisk* town, for long the biggest exporter of Norwegian dried cod. There are only 18,000 inhabitants but, because of the centuries-old links with other countries of its sailors and fishermen, and the foreign merchants who settled here, the atmosphere is cosmopolitan.

Like most Norwegian towns with "Kristian" in their title, Kristiansund was named after a Danish King, Christian VI, who gave it town status in 1742. An excellent introduction is by *sundbåten*, the harbour boat which for more than 100 years has been the link between the town's islands. **Mellomverftet**, once one of four shipyards in Vågen, is working again as a centre for preserving the craft of ship-building, carefully restoring the beautiful lines of traditional Norwegian boats.

Kristiansund consists of three islands. One of them is **Innlandet**, the oldest preserved part of the town with its first customs house (1660–1748), hospital, school and other buildings which are gradually being restored. Walk to the **Sjursvika** on the east side for a look at the old warehouses. These interesting parts of the harbour are

In spring the fjords are carpeted with blossom.

A Country Afloat

To the world, Norway and seafaring are synonymous; the very word Viking means "Men of the Bays." From the age of sail until after World War II, the Norwegian merchant fleet was one of the world's largest, and Norwegian could be heard in ports worldwide. The country's most popular museums by far are the Seafaring Museum on the Bygdøy peninsula in Oslo, the Viking Ship Museum with magnificently preserved long ships, the Kontiki Museum with the rafts that ethnographic explorer Thor Heyerdahl used to prove his theories of the migrations of Pacific Ocean peoples in dangerous journeys across the oceans, and the Fram Museum built around the sturdy vessel that carried Fridtjof Nansen and Roald Amundsen on their heroic polar explorations around the turn of the 19th century.

Although less important than they were before the jet-age, shipping and other sea-going activities still comprise a sizeable portion of the Norwegian economy, especially if one includes offshore oil.

Norwegians seem happiest when they are in, on, or around the sea. Each year, 1.6 million Norwegians, over a third of the population, spend their summer holidays partly or completely in recreational craft that range from small dinghies to large motor launches and ocean-going yachts. Even the most conservative estimates place the number of pleasure craft in Norway at 650,000, about one for every seven Norwegians. The sea is a natural part of life.

Geography and topography are the deciding factors. The country is long and thin; indeed, if it were rotated on its southernmost point, the northern tip would overlap northern Italy. There are thousands upon thousands of islands, ranging in size from mountainous Hinnøya 850 sq. miles (2,200 sq. km) north of the Arctic Circle to flat, rocky specks. In those numbers lie the attraction and popularity of boat sports. The fjords and the coastal archipelago are a paradise for competitive and recreational sailors, king and commoner.

King Olav V is the country's foremost sailor in far more than name only. He won a Gold Medal in sailing in the 1928 Olympics, which makes him the world's only Olympic medallist monarch. He has won gold and bronze medals in the 5.5-metre class in the World Championships in Sailing, in 1971 and 1976.

In founding its first sailing club in 1868 in Tønsberg, then a major merchant fleet port, Norway triggered a long latent urge. The country's first regatta had been held five years previously, in 1863. In 1883 Den Kongelige Norske Seilforening (the Royal Norwegian Sailing Association) was formed in the capital, and in 1900 sailing became an Olympic sport. For years, Norwegians were a major force in Olympic and championship sailing and in regattas worldwide.

By chance, Norway's leading position in international sailing coincides approximately with the country's yacht production. In the days of wooden yachts, Norwegian yards and naval architects were among the world's best, and Colin Archer (1832-1921) stands out. Born in the port of Larvik, Archer grew up with boats and at an early age started building craft to his own design. Among his best known are the stable, sturdy rescue schooners that bear his name and the three-masted Arctic exploration vessel *Fram*, built in 1892. Archer also built regatta-winning yachts, and in so doing set a style for the following generations of Scandinavian naval architects.

The tradition lives, albeit altered. Fibreglass hulls and masts changed the picture completely; motor cruisers are made in a variety of designs to fit an equally large range of pocketbooks; but aside from mass-production dinghies, sailing craft are no longer made in Norway, which now exports motor cruisers and imports yachts.

Wherever there's water, there are all manner of motor and sailing craft. Small boat harbours in and near major cities, particularly Oslo, Kristiansand, Ålesund, Stavanger, and Bergen, never fail to impress visitors by the numbers and types of crafts lying there. Even away from the harbours, boats and the sea are visible in the many small cars towing boats on trailers and in the number of windsurfing boards on car roof racks. From windsurfing in fjords and bays to major regattas, Norwegians love their water racing.

being amalgamated into an emergent coastal culture centre, to tell the history of the maritime people of old, alongside harbour life that continues today.

Kristiansund's main church was destroyed by bombing in 1940. The architect responsible for its replacement named his creation **Rock Crystal in Roses**, and whether you love it or loathe it, you cannot ignore this stark, white building. Inside, the choir wall is a 100-ft (30-metre) sweep of 320 stained glass panels which at the foot symbolise the heavy, dark colours of the earth soaring up to eternal light.

An entirely different church stands on the island of **Grip**, close to Kristiansund, which has a long and eventful history of flood and storm. In 1796, a nor'wester tore down and washed away 100 houses and, when the same thing happened seven years later, the pastor recorded the piteous prayer: "Almighty God, spare us further destruction and misery". Whether it was that plea or not, the ancient little red stave church survived, only 25 ft (8 metres) above the sea. Once 400 souls lived on Grip, scraping a living from fish: today people live there only in summer when it metamorphoses into a holiday island and makes a popular excursion from the town. A wedding in the old church is a very special occasion.

Evocative monuments: The Nordmøre museum includes archaeological finds from the Fosna culture and the history of *klippfisk* processing. But the town's oddest monuments are the tall pointed natural stones, tributes to town dignitaries: Bäckstrøm, who built the reservoirs, Brinchman the provider of the water supply, Bræin, the musical founder of a musical family, which gave birth to an annual Opera Festival, and Hanson, the Polar explorer.

To the north and northeast of Kristiansund, the last big island is Smøla at the mouth of the Trondheimfjord, where the county ends in a gaggle of islands which retain something of the life of the old farmer-fishermen.

Sanden is one of several buildings that form Smøla's scattered museum,

with the main 18th-century building, warehouses, barn and a store house on wooden pillars, just as it was when the last owners left a few years ago. A few of these old fishing grounds where cod was split, salted and dried on the rocks are now marinas with simple accommodation, seafood dishes, and the atmosphere of earlier days. The small idyllic island of Kuli off Smøla is rich in relics, the most famous being the Kuli stone. On this stone the name Norway is mentioned for the first time in an inscription which dates to the first years after the coming of Christianity.

To the east, the northern part of the county ends in a criss-cross of fjords eating into the islands and peninsulas which lead to **Trollheimen**, the "Home of the Trolls," where the mountains reach nearly 6,000 ft (1,600 metres). This haunt of climbers and skiers is bounded by two important valleys, **Surnadalen** and **Sunndalen**, with between them the tiny **Todalfjord**. Beside the last is the surprise of the **Svinvik Arboretum**, beautiful gardens with thousands of rhododendrons, conifers and other plants. Despite the northern latitude, plants from all over the world grow at Svinvik, owned and run today by the University of Trondheim.

On the way to Sunndalen, you come to **Tingvoll**, which has Nordmøre's oldest church in an area with a surprisingly large selection from different centuries and styles. Church historians believe that it was built as long ago as the 12th century, a granite and brick structure which is well preserved as well as beautiful, surrounded by a stone wall with an arched entrance way.

Sunndalen is deep in the Nordmøre wilderness, with narrow valleys between the mountain ranges forming sheltered farming country which supplies grain for most of the county. At the end of the fjord, the main town of **Sunndalsøra** lies below mountains where you might startle reindeer, their white rumps disappearing in a flurry of snow. This is a ruggedly magnificent area for walking, skiing or fishing.

Road 16 follows the course of the valley to **Oppdal** on the third side of Trollheimen. On foot, there are more energetic routes over the mountains, with a mountain centre in **Innerdalen** and ski lifts as well. The River Driva is one of the most famous in a county and country of good salmon and trout rivers. Between the head of Sunndalen and Grødalen, next-door at Åmotan, the spectacular **Jenstadjuvet** (gorge) is the place where five valleys and their watercourses meet in two furious waterfalls. Grødalen has an oddity in **Alfheim**, a small hunting lodge from 1876 built in Scottish Highland style by a Scot, Lady Arbuthnott, who became something of the "laird" of the valley. Her old farm at **Elverhøy** is now the Sunndal Museum.

Surnadal has another good salmon river, the Surna; side valleys lead up to the heart of Trollheimen, and to signposted trails from mountain hut to mountain hut, in what seems like the top of the world. At valley level, the road through Surnadal is the inland route out of West Norway, straight on to the city of Trondheim, the gateway to the north.

Left, in autumn mountains and forests are bright with berries. **Right**, Norway's rushing rivers give splendid fishing for trout and salmon.

PEAK AND PLATEAU

Jotunheimen, which includes Norway's mightiest mountain range, and Hardangervidda, a huge mountain plateau, make up Lower Central Norway, forming an extensive area of outstanding beauty (*see map, page 202*). Centres of population are few, places of interest are also thin on the ground but of superb scenery—mountains, glaciers, lakes and rivers—there is an excess.

Hardangervidda, on average, 3,000 ft (914 metres) above sea level, lies south of **Jotunheimen** and several river-valleys—Begnadalen, the Hallingdal and the Numedal—cut across it in a south-easterly direction. To the south Hardangervidda (*vidde* means a highland plateau) broadens out from **Hallingskarvet**, a rocky wall rising up to a height of 5,700 ft (1,737 metres).

The centre of the plateau with its lakes, waters and streams—a paradise for anglers—forms the source of the mighty watercourses of Hallingdal and Numedal. The attraction of Hardangervidda lies in its wide open spaces while in the west is one of Norway's outstanding waterfalls—**Vøringfoss.** It has a perpendicular drop of 489 ft (149 metres) down to the wild Måbø valley and there is a path at the top overlooking the fall which is not for those who suffer from vertigo. You reach it by a private toll road from highway 7. Another magnificent waterfall in an area of many is the **Valursfoss** which drops 300 ft (91 metres) into the Hjelmodal.

Dizzy descent: The Oslo-Bergen railway line cuts across Vidda keeping road 7 company as far as **Haugastøl** where it goes north of the Hardanger Jøkulen through Finse, Myrdal and Mjølfjell. The road takes a different course, a tarmacadam ribbon heading south across the wide, empty landscape with distant views of mountains, which passes lakes and streams, before making a dizzy descent to sea level via a series of brilliantly engineered tunnels to the end of the Eidfjord.

Hardangervidda is in many ways unique as Europe's largest mountain plateau, covering an area of 3,860 sq. miles (10,000 sq. km) nearly a third of it forming Norway's largest national park. There are tracks and trails galore and isolated cabins provide basic overnight accommodation. These rough trails were once a vital link in east–west communications in a farflung country and a source of cultural development. Nowadays, the trails cater for walkers at all levels of proficiency, as part of the outdoor network that encourages the Norwegian outdoor life.

The flora and fauna of the plateau is Arctic and very varied. Several thousand reindeer roam freely, around 120 species of birds breed on these upland moors and there are over 400 different species of plants, an abundance due to the two distinct climates of Vidda—the gentle western coastal climate and the harsher inland climate of the east.

From Haugastøl, travelling northeast both road and railway pass Ustaoset and the Ustevatn (lake) where the landscape is dominated by the Hal-

lingskarvet mountain. The immediate surroundings become somewhat softer as you reach **Geilo**. Though it lies at a height of 2,642 ft (805 metres) above sea level, and is roughly midway between Oslo and Bergen. Geilo has grown and developed into one of Norway's best-known and most popular international winter sports resorts. It has a good strategic position at the head of the Hallingdal valley and the gateway to Hardangervidda; there are 16 chair lifts which can cope with 14,000 persons an hour, plus ski tows and miles of well-groomed downhill runs.

Winter sports country: Geilo, with its range of hotels, has also become popular as a summer holiday centre and as a base for exploring the region by car (although the choice of roads is limited) or on foot or horseback. In summer it still looks like a winter resort minus snow, with that spread-out, slightly unfinished appearance that characterises many winter sports centres.

From Geilo a road (number 8) goes southeast to an open-air museum which takes the usual form of a collection of old buildings. In this case it includes the **Mostugua** from 1750, the **Hågåstuga** from 1806, a mill from 1774, a stable and grain drier, and furnishings, equipment and implements. Road 8 continues along the eastern edge of Hardangervidda before it follows the Numedal valley to Kongsberg.

Road 7, meanwhile, continues northeast through Hagafoss and winter sports territory, dotted with cabins, and alongside the sizeable lake **Strandavatn**. Beyond this limpid water the scene changes, the views become more exhilarating while nearby is a summer ski centre. Suddenly the road begins to descend through an impressive series of tunnels, including spirals, until the motorist is decanted into the Aurland valley which continues to the village of **Aurland** on the Aurlandfjord. It is an exciting ride made easy by the skill of Norway's road builders.

Unique ceiling: After being separated by the Strandfjorden, road 7 and the railway meet up at **Ål** which has a

<u>Left</u>, all the excitement of summer skiing. <u>Right</u>, first frosts tint the trees red.

museum with 15 buildings at **Leksvold**. There is a fine collection of rose paintings as well as a collection of 2,000 objects. **Torpo** has no museum but a **stave church** which is the oldest building in Hallingdal. It dates back to the second half of the 12th century and has a unique painted ceiling from the second half of the 13th century. The motifs include scenes from the life of St Margaret, to whom the church is dedicated.

At **Nesbyen**, the visitor passes the local shopping centre and on the outskirts among the trees finds Norway's oldest outdoor museum founded in 1889. The **Hallingdal Folk Museum** has 22 buildings, the earliest—the Staveloftet—dating from 1340. All come from different parts of Hallingdal while some interiors are rose painted and the exhibition building houses collections of furniture, textiles and weapons. The road and railway stay with the Hallingdal valley until it ends at Gulsvik at the northern end of Lake Krøderen.

The two other roads at Gol both lead the traveller through more attractive scenery. Road 52 goes north-west along the **Hemsedal** valley through Hemsedal, another winter sports centre with a church which has an altar piece from 1775 and a painting of *The Last Supper* from 1716. From the village a minor road goes past a small open-air museum near the village of Ulsåk and, further on, a private toll road winds its way across superb scenery to Ulnes on road E68. This is the **Panorama Way**, a popular route which links the Valdres and Hemsedal valleys. Although narrow and rough in parts it lives up to its name, threading its way between lakes and providing fine views of the **Skogshorn**, known as the "Queen of the Hemsedal".

Trolls and giants: The Jotunheimen was, in Norwegian mythology, the home of trolls and giants and it is here that Norway's mightiest mountains are to be found. The peaks top 7,000 ft (2,133 metres) while in the east are the two highest mountains in the country: **Galdhøpiggen** 8,100 ft (2,469 metres) and **Glittertind** 8,087 ft (2,465 metres). In west Jotunheimen is another group of

En route for Jotunhiemen.

crevassed mountains which are not far short of the 8,000 footers, of which the highest is **Skagastølstindane**.

The southern part of the Jotunheimen has some major lakes, including **Gjende** which is particularly beautiful with its greenish glacier water and flanked by impressive peaks. These include **Knutsholstind** 7,677 ft (2,340 metres) and **Besshø** 7,408 ft (2,258 metres). Other major lakes are Bygdin, Tyin and Vinstri, while glaciers add to the superb natural attractions.

The northern border of the Jotunheimen is the **Otta river valley** which acts as a natural boundary. From **Otta** the river and road go through fertile countryside, with farms and forests, but beyond Lom the scene gradually changes. The green and lush surroundings give way to forests and rocky outcrops and the river grows more turbulent. Eventually at the tree line the scenery becomes bare and inhospitable.

At **Grotli**, which consists of little more than a large roadside hotel, cafeteria and souvenir shop, highway 15 continues past the junction with the 58—a spectacular road which skirts lake Djupvatnet and then descends steeply to Geiranger. Road 15 meanwhile follows its more recently engineered course through several tunnels until it reaches Stryn on the Innvikfjord.

An alternative to the 15 from Grotli is the old road (number 258) which is a 16 mile (26 km) spectacular journey. It climbs to a height of 3,736 ft (1,139 metres) and although narrow and unsurfaced in parts provides a thrilling journey. West of the summit it passes a summer ski centre and **Snowland**, a summer activity area for the family—with snow thrown in.

There are only two roads between Otta and Grotli bold enough to penetrate the heart of the Jotunheimen. The 51, the most easterly, leaves road 15 at Randen and goes south into the Valdres region. It starts by climbing into a region of upland pastures with a distant backdrop of mountains. A further climb to Darthus brings **Ridderspranget** close at hand, where the river Sjoa is

Fish farming in Sunndals-fjord.

channelled into a narrow gorge. Legend has it that a Valdres knight jumped the gorge with a beautiful maiden in his arms. Hence the name Ridderspranget which means "Knight's Leap".

Kidnap: The knight was Sigvat Kvier and he made the leap to shake off pursuers, lead by Ivar of Sandbu and his followers. They were chasing him for the very good reason that he had kidnapped the betrothed of the knight of Sandbu. In seizing the young lady, Sigvat Kvier tackled the guard with an axe and set fire to a farm; just an everyday story of mountain folk.

Lakes lie scattered across to the west while beyond can be seen the Glittertind. The most important stretch of water is **Lake Gjende**, long and narrow and curving slightly to the south-west. Beyond Bessheim there are more inspiring views and this scenic feast continues for mile after mile.

Bygdin lies between two lakes: Lake Bygdin which stretches like a long finger pointing to more distant mountains in the west; eastwards is the major expanse of Lake Vinstri. There are boat trips on several of the lakes and **Lake Bygdin** has northern Europe's highest scheduled boat service, in waters 3,477 ft (1,060 metres) above sea level.

Between Bessheim and Bygdin the road reaches its highest point—4,557 ft (1,389 metres). From here it descends, first to the tree line, then to more gentle scenery at **Beitostølen**. This winter sports resort got its first ski lift in 1964 and now has seven and over 60 miles (100 km) of marked trails. It is a typical village of its kind with several hotels, very popular for cross-country skiing, and with a school for handicapped and blind skiers, who plunge down the slopes with unbelievable confidence at their annual competition.

Fagernes is in the heart of the Valdres area. The focus of attention is the **Valdres Folk Museum** which has about 70 old buildings. Of particular interest are a 16th-century tapestry, medieval chests, a collection of antique silver, old textiles, folk music instruments and hunting weapons. On a

The visitors stare at the goats, and the goats stare back.

modern note it has one of Norway's newest airports, opened in 1987.

In one direction the E68 goes southeast through the Begnadalen valley and eventually to Hønefoss. In the opposite direction the road goes west through more exciting scenery on the southern edge of the Jotunheimen. At Tyinkrysset a road goes off to Øvre Årdal on the Årdalsfjord while the E68 turns south, descending through forested scenery to Borgund. Apart from the stave church at **Heddal**, the one at **Borgund** is regarded as the most typical and best preserved in Norway. Built in 1150 it is dedicated to St Andrew.

Exciting road: At Sæbø a minor road goes to Aurland, one of the most exciting routes in Norway. It starts to climb almost immediately, through remarkably lush scenery but this gradually changes as the narrow road ascends higher and higher, unfolding a series of stunning panoramas until the summit at 4,284 ft (1,305 metres). It then begins an increasingly steep descent to the village of **Aurland**. "Breathtaking" is an over-

used description but on this road it is justified, especially the view over the Aurlandsfjord from several thousand feet above it. Not for the fainthearted.

The second route through the Jotunheimen region is road 55 from **Lom** to the **Lustrafjord** which is the part of the Sognefjord farthest from the sea. Lom is a typical Norwegian "junction" village with its two or three hotels, shops and garages but it also has one of the finest **stave churches**. This was originally built in 1100 but was enlarged and reconstructed in the 17th century—fortunately without destroying its original architectural form.

Starting out from Lom, you drive through the deceptively placid Bøverdal valley, passing small farms and villages, but the view gradually changes as it gains height and the mountains become more noticeable. At Galdesand there is a toll road to **Juvashytta** which is the nearest point by car to the **Galdhøpiggen** mountain.

At 2,100 ft (640 metres) is **Elveseter**, one of Norway's most unusual hotels. People have lived and farmed here for 1,000 years and the Elveseter family has owned the property for five generations, gradually converting it into an hotel but retaining many old buildings. The oldest is from 1640 and has survived as a wooden building because of the dry mountain air. The first visitors arrived in the 1880s but it was the opening of the Sognefjell road in 1938 that lead to the expansion of tourism.

The road continues its upward ascent past the isolated Jotunheimen Fjellstue to the summit at **Krossbu** a height of 4,593 ft (1,400 metres) amidst superb mountain scenery. From there, make the steep descent to **Turtagrø** where the hotel (which is about all there is to Turtagrø) is a popular base for walkers and climbers; continue the downward course to softer surroundings at Fortun and, a few miles on, to sea level, at the end of the Lustrafjord at Skjolden.

On foot or by car, Jotunheimen and Hardangervidda are two regions that combine to mesmerise and stun the senses with their magnificence, a surfeit of visual delights.

Left, Lustrafjord. Right, Mountain Seter in autumn.

TRONDHEIM

A thousand years ago, **Trondheim**, then Nidaros, was the capital of Norway, Olav Tryggvason's city, and the resting place of King Olav Haraldson, who became St Olav. A thousand years later, it is a 20th-century city, far to the north in European terms yet only midway along Norway's long west coast. Modern though it may be, Trondheim has kept much of the charm of the past.

The heart of the old city lies on what is virtually an island between river (**Nidelva**) and fjord (**Trondheims-fjorden**), joined only by a narrow neck of land to the west, once the western fort. Nowadays the river meanders through a much-extended community with bridges linking this old centre to the wider city.

King Olav Tryggvason founded the settlement as Nidaros in 997. A reminder of those days and of the old harbour is provided by the **Wharves**.

Though they date back only to the 18th century, these coloured, wooden warehouses echo the architecture of medieval times and it is not too difficult to feel what the atmosphere must have been around that busy harbour when fish and timber dominated the city. Also ancient are the narrow streets (*veitene*) which run between the wooden buildings.

In contrast to these recollections of the past is the **Institute of Technology**, part of **Trondheim University** to the southwest of the centre. The University itself has 10,000 students and is the second largest in Norway. As well as the Institute of Technology, it has a faculty of medicine, a college of Arts and Science, and the Royal Norwegian Society for Science and the Humanities. The University Museum, from 1760, is Norway's oldest scientific institution.

Today, Trondheim is in the forefront of Norwegian education and church affairs and is the leader of high-technology research in Norway. Not far from the university is SINTEF, Scandinavia's largest foundation for scientific and industrial research. Both SINTEF and the Institute have encouraged high-technology businesses to open in Trondheim, with the advantage of being able to turn to the research establishments for guidance and development. The city is also the administrative centre of Trøndelag *fylke* (county).

The building that unites past and present is the **Nordenfjeldske Kunstindustrimuseum** on Munkegate, a museum of applied art and craft, both past and present, which has exhibitions of Norwegian and international industrial arts throughout the year.

Saint and martyr: Though Olav Tryggvason had attempted to introduce Christianity to Norway in the late 10th century, many Norwegians still clung to their pagan gods, and it was only after the death of his successor, Olav Haraldson, at the Battle of Stiklestad some 30 years later *(see page 309)* that Christianity acquired a focal point in Norway. Olav's men buried him in sandy ground near the river but when miracles began to happen he was moved to the town's only church. Then, according to the sagas, a spring began to flow near his first grave and "men were healed of their ills by the waters." The king was declared a saint and martyr.

His nephew, Olav Kyrre, built the great stone church over the place where the saint's body had lain which is now **Nidaros Cathedral** and Trondheim's finest building. Once again, the saint's body was moved and the cathedral became a place of pilgrimage, many making the long walk north through Sweden, others arriving by sea.

Until the Reformation, Nidaros Cathedral was the seat of the archbishop, and the setting for the coronation of Norwegian monarchs, a tradition revived after 1814, when Norway shrugged off its 400 years of Danish rule and united with Sweden. The last coronation was 1906, when the Constitution changed; today there is no formal ceremony. In 1988, however, the Norwegian Crown Jewels were placed in the cathedral in a special royal ceremony and the modest but beautiful regalia for King, Queen and Crown Prince are now on display in a side chapel.

The great arched nave is in a Gothic style and, looking back at the main door, the most striking feature is the brilliant stained-glass rose window above the main entrance on the west wall, the work of Gabriel Kjelland in 1930, with the organ below. Both inside and out are many statues of saints and monarchs; but the beautiful interior lines of the cathedral, built in a green-grey soapstone and its finest feature, do not call for over-ornamentation.

As the second oldest city in Norway, Trondheim has a great many buildings and institutions that can be labelled "the first", "the oldest", or "the largest". Next door to the cathedral is Scandinavia's oldest secular building, once the **Archbishop's Palace**, later the residence of the Danish governors, and eventually a military establishment. The oldest part is used for official receptions, and the palace includes **Rustkammeret**, an army museum. Nearby is **Waisenhuset**, a beautiful timber building from 1722.

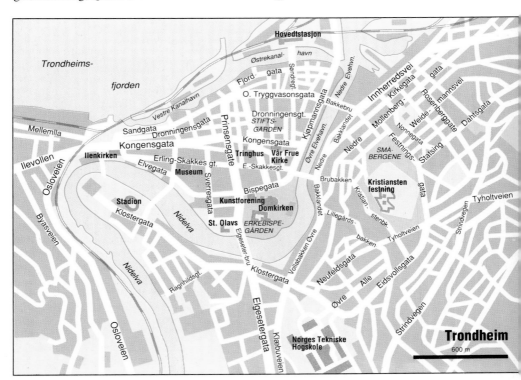

All around the original medieval city are the remains of fortifications, which were reinforced or built in the late 17th century by a military architect from Luxemburg, General Johan Caspar de Cicignon, after the great fire of 1681 devasted most of medieval Trondheim.

From the cathedral area it is just a short walk to **Gamle Bybro**—the old town bridge—also erected after 1681 when de Cicignon was constructing Kristiansten Fort on a hill to the east, at that time outside the city proper. The first bridge had a sentry box and excise house at either end and the western building still remains, now used as a kindergarten. The present bridge and gates were built in 1861.

Best view point: Kristiansten Fort now part of the city, provides one of the best views of Trondheim, spread out below like a map. From here you can see the old stone walls of the 13th-century **Vår Frue Kirke** (The Church of Our Lady) and **Stiftsgården**, Scandinavia's largest timber mansion which was built as a private house in the 1770s. Today it is King Olav's official residence in the city and is open to the public in summer. Both church and residence are near the main city square on Munkegate which looks up to the cathedral.

Further on, and not far from the bustle of the **Ravnkloa** fish market at the lower end of Munkegate and past the ornate railway station, is **Fosenkaia**, where sightseeing and other boats tie up. At midday, the Hurtigrute coastal express will be lying at one of the two main quays, with a half-day to spend in Trondheim before it heads north. Returning south on a summer evening, the ship is outlined against the late sun as its passengers make an excursion to see the midnight sun from the summit of **Mount Storsteinen**. The remains of Trondheim's old defences, **Skansen**, lie to the west where the city gate once stood. Skansen is now a park. Also near the harbour is a curious warehouse built out on iron stilts over the sea; its shape is explained by the fact that it was a World War II U-boat bunker when German forces occupied the city.

Colourful old buildings along Trondheim's waterfront.

Well out into the fjord is **Munkholmen** (Monks' Island) where the Benedictine monks built a monastery very early in the 11th century, one of the first two monasteries in Norway. Even earlier this had been Trondheim's execution ground and in 1658 it became a prison fort. Munkholmen is a favourite spot for a day out and boats leave every hour from Ravnkloa. You can make a tour of the fort and the island offers good sea bathing and a restaurant.

For a bird's-eye view of the city from a modern building, try the 400-ft (120-metre) **Tyholt Tower**. Built by the Telecommunications Authority as a radio and telecommunications link, it is a popular place to look at the city and fjord or for a meal in its rotating restaurant three-quarters of the way up.

From here, it is clear that Trondheim is an easy walking city where many people still live in the centre. Two places best toured on foot are **Hospitalsløkka**, the area around the old Trondheim Hospital, which was founded in 1277 and is Scandinavia's oldest surviving hospital building, now used as a home for elderly people. In the ground is another first: the first octagonal timber church to be built in Norway and Sweden which dates from 1705. The surrounding area is full of typical old timber houses, lovingly restored by their present owners.

On the eastern side of the Nidelva, not far from the old town bridge and opposite the riverside warehouses, **Bakklandet** is another area of old wooden houses, originally the working-class part of the town. **Bakklandet**, and the **Mollenberg** and **Rosenborg** districts, were restored relatively recently as complete communities of houses and shops. Trondheim also has the oldest factory building in Norway: **Sukkerhuset**, the Sugar Factory, dating back to 1752, was later used as a brewery.

For an understanding of the past of this ancient area of Trøndelag, two museums are invaluable. At the **University Museum**, an archaeological exhibition traces the history of the area up to the Middle Ages, and an exhibition of Church history shows Church art from the 13th to 18th centuries. The museum also has a natural history exhibit covering Trøndelag flora and fauna and not far away is the **University Library**. The **Shipping Museum** (Sjøfarts Museum), an old yellow building near the Royal Garden Hotel north of the warehouse waterfront of Kjøpmannsgate, covers shipping, fishing and whaling.

Trøndelag Folk Museum in Sverresborg, on the west side of the city, looks at towns and villages in Trøndelag's rural areas, showing life in coast and country in days gone by. There are old tools used to scrape a meagre living, a ski museum and recollections of old trades and crafts such as the *passementerie* which made trimmings and lace for women's Sunday best. Within the museum are the remains of King Sverre's palace, **Sion**, from around 1180, and the late 18th-century **Tavern** has a good restaurant. There are tours in English, German and Norwegian. (Buses 8 and 9 from Dronningensgate to Wullumsgården.)

A good way to get about in the snow: a *sparkstotting* (kick-sledge).

With all the "oldests" and "firsts", it is no surprise that Trondheim has Norway's oldest theatre building, **Trøndelag Teater** in the centre of the old town, as well as **Teater Avant Garden**. Other arts are represented by institutions, galleries and centres such as the **Trøndelag Kunstnersenter**, the Academy of Art, galleries showing and selling contemporary paintings, the Trondheim Symphony Orchestra, the **Conservatory of Music** and almost more interesting than anything else, the **Museum of Music History** at Ringve.

The Ringve Museum is near the Lade district to the northeast, an ancient manor still run as a farm after the museum came into being. Since the late 19th century, it belonged to the Bache family. In 1943, the last representative, Christian Anker Bache, bequeathed the estate to the Ringve Museum Foundation and, after his death in 1946, his widow, Russian-born "Madame Victoria", worked steadily to build up the collection of musical instruments from all over the world. Her persuasiveness

In winter, when snow covers the mountains, the Hurtigrute is an easy way to travel along the coast.

in prising relics from many countries is legendary and when the museum opened in 1952 the couple's collection had grown magnificently.

Madame Victoria decreed a living museum; almost all the instruments in the beautiful rooms of the main building can be, and are, played by the music-student guides during the tour. In addition to the more formal, classical instruments, there are examples of music boxes, old folk instruments such as the *langeleik*, a sort of Norwegian zither, and clay flutes shaped like birds and soldiers, which delight children. There are also "Aeolian bells", which 18th-century Norwegians used to create music in their gardens; in more superstitious ages the bells were thought to give protection against evil spirits.

Just before her death in 1962, Madame Victoria opened the museum's concert hall, which can seat 350; it was built into the old cow sheds and is used for more formal music. After the museum, leave time for a stroll around the **Ringve Botanic Gardens**, just next

door, and the most northerly botanical garden in the world.

Outdoor Life: As with all Norwegian cities, it doesn't take long to escape to the great outdoors. Trondheim's back garden is **Bymarka** to the west, where **Gråkallen** (The Old Man) at some 1,700 ft (520 metres) is the city's favourite skiing area. In summer, it is a good spot for walking. Its counterpart to the east is **Estenstadmarka**. Both have walking trails, alpine slopes, the ski jumps so beloved of Norwegian youngsters and a **Skistua** (skiing lodge). By contrast, in June you can play golf at midnight on Trondheim's nine-hole course. Fishing is good in Nidelva, which is renowned for the size of its salmon. The Gaula to the south is another fine fishing river. The fjord itself is rich in many species for sea-fishing from boat or shore.

As well as the hourly boats to Munksholmen, Trondheim Tourist Association offers a two-hour summer introduction to Trondheim from the sea, from Ravnkloa; there is a half-day tour to the 17th-century manor and gardens at **Austråtborgen** at Ørland on Trondheimsfjorden, which includes a catamaran tour along the fjord to Brekstad, a tour of the castle and coffee and waffles to finish. Another idea is to take a short leg of the Hurtigrute and return by coach or train.

Trondheim is a mixture of modern and ancient, with its high-technology industries and institutions grafted on to turn-of-the-century ship-building and the sea-trading and fishing that first made it prosperous.

But for most people Trondheim means history and culture. Like the pilgrims of old, visitors come to see the cathedral, the Archbishop's Palace and de Cicignon's 17th-century city, and for historical events such as the annual 10-day **St Olav festival**, known as Olsok (Olav) Days, centred around 29 July, the anniversary of the Battle of Stiklestad. Although Trondheim has long lost its political role, to many Norwegians it is still the country's historical, cultural and ecclesiastical capital.

Below, the old view of Stiklestad by Johannes Flintoe, from *Snorri's Norse Kings*, 1839. Right, the victor of Stiklestad, King Canute of Denmark.

STIKLESTAD

Stiklestad is a name which means nothing to the majority of visitors to Norway but it is known and revered by Norwegians. The ancient battlefield is a milestone in Norwegian history and the church marks the spot where King Olav Haraldson died. For Stiklestad, north of Trondheim, saw the foundation of Norwegian national unity and the adoption of the Christian faith, not through the signing of a treaty or a glorious victory but by the death in battle of the Christian King Olav Haraldson.

In the 11th century Norway was a country constantly disrupted by disputes between rival chieftains, and Olav's ambition was a united Norway. He also aimed to create a Christian country with Christian laws and churches and clergy.

This was the second attempt to introduce Christianity; the first came in the previous century by Olav Tryggvason (a descendant of Harald Hårfagre who in his youth had been on many Viking expeditions). In England, Olav Tryggvason was converted to Christianity and confirmed by the Bishop of Winchester. He returned to his native land in 995 with the express purpose of crushing the chieftains and imposing his new-found faith.

But Olav Tryggvason's conversion had not swept away all his Viking instincts and in his religious zeal he used great cruelty to convert the populace. As a result, he fell in the Battle of Svolder in the year 1000, fighting both the Kings of Denmark and Norway. They were supported by disenchanted Norwegian chieftains whose treachery achieved success for the Danish and Norwegian kings.

Olav Haraldson was also a descendant of Harald Hårfagre and he landed in Norway and ascended the throne in 1015. It was a propitious time as King Canute of Denmark and England, who had long threatened Norway, was out of the country, in England. But, like his predecessor, Olav foolishly made too great a use of the sword to establish Christianity. The result was the same: his evangelistic efforts made him highly unpopular and disaffection grew. With his eye on the Norwegian throne, Canute gave support to dis-

contented factions and in 1028 invaded Norway, which forced King Olav to flee to Russia.

Undaunted, King Olav returned with a few followers but whatever loyalty he had once inspired had been lost through his ruthless methods. He died on 29 July 1030 at the Battle of Stiklestad. Olav's corpse was taken to the then capital, Nidaros, and buried on the banks of the river Nid. When the body was disinterred a year later, it showed no signs of corruption. The face was exactly as it had been in life; his nails and hair had grown, at that time taken as a sign of sanctity.

Following this revelation, many began to reproach themselves for having caused his death. Olav was proclaimed a saint and his body placed in a silver shrine in Nidaros Cathedral in Trondheim. Faith in the holiness of King Olav—or St Olav as he now was—spread and, until the Reformation, his shrine became a goal of Christian pilgrims.

Canute's triumph at the Battle of Stiklestad was but brief. He ceded the reins of power to his son Svejn but, as the rumours of Olav's sanctity gained ground and were declared by a national assembly, popular support for Canute evaporated rapidly.

Svejn attempted to introduce Danish laws, which were at variance with the Norwegian traditions of rights and liberty, and he was exiled to Denmark in 1035. All the while, St Olav's son, Magnus, had also been in exile in Russia, but Norway now invited him to return and accept the crown, an event that marked a major turning point in the history of Norway.

From that time, Stiklestad has been a place of steady pilgrimage. They still come, usually by car, at the end of July each year to commemorate the battle. Stiklestad now also has a very beautiful open-air theatre, the biggest in Scandinavia, and on the anniversary of the battle, a cast of over 300—actors, choristers, dancers and musicians—re-enact the events of July 1030. Once again, the Christian sovereign Olav faces his enemies, to be defeated and slain. Not far from the open-air stage is the stone-built Stiklestad church, only 100 years younger than the event it commemorates but also a place for anyone who knows or wants to know of Norwegian history.

NORTH TO THE ARCTIC CIRCLE

The city of Trondheim is a marker on the map of Norway, the gateway to the north. But anyone who looks for an immediate change in scenery will be disappointed. The first county north of Trondheim, **Nord Trøndelag**, has wide areas of rich agricultural land and prosperous looking farms.

The boundary between Nord and Sør Trøndelag runs across the Trondheim fjord, which cuts deeply into this green and pleasant land, and a large area on its western side is in the county of **Sør Trøndelag**. On the eastern shore is Norway's north-south jugular, the E6 highway, which lures a driver north and ever further north.

But this is also rail country, and the **Nordland railway** follows much the same route. Just north of Trondheim, a branch line (with a companion road) reaches over the border into Sweden. The branch veers off at the small village of **Hell**, whose station must be one of the most photographed by English-speaking visitors and whose tickets are collectors' items.

From a motorist's point of view, there is not a great deal of interest along this section of the E6 and the inclination is to keep going; but make time for **Værnes**, which has an interesting church from the Middle Ages with a fine baroque pulpit. Adjoining that is the Stjørdal open-air museum. Near **Åsen**, you will find a memorial grove to the prisoners of war executed by German occupying forces—unhappily something which is commemorated on more than one occasion further north.

St Olav's battleground: Just north of Verdalsøra is the road to **Stiklestad**, the battleground where King Olav Haraldson was killed on 29 July 1030, and revered by Norwegians as the birthplace of Norwegian national unity and the adoption of the Christian faith.

Near Utøy is **Rostad Gård** which was the home of Ole Richter, the country's prime minister in the middle of the 19th century. His life and that of his family were the subject of a play, *Paul Lange og Tora Parsberg*, by the well-known Norwegian author Bjørn-stjerne Bjørnson.

The first town of any size north of Trondheim is **Steinkjer** on the River Steinkjer by the Beitstadfjord, which has been a centre of commerce for more than 1,000 years. The **Nord Trøndelag county museum** has two branches near the town, one in the former factory of **Dampsaga**, the other a collection of old farm buildings at **Eggemarka**.

War destruction: Like so many northern Norwegian towns, Steinkjer was destroyed in World War II. After the German invasion in 1940, the king and government moved north, eventually to Tromsø, before they left to continue the government in exile from London. This meant that these sparsely populated northern areas suffered dreadful destruction through the bombing which followed the German invasion. All along this coast, you come across memorials and reminders of the years of Occupation, and towns like Steinkjer

that are little more than a modern commercial centre.

Northwest of Steinkjer are interesting rock carvings from the Stone and Bronze Ages; but much the most impressive carvings are around **Bøla** on the opposite (eastern) side of Snåsavatnet, the long narrow lake to the northeast of Steinkjer. Of these, the best is the 6,000-year-old **Bølareinen reindeer**. The scenery around the lake is remarkably soft and gentle for a latitude between 63 and 64 degrees north, and at its northern end is **Snåsa**, the centre of South Sami (Lapp) culture. It has a Sami school and cultural centre which includes a museum. To the east, about 31 miles (50 km) away, the **Gressåmoen National Park** has preserved an area of typically thick Trøndelag forest and mountain landscape.

Dotted throughout Norway—and particularly in the north—are small towns or villages which are essentially centres of communication and crossroads for many forms of transport. Typical is Grong, where the E6 runs north-south and the road and railway to Namsos on the coast goes off to the west, while just south of the town a secondary road runs east through wild countryside to the Swedish frontier at Gæddede. It is also the junction of two rivers, the **Namsen** and the **Sandøla**, both popular with anglers. Each river has an impressive waterfall not far from Grong: **Fiskumfoss** on the Namsen and **Formofoss** on the Sandøla.

This is the beginning of the long valley of Namdalen, while to the northeast is **Røyrvik**, a huge mountainous area which stretches across to the Swedish frontier. Half this region is above the tree line at 2,000 ft (610 metres) above sea level. There are three major lakes within this area: **Tunnsjøen**, Limingen and Store Namsvatnet. The first has an island peak soaring up to 2,700 ft (823 metres), and was once a Sami place of sacrifice to their old gods.

Here the contrast between the east and west of Nord Trøndelag in this area is very marked. The frontier mountains to the east, which bulge into Sweden,

A well-equipped walker starts a day out on Svartisen.

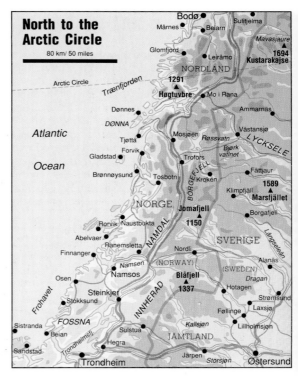

North to the Arctic Circle

have a harsh beauty but much of the land is desolate and empty. To the west, the coastal scenery is a pleasant surprise, green and fertile. All year round, the Gulf Stream warms these western coasts to the very north of Norway, making the climate much gentler at the same latitude than it is further inland, or than you would expect. Even in winter, the waters are ice-free and the ships of the Hurtigrute (the Coastal Steamer route) can travel up the west coast and round the North Cape without difficulty. At the mouth of the Namsen is **Namsos**, which has been destroyed by fire on several occasions in its comparatively short history. Only the last fire, during World War II, was deliberate.

The north end of Namdalen valley marks the border with the county of Nordland, the beginning of the real north. This border is straddled by the **Børgefjell National Park**, a district of high mountains, lakes and numerous watercourses, a backpacker's idyll for walking and to see nature.

Long miles: In these northern territo-ries, distances are long, and **Nordland** stretches 310 miles (500 km) to the north of Narvik. The Arctic Circle runs through the middle and the county includes the long, narrow islands of **Vesterålen**, and the grey peaks of the **Lofoten Islands**. (For the purposes of this chapter, the town of Bodø marks the northernmost point.)

Nordland has immense variety. If you take in all the fjords and islands, Nordland's coastline tots up to 25 percent of Norway's grand total. It includes mountains of more than 6,000 ft (1,900 metres), countless islands and skerries, the second largest glacier in Norway, **Svartisen**, and the largest inland lake, **Røsvatnet**, which covers an area of 81 sq. miles (210 sq. km.) Near the Helgeland coast is the **Bindalen valley**, green with forests. At one time, the discovery of gold turned it into a mini-Klondike. Today, it has gone back to sleep. Close to Bindal, on the side of the fjord that bears its name, is the mountain massif of **Tosenfjellet**, a favourite haunt of potholers and cavers. The big-

gest cave is **Etasjegrotten**, which is 1,531 yards (1,400 metres) long, where cavers have recently discovered an underground lake.

Between Trofors and Mosjøen, is the wide but shallow **Laksfors** waterfall which has a 52 ft (15.8 metre) drop. The best time for Norwegian waterfalls comes in late May, or even June this far north, when summer creeps north melting the snow and ice to swell the cascade, turning every trickle into a torrent.

At the end of the long curve of the Vefsnfjord, which cuts far into the land, lies **Mosjøen**, an industrial town where a splendid location fights for domination with a large aluminium works. However, Mosjøen does have **Dolstad Church**, built in 1734 and the oldest octagonal church in north Norway. Look closely at the traces of the old ornamental decor and at a wooden angel in the ceiling which is lowered for use as a baptismal font.

Near the church is the **Vefsn Museum**, founded in 1909 and one of the ubiquitous open-air museums which Scandinavians love. It brings together 12 buildings from the surrounding district, and the largest holds a collection of 5,000 objects from the olds days of farming, fishing, hunting, and domestic life. There is one old area of the town, near the point where the river Vefsna enters the fjord, where some wooden houses and warehouses have been preserved and restored.

Beyond the town the scenery changes as farmland gives way to bare fjells. There are camping sites with tents and cabins on both sides of the road north from Mosjøen to cater for the outdoor holidaymakers who especially love these northern regions. **Mo-i-Rana** is also on a fjord and, like Mosjøen, is dominated by industry—in this case, the steelworks of Norsk Jernverk. These industries in small remote towns may displease the casual visitor but they illustrate a Norwegian determination to minimise the pull of the more populated south and a sign of success in spreading industry to help people to find work within their home areas.

Though Mo-i-Rana itself may be too modern for a visitor's taste, it is within reasonable distance of several "musts" on the list of many visitors to Norway—caves, a glacier, and the **Arctic Circle**. The **Grønligrotten caves** lie around 13 miles (21 km) from the town and guides shepherd parties through a glittering underground world of stalactite-hung caverns. At **Sætergrotten**, the cave calls for care and is more suitable for expert enthusiasts, with unexplored caves, crevices and passages, and interiors of white marble and limestone.

From Mo-i-Rana, it is also easy to reach Norway's second largest glacier, **Svartisen**, which covers 143 sq miles (370 sq km) with ice up to 328 ft (100 metres) thick in places. Its second distinction is that it is the lowest-lying glacier on the European mainland, and reaches down to within 565 ft (172 metres) of sea level. The route lies off the E6 a short distance north of Mo-i-Rana, which heads northwest to Svartisvatnet. You then cross the water by boat, and walk less than 2 miles (3 km) to the glacier itself.

The edge of the glacier.

Crossing the line: Many try but few have managed to explain why it should be so exciting to cross a line you cannot see. But most people experience an inexplicable thrill and sense of achievement as they cross the Arctic Circle. It seems to mark the end of modern comforts and the beginning of the wild, and nowhere is that sense of entering the unknown stronger than on highway E6 on its long trek north.

From Mo-i-Rana, the road makes its way through the temperate landscape of **Dunderlandsdalen**, past Storsforshei iron ore mine. Then, beyond Krokstrand, the scenery begins to change as the road approaches Saltfjell, a wild and majestic mountain valley flanked by bare, brooding mountains. Apart from the road, railway line and river, there is nothing else until you come to the monuments that mark the Arctic Circle, more than 2,000 ft (650 metres) above sea level.

Alongside the official markers are numerous small stone cairns erected by visitors who felt a common need to mark the event. A café and souvenir shop, a car park and a Sami encampment which sells handicrafts, also mark the Circle. There is a scheme to build an Arctic Circle Centre beside the road which would explain the scenery, flora and fauna, the climate and Sami culture. Nature, it would seem, cannot be left to its own devices.

Slave labour: There is a darker and sadder side to this area, which dates back to World War II when thousands of prisoners of war, mainly Yugoslavs, were used to build the railway. Many perished in the bitter winter conditions, and their memorial stands in the wild mountains where they worked and died.

The summit of the Saltfjell road, at **Stødi**, is 2,320 ft (707 metres) high and these mountains also mark the limit for most temperate flora and fauna, though a few brave exceptions survive. As the road begins to descend, first the trees reappear at Lønsdal and then, as it races down towards sea level at **Rognan**, the vegetation becomes lush and abundant but flanked by impressive mountains on

Late-evening picnic by the light of the midnight sun.

either side. About half-way down, a short detour to the right and a steep climb to Junkerdalen takes you to the "silver road", a historic route from Skellefteå on the Gulf of Bothnia in Sweden, to Bodø.

This dramatic mountain scenery also leads to a unique botanical phenomenon. A bedrock of mica, which provides exceptional growing conditions, has led to a profusion of rare plants such as cyclamens, usually found only in lowland or more temperate regions. Nowhere else can you find similar growth at this height and nearly 67 degrees north. When the road reaches **Rognan** there is the inevitable local museum with 20 old buildings.

A more moving sight, a little further north at **Botn**, is a cemetery for the 1,657 Yugoslav and Russian prisoners of war who died here in World War II. Though these prisoners slaved to build a road and not a railway, the result was the same and the stretch between Rognan to Fauske earned the name of the "blood road". In another cemetery

nearby, 2,700 German soldiers are buried and a plaque commemorates the 2,000 who died in the battle cruiser *Scharnhorst*, sunk off the North Cape in 1943. It is all a sobering reminder of a grim period of recent history.

Silver and gold: Fauske, on the Skjerstadfjord, is another crossroads town. The ever-present E6 goes north to south, while another road disappears east towards the mountains. It stops at **Sulitjelma**, which owes its existence to the discovery of copper by a Lapp in 1858. The mines go down to 1,312 ft (400 metres) and produce half a million tons of ore a year. Copper pyrites, sphalerite and iron pyrites are extracted from the ore, plus a useful haul of silver and gold.

For many years, a railway alone linked the isolated community at Sulitjelma to the outside world,. When the railway closed, the road was built over the former trackbed. The wild and desolate mountain scenery of this remote area is dominated by the **Sulitjelma glacier**, whose melting waters feed

Norlandsbanen stretches hundreds of miles north to Bodø.

Sweden's river Piteå, and **Suliskongen** at 6,276 ft (1,913 metres) above sea level. Scenery like this and the mining museum at Sulitjelma, open during the summer, make a detour worthwhile, and there is tourist accommodation and a camping site.

The quarrying area around Fauske provides the unique reddish marble known as Norwegian rose, which has been used to decorate important buildings throughout the world, including the United Nations building in New York. Fauske itself was destroyed by bombs in 1940 and so, in practical terms, is only 50 years old, though the **Bodin Church** nearby, built in 1200 with additions in 1784, was one of the few buildings to survive the attacks.

In this narrow part of Norway—and even more so as the road heads north—you are never far from either the sea or the Swedish border. At Fauske, midway between both, road 80 and the railway turn west and run along the north of the fjord to **Bodø**, on the west coast.

Modern centre: Bodø is another marker along the way to the far north. Like many of the coastal towns, it began as a small community, a safe place for boats and fishermen, and stayed small until the 1860s and 1870s, when three changes brought prosperity: the herring fisheries developed fast, the Sulitjelma mines started production, and the first coastal steamer service began to link the towns of the west coast. It, too, was largely laid waste in attacks by German forces in May 1940 and today it is essentially a spacious modern town with a population of 32,000.

Bodø is the commercial and administrative centre. It is also a staging post for summer visitors, the end of the Nordland railway line, where the backpackers get down and continue north by coastal steamer or bus. The town has a county museum and the **Bodøsjøen Open Air Museum** by the Saltenfjord, some 2½ miles (4 km) from the centre.

More interesting than either is the old trading centre at **Kjerringøy**, which is on the coast 25 miles (40 km) to the north. Long overtaken by Bodø, Kjer-

Reindeer have right of way.

ringøy was one of the richest trading settlements in northern Norway in the 19th century. It has 15 preserved buildings, all with their furnishings, and some typical Nordland boats.

If you are travelling north by the E6, largely an inland route, when you reach Bodø again on your return journey, you might like to try another route south, although it takes in innumerable ferry crossings: road 17 starts just northeast of the town by bridging the **Saltstraumen**, where a combination of powerful currents and a narrow channel twice a day create a vast rush of water, and violent "kettles" or whirlpools. This is the most powerful maelstrom in Norway, some 480 million cubic yards (372 million cubic metres) of water pour through the sound which is less than 49 ft (15 metres) wide, at a rate of up to 28 knots. Saltstraumen is a joy to anglers and seabirds alike, as the current brings an abundance of fish.

The road follows coast and fjord on its way south, and passes Våg on the island of Sandhornøy, and **Blixgård**

(manor) which has a memorial to the poet Elias Blix, who composed North Norway's national anthem "*Å eg veit meg eit land*", (Oh, I know of a land).

At **Glomfjord** a chair-lift gives wonderful views and you can also reach an arm of the Svartisen glacier. However, it is better to keep to road 17 which goes through a major tunnel under the outer edge of the glacier and comes out alongside Nordfjord, cross the Holandsfjord and then walk to the base of the glacier.

Four ferries later, the road reaches **Sandnessjøen**, on the northern tip of the island of Alsten, a trading centre for more than 300 years.

Alstahaug on the southern point has a 12th-century church and memorial stone to the parson-poet Petter Dass who lived there from 1689 until his death in 1708. Dass was so well-known that, after his death, most Norwegian ships carried a black patch on their sails as a badge of mourning, a practice that continued for over 100 years. Today, the life and work of Petter Dass is commemorated by a biennial four-day cultural event.

A short ferry crossing takes you to the island of Dønna, where **Dønna Manor** has been an estate from saga times until the present day. The 13th-century stone church has secret passages cut into the walls which revealed a hoard of coins, some dating back to the time of King Håkon Håkonsson (1204–63), during restoration work in 1974.

On the eastern side of Alsten is a mountain range with seven peaks known as **De Syv Søstre** (the seven sisters). South of Sandnessjøen is **Tjøtta** which was the home of Hårek, one of the chieftains who killed King Olav at Stiklestad.

This entire area is full of burial mounds and monoliths. There is also a war cemetery for the 7,500 Russians who died as prisoners of war in World War II, and even more heart-rending is the **Riegel Cemetery** which has the graves of over 1,000 of nearly 3,000 Russians, Germans, Poles, Czechs and Norwegians. They died when *Riegel* was sunk in 1945 outside Tjøtta, de-

Many air routes lead to Bodø Airport.

stroyed by allied aircraft unaware of its human cargo.

Old hat: Further south near Brønnøysund and after two more ferry crossings, is another strange natural phenomenon. The high hat-shaped island of **Torghatten** is pierced 525 ft (160 metres) up by a great hole more than 130 ft (40 metres) high. Legend has it that the hole was made by a horseman, thwarted in love, who shot an arrow at his lady, the Maid of Leka.

Just in time, the mountain king of Sømnafjellet saw what was happening and threw his hat in the air to intercept the arrow. At that moment the sun rose and all were transformed into stone. The Maid of Leka stands petrified on the island of **Leka**. Torghatten has its hole and to the north is the island of **Hestmannøy** to represent the horseman.

A more prosaic explanation is action by frost and sea towards the end of the last Ice Age when the island was considerably lower than it is today. A small road takes you to Torhatten, the it is a 30-minute scramble up to the hole.

The **Brønnøysund** area has some of the most fertile land and the largest farms in northern Norway. The island museum of Leka has many curiosities, including boats and fishing equipment. **Herlaugshaugen** has Norway's second largest Viking burial mound. South of Leka is **Vikna**, the largest in this astonishing chain of 6,000 islands and skerries. Vikna is linked to the mainland by a 2,296 ft (700 metre) bridge over the **Nærøysund** which, so the old legends relate, was the battleground of giants and trolls.

After one more ferry, road 17 deserts the coast it has followed so slavishly on its long route south and moves inland through Namsos until it joins the ubiquitous E6 just north of Steinkjer. This is no whistle-stop tour but, if you choose the inland route north and return south along the sea, the journey will bring a wonderful mix of fjords, islands, rivers and waterfalls, lakes and forests, mountains and fertile farmland—almost every facet of the land that lies between Trondheim and Bodø.

Everyone's favourite: the comical puffins abound on the northern coasts.

ISLANDS AND MOUNTAINS

Viewed from the mainland across the broad expanse of the Vestfjord, the Lofoten Islands present an imposing wall of jagged peaks rising up sheer from the sea. On the west these mountains form a mighty breakwater from the onslaught of the Arctic Ocean, a 70-mile (112-km) archipelago which stretches from the waters of the narrow Raftsund in the north to the tiny island of Røst in the south. In winter the coast is one of the stormiest in Europe while the unsurpassed summer beauty of the islands makes them one of Norway's major tourist attractions.

Between the mountains, which are composed of some of the oldest rocks in the world, are stretches of fertile farmland, fjords and deep ravines while the coastline is sprinkled with fishing villages and one or two small towns.

A phenomenon peculiar to the Lofotens is the annual cod fishing which in the past involved up to 6,000 boats and 30,000 fishermen. Between January and March these migrant fishermen lived in simple waterside wooden cabins called *rorbuer*. By 1947 the number of fishermen was declining and today it is down to 2,000, and this seasonal event has been replaced by a year-round fishing fleet. The *rorbuer* have been spruced up and provided with additional modern conveniences and are now rented to summer visitors.

Svolvær, the principal town, is on the island of Austvågøy and has been a trading centre since the 17th century. Virtually surrounded by water—and confusing to the visitor on that account—it is flanked by sharp pointed rocky peaks. Some of these rise almost straight up from the gardens while the **Svolværgeita** (the Svolvær goat) is the town's own special mountain.

The town has connections to the mainland by ferry to Skutvik, and by coastal steamer to Bodø. Svolvær, like the Lofotens as a whole, has become a major attraction for artists and craftsmen and there is now an artists' centre

and, at nearby **Kabelvåg**, a school of art. Kabelvåg's impressive wooden church looks old but was in fact built in 1898. On the outskirts is the **Lofot Museum** on historical ground where **Vågar**, the first town north of the Arctic Circle, existed in the Middle Ages.

Payment in fish: The main museum building was originally in the centre of the thriving fishing community and one room is furnished as a fish station owner's office in the 1880's. He would own all the *rorbuer* and the fishermen who rented them would pay in fish from their catches. There is a typical *rorbu* from 1789, with its primitive and crowded living conditions, and a boathouse with three traditional boats of various sizes. Another building is devoted to the development of the Lofoten fishing industry which in its modernised form plays a vital role in the economy of the islands.

Kabelvåg gained a new attraction in 1989 with the opening of a **Lofoten aquarium**, which is designed as a small fishing village with wharves, and in-

Preceding pages: Røost in Lofoten; night over the Tjelsund Bridge and the Ice Cathedral in Tromsø. **Left**, small boats and *rorbuer* (old fishing cottages) in Stamsund. **Right**, island fisherman.

cludes both salt and fresh water fish and a seal tank.

To journey south means going from island to island, all of which, bar one, have gradually been linked by impressive bridges. The one remaining ferry connection is due to be replaced by an undersea road tunnel in 1990.

On the southern tip of Austvågøy is **Henningsvær**, one of numerous Lofoten fishing villages, while the imposing bridge over the Gimsøystraumen, 2,756 ft (840 metres) long, provides access to the small island of Gimsøya. From here a second bridge takes the road across the Sundklakkstraumen to Vestvågøy. Stamsund, on a secondary road, is a coastal village and a port of call for the coastal steamer.

The **Vestvågøy Museum** is at Fygle, near Leknes, and has exhibits showing how the fisherman-farmer's life has changed over the years. **Leknes** is the main centre of population on the island and a typical small Norwegian town with a long straggling main street. A few miles south at **Lilleeidet** is the ferry to Napp on **Flakstadøya**. It became redundant in July 1990 with the opening of the tunnel 164 ft (50 metres) below the surface of Nappstraumen.

Paddling north of the Arctic: The west coast of Flakstadøya provides the surprise of wide sandy beaches. On a sunny summer's day, the sight of children playing and paddling belies the fact that it is several hundred miles north of the Arctic Circle. The hamlet of **Flakstad** has a pretty little 18th-century church with an onion dome while nearby are monuments to those who died in World War II and fishermen whose lives were lost at sea.

Nusfjord and **Sund** are two other fishing villages on the island. The former is on UNESCO's list of preservation-worthy environments while Sund has a small fisheries museum. One section is devoted to early marine engines while the adjoining **Smithy** is now used by the artist Hans Gjertsen who is well-known for his stylishly crafted steel cormorants. Also on the island is **Storbåthallaren**, the oldest known stone age set-

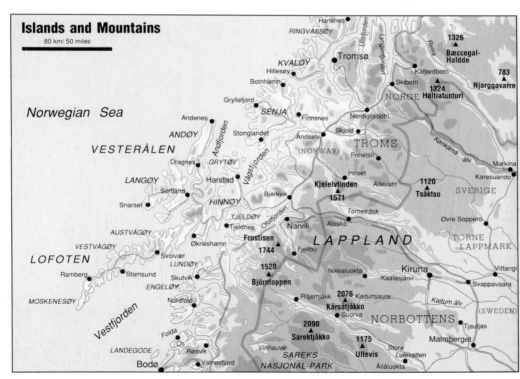

tlement in Northern Norway populated 6,000 years ago. More recent is **Østre Nesland**, a derelict fishing and farming hamlet with some preserved buildings.

The last bridge takes the road across to the island of **Moskensøy**. This also has its quota of fishing villages of which the most picturesque is **Reine**. The road clings close to the coast and looks towards the mainland mountains clear across the Vestfjord.

Road 19 finally runs out at Å, the village with the shortest name in the world. The sign on the outskirts must be the most photographed in the Lofotens. Å marks the end of the Lofoten "wall" and the village has some old buildings and one of the few trading posts to be preserved in its original condition. There is a small **Fishery and Farming Museum** in a 19th-century barn, and the white painted wooden café opposite offers coffee and home-made cakes.

Beyond the tip of Moskensøy is the **Moskenstraumen**, a maelstrom which may not match the Saltstraumen near Bodø but which was once greatly feared by sailors. Even in calm weather it seethes and boils and was made famous through the works of Jules Verne and Edgar Allan Poe.

For the birds: The maelstrom separates Moskensøy from the small island of **Værøy**, beyond which is the even smaller island of **Røst**. These are the "bird islands", which attract thousands of different birds of various species including puffin, auk, eider, guillemot, kittiwake and cormorant.

Both islands have small airfields with scheduled flights to Bodø, obviating a sea trip which, because of the rapidly changing sea conditions, can be unpleasant. It never gets very cold on Røst or Værøy and sheep can graze on the meadows throughout the winter. The January temperatures are, on average, 20° C (68° F), higher than in other places in the same latitude.

The journey south from Svolvær to Å must rank as one of the most outstanding in Norway. At every turn the traveller is confronted with another seemingly haphazard series of jagged peaks

Leknes.

rising to a height of between 2,000 ft (609 metres) and 3,000 ft (914 metres) and possessing a stark beauty which contrasts with the green and benign scenery at sea level.

North of Svolvær the views may be splendid but they do not quite measure up to those in the south. In truth, this is only a question of degree because the Lofoten Islands have such a richness of views that they almost give you scenic indigestion. Heading north, the road keeps close to the Austnesfjord, beyond which, to the northeast, is the Raftsund and the narrow, grim Trollfjord which is used by the coastal steamer in summer.

At Fiskebøl the ferry takes the visitor away from the Lofotens to **Melbu** on the first of the **Vesterålen Islands**, Hadseløya. As if to emphasise that you have left the Lofotens behind, **Melbu** has the **Vesterålen Museum**, housed in an Empire-style manor house. Among the exhibits is an interesting collection of 18th-century costumes.

Between Melbu and Stokmarknes on the northern side of the island is **Hadsel Church** (1824), distinctive in style and with an altar piece from 1520. **Stokmarknes** was a trading post in the 18th century and is also the headquarters of the Vesteraalen Steamship Company, founded by Richard With, sometimes called the father of the coastal steamer.

The little town lacks character, the most impressive thing being the Hadsel Bridge 3,937 ft (1,200 metres) in length which carries the main road to the island of Langøya. Here the principal town is **Sortland**, a commercial centre with a fishing harbour that has a busy and pleasant atmosphere.

The western side of the island has imposing mountains, the most unusual being the sway-backed **Reka** at 1,991 ft (607 metres) which is popular with climbers. The most northerly point is **Langenes** with its early 16th-century church and in the south west is **Vinjesjøen** which has a fishing museum.

The Sortland Bridge, 3,153 ft (961 metres) long is the link to **Hinnøya**, Norway's largest island. Away to the north west is the long island of **Andøya**,

Restored *rorbuer* are very popular with holiday-makers.

which is also connected by bridge and, unlike most other Vesterålen islands, is flat. Much of the land is peat, renowned for its cloudberries. **Andenes**, at the northwestern extremity, is a large fishing village with a **Polar Museum**. It was a fishing village in the Middle Ages and then a Dutch whaling base in the 17th century. The most noticeable feature is the lighthouse, 157 ft (48 metres) high and built in 1856.

Hinnøya's scenery varies: farmland along the coastal fringe, green valleys, rugged mountains and fjords. On its eastern coast is **Lødingen** with a ferry service to Bognes on the mainland. To the north is **Harstad**, the principal Vesterålen town with a population of 22,000. Originally devoted to fishing it is now a commercial and administrative centre with a shipyard, engineering works and a base for the offshore oil industry; it is also a garrison town.

Adolf's guns: A little to the north is **Trondenes** which has a stone-built 13th-century church, the most northerly example in Romanesque/Gothic style.

In the bay below there are Viking burial mounds. Also here are the Adolf Cannons, massive long-range guns installed by the German forces in World War II to protect the approaches to Narvik. Visits can be made but only accompanied by a local guide.

A final lengthy bridge 3,284 ft (1,000 metres) long carries the main road over the Tjeldsundet and on to the mainland, although to the confused motorist it may appear to be another island. This extensive area of Nordland is separated from the rest of the county by the wide expanse of the **Ofotfjord** which provides deep-water access to Narvik.

If the Lofoten and Vesterålen islands are ignored the only alternative way north is by the inevitable E6. From Fauske it clings to the side of fjords, going through a succession of tunnels, with the **Rago National Park** away to the east stretching as far as the Swedish frontier. This is a vast mountainous area with no roads, judged to be the most magnificent but least accessible of all Norway's National Parks.

Morning service at Hadsel Church, Vesterålen.

A superb new section of highway has been built from Sommarset, where formerly there was a ferry, which cuts across exciting mountainous country. In many areas of the north these new roads have given exciting new access to country that, in earlier days, had been seen only by a few hardy walkers. There are several tunnels, the longest being below the **Sildhopfjell**. North of Kråkmo, at **Sagelv**, there are 5,000-year-old rock carvings of reindeer (early man was a prolific graffiti artist in this part of Norway).

At Ulsvåg a road goes off west across Hamarøy to Skutvik for the ferry to **Svolvær**. Until recently another ferry provided the only link with a number of small communities which, although close to the fjord, were actually on the mainland and also the island of **Engeløya**, but now a new road provides an alternative.

Hamarøy is the childhood home of Nordland's greatest author and poet, Knut Hamsun. A biennial cultural event, *The Hamsun Days*, commemo-rates his life and work. Engeløya island was a seat of power many centuries ago and there are numerous graves and burial mounds, the biggest being at **Sigarshaugen**.

A little north of Bognes are more rock carvings depicting 40 different subjects. To the east of the Tysfjord is a mountainous section popular with climbers, especially **Stetind**, 4,567 ft (1,392 metres) high which is called the "world's greatest obelisk". There are numerous caves for those who prefer to go down rather than up, the best known being **Råggejavie**, 2,034 ft (620 metres) deep. For the remaining miles to Narvik the road clings to the side of the Ofotfjord, providing some outstanding views to the west.

The deep, ice-free waters of the Ofotfjord were the reason for **Narvik** becoming a major centre for the export of the iron ore mined in northern Sweden, and a railway was completed from the mining town of Kiruna to the port in 1883. In World War II Narvik was the scene of bitter fighting and these events

Students celebrate the end of the academic year. Tromsø University is the most northerly in Europe.

are portrayed in the local **War Museum**. Today the town is a staging post for tourists. For an overview of Narvik and its surroundings take the cable car to the top of **Fagernes** 2,296 ft (700 metres) high, but at ground level Narvik is uninteresting.

North of Narvik the E6 crosses the Rombakfjord over another major bridge, passes the junction with the road to Sweden which was opened in 1984, and joins with road 19 at Bjerkvik. Then follows a climb up the **Gratangseidet** county boundary into Troms.

Troms is one of the three northern counties, sandwiched between Nordland and Finnmark. It has widely contrasting scenery, all typically North Norwegian: rugged mountains, with sharp peaks, countless islands and skerries, a softer landscape at sea level and fast-flowing rivers and numerous lakes. The county is split up by a number of major fjords and is also notable for its extensively forested valleys.

Setermoen, the first town north of Narvik, lies in the heart of a military area and has a large garrison. The military presence is also apparent further north at **Andselv**, with its major airbase at Bardufoss.

To the south of Andselv at **Elverum** a road goes east from which you can reach **Målselvfossen Waterfall**. It may only have a drop of 50 ft (15 metres) but it extends over 1,968 ft (600 metres). There are salmon ladders and the Målselv river, which is renowned for its salmon, was discovered by English anglers as early as the 1840s.

At Rundhaug a secondary road follows the Målselv to Øverbygd, then continues along **Tamokdalen** with its strangely shaped mountains until it rejoins the E6 near Øvergård. The river meanwhile continues eastward to the Store Rostavatn, a lake bordering Sweden. To the south lies the **Rostadalen and Dividalen National Park** where all four of Norway's major predators— bear, wolf, lynx and wolverine— have their habitat. Some 2½ miles (4 km) from Andselv is the **Målselv Bygdemuseum** which has a small collection of local buildings from 1820 to 1900.

To the west, on the Solbergfjord, Sørreisa is the junction of two roads, one threading its way south to Salangen and eventually looping back to the E6. In the opposite direction the second road goes to **Finnsnes**, an important traffic centre facing **Senja**, Norway's second largest island. It is a natural starting point for the exploration of this island, which you reach across the Gisund bridge 3,759 ft (1,146 metres) in length. There is a mix of scenery on the island which also includes the **Anderdalen National Park**.

Road builders' gift: From Andselv the E6 follows the Målselv river until it turns abruptly east past Takvatnet (lake) where a major new cut-off provides some stunning views of distant mountains, a bounty conferred on the motorist by the road builders. The new road bypasses **Storsteinnes**, on the Balsfjord, which is a major producer of goat's cheese. Near **Balsfjord Church** about 6¼ miles (10 km) from Storsteinnes are rock carvings which are 2,500 to 4,000 years old.

Boatbuilder with a Norlandsbåt, the traditional northern craft.

The area around Balsfjord has some of the richest farming land in Troms and goat herding and breeding is a major activity in this green and fertile district.

Tromsø occupies most of the island of Tromsøya and overflows on to the adjoining island of Kvaløya. With a population of 45,000 it is by far the largest town in Northern Norway and, until the opening of the bridge in 1960, everything had to be ferried across from the mainland.

The town has variously been called the Gateway to the Arctic, the Arctic Ocean city and the Paris of the North. The first two names may have some justification but the third sobriquet requires an extensive imagination. Fishing is of prime importance and today the centre of the town boasts four large fish filleting factories as well as the country's largest shrimp processing plant and three herring oil factories. These make Tromsø's other nickname as Norway's "largest fishing village" the most believable.

Trappers' territory: In the early 19th century it was the natural starting point for trapping expeditions to the pack ice both to the north and the east to Spitsbergen. The trappers would set sail to the White Sea, Greenland and Newfoundland, returning months later with their spoils.

Today Tromsø, which fortunately was not laid to waste in World War II, has North Norway's only university (established in 1972) and the country's northernmost brewery—Mack, famous for its Arctic Ale, with a beer hall below the premises. The town is well endowed with museums, the old established **Town Museum** being the largest in this part of Norway. There is also a **Polar Museum**, a **Marine Aquarium** and the **Troms Folk Museum**.

In the centre of the town is the **Cathedral** completed in 1861, which is one of the country's largest wooden churches, seating 750. On the mainland is the modern **Tromsdal Church**, opened in 1965 and usually referred to as the **Arctic Ocean Cathedral**. Near it is the cable car to the top of the **Storsteinen,**

Left, racks of drying fish have their own "guard" to deter hungry birds. **Right,** Tromsø church in winter.

1,378 ft (420 metres) where there are magnificent views over the town and the surrounding area.

On the island of **Kvaløya**, which is reached by another imposing bridge opened in 1975, is the **Northern Light Planetarium** at Breivika while at Straumen farm there is a collection of 10 period buildings. To the north west of Tromsø lie a number of islands which stand guard where the lengthy Ullsfjord and Lyngenfjord reach the sea.

Between these two major fjords is a long wide peninsula with, on its eastern side, the range of mountains known as the **Lyngen Alps** which are a favourite haunt of climbers. The full majesty of these snow-capped peaks and glaciers, some of which are over 5,000 ft (1,524 metres) high is best seen from the eastern side of the Lyngenfjord.

From Tromsø there is an attractive alternative route which avoids the main road and affords additional fine views of the Lyngen Alps. It involves road 91 through the Breivik valley, a ferry across the Ullsfjord to **Svensby** then a drive to **Lyngseidet** and a second ferry crossing to **Olderdalen** on the mainland and on the E6.

The more obvious route is along the E78 to where it joins the E6 at **Nordkjosbotn** and then through **Skibotn**, keeping along the shore of the Lyngenfjord with its views of the Lyngen mountains across the water. After changing direction along the side of the Rotsundet, opposite the island of Uløya, the road swings inland before meeting the Reisafjord. There are fine views to the west which are even better after climbing over the summit of **Kvænangsfjellet** 1,319 ft (402 metres) above sea level.

There is an impressive panorama of islands and mainland mountains before descending to Burfjord. Away to the west of Alteidet a minor road goes to the Jøkelfjord where the **Øksjord Glacier** calves into the sea, the only one in Norway to do so. A short distance beyond Alteidet is the boundary into Norway's most remote northerly county, Finnmark.

Tromsø Ice Cathedral.

NORTH CAPE
AND BEYOND

No-one describes Finnmark without a combination of superlatives and impressive statistics. It is Norway's most northerly county and the largest; it covers 18,528 sq. miles (48,000 sq. km) equal to 15 percent of the entire country and yet it has only 75,000 inhabitants— 2 percent of the population.

Finnmark lies along the same latitude as Alaska and Siberia but the Gulf Stream ensures that the harbours do not freeze even in the depths of winter. Inland the temperature can drop to a chilling –50° C (–70° F). During the short summer, it may nit 32° C (90° F). Between mid-May and the end of July, the sun never sets, and gives 24 hours of daylight, clear enough to read a newspaper outside, while in winter the sun stays snug below the horizon from the end of November to the end of January.

The scenery is spectacular with the highest areas in the northwest and the less mountainous regions to the east and southeast. The bare grey rocks of the coast take the full force of the winter storms that sweep in from the Arctic.

It is the vastness of the uninhabited areas that make the greatest impression: ranges of mountains and fjells stretch away to the horizon, seemingly without end, silent and awe-inspiring. The coast has its own gaunt beauty with sudden patches of green and pleasant scenery which catches the visitor unawares.

Much of this wonderful county is now easily accessible by car or public transport on well-surfaced main roads, while there is an extensive network of air services which land at tiny airports dotted all over the area, and the ubiquitous coastal steamer serves towns and villages along the coast.

Ancient people: Despite the inhospitable nature of the region and the ferocity of the winter, the people of Finnmark are greatly attached to their part of Norway, which has been inhabited for 10,000 years. They include not only Norwegians and Sami (Lapps) but also many Finns. The Norwegians settled along the coast in the 14th century but major changes in the 18th and 19th centuries brought in people from the south of the country. At the same time came a large migration from Finland and Sweden.

Scorched earth: World War II was a nightmare for the county when, as Soviet liberators crossed the northern border in the autumn of 1944, the German occupation forces began a scorched earth policy as they retreated south, burning towns and villages and even individual farms as they went.

Alta, the first town across the country border from Troms is also the biggest, with a population of 14,000. It is really several places linked together: Aparnes, Bossekop, Sentrum, Bukta, and Elvebakken. Some of the architecture is undistinguished, often the case in north Norwegian towns which had to rebuild rapidly after World War II.

But if parts of Alta are less than imposing, it does have a major archaeological attraction. On the southern outskirts is an outstanding collection of

prehistoric rock carvings at **Hjemmeluft**. They were discovered in 1973 and are now on UNESCO's World Heritage list. Some 2,500 to 3,000 lie on four different sites, with the biggest concentration at Hjemmeluft.

These "stories in pictures" are estimated at 2,500 to 6,000 years old and depict people, animals (particularly reindeer) boats, weapons, and some which have yet to be identified. Traces of these early inhabitants, the Komsa people, were discovered in 1925 on **Komsafjell**, which bulges out into the Altafjord. Here the dwelling sites go back some 10,000 years, a sobering reminder of how long human beings have lived in this apparently inhospitable region.

Alta Museum has historical exhibits relating to fjord and river fishing, slate quarrying (still carried on today), Sami costumes and the Alta forest. The church, built in 1850, was the only building to survive the war. This town is an important communications centre and is developing local industries, while the Alta river is famous for its salmon fishing.

Sami culture: Finnmark has few roads, so it is easy to find your way. Going south from Alta is road 93 to **Kautakeino** and the Finnish frontier. Kautakeino is the largest Sami community in the county and the centre of Sami education. The **Kulturhus** has the only Sami theatre in Norway, and the museum has indoor and outdoor exhibits showing Sami life in old Kautokeino.

Northwards from **Leirbotnvatn** (around the fjord from Alta) to the village of Skaidi is 55 miles (89 km) of sheer emptiness. The ever-present E6 takes a lonely course through the wonderful, if awesome, stretch of wild countryside. Almost the only building is the small **Sami chapel**, completely dwarfed by the immensity of its surroundings. The only signs of life away from the road are the vast herds of reindeer. Despite today's roads and vehicles, on a first journey through this huge territory, you find yourself constantly aware of how little human activ-

<u>Left</u>, old print of a Sami woman and child. <u>Right</u>, selling skins and other Sami goods.

ity has impinged on the grandeur of its great empty spaces. Outside the modern life of the coastal towns, villages cling close and even a lonely church merits a mention on the map.

Skaidi is a popular base for local anglers, hunters and winter sports enthusiasts. It is also the junction of the E6 and the road to Hammerfest (35 miles (56 km) away on the island of Kvaløya) through the Repparfjord valley, and along the southern bank of the fjord to the lengthy suspension bridge which connects the mainland to the island.

Hammerfest on its bare rocky island is the world's most northerly town. It was founded in 1789. For centuries it was the best ice-free harbour in northern waters, although storms and hurricanes plus many man-made disasters have repeatedly wrought havoc on the town. In 1825, a hurricane destroyed houses and boats, and an even more ferocious storm in 1882 moved the German Kaiser, Queen Victoria, and the Tsar of Russia to donate money to repair the damage. In 1890, the town had ambitious plans for a hydro-electric power station but, only a month after work started, fire again destroyed two-thirds of the town. In the following year, nevertheless, Hammerfest became the first European town to have electric street and domestic lighting.

Destruction by fire: The harbour has always been of importance both commercially and strategically and ships have long called there. For over 100 years it was also the principal Norwegian base for hunting and fishing. When Norway was invaded in 1940, it was a growing and flourishing community. The retreating Germans burned down the entire town and by 10 February 1945 it had been wiped out except for the chapel in the graveyard. Today it is Norway's main trawler port, devoted to all aspects of the fishing industry.

Hammerfest clings to the curving shore line which is backed by a steep escarpment. Its most notable monument is the **Meridian Column** which was erected by King Oskar II to commemorate the first international meas-

Contrasting styles at the Sami market in Hammerfest.

urement of the earth, a joint enterprise by Russia, Norway, and Sweden. On the highest point of a walk from town centre up the escarpment is the **Midday Pole**, erected at the end of the 19th century and topped by a cannonball. When the shadow from the Midday Pole points directly to the Meridian Column, the time is 12 noon precisely. The cannonball itself is a reminder of another episode in Hammerfest's history.

In 1809, after Norway became involved in the Napoleonic wars, two British warships attacked Hammerfest. The town fell to the British who stayed for a week of plunder and destruction. The British cannonball is the permanent reminder of this unhappy event. To prevent any further attack the military built a redoubt or **Skansen** in 1810 with eight guns, which Hammerfest folk are happy to report never fired in anger. This walk also passes a beacon built by the young people of the town in 1882–83 "as they had no other amusements." The occupation forces pulled it down but the town rebuilt it in 1982–83,

though by this time the young people had other amusements.

More noticeable today is the circular **Isbjørnhallen** (Polar Bear Hall) used for sporting events and exhibitions. At the opposite end of the town is the equally striking **church**, its form inspired by traditional wooden fish-drying racks, which was consecrated in 1961. Its altar piece, which dates back to 1632 comes from Hammerfest's first church. The fountain in the town centre was a gift from Charles Ulrick Bay, a former US Ambassador whose mother came from Hammerfest. The sculpture on the fountain—"mother and children"—is the work of Ørnulf Bast.

Profitable polar bears: In a shrewd move in 1963, Hammerfest created the **Royal and Ancient Polar Bear Society**, which must earn the town a tidy sum, and offers one of the more attractive souvenirs of its kind. To get this certificate of membership, you must apply in person to the Polar Bear Society's Museum in the Town Hall.

From Skaidi the E6 goes northeast

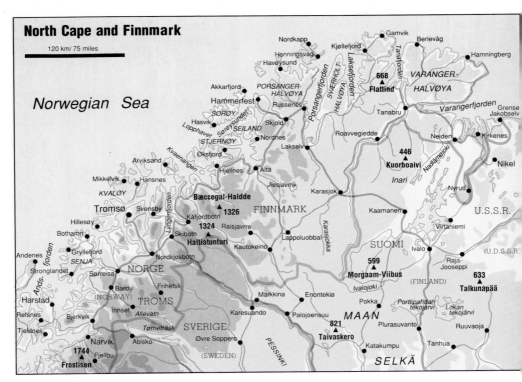

North Cape and Finnmark

120 km/ 75 miles

across another stretch of wild, uninhabited landscape before the road descends to the sea at Olderfjord. Here the majority of visitors turn north for Finnmark's overwhelming attraction: **North Cape**.

Nordkapp or North Cape is for many the Holy Grail, the end of their pilgrimage by car, motor-home, motor bike, bus or even bicycle. The alternative is to fly to Honningsvåg or sail there by coastal steamer or cruise liner.

The road hugs the edge of the huge Porsanger fjord, with rugged country to the landward side, and ends at the ferry terminal at **Kåfjord** where the ferries run to Honningsvåg on the island of **Magerøya**. This is the last obstacle before North Cape and in the peak summer season, you may face a lengthy delay before making the 55 minute crossing. But take heart; an undersea tunnel 4½ miles (7 km) long is planned, and due for completion in 1997 when North Cape will become a year-round instead of a summer only attraction.

Between Honningsvåg and the North Cape lie 21 miles (35 km) of the only genuine **Arctic scenery** in Europe. It may be bare and treeless but there is a stark beauty about the island which, on a sunny day, is emphasised by the clarity of the atmosphere; too often, alas, misty conditions prevail.

China route: The name North Cape was given to this imposing headland by an Englishman, Captain Richard Chancellor. In 1553, as master of the *Edward Bonaventure*, he was seeking a new route to China when he rounded Europe's most dramatic northern cape, but it was not until the 19th century that the Cape began to attract visitors. In 1845, passengers from the *Prinds Gustav*, were rowed ashore and then had to struggle up 1,000 ft (300 metres) to the plateau at the top. After a visit by the intrepid King Oskar II in 1873, Thomas Cook arranged the first organised tour for 24 Englishmen in 1875.

By 1880, a path with primitive railings from **Horn Bay** to the top had appeared and you can still see the remains of the quay by taking the 7-mile (11-km) walk from the plateau. The

Hammerfest Harbour.

coastal steamers have provided the biggest impetus to tourist traffic and by 1920, the wild grandeur of North Cape had learned to live with the incongruity of its first building, an eight-sided pavilion with a post office and refreshments.

The road from Honningsvåg opened in 1956, as did a centre, **Nordkapp-huset**, with the usual souvenir shop, cafeteria and post office. In 1988–89, this earlier building gave way to the new centre, with its circular **Compass Restaurant** and, below, the **Supervideograph**, where a 225-degree screen and wrap-around sound bring the four seasons of Finnmark to the visitor, whatever the time of year.

An underground tunnel leads from the new building to the **North Cape Hall** and champagne bar, which is like an amphitheatre cut out of the rock and overlooks the Arctic Ocean. Even if you suffer from vertigo, look briefly from the balcony which provides a spectacular view straight down to the sea far below. Along the tunnel are tableaux depicting historical events at the North

Cape, such as the visit of King Oskar II, who also has a monument on the plateau to commemorate the same occasion.

Too many people: On what is in danger of becoming a crowded plateau are seven circular, wheel-like sculptures. They are monuments to the children of the world, sculpted by seven children, aged between eight and 12 years, from seven lands. In 1988, they spent seven days at North Cape, to carve the sculptures as monuments to joy, friendship, and working together. A monument nearby entitled *Mother and Child* is by the sculptor Eva Rybakken.

Apart from the main road to Nordkapp itself, there is only one other road on the island, which leads to the village of **Gjesvær** on the west coast. On the eastern side of Magerøya is the little fishing community of **Skarsvåg**. **Honningsvåg**, where the ferry arrives, has been a fishing harbour for many years and an important pilot station. In the old days, the trawlers were the most frequent visitors, and up to 4,000 called each year at this remote northerly port.

Europe's most famous headland, Nordkapp (North Cape).

Most were British and through their visits, Honningsvåg developed "haddock English," a mixture of sign language and occasional English words. Like other centres in the north, Honningsvåg burned down during hostilities and by the end of World War II the 1884 church was the only building left standing on the island. Honningsvåg today also has a small local museum.

Most villages and towns in Finnmark sit along the coast but the two main Sami communities are the exception. Kautokeino and Karasjok are deep inland. Returning from North Cape, continue south through Lakselv at the end of the Porsangerfjord, to Karasjok, the second important Sami centre. The town's 1807 church is the oldest in Finnmark, and was lucky enough to survive the war, and the Sami Museum and Library has a unique collection of Sami literature. At Karasjok the main E6 road makes a massive U-turn and heads north again, keeping company with the Tana river through its every twist and turn, all the way to Tana Bru,

some 112 miles (180 km) to the north.

Tana Bru, at the first bridge across the river, is also a meeting place of four roads. One is the alternative route north, which veers away from the E6 at the head of the Porsanger fjord. This long road has few communities but an abundance of beautiful scenery and it rolls ahead across two magnificent inland stretches—from **Børselv** to **Adamsfjord** and across the **Ifjordfjell**. At Ifjord a road pushes even further north to the **Nordkyn** peninsula, to reach Kjøllefjord, Mehamn and Gamvik, across the very top of the country.

Over the bridge at Tana Bru, the E6 divides; the main road winds a long route east towards Kirkenes, only 3 miles (5 km) from the Russian border, while another road heads north until it reaches Berlevåg, and also Båtsfjord, on a magnificent offshoot road only opened in 1961, which crosses the highest pass in Finnmark, the **Oarddojokke** at 1,312 ft (400 metres) above sea level. Berlevåg and Båtsfjord are fishing villages, both on the far coast of the Var-

The children's statues at Nordkapp.

North Cape and Beyond 345

anger peninsula, last of the three that stand out from the north of Norway.

As the road travels east, it divides yet again at Varangerbotn, after the narrow neck of land that joins the Varanger peninsula to the mainland. In this part of Norway, where the fjords and coastline bite deep into the land, you are rarely far from water. **Varangerbotn** has a small but interesting **Sami Museum** and it is worth making a detour along the north coast of the Varangerfjord on road 98 to **Vadsø**, the administrative centre of Finnmark. On the way, at **Nesseby**, you find a small wooden church built in 1858 and Varanger's oldest log cabin, from 1700. The surprise of this whole remote area is that it is rich in archaeological finds, with graves and places of sacrifice to indicate human occupation as early as 9,000 BC.

Finns too: A monument to Finnish immigration in Vadsø explains why many inhabitants are of Finnish origin and Finnish-speaking, and the local museum highlights the two nationalities. It is housed in two buildings, one a Finnish style dwelling (Tuoainen-gården) and the other a patrician house from 1840 (Esbensengården). Vadsø's church, built in 1958, is of striking appearance. In front, the **King Stone** bears the signatures of King Olav V of Norway, President Kekkonen of Finland, and King Carl Gustav of Sweden, who all visited the town in 1977, to commemorate the unveiling of the **Immigrant Monument** to the Finns who came to find food and work in Finnmark in the 1800s. Another landmark is **the mooring mast** used by Amundsen's airship, *Norge*, in 1926 and by Nobile's airship *Italia*, two years later.

Beyond Vadsø there is only the town of Vardø, on an island connected to the mainland by an undersea tunnel 1½ miles (2.5 km) long. The easternmost town in Norway, it is the only one situated in the Arctic climate zone. There have been fortifications at Vardø since around 1300 but the present octagonal star-shaped redoubt with four bastions was built in 1734. The only remnant of the original fortress is a beam which

A good catch: Atlantic salmon at Honningsvåg.

bears the signature of King Christian IV and is dated 1599, while later monarchs have added their names: King Oskar II (in 1873), King Haakon VII (in 1907) and King Olav V (in 1959).

Vardø's only tree, a rowan, grows in the fort. It is wrapped up every winter to ensure its survival. Another important ritual celebrates the return of the sun, with a gun salute on the first day that the entire disc is visible after two months of winter darkness. Usually, this ceremony takes place around 20 January.

Bird-watching: Along the coast to the west of Vardø, you come to the abandoned fishing village of **Hamningberg** with its old architecture and church, paradoxically, one of the few not destroyed in World War II. Norway's most easterly point is Hornøya, off Vardø. As you return south again, you come to **Domen mountain** where, legend tells, the witches assembled to meet the Devil. Next at Kiberg is **Kibergnesset**, the remains of a major World War II gun site. This coast between Vardø and Vadsø has Ekkerøya,

Fishing trawlers at Lebesby, 70° 30' North, on the Arctic coast.

Finnmark's only bird rock accessible by car. Here birdwatchers gather to watch breeding kittiwake, black guillemot, Steller's eider and grey phalarope, and the small harbours of the two towns are also profitable for binoculars.

Beyond Varangerbotn, the E6 follows the coast through another huge, uninhabited area to the southeast and some beautiful views across the waters of the Varanger fjord. **Bugøynes** is an old fishing village on the coast which, like Hamingborg, escaped destruction in the war and is in a Finnish-speaking area. Further east, **Bugøyfjord** is an old trading centre and birthplace of the Sami artist John Savio.

Only 5 miles (8 km) from the Finnish border to the southwest, the little town of **Neiden** has the distinction of having the only **Greek Orthodox Church** in Norway, where the Skollé Lapps worship. Each year since 1965, the church has held a service to bless the waters of the Neiden river and ensure that their reputed healing powers continue, a service which attracts believers from

many areas. The restored **Labahå farm** at Neiden, built by Finnish immigrants, is part of the Sør-Varanger Museum.

This easternmost wedge of Norwegian territory became important with the discovery of iron ore at **Bjørnevatn** and, since 1906, it has been mined and shipped from the port of Kirkenes some 4 miles (7 km) away. The region is also a centre for fishing, farming, forestry and reindeer husbandry.

Kirkenes, a town of 5,000 inhabitants, is dominated by the installations of the Sydvaranger Iron Ore Company. Although it has recently acquired a new luxury hotel, the **Rica Arctic**, the town's somewhat rough and ready appearance is explained and easily forgiven when you learn that the 20th century has brought no less than four wars fought in or near it. World War II brought the most suffering when, apart from Malta, Kirkenes acquired the unsolicited honour of being the most bombed centre in Europe. It was liberated by the Russians in 1944. They withdrew in 1944 and left behind a rare

lack of nervousness of, and sympathy for, the "Russian Bear," and a memorial built by the town. Kirkenes is the final point of call for the coastal steamer before it returns south to Bergen.

Glimpses of Russia: East of Kirkenes, at **Storskog**, is the only official border crossing to the Soviet Union, while at **Skafferhullet** the viewpoint is an obligatory trip for most visitors who gaze across to Boris Gleb in the USSR, though there are other viewpoints, such as Høyde 96 (Hill 96) which looks across to the Soviet town of Nikel. You can also take a weekly sight-seeing flight over the iron-ore mines and along the Norwegian–Soviet border and, with the coming of *glasnost*, take a boat excursion to Murmansk.

The extreme eastern tip of Norway, at **Grense Jakobselv** has a chapel built on the order of King Oskar II in 1869 as an unusual means of protecting Norwegian interests. The idea of a chapel rather than a fort at this strategic location came about when the Norwegians noticed that the Russians attended their own Orthodox church not far over the border. Faced with a Protestant church, the argument ran, the Russians would realise they had strayed into Norwegian territory and this somewhat unusual approach to maintaining the frontier was highly successful.

In the extreme north of Finnmark, Norway is sometimes only a mile or two wide between the border and the sea, and a long pocket of the country hangs south between the Soviet Union and Finland. Here the **Øvre Pasvik National Park** includes the largest virgin forest in the country. This comparatively flat area has pine forests, bare rock, swamps and two watercourses which are tributaries of the Pasvik river (the official boundary between Norway and the Soviet Union).

Wildlife in the park includes moose, reindeer, bear and wolverine; there are whooper swans, great grey owls, the bean goose, sea eagles, gyr falcons, spotted redshanks and cranes and the whole area is protected from development and pollution to form a peaceful border between East and West.

Left, the miners' statue at Kirkenes. Right, winter in Kautokeino.

SPITSBERGEN

Preceding
pages: rock
formations at
Spitsbergen.
Left, King of
the Arctic, a
young Polar
bear. Below,
Saxifrage
Herculus.

From Tromsø in the north of Norway, the big airliner drones almost due north for an hour and a half. Far below is a seemingly empty sea, hidden here and there by banks of clouds.

Suddenly the traveller becomes aware that through the clouds, stark, jagged mountain peaks project like huge fangs, and that the clouds in between are in reality great sheets of snow-covered glaciers. This is **Svalbard**, better known to English-speakers as **Spitsbergen**, the land of the pointed mountains. The archipelago lies 400 miles (640 km) north of the mainland of Norway and has two main islands, West Spitsbergen and Nordaustland, with numerous smaller islands dotted around in the seas nearby. In winter, the pack ice of the Arctic is all around and only some 600 miles (960 km) separate the islands from the North Pole.

The smooth asphalt runway, long

enough to take the big jetliners, lies on the narrow coastal plain between the mountains of West Spitsbergen and the sea of **Isfjord**. With a minimum of formality, you are through customs and on to a land where the forces of nature are still in control. On the landward side, the mountain slopes darkly up in to the clouds, traversed by a row of pylons; now disused, they carried coal from the mines down to the loading jetties.

The Spitsbergen coal mines are rare in that the mine shafts do not go *down* into the ground but are driven horizontally into the mountains. The coal mountain overlooks **Adventfjord**, a subsidiary of Isfjord, a great arm of the sea which offers comparative shelter in the harbour of Longyearbyen.

Why an airport?: During the Arctic summer, the fjord most often lies calm and unruffled, the surface broken only occasionally as a seal surfaces, an eider duck dives, or a kittiwake dips to pick up some morsel of food. A mile or so along the road—which, like the curate's egg, is good in parts— a valley opens up to explain why the airport exists.

For here lies the township of **Longyearbyen**, built solely to accommodate the people who came north—mainly from Norway—to work at the hard and dangerous job of winning coal from the inside of the mountains of Spitsbergen. Coal was first discovered in the early 17th century but for many years it remained unexploited except as a source of fuel for trappers. Only since around 1900 have serious attempts been made to exploit this resource, and the first to claim mining rights was a Norwegian skipper from Tromsø, called Zakariasen. He was followed by others including John Longyear, an American after whom the village is named.

Around 2,000 people live in the village, mainly in modern, well-insulated houses, served by facilities such as shops, a bank, a café, and even a fine little museum which, as well as stuffed examples of the Spitsbergen birds and mammals, displays many artefacts from the days when the only people to live in these Arctic islands were a few hunters and trappers.

As if to remind you that summer, if sweet, is short, in front of most houses you will see a parked "skidoo," a motor scooter with rubber tracks and steering "skis," which is the only means of transport in winter when snow lies thick on the ground and ice covers the fjord.

Nature in the raw: With less than one mile of road for every 1,000 sq. miles (2,590 sq. km) of land, it is obvious that Svalbard should not, and is unlikely ever to become a place for mass tourism. The islands could not support it and, in any case, the appeal is to people who like to find their own wildlife and explore nature in the raw. Perhaps this is no bad thing as a former Sysselmann (mayor) of Svalbard expressed it: "Since we have no hotels or restaurants, cruise ships provide the best way to visit Svalbard. Some campers arrive each summer but they must bring their own food as well as tents. It is for the best; the ecology is too fragile to withstand anything but controlled tourism."

That situation hasn't changed much but in summer, the area round Lon-gyearbyen is a pleasant place, the stark mountains offset by a valley which has meadows spangled with flowers to make it popular with naturalists of all sorts. Here, you will find the tiny bells of *Cassiope* mixed with purple saxifrage, *S. oppositifolia*, and, if you are very lucky, a patch of Boreal Jacob's Ladder, *Polemonium boreale*, an Arctic rarity with beautiful flowers. Near the shores where the glaucous gulls congregate, look for the fleshy leaved *Mertensia maritima*, or oyster plant, in one of its most northerly stations.

The polar winter is a different matter. The sun does not rise above the horizon at Svalbard and everything is locked in darkness, lit only by the moon and the multi-coloured rays of the **Aurora Borealis**, or Northern Lights.

When the sun reappears and gathers strength, the ice pack retreats north, speeded by the warming influence of the Gulf Stream. This great tidal current, which has its origin in the warm waters of the tropical South Atlantic Ocean, flows northwards past the west

The spiky peaks that gave Spitsbergen its non-Norwegian name.

coast of Great Britain, spilling a tributary into the North Sea and along the Norwegian coast. Still with enough strength to exert pressure on the ice waters of the Arctic Ocean, this great "river" flows up the coast of West Spitsbergen and ensures that, in summer, ships can have an ice-free passage right to the north shores of the islands. Even so, in places the ice never melts.

In general, West Spitsbergen is mountainous and glaciated with around 60 percent covered in permanent ice. The highest mountain, **Newtoppen**, is over 5,500 ft (1,717 metres) high. Farthest from the influence of the Gulf Stream, the second largest island, **Nordaustlandet**, although about 5,800 sq. miles (15,000 sq. km) in extent, is almost completely covered in an enormous layer of ice, said to be over 2,300 ft (700 metres) thick in places.

Mineral rights: After World War I, Norway was granted sovereignty over the archipelago of Svalbard, though the various countries who agreed to the treaty reserved the right to exploit minerals. Sweden already operated a coal mining business but sold out to the Norwegian company in 1934.

Today, Russia is the only one of the original signatories to the Svalbard Treaty to retain an interest in coal mining, and has a substantial operation at **Barentsburg**, only a few miles further down the fjord from Longyearbyen. Around 2,000 people live in a village set on a steeply sloping fjordside, where groups of well-dressed, fur-hatted people chat beneath hoardings which display large photographs of the most virtuous workers; kittiwakes scream from their nests on the window ledges above, while the whole scene, somewhat incongruously, is overlooked by a huge smiling portrait of Lenin!

As there is no land access, the only "foreign" visitors to Barentsburg are passengers of an occasional summer cruise ship, who are greeted pleasantly, if somewhat warily, by the Russians.

Unknown and unexplored: According to the old Icelandic annals, in 1194 land was found to lie "four days sailing from

Signs of the Soviets.

Langanes, at the northern end of the sea." They called it Svalbard but, after that first mention, the islands lay unknown and unexplored for several hundred years. The next mention was in the journals of the great Dutch explorer, Willem Barents, in 1596. Barents, with two ships under his command, was on a voyage to try to find a northern route to China, when he sighted an island which, from the shape of its mountains, he named Spitsbergen.

The two ships of the expedition then parted, one to carry news of fjords filled with whales and walrus back to Holland, while the other ship with Barents on board continued eastward. They got as far as Novaja Zemljej before become trapped in the pack ice, where they were forced to spend the winter. During those long, harsh months many of the crew perished, including Barents himself.

In the years that followed a number of hunting expeditions went north. At first they seldom ventured further than **Bear Island** but, by 1610, they had begun to hunt around the coast of Spitsbergen. News of the amazing numbers of whales spread and soon the Dutch whalers were joined by English, French, Basques, and Danes. Inevitably trouble flared as they disputed rights and fought pitched battles when warships came north to defend the claims of the whalers.

The butter mountain: English and Dutch at last agreed on a division of hunting territories and some peace was restored. The Dutch established a shore base on **Amsterdam Island**, which grew to be almost a town with a fort, church and whale-oil refinery, and a summer population of a couple of thousand. They called it **Smeerenburg**, the "butter-mountain," and you can still find traces of the Dutch operations, mainly outlines of stone buildings and the furnaces built to render the whale blubber into oil. The large numbers of bleached bones of thousands of whales testify to the growing demands for whale oil and in some places further mute testimony in the graves of men who died, either in battles or from more natural causes in this stern territory.

Under the pressure of all the killing, it was inevitable that whale stock should decline and by the middle of the 18th century whaling at Spitsbergen had ceased. The focus of the industry shifted to an area west of Greenland, until that region too was fished to extinction around the turn of the 20th century. This intensive whaling was purely a summer activity. In winter the islands were deserted except by accident.

In 1630, an English ship was wrecked and the crew managed to cling to life throughout the winter. In 1633, some Dutchmen wintered at Smeerenberg, but the following year those who attempted to stay on all died of scurvy. The English had intended to colonise the archipelago but even prisoners under sentence of death refused to face the prospect of the Arctic night.

Tough life: The Russians were made of sterner stuff, however, and in the early part of the 18th century a number of hunting parties built houses in Spitsbergen and continued to hunt bear, fox, walrus, and seals throughout the winter

Norwegian botanist Hanna Resvoll-Holmsen, a self-portrait in camp at Colbay, 1908.

darkness. Not until the late 18th century did Norwegian hunters first arrive in Svalbard. They too over-wintered and today their cabins still lie along the shores of many fjords. Though mainly deserted, scientists and explorers often make use of the huts and many are kept in a good state of repair.

A trapper led a tough and rigorous life. He had to set his traps, mainly for Arctic fox whose beautiful pelts were most valuable in winter in a hunting territory that covered many square miles. He also shot or caught polar bears in baited "fell-traps," and hunted seals not just for food and skins but for the oil which he then extracted from the blubber. Mile after mile the hunter would walk through the winter storms and darkness, always anticipating a dangerous face-to-face encounter with a hungry polar bear.

Ever since its discovery Svalbard has attracted scientific expeditions. The first on record was in 1773 and included **At the edge of** no less a personage than Horatio Nelson, then a midshipman. In 1827, the

first Norwegian geological expedition took place under Professor B.M. Keilhau, and this was soon followed by expeditions from many of nations. Today, the Norsk Polarinstitut is the "clearing house" for all expeditions which visit this fascinating Arctic outpost.

Natural laboratory: Svalbard offers a unique environment for the study of ecology and natural history by scientist and amateur alike. Almost every visitor who makes the long journey to this distant archipelago has more than a passing interest in wildlife in general and birds in particular, and Svalbard's short Arctic summer offers a rich feast. For though the archipelago can seem desperately inhospitable, in the 24-hour days of summer the tundra slopes between the mountains and near the sea offer enough thin soil to encourage and support a surprising number of plants.

These, in turn, encourage other wildlife such as insects, birds and a few mammals. The surrounding seas, although cold, are rich in fish and invertebrates which attract sea birds and sea

At the edge of the ice pack.

mammals who use the shores and cliffs for breeding and resting.

With their great mobility, birds are able to explore almost every food-providing niche. Kittiwakes, glaucous and ivory gulls push north as soon as daylight allows and are soon followed by Arctic terns, all the way from the southern hemisphere.

The kittiwake, on the other hand, is essentially an ocean bird which feeds almost exclusively at sea. At nesting time they set up huge noisy colonies on suitable cliffs, or even on window ledges in some places. The unmistakable cry that gives them the name *kitti-wake, kitti-wake* is everywhere. Another ocean wanderer is the fulmar. Most of the Svalbard population is the dark grey phase, largely confined to Arctic waters, and this at first puzzles some birdwatchers from further south.

Four species of auks breed in Svalbard: Brünnich's guillemot, the little auk, puffin and black guillemot. While Brünnich's guillemot nest on open but inaccessible ledges, the others seek the safety of crevices or burrows, where predators such as Arctic fox and glaucous gulls have less chance of getting at their eggs or young. Again, Svalbard has almost all the European population of the rare little auk.

Binoculars ready: The large expanses of barren mountains do not offer much in the way of food for land birds, but try the slopes and valleys which are often carpeted in dwarf birch and polar willow, with many species of alpine plants such as saxifrages underfoot, and you will find snow buntings foraging for seeds and singing from the rocks. Ptarmigan, that hardiest member of the grouse family, also uses this habitat. It is the only bird to stay through the winter, hard to spot against the snow in its winter coat of white.

Some waders also nest on these tundra plains near the sea. Purple sandpiper, turnstone, ringed plover and grey phalarope are regulars and others, such as knot and sanderling, have been recorded. Inland lakes and pools are not common but, where they have formed, they are often tenanted by red-throated divers, their haunting wild cries the very epitome of the Arctic.

Three kinds of geese breed in Svalbard, and the many naturalists who have studied the barnacle geese now realise that the entire Svalbard population flies all the way to and from Scotland each year, to spend the winter in the Solway area in the southwest, then return in spring to their breeding place in the north. You will find pink-footed geese in considerable numbers and smaller colonies of Brent geese of the pale-bellied variety. When you spot the plentiful flocks of common eider along the shores, look closely because you may be lucky enough to find a few of the oustandingly handsome king eiders, showing off their superior plumage to their less flashy kin.

Arctic monarch: There is only one kind of grazing mammal in the islands and that is the hardy Svalbard reindeer. Smaller than the Lappland reindeer, you come across groups, which seem quite tame, living a spartan life off plants and lichens in the valley bottoms.

The beautiful ivory gull nests everywhere in Spitsbergen.

The only other land mammals are the two carnivores, the fox and the bear. The Arctic fox is a very attractive looking little animal, with a coat of varying shades of white and grey in summer and pure white in winter. Though it was hunted heavily in the past, it is still remarkably tolerant and curious about humans and will scavenge round the townships in the winter. Even in summer, the foxes are not too difficult to find on the sea-bird cliffs, where they dig out nests or pick up any young birds that have fallen from the ledges.

The undoubted king of the Arctic is the polar bear. Adult males especially lead a nomadic life on the pack ice for much of the year and live mainly on seals, while young males and females with cubs tend to spend the summer on the island. Polar bears are said to be the fiercest animal of all, but these younger males and females exist largely on a vegetarian summer diet. Though they were formerly hunted for their skins, polar bears are now protected and can be killed only if they threaten human life. Their numbers on Svalbard vary according to the proximity of the pack ice but they are not uncommon, especially on favourite breeding islands, such as **Barentsøya** and **Edgeøya**.

Whales and walrus: Though the fjords of Spitsbergen may no longer be "filled with whales and walrus," as they were said to be in the 15th century, you will certainly find sea mammals around the islands. In the same way, though it is now rare to see any of the "great" whales in Arctic waters, species such as the lesser rorqhual or minke whales come into the fjord quite often. But the one you are most likely to spot is the beluga or white whale, easy to identify with its white body and lack of a dorsal fin. Now and then you might be lucky enough to sight the remarkable narwhale, small and dapple-skinned with a spear-like tusk projecting out in front.

The immense herds of walrus which in days past thronged places like Moffen Island, off the south coast of West Spitsbergen, have never fully recovered from over-hunting but sometimes small groups appear at **Moffen Island** or on the south of **Edgeøya**, where they feast on the clam beds or rest on the shore. Spitsbergen's two most common species of seal are the ringed and the bearded seal. The sealers of old used to call the ringed seal the "floe rat". It is the smaller of the two with a dark speckled coat, whereas the bearded seal is larger and generally a sandy brown colour.

Creature comforts: For anyone other than the young, fit and dedicated explorer, cruise ships offer the best of both worlds when visiting these islands. The ships separate into two groups. First come the larger ships whose itinerary includes a visit to Svalbard as part of a more extensive tour; the smaller ships stay in Svalbard for the summer season and can offer extended voyages.

If you want a more intimate look at the flora, fauna or geology of Svalbard, the smaller ships are probably the best bet. They can get nearer to the shores and into secluded fjords denied to the bigger craft and, while their standard of luxury may not match that of the big cruise liners, it is entirely adequate.

Right, a kayak in icy waters. **Overpage**, wrought-iron gates at Vigeland Park in Oslo.

TRAVEL TIPS

GETTING THERE

BY AIR

Scandinavia's flagship carrier, SAS, runs a wide range of flights between Oslo and other world capitals, with many direct services to and from Oslo. Major commercial carriers for Oslo stop at Fornebu airport, and charters land at Gardermoen. In addition, several large European carriers connect Norway to their home cities. Air Europe, which flies daily to Oslo from London, started service with low APEX fares in June 1989. Bergen and Stavanger are the other airports with international connections.

Norway's domestic flight network is comprehensive. Braathens, NorskAir, and Wideroes are the domestic carriers.

BY SEA

Fred Olsen Line sails from Newcastle (in Britain) to Bergen, then north to Ålesund and Molde twice a week all year round. The crossing to Bergen takes about 21 hours.

Norway Line sails direct to Stavanger/Bergen. The crossing takes about 22 hours to Bergen. Early February–end September, twice weekly; October–end December, weekly.

Scandinavian Seaways offer a longer route via Denmark. From Harwich (all year round) and Newcastle (summer only) to Esbjerg on Denmark's west coast then by train to Copenhagen (5 hours). Inclusive "Seapex" price boat/train to Copenhagen. Separate Scandinavian Seaways sailings Copenhagen/Oslo take 16 sea hours.

Stena Line also run ferries between Denmark, Norway and Sweden.

BY RAIL

Trains from Stockholm and Copenhagen to Oslo usually run twice a day. You can also get to northern Norway from Stockholm, with Trondheim and Narvik the principal destinations, again usually twice daily. There are also several daily Copenhagen and Gothenberg connections. International arrivals and departures at Sentralstasjon (Oslo-S). The Norwegian State Railways (NSB) have train information and also operate as a travel bureau across Norway. In Oslo they're at Jernbanetorget 1, Oslo, tel: 02-36 37 80, in London (under the name NSR) at 21–24 Cockspur Street, London SW1 5DA, tel: 071-930 6666 (no USA office).

BY ROAD

Most major shipping lines to Norway allow passengers to bring their cars. Bringing a car increases sea travel costs, and petrol is very highly priced in Norway—about 5.30 Nkr per litre.

Two Oslo-based organisations can help with queries concerning driving: the Norges Automobil Forbund (NAF or Norwegian Automobile Association) at Storgate 2-6, Oslo 1, tel: 02-33 70 80; and the Kongelig Norsk Automobilklub (KNA or Royal Norwegian Automobile Club) at Parkveien 68, Oslo 2, tel: 02-56 26 90. Car hire in Norway can be expensive (up to 3,000 Nkr a week), but may be worthwhile if shared between several people. Otherwise watch for weekend and summer special prices; Budget for example has a very low Friday to Monday rate (550 Nkr with the first 250 km free; tel: at Fornebu airport 02-53 79 24).

Be aware, at least, of these three rules of the highway code:
• Dipped headlights are required at all times from 1 September to 30 April (right-hand drive vehicles must adjust the sweep of the lights to the right);
• Cars approaching from the right always have right of way;
• Seat belts must be worn.

Travel Essentials

VISAS & PASSPORTS

A valid passport is all that is necessary for citizens of most countries to enter Norway. Visas are not required. If you enter from another Nordic country (Denmark, Finland, Iceland, Sweden), you won't get a new entry stamp. Stays for tourists are generally limited to three months; it is possible to stay longer, but you must apply for a visa after the initial three-month stay (Scandinavian passport holders are exempt from this requirement) or if you plan to work.

MONEY MATTERS

The Norwegian krone (Nkr) is divided into 100 ore. Notes come in denominations of 10, 50, 100, 500, and 1,000 Nkr (you may occasionally see higher) and coins are 1, 5, 10, 50, and 100 ore.

You can change currency at post offices, the Oslo S train station, international airports, some hotels, and commerical banks. Bank opening hours are Monday to Friday only, 8.15 a.m.–3 p.m.

There is no limit on the amount of currency you carry into Norway, but no more than 5,000 Nkr may be taken out. You may leave with any foreign currency you brought in.

Eurocheques are accepted in banks up to the equivalent of 1,300 Nkr.

In most banks you can get cash advances on a Visa card, up to a limit of 2,000 Nkr a week.

HEALTH

No vaccinations are necessary to enter Norway and the tap water is very good. A first aid kit is recommended to those who plan trips to remoter parts, and be sure to include prevention and treatment potions for mosquito bites—from mid-summer into early autumn, Lappland is rife with biting insects.

Hospital treatment: Norway has reciprocal treatment agreements with the UK and many other European countries; in other words, your own National Insurance should cover you. People from countries without such agreements will have to pay a small fee. A visit to a doctor in a clinic will cost 50–100 Nkr. If you are concerned whether you need extra coverage you are advised to check in your own country before you go.

To make an appointment with a doctor in Oslo, dial the general number, 02-20 10 90. The phone number for medical emergencies in Oslo is 003; in other parts of the country, look at the front of the local phone book. If you don't have one, you'll have to dial an operator on 0180 and ask for the local emergency number (*Nødhjelp* = emergency assistance).

WHAT TO WEAR

You're in for a pleasant surprise if travelling to Norway in summer. As it is protected by the Gulf Stream it can get even warmer than some of its southern neighbours. In the south, temperatures in the upper 20s C (80s F) are not unusual. The average temperature for the country as a whole in July, including the far north, is about 16° C (60° F), 22° C (71° F) in Oslo. Spring and autumn are rainy, and nights can be brisk.

In winter bring very warm clothing and dress in layers. Woollen mittens or gloves and hats are strongly advised (and face cover, if you are skiing). In the far north, temperatures drop to below –20° C (–68° F). In January, the average day time temperature in Oslo is –2° C (–35° F); night time, –7° C (–44° F).

CUSTOMS

Duty-free allowances are as follows for alcohol and tobacco:

Anyone over 20 may bring one litre of wine and one litre of liquor or two litres of wine. In addition you may bring two litres of beer.

European residents over 16 may bring 200 cigarettes or 250 gm of other tobacco goods. Residents of non-European countries over 16 may bring 400 cigarettes or 500 gm of other tobacco goods.

In addition to the tax-free quota you may bring in four litres of wine or liquor against payment of duty.

One kilo of chocolate and sweets can be brought in duty-free. Goods other than those mentioned above may be brought in duty-free up to a total value of 1,200 Nkr, but this restriction is not usually applied to articles strictly for your personal use. Importation of narcotics, medicines (except for personal use) and poisons, firearms, ammunition and explosives is prohibited.

Agricultural importation comes under strict surveillance (if this concerns you, get specific information before you leave your own country), as does the import of animals. Most animals must be quarantined, dogs and cats for four months. Dogs and cats from rabies-free countries are kept in isolation for 30 days. Animals leaving Britain may need rabies shots because they will be specially vulnerable.

GETTING ACQUAINTED

GOVERNMENT & ECONOMY

Norway's national assembly, the Storting, is the mainstay of its political system. There are 157 members who sit in two chambers (Odelsting and Lagting); elections occur every four years. There are 19 major local government sub-divisions, all of which are divided into smaller municipalities. The government is headed by a prime minister who leads the majority party or a coalition of parties in the Storting. The Norwegian monarch fulfills a symbolic role as the country's Head of State.

The Labour Party and the Conservative Party are the two major parties; others represented in the Storting are the Christian Democratic Party, the Centre Party, the Socialist Left Party, and the Progress Party. Norway's constitution dates from 17 May 1814; a painting of its signing hangs in the Storting chamber. Previously, Norwegians were subject to Danish rule for many centuries, and then entered a union with Sweden which lasted from 1814 until 1905.

National Day is celebrated across the nation on the constitution's anniversary, 17 May, with parades, music, and dance.

Norway is a member of NATO and OECD and spends more money per capita on foreign aid, mainly for the Third World, than any other country. It is also a member of the Council of Europe and EFTA; it is not a European Community member but has trade agreements with the EC.

With Denmark, Sweden, Iceland, Finland, the Faroe Islands and Greenland, Norway is also a member of the Nordic Council (founded 1952). The Council has 87 members, meets once a year in full session, and has a permanent secretariat in Copenhagen.

Its most successful agreement is the freedom of all Nordic citizens to travel without passports within *Norden* (the Nordic area) and work without a work permit. The 1955 social security convention also guarantees them the welfare benefits, from unemployment to health care, of the country in which they are working. Discussions on a customs union have not had similar success. Most recent are talks to find a common Nordic policy on matters outside Norden, eg. assistance to Central America.

Among a mass of technical, educational and arts co-operation are NORDUNET, a communications network for education; educational exchanges; information networks for medical data, facilities for the handicapped, and public administration; environmental programmes including a Nordic convention on world environment.

Individual subjects are based in different centres, such as Helsinki's studies on environmental monitoring, Oslo's Nordic Industrial Council which co-ordinates industrial collaborations.

The economy has boomed due to North Sea oil. Other products from natural resources include timber, pulp and paper, hydro-electric power, gas, shipping, and some mining. Fish and agricultural products have long been staples of the Norwegian economy. Newer industry revolves around computers and business services. Tourism is a continually increasing source of capital, too. Some of

Norway's most successful ventures include Statoil, Elektrikbyra (electrical and electronic), and Royal Caribbean Cruise Lines.

GEOGRAPHY & POPULATION

Norway is a narrow country 1,600 miles (2,600 km) long, shaped like a tadpole swimming south. At points along the tail it narrows down to as little as 1¼ miles (2 km) wide. It stretches from latitude 57°57' North to 71°11' North. A few islands within the Arctic Circle are also part of Norway, the largest being Spitzbergen, jointly administered with the Soviet Union. Most of the coast lies along the North Sea. Bordering countries are Sweden, Finland and, in the north, the Soviet Union. Norway is mountainous, with elevations ranging to around 6,500 ft (2,000 metres).

The country's total population is just over 4 million. At about 27 people per sq. mile (10 people per sq. km), Norway has the second lowest population density after Iceland. (Norway's total area is 386,958 sq km or 150,000 sq miles.)

The south is hilly and partially forested. The most fertile food-growing region is the southern quarter of the country. Although indented with fjords all around its coast (a fjord is a narrow finger of the sea that cuts in between coastal mountains), the west coast area from Stavanger to Bergen and Bergen to Trondheim contains the most visited fjords. The north is very sparsely populated.

The capital, Oslo, is on the southeast coast at the head of Oslofjord and is home to about 450,000 people—over 10 percent of the national total. English is widely spoken here and in other sizeable towns throughout Norway.

Other major cities' estimated populations: Bergen 209,000, Stavanger 90,000, Trondheim 135,000.

TIME ZONES

Norway is on Central European Time, which is one hour ahead of Greenwich Mean Time and six hours ahead of Eastern Standard Time. The clock is set forward an hour to "summer time" at the end of March, and set back an hour at the end of September.

CLIMATE

Oslo is one of the warmest locations in Norway during winter; in January the average 24-hour high is –2° C (28° F) and the low is –7° C (19° F). Up north it's a different story, however, with sub-zero temperatures reigning for months and a good number of roads shut down due to long-term snow. February and March are the best skiing months. March and April and sometimes even early May are the wet spring months when skies are grey and roads are buckled due to thaws and re-freezes; during this time the daily high temperature slowly lifts from about 4° C (39° F) to 16° C (61° F).

Come summer-time and the season of the midnight sun, Oslo enjoys daily average temperatures in the low to mid-20s C (70s F), while the sunlight-bathed north is perfect hiking temperature, hovering around or just below 20° C (68° F). October is the time for the autumn rains to begin as temperatures dip below 10° C (50° F), then continue their slide toward zero. The first snow can be expected any time from mid-October to early December, depending on location.

May and September are very popular with visitors—transportation, hotels, and museums are often crowded in these two months. The Easter ski break is a time of mass exodus from schools and jobs to the slopes and trails. Otherwise, Norwegians mainly holiday in July or August.

CULTURE & CUSTOMS

Norwegians are great hand shakers. Whenever strangers meet, there is always a handshake accompanied by an exchange of full names. Also, when meeting casual acquaintances subsequently, you usually shake hands when greeting and parting.

Norwegians are pleasantly polite. Any time you are served you will hear the phrase *Vær så god,* which basically means "You are welcome" and "It is a pleasure to serve you" all rolled up in one. The only equivalent to "please" in Norwegian is *vennligst*, which is formal and not frequently used.

The only thing remotely unruly in Norwegians' manners occurs in the busy streets of Oslo. People seem to jostle a bit more, and apologies are not usual, so don't be offended if you don't get one after someone bumps into you—as long as it's gentle. Of more concern, especially if you are driving, is the mad darts and leaps people take into and across streets, without regard for traffic lights or the fact that Scandinavians are supposed to be the world's best- behaved pedestrians.

Coffee is the national narcotic and served whenever people meet—you may end up awash with coffee if you're doing the rounds in a given day. But the real difficulty is coping with the mounds of pastry often served with the coffee; if you must refuse, do so politely, especially if you are turning down home-made pastries! If you are invited to someone's home for a full meal, a gift of flowers or sweets is customary.

There is an intricate ritual of eye contact while "skåling," or toasting when drinking. Lift glass, look drinking partner in the eye, say *Skål*, clink glasses, look each other in the eye one more time, and then down it (or perhaps nursing it would be a better idea, considering the cost).

Tipping is easy. Hotels include a service charge and tipping is generally not expected. Restaurants usually have the service charge included, in which case it's your choice to add anything extra. However, 5–10 percent is customary. The same applies to taxi drivers. With hairdressers a tip isn't quite as customary, but again 5–10 percent would be appropriate—and appreciated. Cloakrooms usually have a fixed fee of about 5–10 Nkr; if not a round figure, you might leave a few krone for the attendant.

ELECTRICITY

The supply in Norway is 220 volts AC. Plugs have two small round pins, so you may need a plug adaptor for the appliances you bring with you.

BUSINESS

Office hours in Norway are 9 a.m.–4 p.m. or 8 a.m.–4 p.m; lunch is taken early, usually 11.30 a.m.–12.30 p.m., or 12–2 p.m. for a restaurant lunch or lunch meeting. Stores are open Monday–Friday 9 a.m.–5 p.m., Saturday from 9 a.m. until 1, 2 or even 3 p.m. The exceptions are the Oslo City and Aker Brygge malls, open until 8 p.m. or 9 p.m. on weekdays and until 6 p.m. on Saturday. Banks are open 8.15 a.m.–3 p.m., weekdays only.

HOLIDAYS

New Year's Day, Maundy Thursday, Good Friday, Easter Monday (making Easter a five-day Thursday to Monday holiday block), 1 May (Labour Day), 17 May (Independence or Constitution Day), Ascension Day, Whit Monday, Christmas and Boxing Day.

RELIGIOUS SERVICES

The Lutheran church is Norway's state church, with around 94 percent of the population registered as Lutherans. Oslo has many Lutheran churches, including one American Lutheran church.

There is also a Quaker Friends Society, a Swedish church, a German Evangelical church, an Anglican/Episcopalian church, a synagogue and a mosque. Services are held in English at the American Lutheran church and the Anglican/Episcopalian church (St Edmund's). Minority religious groups are Pentecostalists, Baptists, Evangelical Lutherans, Methodists, Catholics, Jews, and Moslems.

COMMUNICATIONS

MEDIA

Most larger kiosks (like Narvesen) and some bookshops sell English-language newspapers. Deichmanske Bibliotek, the main public library, is at Henrik Ibsen's gate 1 in Oslo; you'll find a selection of international papers and periodicals in its reading rooms. Some of the larger newspapers feature a page or two in English in summer.

You can hear English on the radio in the summer on 106.8 FM. The NATO station broadcasts in English, year-round, on 105.5 FM. Hotels with radios in rooms will also give a schedule of broadcasts.

There are several bookshops in Oslo with English-language sections; Erik Qvist on

Drammsveien 16, tel: 02-44 52 69 and Tanum Karl Johan on Karl Johansgate 43, tel: 02-42 93 10.

POSTAL SERVICES

The central post office, at Dronningensgate 15 (entrance corner Prinsensgate) is open Monday–Friday 8 a.m.–8 p.m. and Saturday 9 a.m.–3 p.m. Other post offices are open weekdays 8 a.m.–4 p.m., Saturday 8 a.m.–1 p.m. At press time, letters and postcards were 4 Nkr for the first 50 gm to the UK and Europe and 5 Nkr for the first 20 gm to North America, air mail.

TELEPHONE SERVICES

Calls abroad can be made from hotels—with a surcharge—or from phone booths or the main telegraph office at Kongensgate 21 (entrance Prinsensgate). You can also send faxes, telexes and telegrams from this office. Most older payphones take 1 krone and 5 krone coins (some take 10 krone coins) and minimum deposit is 2 krone. Cheapest calling times are outside business hours: 5 p.m.–8 a.m.

Oslo's code is 02, unnecessary inside the city. For other parts of the country, or dialling abroad, see the phone directory. Directories have a page of instructions in English, listed in the index. Most cities' phone numbers have six digits, but there are fewer digits for smaller towns. Remember the vowels æ, ø, and å come at the end of the alphabet, in that order.

EMERGENCIES

SECURITY & CRIME

The streets of Oslo are very safe compared with the bigger cities of Europe and North America. (When unemployment rises, street crime goes up slightly.) Crime against foreigners is even rarer in smaller places. The only threat you may feel is from drunks. Most bars have good bouncers, so alert them if you're having trouble. Out in the street, you're more in danger of verbal harassment from drunks than bodily harm; often you'll just be asked for a cigarette or matches.

Dial the police on 002, in emergencies only. Call 001 to report fire, 003 to call an ambulance (no coins required on any of these). Private doctors are listed in the directory under *Leger* (doctor). Outside Oslo, dial an operator on 0180 for local emergency numbers (*Nødhjelp* = Emergency assistance). If you have a local phone book seek out the full local listings for police, fire, doctor on duty (*Lækjarvakt*), first aid, and ambulance in its first pages.

MEDICAL SERVICES

Most larger cities have all-night pharmacies; in Oslo it's Jernbanetorgets Apotek, tel: 02-41 24 82, fax 02-36 34 10—across from central train station at Jernbanetorget 4B; in Bergen, Apotek Nordstjernen, Bus Station, tel: 05-31 68 84; in Stavanger phone for 24-hour pharmacy service on 04-52 01 28; in Trondheim, St Olav's Apotek, Kjøpmannsgate 65, tel: 07-52 31 22.

In other cities enquire at your hotel; if no luck here, you could try the emergency number in the phone book marked with a cross and the word *Lækjarvakt*—doctor on duty. Where there is a rotating schedule of 24-hour pharmacies in a city, these will usually be posted on the door of them all.

Emergency dental treatment in Oslo (for

the times outside regular dentists' office hours) is available from Oslo Kommunale Tannlegevakt, Tøyen Senter, Kolstadgata 18, tel: 02-67 48 46. Open: weeknights 8 p.m.–11 p.m., weekends and holidays 11 a.m.–3 p.m. and 8 p.m.–11 p.m. (near Tøyen T-bane station).

GETTING AROUND

FROM THE AIRPORT

Oslo has two airports (a third had been proposed at press time, against great resistance from local residents and the Socialist Party). Fornebu, the international airport, is only 6 miles (9 km) from central Oslo. Airport left luggage room is open 6.30 a.m.–11 p.m. daily.

SAS buses (cost 30 Nkr) run to and from Fornebu every 15 minutes; one public bus goes to the airport about once every hour (No. 31, marked *Snarøya* from Jernbanetorget, opposite Oslo-S); fare 13 Nkr. Travel time to and from Fornebu is about 25 minutes. Fare by taxi would be approximately 100–200 Nkr. There is also a stop called *Lysaker* about a mile (2 km) from the airport on the T-bane and the Oslo-Skien long distance train line. Cabs and buses stop at Lysaker for passengers to the airport on a fairly regular basis.

Gardermoen airport, 30 miles (50 km) from Oslo, receives European charter flights and some flights from North America. Buses meet incoming flights, leaving from Oslo-S central train station two hours before the departure of any scheduled flights. Fare 50 Nkr; duration of trip 50 minutes.

DOMESTIC TRAVEL

Within Norway, there is an excellent network of domestic transport services, a necessity in a country so large and often impassable by land. You may have to use more than one means (for example, train and bus or plane and bus) but if you're determined to travel beyond Oslo you'll find these services indispensable.

Although covering great distances can be expensive, Norway offers transport bargains through special tourist cards like the Fjord Pass, the Bonus Pass (all Scandinavia) plus some of the pan-European programmes like InterRail and Eurail. Within larger cities, tourist passes cover urban transportation and many museums.

AIR TRAVEL

With car travel so costly and distances so tremendous, flying is actually not the extravagance you might think, especially if you take advantage of a "Visit Norway" pass. This gives you flight coupons valid for domestic travel in summer.

The following airlines, in addition to SAS (SAS Building, Ruseløkkveien 6, Oslo 2, tel: 02-42 99 70) serve inside Norway: Braathens SAFE AS, Ruseløkkveien 26, Oslo 2, tel: 02-41 10 20; NorskAir at Gardermoen tel: 06-97 82 20, in Bergen tel: 05-99 82 20, in Sandefjord tel: 034-70 230, in Skien tel: 03-54 65 55, in Stavanger tel: 04-65 29 55, in Trondheim tel: 07-82 60 22; Wideroes Flyveselskap AS, Mustadsveien 1, Oslo 2, tel: 02-55 59 60.

RAIL

Rail service is far more comprehensive in the south than in the north, and tends to fan out from Oslo, so you will have to supplement your trip with ferries and buses, unless you are travelling strictly in the south or to the biggest towns. The Oslo-Bergen rail trip is hailed as one of the world's most spectacular for its scenery. Oslo-S (Oslo Sentralstasjon) is Norway's busiest railway station, located in central Oslo at the eastern end of Karl Johansgate on Jernbanetorget. Long-distance and express trains leave mainly from here, although a few trains— mainly the suburban trains—leave from Oslo-V (west), at Vestbaneplassen near the Rådhus (City Hall).

If you plan to take special fast trains, you must book ahead. Ticket sales are from the main hall of the train station (tickets for ordinary trains may also be bought on board).

Trafikanten, in the bottom of the glass tower at the front of Oslo-S, also helps with transportation and booking queries. Open: weekdays 7 a.m.–8 p.m., weekends 8 a.m.–6 p.m., tel: 02-41 70 30.

WATER TRANSPORT

Ferries: Norway is a country where you are never very far from the sea. Ferries are an invaluable means of transport that allow short cuts across fjords to eliminate many road miles. In Oslo, ferries to the fjord islands leave from the quay near Aker Brygge.

Ferries are crucial to commuters in busy areas, for example the Horten-Moss ferry across Oslofjord between Vestfold and Østfold. Almost all town marinas have places for guest boats, with tying up fees running from 30 Nkr a night.

Long-distance boats: The Hurtigrute, Norway's coastal steamer route, is a vital means of water transport for Norwegians, but also a superb way for visitors to see Norway's dramatic coast. In summer, boats leave daily, travelling between Bergen and Kirkenes in 11 days and putting in at 35 ports. Travel agents can give details, and sell Coastal Passes to 16–26 year olds for around 1400 Nkr—good for 21 days of unlimited travel. The steamers take cars, but only newer boats have "drive-on" facilities (as opposed to winching). The drawback is that you may have to book up to six months ahead.

PUBLIC TRANSPORT

The Oslo Card (Osloskortet—one day 80 Nkr, two days 120 Nkr, three days 150 Nkr, half price for children) is your ticket to unlimited public transport (including city ferries) and free entry to many museums. If you want a card for travel only, there are all kinds of passes including a *Minikort* (4 rides; discount) and *Maxikort* (14 rides; discount) plus passes appropriate for longer stays. Queries by phone are taken by Oslo Sporveier, tel: 02-41 70 30.

Buses and trams: Oslo's bus and tram system is comprehensive and runs on schedule; there are detailed timetables at every stop. Single fares range up to 14 Nkr; with an Oslo Card you pay nothing.

Trafikanten or (tourist information) in the main concourse at Oslo-S can suggest bus or tram routes to get you where you're going. There are night buses on some routes and very early morning buses (starting at 4 a.m.) so that public transport is available virtually around the clock.

Underground: Oslo's underground is called the T-bane. There are eight lines that run through central Oslo out to some far-flung suburbs. Station entrances are marked with "T." *Trafikanten* has route maps. To continue east-west travel through the centre, you must always change trains at Stortinget—a short walk underground to the next track.

PRIVATE TRANSPORT

Car: Driving in Norway can be a real pleasure—if the weather conditions are right and the distance you have to travel not too daunting. Speed limits are 30 mph (50 kph) in built-up areas and 50–60 mph (80–90 kph) on highways. Traffic coming from the right in an intersection always has right of way. For drivers of right-hand drive cars, remember that headlights must be adjusted to sweep right. Dipped headlights must be used at all times from 1 September to 30 April. Seat belts msut be used, front and back.

If you are involved in an accident where there are no injuries, tel: 23 20 85 or 42 94 00 from anywhere for vehicle breakdown assistance. It is not necessary to call the police for minor accidents, but drivers must exchange names and addresses; leaving the scene without doing so is a crime. Only call police (on 002) or ambulance (on 003) if it's a real emergency.

Alcohol: Under no circumstances should you drink and drive in Norway. The new penalties include (maximum) fines over 10,000 Nkr (£1,000) and, in some cases, imprisonment. The allowable level is extremely low: even a single half-litre (the typical serving of beer in a bar) can get you into trouble.

Car hire: There are a number of car hire desks at Fornebu airport, and several more with downtown offices:

ANSA (car and coach hire), Pilestredet 70.

Tel: 02-60 00 00 or 60 27 70.

Avis, Munkedamsveien 27. Tel: 02-84 90 60; at Fornebu airport tel: 02-53 05 57.

Budget, Fornebu Airport. Tel: 02-53 79 24.

Europcar, Fornebu Airport. Tel: 02-53 09 39.

Hertz, Hotel Scandinavia. Tel: 02-20 01 21.

Bergen, Stavanger, and Trondheim all have their own city guides which should list local hire firms, or you can look in the phone book (yellow pages) under *Bilutleie*.

Taxis: Taxis are widely available, even in many suburban and rural areas, so you need never risk getting caught for drunken driving. In Oslo, they can be telephoned on 02-38 80 90 for service within an hour, or you can get a cab from a cab rank or in the street. In Oslo cab meters start at 15 Nkr in the day, 20 Nkr at night, 33 Nkr if ordered by phone.

Cycling: A lot of people cycle in Oslo, but you must go with caution. There are a few cycle lanes, but it is not an integrated system. Out in the countryside you'll find paved cycle paths. Bicycles are allowed on most trains and buses, making cycling an excellent way of exploring outside Oslo. *The Oslo Guide*, under *Outdoor Activities*, gives detailed suggestions for a Nordmarka (Oslo's forest land) route.

The Syklistens Landsforening (Cycling Association) can help with planning tours and cycling holidays; at Maridalsveien 60, tel: 02-71 92 93. Behind the Royal Palace is Den Rustne Eike (the Rusty Spoke), Oscarsgate 32, tel: 02-44 18 80, which rents bikes out for 60 Nkr/day and 300 Nkr/week. A security deposit of 500 Nkr is required. Off-road and mountain bikes are available for hire, too.

On foot: There is nowhere in Norway you can't go happily on foot; it is a nation of devout walkers, and walking is still probably the most popular weekend outdoor activity. You can walk on fine gravel paths, on lakeside trails, or cut through the forest on your own.

Detailed maps are available from Den Norske Turistforening (Touring Association), Stortingsgate 28, tel: 02-41 80 20 (closed weekends). Anyone can join; write for an application at the above address (fees

are from 120 Nkr per individual, cheaper for family membership). Membership gives you rights to use the association's huts. If you subscribe at a slightly higher rate, you'll get the magazine and yearbook. The map and guidebook selection is excellent; survey maps of all Norway are sold; sketch maps are free.

If you read Norwegian, there is a very good guide for long tours in the Oslo area called *40 Trivelege Turer i Oslo og Omegn*.

Hitchhiking: Hitching is not as common a practice here as it is in elsewhere in Europe; this is not to say it is impossible to get a ride. You'll have the best chance on busier south and west coast roads. Using a sign is recommended.

WHERE TO STAY

If you haven't booked in advance, it's helpful to know that most tourist information offices will book local accommodation.

HOTELS

Norwegian hotels are notoriously expensive, but, in common with the rest of Scandinavia, they slash their rates during the outdoor summer holiday period when business decreases. This makes the summer holidays (mid-June to mid-August) seem attractive when compared with standard rates. Weekend rates are usually halved.

The hotel standards are high, and a lot of hotels provide luxury attractions like fitness centres and secretarial services. The normal weekday rates outside summer are geared toward business occupants, which partially explains why they're so high; newer Norwegian hotels are very business conference-orientated. Another way to save is to stay several nights in the same place, which qualifies you for lower *en pension* rates.

Best Western, Inter Nor, Rica, SAS, and Scandic are some of the larger hotel chains in

Norway (see *Norway Accommodation Guide*, available from tourist offices—free abroad, 5 Nkr in Norway—for full list). Best Western and Rica have their own discount pass programmes, and the Scandinavia Bonus Pass is good for discounts of 15–40 percent in many hotels (another pass is the Scandinavian Passepartout).

MOTELS/BUDGET ACCOMMODATION

Motels are not plentiful. One motel chain called Høk operates clean, modern motels where you have a choice of a regular motel room or small cabins. They also have good cafeterias.

CAMPING SITES/SELF-CATERING

Camping is a tremendously popular way to spend summer holidays in Norway; request the *Norway Camping Guide* from any tourist office. There are over 1,400 sites, and they are rated with a star system, explained in the guide.

Self-catering chalets are called *hytter* in Norway—the easiest way to find a *hytte* is through the Hytte Formidlingen, Kierschowsgate 7, 0405 Oslo 4, tel: 02-35 67 10, and you can ask for their guide from tourist offices. *Rorbus* are simple fishermen's homes, available for rent mainly in the Lofoten Islands in the far north. You should bring your own bedding and towels for a self-catering stay. *Pensjonat* is a room in a private house—check with accommodation bureau.

YOUTH HOSTELS

Norway is well supplied with youth hostels, especially in the popular hiking district around the west coast fjords. Norske Ungdomsherberger (NUH) is part of the international Youth Hostel Association; its headquarters are at Dronningensgate 26, Oslo, tel: 02-42 14 10. Their free booklet gives prices and locations.

Some hostels serve breakfast (usually included in the fee). Reserving space during the high season is a must, as hostel accommodation is the cheapest way to travel and everyone knows it.

ACCOMMODATION INFORMATION

Best Western Hotels Norway, Storgata 117, Box 25, N-2601 Lillehammer. Tel: 062-57 266.
Inter Nor Hotels A/L, Dronningensgate 40, Oslo 1. Tel: 02-36 33 35.
Rica Hotel og Restaurantkjelde, Box 453, N 1301 Sandvika. Tel: 02-54 62 40.
SAS International Hotels, Box 325, N 1324 Lysaker. Tel: 02-53 18 00.
Scandic Hotels A/S, Askerveien 61, N 1370 Asker. Tel: 02-78 47 80.
Oslo Hotel Booking, Centrem Grensen 5/7, tel: 02-42 62 62 for hotels in Norway and the rest of Scandinavia. No booking fee.

In Oslo, the city central accommodation bureau is at the tourist information office in Oslo-S train station on Jernbanetorget at the eastern end of Karl Johansgate. It's open every day 8 a.m.–11 p.m. and can book all grades of accommodation from private rooms in houses to pensions and hotels in the Oslo area. Booking fee is 10 Nkr; some rooms have a two-night minimum.

Below is a sampling of hotels in Norway's main cities; prices given are total for two people in a double room and (usually) breakfast. Prices were correct at press time, but they increase slightly each year; where there is a range of room prices, the average price is given.

OSLO

Akershus Hotel, Akershuskaia, Oslo 1. Tel: 02-42 86 60. You can't beat the setting; this hotel is an old German passenger ship docked right off Akershus fortress. The rooms are rather bunker-like. Active bar. 520 Nkr.
Bristol, Kristian IV's gate 7, Oslo 1. Tel: 02-41 58 40. Superb Moorish-style lobby and right on Oslo's main shopping street. Rooms decorated with antiques. Patronised by the wealthy. 1240 Nkr.
Continental, Stortingsgaten 24–26, Oslo 1. Tel: 02-41 90 60. Established 1909 and still run by the family of the founders, the place where Norwegian guests of state are accomodated. The splendid Viennese-style Theatercaféen is where Oslo socialites meet after a night at the National Theatre opposite. 1,300 Nkr.
Grand, Karl Johansgate 31, Oslo 1. Tel: 02-42 93 90. Opposite the Stortinget, one suite

is reserved for the winner of the Nobel Peace Prize in December, and official government receptions are held in the rococo banqueting hall. Spacious contemporary-style decor in the bedrooms and a roof-top pool. 1,760 Nkr.

Holmenkollen Park Hotel Rica, Kongveien 26, Oslo 3. Tel: 02-14 60 90. Set high in the leafy Holmenkollen district, this grand old-style, wooden building looks right out over Norway's most famous ski jump; a modern annex was added in the 1980s. Excellent facilities. 800 Nkr.

Majorstuen, Bogstadveien 64, Oslo 3. Tel: 02-69 34 95. Reasonably priced and friendly, this hotel near Frogner Park is in a good, lively shopping district and convenient to trams, buses and the T-bane (one stop from Nationaltheateret). 540 Nkr.

Norum, Bygøy Alle 53. Tel: 02-44 79 90. Beautiful old building just west of the centre; quiet, with cosy bistro. 520 Nkr.

Royal Christiania Hotel (formerly Sara), Biskop Gunnerus' gate 3, Oslo. Tel: 02-43 04 85. Restored luxuriantly in 1989–90; magnificent atrium, spacious rooms, wonderful service and breakfasts, and convenient location near Oslo-S. 1,200 Nkr.

SAS Scandinavia Hotel, Holbergsgate 30, Oslo 1. Tel: 02-11 30 00. Luxurious, like all SAS hotels, this one also has very fine restaurants and a rooftop bar. Buses to and from airport. 1,500 Nkr.

Stefanhotellet, Rosenkrantzgate 1. Tel: 02-42 92 50. No alcohol is allowed here, but the location couldn't be more central and the lunch buffets are great. 650 Nkr.

OSLO OMEGAN (OSLO AREA)

Rica Hotel Oslofjord, PO Box 160, Sandvika 1330. Tel: 02-54 57 00. Set in handsome fjord town only 4 miles (7 km) from airport, 9 miles (15 km) from central Oslo (shuttle buses and public transport). Great views over fjord and islands; pretty marble atrium. 660 Nkr.

Scandic Hotel Oslo, Drammensveien, 1322 Høvik. Tel: 02-12 17 40. Attractive hotel with good dining and bar facilities; 1 mile (3 km) from airport, 4 miles (6 km) from centre. 500 Nkr.

BERGEN

Admiral Hotel, C Sundtsgate 9. Tel: 05-32 47 30. One of Bergen's finest. Restaurant Emily has superb views and cuisine. 1,100 Nkr.

Fagerheim Pensjonat, Kalvedalsveien 49A. Tel: 05-31 01 72. A friendly pension with a good central location. 300 Nkr.

Hotel Norge, Ole Bulls Plass. Tel: 05-21 02 99. One of Bergen's best-loved hotels and meeting places, right in the centre, now owned and restored by Reso Hotels, with 350 rooms and suites of highest standard. Four restaurants including gourmet *Grillen*. Winter garden, swimming pool. 1,100 Nkr.

Hotel Park Pension, Harald Hårfagresgt 35. Tel: 05-32 09 60. You can choose between rooms with or without their own facilities. 550 Nkr.

Hotel Rosenkrantz, Rosenkrantz 7. Tel: 05-31 50 00. Comfortable, early-20th-century hotel, in street behind Bryggen (the wharf) in heart of old town; 129 rooms, well-modernised in light airy colours. Restaurant and piano bar. Hotel night club entrance next door. 900 Nkr.

SAS Royal, Bryggen. Tel: 05-31 80 00. The influence on the hotel's architecture of the classic Norwegian building style makes this an unusually handsome hotel. High grade facilities. 1,260 Nkr.

Strand Hotel, Strandkaien 2. Tel: 05-31 08 15. Superb harbour views make for a pleasant stay. 720 Nkr.

Victoria Hotel, Kong Oscarsgate 29. Tel: 05-31 50 30. Once a staging-post inn, 43 comfortable, modern rooms with own facilities. Full of character. Central. 750 Nkr.

STAVANGER

City Gjestehuset, Madlavn 20. Tel: 04-52 04 37. Typical guest house. 470 Nkr.

SAS Royal Hotel, Løkkeveien 26. Tel: 04-56 70 00. With SAS's usual complement of excellent services. 590 Nkr.

Stavanger Somerhotell, Madlamarkveien 6 (Hafrsfjord). Tel: 04-55 70 00. One of the cheapest places to stay in this oil-rich town. 300 Nkr.

WELCOME TO THE KILDE HOTELS

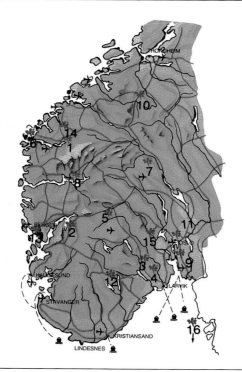

HIGHLIGHTS:

* Oslo
* Bergen – Capital of the Fjords
* The Hardanger Fjord
* The Sogne Fjord
* The West Cape
* Summer Skiing
* Briksdal Glacier
* The Geiranger Fjord
* The Telemark Channel

Kilde Hotels A.L.
Dronningensgt. 40, N-0154
Oslo 1, Norway
Tel: 47 2 42 11 77.
Fax: 47 2 42 25 66.
Telex: 71 841 kilde n

---

otel Alexandra

878 Loen.
(057) 77 660
x 42 665 alex n.
(057) 77 770

ogndal Hotel

800 Sogndal.
(056) 72 311
x 42 727 soho n
(056) 72 665

Union Hotel

216 Geiranger.
(071) 63 000
x 42 339 union n
(071) 63 161

2. Hotel Ullensvang

N-5774 Lofthus.
Tel. (054) 61 100
Telex 42 659 fjord n
Fax (054) 61 520

8. Hotell Refsnes Gods

N-1500 Moss.
Tel. (09) 27 04 11
Telex 74 353 rgods n
Fax (09) 27 25 42

14. Sole Hotel

N-3516 Noresund.
Tel. (067) 46 188
Fax (067) 46 525

3. Bolkesjø Hotel

N-3654 Bolkesjø.
Tel. (036) 18 600
Telex 21 007 bolke n
Fax (036) 18 714

9. Hotel Nor Alpin

N-7341 Oppdal.
Tel. (074) 21 611
Teletex 85 20 876 noral n
Fax (074) 20 730

15. Hotel Norge

2-Hamburg-6,
Schäferkampsallee 49
Deutschland.
Tel. (040) 44 11 50
Telex (0) 21 49 42
Fax (040) 44 11 55 77

4. Bardøla Høyfjellshotel

N-3850 Geilo.
Tel. (067) 85 400
Telex 78 771 bardo n
Fax (067) 86 679

10. Hotel Continental

Stortingsgt. 24/26,
N-0161 Oslo 1, Tel (02)41 90 60
Telex 71 012 conti n
Fax (02) 42 96 89

5. Selje Hotel

N-6740 Selje.
Tel. (057) 56 107
Teletex 84 80 200
Fax (057) 56 272

11. Morgedal Turisthotell

N-3848 Morgedal.
Tel. (036) 54 144
Telex 21 712 morg n
Fax (036) 54 288

6. Wadahl Høgfjellshotell

N-2654 Harpefoss.
Tel. (062) 98 300
Telex 72 534 wadal n
Fax (062) 98 360

12. Sølstrand Fjord Hotel

N-5200 Os.
Tel. (05) 30 00 99
Telex 42 050 solstr n.
Fax (05) 30 00 99 lj 230

KILDE HOTELS

Ambassadeur, Elvegate 18. Tel: 07-52 70 50. Not only is this one of Trondheim's most reasonably priced hotels, it also has a roof terrace. 540 Nkr.

Elgeseter "Bed & Breakfast", Tormodsgate 3. Tel: 07-94 25 40. A convenient location for what could be Norway's only B&B. (Prices not yet available.)

Prinsen, Kongensgate 30. Tel: 07-53 06 50. A wealth of facilities here includes the fine Coq D'Or restaurant, a bistro, bar, grill room, wine tavern, and beer garden. 540 Nkr.

Royal Garden Hotel, Kjøpmannsgt 73. Tel: 07-52 11 00. Lovely guest rooms plus more: solarium, indoor pool, gymnasium, sauna, and several restaurants. 1,100 Nkr.

FOOD DIGEST

WHAT TO EAT

Norwegians eat hearty-breakfasts, but light lunches; the size of the evening meal (*middag*) depends on the day of the week and the occasion. With the abundant supply of seafood and what can be gleaned from forest and field, the Norwegian diet is in the main healthy and appetising, and is becoming more so as Norwegians get more diet-conscious—advertisements for non-greasy, non-fat, non-sugar products are on the increase.

The hunting season (early autumn) throws up some irresistible temptations: pheasant, grouse, and fresh elk and reindeer steaks served with peppercorns and rich wild mushroom sauces. Autumn is also a good time of year for seafoods (available in months with an "R" in them).

Outside main meals, there are many coffee breaks. Inevitably pastries will be served, too, if you are in someone's home or having an informal meeting. The dish may be laden with *bolle*, raisin buns, and *vienerbrød*, lighter pastries laced with fruit or nuts, and anything else the baker can conjure up.

Frokost (breakfast) is more or less a variation of the lunch *Koldtbord*, a spread including breads (try *grovbrød*) and *flatbrød* (oblongs of crisp cracker), sausages, cheeses (try the piquant *Gudbrandalsost*, a delicious burnt goats' milk cheese with a dark golden colour), eggs, herrings, cereal, *gravlax* (marinated salmon), cereals, and coffee and tea. The lunch version has hot dishes, such as sliced roast meats, meatballs, or fish. *Øllebrød*, beef marinated in beer and served inside pitta bread with salad, makes a hearty inexpensive lunch; an open-faced shrimp or ham sandwich is another staple.

Dinner in a city restaurant these days can be anything you wish. In someone's home you might eat mutton stew or a fish ragout. Boiled potatoes with dill or parsley usually accompany a hot main course. When dining in more remote places, the menus will invariably be limited by availablity. *Smørbrød* is a snack (called *aftens* when eaten late at night), usually of rye crackers with butter, cheese, and salami or ham.

For dessert, ice cream is a favourite, as is apple pie. In summer there are all kinds of sweets based on the fresh berries that grow so profusely in the Norwegian woods.

WHERE TO EAT

There has been a significant increase in the variety of what's on offer if you eat out. Pizza is very popular, and oriental food is becoming so. Continental European cuisine has always played a role, too (e.g. Viennese and French styles). But pride in the native cuisine is growing apace with the competition from foreign foods.

At lunchtime, many restaurants offer special fixed-price menus; more casual meals can be had from more informal establishments which come under a range of names such as *stovas, kaffistovas, kros*, bistros, kafés, kafeterias, and *gjæstgiveris* and may sell beer and wine as well as coffee and soft drinks. For an even more casual meal buy a hot dog (*pølser*) or a waffle from a kiosk; kiosks stay open late to catch the traffic going to and from bars and nightclubs. And yes, there is McDonald's.

Evening dining yields up some wonderful surprises in terms of choice, some unpleasant ones in terms of cost. Any large city should give the best cross-section of what you can get throughout the country.

The symbols which follow each entry give a rough indication of prices, based on the typical three-course evening meal per head, excluding wine. * = less than 100 Nkr; ** = 100–250 Nkr; *** more than 250 Nkr.

OSLO

Brasseriet (SAS Hotel), Holbergsgate 30. Tel: 02-11 30 00. Continental menu interspersed with Norwegian seafood specialities. Fish and meats served with delicious sauces. ***

Café de Stijl, Rådhusgate 5 (entrance Skippergate). Tel: 02-42 44 47. A bistro and bar serving wonderfully fresh meals—a chunky Greek salad, wok-steamed chicken, enormous slabs of quiche and green salads. Giant cups of coffee, tea, and cocoa. *

Costas Brasserie & Bar, Klingenberggate 4. Tel: 02-42 41 30. Tremendous Italian-style eatery with front section a handsome brasserie; light, fresh meals. Bruce Springsteen has been here. **

Gamle Raadhus, Nedre Slottsgate 1. Tel: 02-42 01 07. Old-style restaurant in 17th-century building serving hearty Norwegian specialities plus surprises like catfish. **

Grand Café, Karl Johansgate 31. Tel: 02-33 48 70. A virtual shrine to Ibsen, who spent many hours of his life here. Choose anything from pastry and coffee to elk stew and whalemeat platter; salad bar. **

Harlekin Homansbyen, Hegdehaugsveien 30B. Tel: 02-60 75 90. There's a definite French flavour to this menu, blended with Norwegian features like ox fillet. Also, "small plates," pizza, pasta, fresh fish, and roasts. **

Holberg's Arstidene, SAS Hotel, Holbergsgate 30. Tel: 02-11 30 00. Imaginative menu with unusual veal and game dishes. ***

Hotel Bondeheimen/Kaffistova, Rosenkrantzgate 8. Tel: 02-42 95 30. This restaurant, owned by the Farmers' Association, is known for its enticing Norwegian fare served cafeteria style; portions are generous.

Hotel Stefan, Rosenkrantzgate 1. Tel: 02-42 92 50. Justifiably famous lunch buffet selection. **

Kafé Celsius, Rådhusgate 19. Tel: 02-42 45 39. Lunch and dinner, or coffee/snacks/wine

and beer. Wild mushroom pie, pasta selections, salads, and seafood soups. **

L'Ocean, Rådhusbrygge 4. Tel: 02-41 99 97. Dine on seafood in this quayside boat-cum-restaurant; summertime cruise meals. ***

Markveien Mat og Vinhus, Torvbakkgate 12 (entrance Markveien 57). Tel: 02-37 22 97. No fixed menu because the owners pick what looks best at the market each day; fresh salads, excellent game steaks in season. Arty decor. ***

Restaurant Blom, Karl Johansgate 41B. Tel: 02-41 58 40. A large selection of savoury classic Norwegian dishes, like reindeer in pastry with port. ***

Stortorvets Gjæstgiveri, Grensen 1. Tel: 02-42 88 53. Within the warm atmosphere of this authentic Kristiania inn, you can eat traditional lunches and dinners to the accompaniment of live jazz tunes. **

Teppanyaki, Aker Brygge Stranden 3. Tel: 02-83 05 79. Enormous menu of tasty Japanese fare; excellent service. **

Vegeta Vertshus, Munkedamsveien 3B. Tel: 02-41 29 13. Vegetarian heaven; this place even got a *New York Times* write-up. "Help yourself" service lets you taste the variety. *

BERGEN

Bellevue, Bellevuebakken 9. Tel: 05-31 02 40. The fjord view from this restaurant in a 17th-century building is superb; Norwegian and Continental. ***

Bryggen Tracteursted, Bryggen 6. Tel: 05-31 40 46. Your selection from the fish market will be prepared to your specifications by the cook; beautiful old Hanseatic district. **

Holbergstuen, Torvalmenning 6. Tel: 05-31 80 15. Another restaurant that will cook fresh fish from the market to your specifications; lively. **

Wesselstuen, Engen 14. Tel: 05-32 39 00. Fish and stews are served here to a loyal local crowd. **

STAVANGER

La Gondola, Nytorget 8 . Tel: 04-53 42 35. Piquant fish ragouts and soups and a full-blown assortment of seafood dishes prepared Norwegian or Italian style; steaks and pizzas, too. **

Sjøhuset Skagen, Skagenkaien. Tel: 04-52

61 90. Seafood specialities are served in an old boathouse restaurant crammed with antiques. **
Viking, Jernbaven 15. Tel: 04-58 87 47. If you're in Stavanger in autumn, don't miss out on the game and wild specialities here; fine all-year seafood selection, too. **

TRONDHEIM

Bryggen, Bakklandet 66. Tel: 07-53 40 55. French cuisine. ***
Coq D'Or, Prinsen Hotel, Kongensgate 30. Tel: 07-53 06 50. Continental. ***
Daniel, Tinghusplass 1. Tel: 07-52 47 30. Steaks are the speciality. **
Grenaderen, Kongsgården. Tel: 07-52 20 06. Enjoy local dishes, including seafood, at this open air restaurant. Live music in summer. **
Peppe's Pizza Pub, Kjøpmannsgate 25. Tel: 07-53 29 20. Lively pizza tavern in an old warehouse. **

DRINKING NOTES

No one talks about a trip to Norway without complaining of the high cost of alcohol. Stronger beer costs about 30 Nkr for a half litre (about 15 percent larger than the British pint); *lettøl* (low alcohol beer) is about 25 Nkr. From here it gets worse. A single glass of wine costs 20–30 Nkr; wines by the bottle on a restaurant's menu start at about 120 Nkr. Spirit prices are through the roof. (It's no wonder home brews are common.)

For those who can afford the prices, serving hours are long; in Oslo you can drink spirits until midnight and wine or beer until 6 a.m. Outside Oslo, it's unpredictable; the Kristlig Folket Parte (Christian Democratic Party a member of the governing coalition) is virulently anti-alcohol and holds sway in many west coast areas, rendering some counties virtually dry. Some hotels, and consequently their restaurants, are the exception to the area they are in: in Oslo there are some no alcohol hotel/restaurants and in the "dry" counties it is possible to find a hotel/restaurant serving some form of alcohol. The Vinmonopolet (state liquor stores) in cities are open weekdays 9 a.m.–5 p.m. and Saturday 9 a.m.–2 p.m; closed on election days, holidays and the day preceding.

Most Norwegians drink beer—although *akevitt*, derived from potato and caraway seeds, is a favourite for anyone doing hardcore drinking. *Akevitt* is usually followed by a beer chaser.

THINGS TO DO

MUSEUMS & ART GALLERIES

Norway's museums tend to be small and focused on one subject rather than vast masoleums. A Norwegian museum speciality is collections based around explorers—as some of the most famous Norwegians were explorers, this isn't surprising. Museums in cities will almost always have English text, or English-speaking guides.

Some museums are free, but for free admission or discounts on those that charge admission, get an Oslo Card, Stavanger's Museumskort, or the equivalent. Summer opening times, listed here, are longer than in other seasons:

OSLO

(*What's On in Oslo* and *Oslo Guide* have full listings.)
Applied Art Museum, St. Olavsgaate 1. A bright collection of contemporary and older tapestries, costumes, gadgets, china and glass, and furniture—emphasis is on the design. Open: Tuesday–Sunday 11 a.m.–3 p.m. and Tuesday evening 7 p.m.–9 p.m.
Nasjonalgalleriet, Universitetsgate 13. Expansive collection of Norwegian art, past and present; strong representation by the Norwegian Romantic school, a Munch room, and good international selections. Much of the contemporary collection moved to the new Modern Art Museum at Bankplassen. Open: Monday, Wednesday, Friday and Saturday 10 a.m.–4 p.m., Thursday 10 a.m.–8 p.m., Sunday 11 a.m.–3 p.m.
Resistance Museum, Akershus Fortress, Building 21. A starkly drawn picture of the

Nazi's vice-like grip on Norway and the brave Resistance fighters who sought to break it. Excellent English text detailing the crucial relationship between Britain and Norway. Displays on battles, the ingenious distribution of underground newspapers, the teachers' movement against the Nazi creed, and much more.

Munchmuseet, Tøyengate 53. Hundreds of paintings and drawings by the father of Expressionism, Edvard Munch; prints sold in the museum shop. Open: Monday–Saturday 10 a.m.–8 p.m., Sunday 12 p.m.–8 p.m.

Theatermuseum, Nedre Slottsgate 1. For any Ibsen fan, the rich and sometimes sordid details of his life as a playwright. Norwegian theatre history from the 1800s—in a 17th-century building, one of Oslo's oldest surviving. Open: Wednesday 11 a.m.–3 p.m. and Sunday 12 p.m.–8 p.m.

Ski Museum, Hollmenkollen Ski Center. Norwegian ski history (1,000 years' worth), daring tales of intrepid explorers, and the famous ski jump. Open: daily 9 a.m.–8 p.m.

BYGDØY MUSEUMS (all on Bygdøy peninsula):

Folk Museum, Museumsveien 10. Traditional farmhouses and odd, interesting bits of cultural and folkloric history; occasional symposia (example: "Ibsen, Freud, and Psychoanalysis"). Open: Monday–Saturday 10 a.m.–6 p.m., Sunday 11 a.m.–6 p.m.

SHIPS:

Fram Museum, Bygdøynes. The very ship Amundsen and Nansen used on polar expeditions. Open: daily 10 a.m.–5.45 p.m.

Kontiki Museum, Bygdøynes. Thor Heyerdahl's incredible sea journeys and the boats he used. Open: daily 10 a.m.–6 p.m.

Maritime Museum, Bygdøynesveien 37. Norwegian maritime history. Open: daily 10 a.m.–8 p.m.

Viking Ships Museum, Huk Aveny 35. The restored *Oseberg*, *Gokstad*, and *Tune Viking* ships, plus some artefacts. Open: daily 10 a.m.–6 p.m.

See also Galleries section in the *Oslo Guide* for a list of private art galleries.

BERGEN

Bergen Municipal Art Museum, Municipal Park (Permanenten). Two centuries of Norwegian art mixed with a sampling of other European artists' work. Open: Monday–Saturday 11 a.m.–4 p.m., Sunday 12 p.m.–3 p.m.

Hanseatic Museum, Bryggen. Artefacts of the Hansa days inside finely preserved wooden buildings with 1500s-style interiors. Open: daily 10 a.m.–4 p.m.

Historical Museum, Sydneshaugen. The west coast's history and ethnography, going back to pre-history. Open: Saturday–Thursday 11 a.m.–2 p.m.

Ole Bull Monument at Lysøen (ferries from Buena pier/Sorestraumen). The beloved violinist's former home, now a monument to him, surrounded by 8 miles (13 km) of nature trails. Check opening hours, ferry schedule.

Troldhaugen (Grieg's home), Nordås Lake, Hopsvegen. The composer's former home is now a music museum with a chamber concert hall. Summer recitals Wednesday and Sunday evening. Open: daily 10.30 a.m.–1.30 p.m. and 2.30 p.m.–5.30 p.m.

STAVANGER

Arts and handicrafts; phone the tourist office (04-52 84 37) if you're interested in seeing artists' and craftworkers' *ateliers*.

Stavanger Museum, Musegate 16, Strandgaten 17-19, and Øvre Strandgaten 88. This museum complex includes cultural, historical, archaeological, maritime, and fisheries collections. Open: Tuesday–Sunday 11 a.m.–3 p.m.

TRONDHEIM

Museum of Music History, Ringve Manor, Sverresborg. A fantastic collection of old and new instruments, on view only via conducted tours (hourly in summer). Open: weekdays 10 a.m.–3 p.m., weekends 10 a.m.–2 p.m.

Trondelag Folk Museum, Wullums–gaarden. A wonderful collection of old churches, houses, and barns. Phone for hours, tel: 07-52 21 28.

University of Trondheim Museum, Erling Skakkesgate 47. Zoological and natural history collection from prehistoric times onward plus Lapp (Sami is what they call themselves) culture, and a stamp collection. Open: weekdays 11 a.m.–3 p.m.

MUSIC & OPERA

In summer the arts take to the outdoors in Norway, and classical music and opera are no exception. For Oslo dates, pick up the *What's on in Oslo* guide. The very active **Oslo Philharmonic**, founded by Edvard Grieg, is conducted by Mariss Jansons, with frequent visits by acclaimed guest conductors and soloists.

At **Holmenkollen** in summer, orchestral and operatic performances are given from a floating stage on the lake. Each September, a "drive-in" opera performance is given at **Youngstorvet** (Young's market square), outside the Opera House in the open air. **Akershus Fortress** and the **Henie Onstad Art Centre** (Høvikodden) are two other fine settings for summer concerts. Bergen's splendid **International Festival** in late May offers music, drama, ballet, opera, and folk arts performances (for information, tel: 05-32 04 00).

Whether the performers are Norwegian or foreign, the season winter or summer, Norway has a rich and varied musical and operatic life (consult area guide for festivals schedule; some English and American newspapers do a pan-European list of festivals at the start of each summer). This may be your chance to see some of the conductors and performers you'd previously only seen on Deutsche Gramophone album jackets, or a first chance to see Grieg performed by Norwegian musicians.

THEATRE & DANCE

Theatre is booming in Norway, with small, contemporary theatres springing up everywhere; but performances are in Norwegian. The exception is September's **Gløgerne Kommer Festival** of performing arts, when dramatists from around the world take the stage.

Dance is also coming into its own here and is now a significant part of the Gløgerne Kommer. Classical ballet is performed at the Oslo Opera House. Traditional folk dances can be seen in many towns on National Day (17 May), or at **Oslo's Konserthus** on Mondays and Thursdays at 9 p.m. in July and August, when the Young Farmer's Union Folk Dance Group performs.

CINEMA & FILMS

The Norwegians love films, a fact attested by the vast number of cinemas; Oslo has 30 screens. First-run and repertory films are always shown in original language, with Norwegian subtitles. Kiosks, newspapers, and local city guides have listings. Booking is possible and recommended for Sunday nights, the traditional night for going to the movies.

NIGHTLIFE

Oslo, once considered a big yawn at night, is now vying with Stockholm and Copenhagen to be Scandinavia's nightlife capital, and the effort may just work. Loads of new clubs have come on the scene, but many can't recoup their investments quickly enough and go out of business, so check locally for up-to-date venue listings.

In Bergen, Stavanger, and Trondheim, nightlife exists to a much lesser extent. In small towns, you may be out of luck altogether—unless you have a locally compatible video recorder, for video clubs have infiltrated, and probably forever changed, rural Norway.

Famed non-classical musicians (rock, folk, and jazz groups) often stop in Oslo on European tours. Paul McCartney began his 1989 tour here. Miles Davis comes twice a year.

Only two things you need warning about before investing in a night out: the high cost of drinking, and age restrictions: some clubs have minimum ages as high as 26 (although 21 and 23 are more common).

OSLO

Jazz:

Amalienborg Jazzhouse, Arbeidergate 2. Tel: 02-42 30 24.

Guldfisken, Rådhusgate 2. Tel: 02-41 14 89.

Hot House, Rosenkrantzgate Pilestredet 15B. Tel: 02-20 39 89.

Oslo Jazzhus, Toftesgate 69. Tel: 02-38 37 65.

Stortorvets Gjæstgiveri, Grensen 1. Tel: 02-42 88 63.

Storyville, Universitetsgate 26. Tel: 02-42 96 35 (attached to the Creole/New Orleans restaurant, Chez Bendriss).

Rock and Mixed Music Bars, Clubs, and Taverns:

Barock, Universitetsgate 26. Tel: 02-42 44 20. Huge, sleek rock bar (bar-rock, get it?) and restaurant.

Brødrene Berg, Søstrene Larsson, Victoria på Karl Johan, Karl Johansgate 35. Tel: 02-42 97 10. Chagall-decorated piano bar.

Café Celsius, Rådhusgate 19. Tel: 02-42 45 39. Roomy café with fireplace sharing a building with the Art Association.

Café Frølich, Drammensveien 20. Tel: 02-44 06 17. Two-level black-and-white tile café with occasional jazz and compulsory meal.

Costas Brasserie & Bar, Klingenberggate 4. Tel: 02-42 41 30. Popular after-cinema brasserie.

Cruise Kafé, Aker Brygge 1. Tel: 02-41 03 69. Crowds pack in when Cruise headlines an out-of-town band.

Eilefs Landhandleri, Kristian IV's gate 1. Tel: 02-42 53 47. Handsomely decorated tavern—check out the costumes on the ceilings.

Kafé de Stijl, Rådhusgate 5 (entrance Skippergate). This bistro turns into a kind of funky place to dance after twilight; mixed gay and straight.

Metropol, Akersgate 8. Tel: 02-42 17 67. Gay discotheque nightly.

Nordraak, St. Olav's gate 32 (entrance Kristian IV's gate). Tel: 02-42 10 59. Artists' afternoon and night-time haunt; poster-bedecked cafeteria.

Rockefeller, Torgata 16 (entrance Marieboesgate). Tel: 02-20 32 32. Stupendously set in old Torgata baths; very active schedule of live entertainment plus campy stage shows.

Sardine's, Munkedamsveien 15. Tel: 02-83 00 75. Grand-scale musical events take place here, including the wildly popular bi-annual appearances by Miles Davis.

Smuget, Kirkegate 34. Tel: 02-42 52 02. Three settings: bistro, disco, plus small stage for live performances, varied music.

BERGEN

(Two hotels, **Norge** and **SAS**, have clubs open until 3 a.m. for dancing.)

Christian Nattklub, Chr Michelsensgate 4. Tel: 05-32 02 62. Crowded and comfortable place to throw back a few.

Holms Discotek Steakhouse, Kong Oscarsgate 45. Tel: 05-31 59 30. Major eating, drinking, and dancing action under one roof.

Hulen Studentkro, Nygårdsparken, Olaf Ryes veien 47. Tel: 05-32 32 87. Students' sprawling underground nightspot with live bands on weekdays and weekend disco nights—student ID may be required.

Theaterkafeen, Chr Michelsensgate 10. Tel: 05-32 78 32. A lively brasserie.

STAVANGER

(Most large hotels have late-night clubs.)

Cobra Club, Atlantic Hotel, Jernbaneveien 1. Tel: 04-52 75 20. An expensively decorated disco.

TRONDHEIM

Café Beverly, Handelsstandens Hus. Tel: 07-52 24 23. Soothing atmosphere.

Gatsby Club, Handelsstandens Hus. Tel: 07-53 17 97. A little rowdier.

Hollywood, Handelsstandens Hus. Tel: 07-52 31 45. Light & sound disco.

Sommerrestauranten, Prinsen Hotel, Kongensgate 30. Tel: 07-53 06 50. Choice of live music room or disco.

Studenteramsfunnet, Elgersgt. Tel: 07-52 21 57. University-aged crowd, occasional live British bands, open seven nights.

Studio Horten, Royal Garden Hotel, Kjøpmannsgate 73. Tel: 07-52 11 00. Dancing 'til all hours against shimmery backdrop.

SHOPPING

Ceramics, glass, pewter, woven and knitted goods, and for some, furs, are the things worth shopping for in Norway. The major department stores are **Glasmagasin** and **Steen & Strøm**, both of which will have a good selection of most of these items. However, if you want specialty stores in Oslo, there is a *Where to Shop* guide, as well as a detailed "Shopping" section in the *Oslo Guide*. Karl Johansgate, Grensen, and Bogstadveien are all major shopping streets.

With the exception of Oslo, most Norwegian towns are so compact that your best bet is to window shop and go into the places that look most appealing.

Anyone interested in buying Norwegian art will have ample prospects—from south to north, Norway abounds in galleries. Get a local recommendation.

SHOPPING AREAS

Offbeat Shopping: Most of Norway's towns still have market days. Some markets are very specialised (e.g. flowers or fish only) while others will have stalls selling practically everything. In Oslo, **Basarhallene** is a fine old collection of boutiques behind the Domkirke; or try the **Grünerløkka** district (Markveien). Grensen is a street of bargain alleys for everything from clothes to records; try "Utopia" pop and rock record shop on Pilestredet 15. Outside Oslo, check locally for special market days and seasonal markets.

SHOPPING HOURS/TAX-FREE SHOPPING

Shopping hours are generally 9 a.m.–5 p.m. on weekdays, with late Thursday opening for many stores until 7 p.m; stores may close earlier in summer, especially Fridays. Saturday hours are approximately 9 a.m.–2 p.m. Malls like **Aker Brygge** and **Oslo City** are open later, until 8 p.m. some nights.

To shop tax-free, i.e. to get your VAT refunded, ask for a tax-free cheque whenever you buy more than 300 Nkr worth of goods in any one establishment. (Carry proof that you are not a resident of Scandinavia.) The items will be sealed, and you carry them away with you, to be presented—still sealed—at the VAT refund desk at the airport, ferry or border crossing when you leave Norway. Enter your name, address, and passport number on the back of the tax free cheque before presenting it for refund. Refunds can often be made in your national currency (eg sterling, dollars, etc).

SPORTS

PARTICIPANT

If Norwegians can contrive a sport as an excuse to be outdoors, they'll do it. That's why there are such great facilities here; all Norwegians love sport. (For a full listing of the range of sports and sports facilites in the Oslo region, see the "Outdoor Activities" pages of the *Oslo Guide*. There is a "Forest Safari" programme, where for a half or whole day you can partake in a range of activities in the "Marka" (Oslo's forest) in between which you are carted around by Land-Rover—visit the main tourist information office for details.

Skiing and hiking: These are the primary participant sports. The ski resorts are too numerous to name here; all tourist offices can advise on local ski facilities for cross country and slalom. Hiking can be done anywhere and combined with another activity like berry-gathering or a swim in a lake; Den Norske Turistforening (Stortingsgate 28, Oslo 1, tel: 02-41 80 20) has a wealth of information and maps for all Norway and can recommend hut-to-hut hiking holidays. Foreigners can write requesting membership, which gives you certain free publications and hut access.

Swimming: This is another passion. Oslo has more than 30 public pools. Though Greenpeace-Norway's main issue at the moment is pollution of the Oslofjord, most bathers consider the risk negligible; everyone living on the fjord has their favourite beach or "strand". Inland, lakes are plentiful.

Boating: *Det Kongelige Norske Motorbåt-Forbund* (the Royal Norwegian Motorboat Association) is the national organisation for recreational and competitive motor-boating. Throughout the country, hundreds of sailing and motorboat clubs and associations cater to local and regional interests.

Foreign visitors are always welcome in boating circles, and the Norwegians are taking steps to make the welcome even better. The traditional, reliable guide to Norwegian small-boat harbours, *Guest Harbours in Norway* (Oslo, 1987, NORTRA Publications, ISBN 82-90103-39-5) is now published in three languages, with texts in Norwegian, English and German. In it, you will find all you need to know about the facilities and amenities of harbours.

The most popular volumes of the six-volume *Den Norske Los* (Norwegian Pilot), the meticulously-detailed manual of all navigable waters, will soon be available with Norwegian and English texts. Volume 3, covering the southwest coast from south of Stavanger to north of Bergen, has a 1990 publication date; Volume 2, covering the Oslo Fjord and the south coast, will appear in 1991–92.

But without your own boat, sailing of any sort can be expensive, and the closest you may get is a small catamaran or even a windsurfer; you can hire equipment from the Seasport and Windsurfing Centre in Oslo, Bygdøyakkëe 60A. Tel: 02-44 79 78.

Fishing: In summer, there are many boat cruises, and in some fjord towns groups can charter boats for fishing or pleasure excursions. The fishing is excellent in Norway, whether you're at sea or on a fjord, lake or river; enquire locally about short-term permits (see tourist board's *Angling in Norway*).

SPECTATOR

Lillehammer, Norway will be the site of the 1994 Winter Olympics. Set at the north end of Lake Mjøsa, it is Norway's longest lake, and one of its most visited; a steamer tours it in summer. At the south end of the lake is Eidsvoll, birthplace of the Norwegian constitution.

For annual ski competitions, check local guides or consult the *Winter in Oslo* brochure.

There are several horse trotting and race tracks in Norway. Other popular spectator sports include marathon running, soccer, ice hockey, and boat races. Again, check Oslo or local area guide for details.

SPECIAL INFORMATION

DOING BUSINESS

Norwegians have all the state-of-the-art props when it comes to doing business. Don't be caught out without a firm handshake, a good-looking business card, and, if possible, a car phone (car fax an added bonus).

Like all Scandinavians, Norwegians take their summer holiday very seriously as a time for fjord or mountain *hytte* (wooden summer house). From mid-June to the end of July/first week in August, offices and factories empty, and it is almost impossible to get an appointment or do any business. May, with its many public holidays can also be a difficult time (see *National Day* page 74).

Nothing about doing business should take you too much by surprise here. People take work seriously, but also know how to maintain a pleasantly relaxed business atmosphere. Norwegians dress for business much as they do elsewhere; but, come summer time, there seems to be a bit of slack in the dress code to allow for the warmth.

Norwegians, in common with other Scandinavians, are rarely duplicitous. They may well mention the bad points of something first, so as to get them out of the way; then it's on to the sell. In other words, you won't be drowned in a sea of impossible hype, and the honesty's a little hard to get used to. Ultimately you'll appreciate not having to figure out the pitfalls for yourself.

If you are searching for someone in a phone book, you'll find his or her profession listed next to the name; not only is it a matter of professional pride, but a real help in a country with a limited number of surnames.

So much for generalisations; there will always be exceptions. The only really important things to remember are that liquid lunches are unusual, and that the work day ends at 3.30 or 4 p.m.

Two organisations deal with tourism, business, service, and trading matters in Oslo. They are:

NORTRA (Norwegian Trade Association and Tourist Board), Havnelageret, Langkaia 1, PO Box 499 Sentrum, Oslo 1. Tel: 02-42 70 44.

Oslo Promotion, Rådhusgate 23, Oslo 1. Tel: 02-33 43 86.

CHILDREN

Norway is a welcoming and safe place for children; this is one reason why you will see children here out on their own at a young age. Children can usually travel and stay in hotels for less than the adult tariffs.

To keep costs down, there are always outdoor activities for the entire family: walking, skating, skiing, or swimming, for instance. Below are listed a few attractions in and around Oslo designed especially with children in mind.

Bogstadveien Aquarium and Zoo, Bogstadveien 53, Oslo.

International Children's Art Museum (exhibits and workshops), Lille Frøensveien 4, Oslo 3.

Minigolf and Minizoo Ekeberg, near Ekeberghallen. Tel: 02-68 26 69.

Tusen Fryd Amusement Park, Ås, Østfold. Tel: 09-94 63 63; transport by bus 541 from Oslo-S or Rådhuset.

DISABLED

The directory for the disabled is no longer available from tourist information, but visitors in need of guidance could contact the Norwegian Association for the Disabled, Nils Hansensvei 2, Oslo 6, tel: 02-15 12 14 for Oslo; tel: 02-64 86 10 for all Norway. Hotel listings in the accommodation guides have symbols designating disabled access and toilets. In the *Oslo Guide* under "Outdoor Activities" you'll find some listings that specially mention capacity for disabled visitors, such as the Bogstad ski area, Nordmarka.

LANGUAGE

Yes	*Ja*
No	*Nei*
Good morning	*God morgen*
Good afternoon	*God eftermiddag*
Good evening	*God kveld*
Today	*I dag*
Tomorrow	*I morgen*
Yesterday	*I går*
Hello	*Hei*
How do you do?	*Goddag*
Goodbye	*Adjø*
Thank you	*Takk*
How much is this?	*Hvor mye koster de?*
It costs	*Det koster*
How do I get to…?	*Hvordan kommer jeg til…?*
Where is…?	*Hvor er…?*
Right	*Høyre*
To the right	*Til høyre*
Left	*venstre*
To the left	*Til venstre*
Straight on	*Rett frem*
Phrase book	*Parlør*
Dictionary	*Ordbok*

Money	*Penger*	Clothes	*Klær*
		Overcoat	*Frakk*
Can I order please?	*Kan jeg få bestille?*	Jacket	*Jakke*
Could I have		Suit	*Dress*
the bill please?	*Kan jeg få regningen?*	Shoes	*Sko*
Could I have		Skirt	*Skjørt*
the key please?	*Kan jeg få nøkkelen?*	Blouse	*Bluse*
What time is it?	*Hvor mye er klokken?*	Jersey	*Genser*
It is (the time is)	*Det er (klokken er)*		
Could I have		To rent	*Leie*
your name please?	*Hva er navnet?*	Free	*Ledig*
My name is	*Mitt navn er*	Room to rent	*Rum til leie*
Do you have		Chalet	*Hytte*
English newspapers?	*Har du engelske*	Grocery store	
	aviser?	(in countryside)	*Landhandel*
Do you speak English?	*Snakker du engelsk?*	Shop	*Butikk*
I only speak English	*Jeg snakker bare*	Food	*Matt*
	engelsk	To buy	*Kjøpe*
Can I help you?	*Kan jeg hjelpe?*	Sauna	*Badstue*
I do not understand	*Jeg forstår ikke*	Off licence	*Vinmonopol*
I do not know	*Jeg vet ikke*		
It has disappeared	*Den har forsvunnet*	Wash	*Vaske*
		Launderette	*Vaskeri*
Chemist	*Apotek*	Dry cleaning	*Renseri*
Hospital	*Sykehus*	Dirty	*Sølet*
Doctor	*Lege*	Clean	*Ren*
		Stain	*Flekk*
Police station	*Politistation*		
Parking	*Parkering*	1	*en*
Department store	*Kjopesenter*	2	*to*
Toilet	*Toalett*	3	*tre*
Gentlemen	*Herrer*	4	*fire*
Ladies	*Damer*	5	*fem*
Vacant	*Ledig*	6	*seks*
Engaged	*Opptatt*	7	*syv*
Entrance	*Inngang*	8	*åtte*
Exit	*Utgang*	9	*ni*
No entry	*Ingen adgang*	10	*ti*
Open	*Åpent*	11	*eleve*
Closed	*Stengt*	12	*tolv*
Push	*Skyv*	13	*tretten*
Pull	*Trekk*	14	*fjorten*
No smoking	*Røyking forbudt*	15	*femten*
		16	*seksten*
Breakfast	*Frokost*	17	*sytten*
Lunch	*Lunsj*	18	*atten*
Dinner	*Middag*	19	*nitten*
Eat	*Spise*	20	*tjue*
Drink	*Drikke*	21	*tjue-en*
Cheers!	*Skål!*	22	*tjue-to*
		30	*tretti*
Aircraft	*Fly*	40	*førti*
Bus/coach	*Buss*	50	*femti*
Car	*Bil*	60	*seksti*
Train	*Tog*	70	*sytti*

80	*åtti*
90	*nitti*
100	*hündre*
200	*tohundre*
1,000	*tusen*

USEFUL ADDRESSES

Tourist Information and Accommodation Bureau, Sentralstasjon (Oslo-S), Jernbanetorget, tel: 02-42 44 60. Open: daily all year, 8 a.m.–11 p.m.
Tourist Information, City Hall (Rådhuset). Tel: 02-42 71 70. Open: Monday–Friday 8.30 a.m.–4 p.m. winter, Saturday 8.30 a.m.–2.30 p.m. Open: Monday–Saturday 8.30 a.m.–7 p.m., Sunday 9 a.m.–5 p.m. summer.
Landslaget for Reiselivet i Norge (Norway Travel Association/NTA), Langkaia 1, Oslo 1 Tel: 02-42 70 44; branches in large towns and resorts. Most open weekdays 9 a.m.–5 p.m., some also open part of Saturday.
Norwegian Tourist Board (NORTRA), Havnelageret, Langkaia 1, Postboks 499 Sentrum, 0105 Oslo 1.
The Export Council of Norway, Drammensveien 40, 0255 Oslo 2. Tel: 02-11 40 30.
Oslo Chamber of Commerce, Drammensveien 30, 0255 Oslo 2. Tel: 02-56 36 29.

Foreign Offices of the Norwegian Tourist Board
Norwegian Tourist Board, 5-11 Lower Regent Street, London SW1Y 4LX, United Kingdom.
Norwegian Tourist Board/North America, 655 Third Avenue, New York, NY 10017, U.S.A.
Norska Turistbyrån, Brunnsgatan 21 B, S-111 38 Stockholm, Sweden.
Norges Turistkonto, Trondhjems Plads 4, DK-2100 København Ø, Denmark.
Norges Turistbyrå, Georgsgatan (Yrjönkatu) 23, PB 709, SF-00101 Helsinki, Finland.

Norwegisches Fremdenverkehrsamt, Norwegen Zentrum, Mundsburger Damm 27, D-2000 Hamburg 76, Federal Republic of Germany (for FRG, Switzerland, and Austria).
Office Nationale du Tourisme de Norvege, 88 Ave Charles de Gaulle, F-92200 Neuilly-sur-Seine, France.
Noors Nationaal Verkeersbureau, Saxen Weimarlaan 58, NL-1075, CE Amsterdam, Netherlands.
Noors Verkersbureau, Louizalaan 130A, B-1050 Brussels, Belgium.
Ufficio Nazionale Norvegese per il Turismo, Piazza Castello 20, I-20121 Milan, Italy.
Scandinavian Tourist Board/Norway, Sanno Grand Building, Room 401, 14-2 Nagatacho 2-chome, Chiyodaku, Tokyo 100, Japan.

Tourist Information in Norway
There are hundreds of tourist information offices throughout Norway, marked with a letter "I" on signs and maps.

Embassies in Oslo
British: Thomas Heftyesgate 8, Oslo 2. Tel: 02-56 38 90 or 56 38 97.
American: Drammensveien 18, Oslo 1. Tel: 02-56 68 80.
Canadian: Oscarsgate 20, Oslo 3. Tel: 02-46 69 55.

Art/Photo Credits

THE COLOUR OF LIFE.

A holiday may last just a week or so, but the memories of those happy, colourful days will last forever, because together you and Kodak Ektachrome films will capture, as large as life, the wondrous sights, the breathtaking scenery and the magical moments. For you to relive over and over again.

The Kodak Ektachrome range of slide films offers a choice of light source, speed and colour rendition and features extremely fine grain, very high sharpness and high resolving power.

Take home the real colour of life with Kodak Ektachrome films.

LIKE THIS?

OR LIKE THIS?

A KODAK FUN PANORAMIC CAMERA
BROADENS YOUR VIEW

The holiday you and your camera have been looking forward to all year; and a stunning panoramic view appears. "Fabulous", you think to yourself, "must take that one".

Unfortunately, your lens is just not wide enough. And three-in-a-row is a poor substitute.

That's when you take out your pocket-size, 'single use' Kodak Fun Panoramic Camera. A film and a camera, all in one, and it works miracles. You won't need to focus, you don't need special lenses. Just aim, click and... it's all yours. The total picture.

You take twelve panoramic pictures with one Kodak Fun Panoramic Camera. Then put the camera in for developing and printing.

Each print is 25 by 9 centimetres. Excellent depth of field. True Kodak Gold colours.

The Kodak Fun Panoramic Camera itself goes back to the factory, to be recycled. So that others too can capture one of those spectacular phooooooooootooooooooooooos.

INDEX

THE KODAK GOLD GUIDE TO BETTER PICTURES.

Good photography is not difficult. Use these practical hints and Kodak Gold II Film: then notice the improvement.

Move in close. Get close enough to capture only the important elements.

Frame your Pictures. Look out for natural frames such as archways or tree branches to add an interesting foreground. Frames help create a sensation of depth and direct attention into the picture.

One centre of interest. Ensure you have one focus of interest and avoid distracting features that can confuse the viewer.

Use leading lines. Leading lines direct attention to your subject i.e. — a stream, a fence, a pathway; or the less obvious such as light beams or shadows.

Maintain activity. Pictures are more appealing if the subject is involved in some natural action.

Keep within the flash range. Ensure subject is within flash range for your camera (generally 4 metres). With groups make sure everyone is the same distance from the camera to receive the same amount of light.

Check the light direction. People tend to squint in bright direct light. Light from the side creates highlights and shadows that reveal texture and help to show the shapes of the subject. If shooting into direct sunlight fill-in flash can be effective to light the subject from the front.

CHOOSING YOUR KODAK GOLD II FILM.

Choosing the correct speed of colour print film for the type of photographs you will be taking is essential to achieve the best colourful results.

Basically the more intricate your needs in terms of capturing speed or low-light situations the higher speed film you require.

Kodak Gold II 100. Use in bright outdoor light or indoors with electronic flash. Fine grain, ideal for enlargements and close-ups. Ideal for beaches, snow scenes and posed shots.

Kodak Gold II 200. A multipurpose film for general lighting conditions and slow to moderate action. Recommended for automatic 35mm cameras. Ideal for walks, bike rides and parties.

Kodak Gold II 400. Provides the best colour accuracy as well as the richest, most saturated colours of any 400 speed film. Outstanding flash-taking capabilities for low-light and fast-action situations; excellent exposure latitude. Ideal for outdoor or well-lit indoor sports, stage shows or sunsets.

ARE Going Places: ↙

Asia & Pacific
East Asia
South Asia
South East Asian Wildlife
South East Asia
★Marine Life
Australia
Great Barrier Reef
Melbourne
★★Sydney
★Bhutan
Burma/Myanmar
China
Beijing
India
Calcutta
Delhi, Jaipur, Agra
India's Western Himalaya
Indian Wildlife
★New Delhi
Rajasthan
South India
Indonesia
★★Bali
★Bali Bird Walks
Java
★Jakarta
★Yogyakarta
Korea
Japan
Tokyo
Malaysia
★Kuala Lumpur
★Malacca
★Penang
★★Nepal
Kathmandu
Kathmandu Bikes & Hikes
New Zealand
Pakistan
Philippines
★Sikkim
★★Singapore
Sri Lanka
Taiwan

Thailand
★★Bangkok
★Chiang Mai
★Phuket
★Tibet
Turkey
★★Istanbul
Turkish Coast
★Turquoise Coast
Vietnam

Africa
East African Wildlife
South Africa
Egypt
Cairo
The Nile
Israel
Jerusalem
Kenya
Morocco
Namibia
The Gambia & Senegal
Tunisia
Yemen

Europe
Austria
★★Vienna
Belgium
Brussels
Channel Islands
Continental Europe
Cyprus
Czechoslovakia
★★Prague
Denmark
Eastern Europe
Finland
France
★★Alsace
★★Brittany
★★Cote d'Azur
★★Loire Valley
★★Paris

Provence
Germany
★★Berlin
Cologne
Düsseldorf
Frankfurt
Hamburg
★★Munich
The Rhine
Great Britain
Edinburg
Glasgow
★★Ireland
★★London
Oxford
Scotland
Wales
Greece
★★Athens
★★Crete
★Rhodes
Greek Islands
Hungary
★★Budapest
Iceland
Italy
Florence
★Rome
★★Sardinia
★★Tuscany
Umbria
★★Venice
Netherlands
Amsterdam
Norway
Poland
Portugal
★★Lisbon
Madeira
Spain
★★Barcelona
★Costa Blanca
★Costa Brava
★Costa del Sol/Marbella
Catalonia

Gran Canaria
★Ibiza
Madrid
Mallorca & Ibiza
★Mallorca
★Seville
Southern Spain
Tenerife
Sweden
Switzerland
(Ex) USSR
Moscow
St. Petersburg
Waterways of Europe
Yugoslavia
★Yugoslavia's Adriatic
Coast

The Americas
Bermuda
Canada
Montreal
Caribbean
Bahamas
Barbados
Jamaica
Trinidad & Tobago
Puerto Rico
Costa Rica
Mexico
Mexico City
South America
Argentina
Amazon Wildlife
Brazil
Buenos Aires
Chile
Ecuador
Peru
Rio

USA/Crossing America
Alaska
American Southwest
Boston
California
Chicago
Florida
Hawaii
Los Angeles
Miami
Native America
New England
New Orleans
★★New York City
New York State
Northern California
Pacific Northwest
★★San Francisco
Southern California
Texas
The Rockies
Washington D.C.

★★Also available as
Insight Pocket Guide

★Available as Insight
Pocket Guide only

Ci VEDREMO·
PRESTO!

See You Soon! In Italy

A
B
D
E
F
G
H
I
J
a
b
c
d
e
f
h
i
j
k
l

A P A
INSIGHT
GUIDES

ARE Going Places:

Asia & Pacific
East Asia
South Asia
South East Asian Wildlife
South East Asia
★ Marine Life
Australia
Great Barrier Reef
Melbourne
★★ Sydney
★ Bhutan
Burma/Myanmar
China
Beijing
India
Calcutta
Delhi, Jaipur, Agra
India's Western Himalaya
Indian Wildlife
★ New Delhi
Rajasthan
South India
Indonesia
★★ Bali
★ Bali Bird Walks
Java
★ Jakarta
★ Yogyakarta
Korea
Japan
Tokyo
Malaysia
★ Kuala Lumpur
★ Malacca
★ Penang
★★ Nepal
Kathmandu
Kathmandu Bikes & Hikes
New Zealand
Pakistan
Philippines
★ Sikkim
★★ Singapore
Sri Lanka
Taiwan

Thailand
★★ Bangkok
★ Chiang Mai
★ Phuket
★ Tibet
Turkey
★★ Istanbul
Turkish Coast
★ Turquoise Coast
Vietnam

Africa
East African Wildlife
South Africa
Egypt
Cairo
The Nile
Israel
Jerusalem
Kenya
Morocco
Namibia
The Gambia & Senegal
Tunisia
Yemen

Europe
Austria
★★ Vienna
Belgium
Brussels
Channel Islands
Continental Europe
Cyprus
Czechoslovakia
★★ Prague
Denmark
Eastern Europe
Finland
France
★ Alsace
★★ Brittany
★★ Cote d'Azur
★★ Loire Valley
★★ Paris

Provence
Germany
★★ Berlin
Cologne
Düsseldorf
Frankfurt
Hamburg
★★ Munich
The Rhine
Great Britain
Edinburg
Glasgow
★★ Ireland
★★ London
Oxford
Scotland
Wales
Greece
★★ Athens
★★ Crete
★ Rhodes
Greek Islands
Hungary
★★ Budapest
Iceland
Italy
Florence
★★ Rome
★★ Sardinia
★★ Tuscany
Umbria
★★ Venice
Netherlands
Amsterdam
Norway
Poland
Portugal
★★ Lisbon
★★ Madeira
Spain
★★ Barcelona
★ Costa Blanca
★ Costa Brava
★ Costa del Sol/Marbella
Catalonia

Gran Canaria
★ Ibiza
Madrid
Mallorca & Ibiza
★ Mallorca
★ Seville
Southern Spain
Tenerife
Sweden
Switzerland
(Ex) USSR
Moscow
St. Petersburg
Waterways of Europe
Yugoslavia
★ Yugoslavia's Adriatic
Coast

The Americas
Bermuda
Canada
Montreal
Caribbean
Bahamas
Barbados
Jamaica
Trinidad & Tobago
Puerto Rico
Costa Rica
Mexico
Mexico City
South America
Argentina
Amazon Wildlife
Brazil
Buenos Aires
Chile
Ecuador
Peru
Rio

USA/Crossing America
Alaska
American Southwest
Boston
California
Chicago
Florida
Hawaii
Los Angeles
Miami
Native America
New England
New Orleans
★★ New York City
New York State
Northern California
Pacific Northwest
★★ San Francisco
Southern California
Texas
The Rockies
Washington D.C.

★★ Also available as
Insight Pocket Guide

★ Available as Insight
Pocket Guide only

INSIGHT
pocket
GUIDES

Ci VEDREMO·
PRESTO!

See You Soon! In Italy